Children and their Books

Iona and Peter Opie in the playground.

CHILDREN AND THEIR BOOKS

A Celebration of the Work of
Iona and Peter Opie

Edited by

GILLIAN AVERY *and* JULIA BRIGGS

with a foreword by

IONA OPIE

CLARENDON PRESS · OXFORD

1989

Oxford University Press, Walton Street, Oxford OX2 6DP

Oxford New York Toronto
Delhi Bombay Calcutta Madras Karachi
Petaling Jaya Singapore Hong Kong Tokyo
Nairobi Dar es Salaam Cape Town
Melbourne Auckland

and associated companies in
Berlin Ibadan

Oxford is a trade mark of Oxford University Press

Published in the United States
by Oxford University Press, New York

British Library Cataloguing in Publication Data
Children and their books: a collection of
essays to celebrate the work of Iona and
Peter Opie
1. Children's literature in English, to
1982 – Critical studies
I. Avery, Gillian, 1926–   II. Briggs,
Julia
820.9'9282
ISBN 0-19-812991-2

Library of Congress Cataloging in Publication Data
Children and their books: a collection of essays to celebrate the
work of Iona and Peter Opie / edited by Gillian Avery and Julia
Briggs; with a foreword by Iona Opie.
p.   cm.
Includes index.
1. Children's literature, English—History and criticism.
2. Children—Great Britain—Books and reading—History.
3. Children's literature—Collectors and collecting. 4. Opie, Iona
Archibald. 5. Opie, Peter. I. Opie, Iona Archibald. II. Opie, Peter.
III. Avery, Gillian, 1926– . IV. Briggs, Julia.
PR990.C49   1989
820'.9'9282—dc 19   88-27005   CIP
ISBN 0-19-812991-2

Typeset by Latimer Trend & Company Ltd, Plymouth
Printed in Great Britain by
Bookcraft Ltd, Bath, Avon

For Iona, with love

·FOREWORD

WHEN I was seven I went to a school called The Haven, whose colours were green and blue, whose badge was a ship, and whose motto, emblazoned over the fireplace in the school hall, was 'More Beyond'. I received these words as from an oracle, and I have lived by them ever since.

One cannot know what lies beyond, one can only believe that more is there, and adventure in search of it. When Peter bought *The Cheerful Warbler* for 5*s.* at Hatchards in 1945 he had not already decided to create the finest private collection of children's books in England. He only knew that the fragile, absurd little nursery rhyme book enchanted us both, and he must go out and find more books like it.

He went to Red Lion Court, to forage in Henry Lyon's cellar, where early children's books were to be had for 3*s. 6d.* each. He frequented the Beauchamp bookshop, near South Kensington station, where he bought our first copy of Halliwell's nursery rhymes; returning home triumphant one day because he had been talking to the bookseller about children's books for over an hour and, he said, 'I could follow everything he said—I knew every book he mentioned.'

Thus the journey began: but what can I say about the next forty years, except that as the 'beyond' gradually became visible it did indeed contain more, and more, and more, until the collection finally numbered 20,000 items. As Peter's knowledge and passion grew, so did the sheet files and card files that now accompany the books to the Bodleian; and the terse entries in his accession books expanded into book-collector's anecdotes. Along the way, too, the book collection earned its keep, providing illustrations for *The Oxford Nursery Rhyme Book*, verses for *The Oxford Book of Children's Verse*, and both illustrations and text for *The Classic Fairy Tales* and *A Nursery Companion*.

We often talked about the future of Westerfield and its contents. We spied out the possibility of turning it into a Centre

vii

of Child Life and Literature (ourselves retreating to a bungalow in the orchard); and we were short-listed for a benefaction which would have taken the books to the Bodleian in Peter's lifetime.

What we could not foresee was the advent of the Opie Appeal, and the wave of support and enthusiasm which carried it beyond its original target, so that additional monies for the fund will establish an endowment for the Collection: for cataloguing, conservation, and—who knows?—subsidy for research.

Nor, perhaps, could anyone have foreseen the good that would grow from the Appeal: the splendid lectures given in Oxford during May last year are an example, and it is from the lectures that this book has grown. I am immensely grateful to all the distinguished authors who have contributed essays to *Children and their Books*, which is a major addition to the existing literature on the subject. The relationship which exists between children and their books is one which lasts through life, and has many repercussions. If Peter had not fallen in love with *The Animal 'Why' Book*—as an artefact, and not only for its subject-matter— the Opie Collection of Children's Literature might never have come into being.

Iona Opie

CONTENTS

Contents

LIST OF ILLUSTRATIONS

The authors and publishers are grateful to the owners of copyright illustrations for permission to reproduce them free of charge.

List of Illustrations

List of Illustrations

[Photographs on pages 12, 23, 64, 81, 111 (top), 172, 204, 236, 359,
393, 402, and 409 are by courtesy of the Bodleian Library.]

NOTES ON CONTRIBUTORS

BRIAN ALDERSON has been associated with children's literature studies for a number of years, lecturing, translating, and reviewing. He revised F. J. Harvey Darton's *Children's Books in England* (1983) and he has organized various exhibitions on the subject. Two of these led to the publication of discursive handbooks: *Looking at Picture Books* (1973) and *Sing a Song for Sixpence* (1986).

GILLIAN AVERY is the author of children's books and a historian of children's literature. Her books include *Nineteenth Century Children* (1965) and *Childhood's Pattern* (1975).

GILES BARBER is Librarian of the Taylor Institution, Oxford. He has written extensively on eighteenth-century bibliography and hopes to write more, both on 'Malbrouck' and on cup and ball games world-wide.

JOHN BATCHELOR is a fellow of New College, Oxford, and the author of books on Mervyn Peake, H. G. Wells and Joseph Conrad, and a literary history, *The Edwardian Novelists*.

JOHN BAYLEY is Thomas Wharton Professor of English at the University of Oxford, and is the author of books on Shakespeare, Thomas Hardy, and has written most recently on the short story.

OLIVIA BELL *and* ALAN BELL Olivia Bell is a graduate of the Open University and a primary-school teacher in Oxford. Alan Bell is Librarian of Rhodes House Library, Oxford, and author of a biography of Sidney Smith (1980).

JULIA BRIGGS is a fellow and tutor at Hertford College, Oxford, and has written on nineteenth-century ghost stories, Renaissance literature and, most recently, a biography of E. Nesbit.

HUGH BROGAN has been a fellow of St John's College, Cambridge, and is currently a lecturer in American history at the University of Essex. He has written a history of the United States and a biography of Arthur Ransome.

HUMPHREY CARPENTER is the co-author of the *Oxford Companion to*

Children's Literature, and the author of *Secret Gardens*. He has written biographies of J. R. R. Tolkien, W. H. Auden, and Ezra Pound.

A. O. J. COCKSHUT is G. M. Young Lecturer in Nineteenth-century English Literature and fellow of Hertford College, Oxford. He is the author of books on Scott, Dickens, Trollope, and on biography and autobiography.

BARBARA EVERETT lectures at Oxford University and is Senior Research Fellow at Somerville College. Her most recent book is *Poets in Their Time: English Poetry from Donne to Larkin*.

KATE FLINT, fellow and tutor at Mansfield College, Oxford, is the author of *Dickens* (1986) and editor of *Impressionists in England* (1984) and *The Victorian Novel: Social Problems and Social Change* (1987). She is currently completing a study of *The Woman Reader 1837–1914*.

CLIVE HURST is head of Special Collections at the Bodleian Library and is in charge of the Opie books.

ALISON LURIE teaches children's literature at Cornell University and is co-editor of *The Garland Library of Children's Classics*. Her most recent novel is *The Truth About Lorin Jones*.

NEIL PHILIP is a writer and publisher. Among his books are *A Fine Anger* (1981, winner of the first ChLA Literary Criticism Book Award), *Between Earth and Sky* (1984), and *The Tale of Sir Gawain* (1987).

W. W. ROBSON was a fellow of Lincoln College, Oxford, from 1948–70, and a professor of English literature at Sussex University from 1970 to 1972. He has been Masson Professor of English Literature at the University of Edinburgh since 1972. His recent publications include *A Prologue to English Literature* (1986).

WILLIAM ST CLAIR is the author of *Lord Elgin and the Marbles, That Greece Might Still Be Free*, and other works concerned with Byron and Shelley and their times. His life of Godwin, *The Godwins and the Shelleys: the Biography of a Family*, was published in 1989.

NIGEL SMITH is fellow and tutor in English at Keble College, Oxford. He has published on Shakespeare, seventeenth-century literature, and Puritanism and is currently writing a history of literature during the English Civil War.

SIR KEITH THOMAS, FBA, is President of Corpus Christi College,

Oxford. He is the author of *Religion and the Decline of Magic* (1971) and *Man and the Natural World* (1983).

JACK ZIPES is professor of German at the University of Florida and co-director of the Institute for European and Comparative Studies. Among his major publications are *Breaking the Magic Spell: Radical Theories of Folk and Fairy Tales* (1979), *Fairy Tales and the Art of Subversion* (1983), *Victorian Fairy Tales* (1987), and *The Brothers Grimm: From Enchanted Forests to the Modern World* (1988).

INTRODUCTION

THE essays in this volume have been assembled as a tribute to the achievement of Iona and Peter Opie, as a memorial to Peter's work which Iona has carried on alone since his death in 1982, and as a celebration of the success of the Opie Appeal—launched in 1986 and completed in spring 1988—which set out to secure the Opies' incomparable collection of historical children's books for the Bodleian Library.

To stand outside the Sheldonian Theatre on a crisp and sunny February day in 1987, and shake collecting boxes at the queues of senior members of Oxford University waiting to vote for a new Chancellor, was to discover just how much impact the Opies' work had made on that particular academic community. Many of those who contributed spoke of their gratitude for the way the Opies had enriched the lives of their children, and enlarged their own sense of their children's lives through their studies of nursery rhymes, games, and fairy tales; all felt strongly that the Bodleian Library was the place for the magnificent collection of children's books that the Opies had acquired over some forty years to back up their study of the literature and lore of childhood. It is particularly appropriate that their collection should come to the Bodleian, because it was through that library that the Opies' connection with the Oxford University Press was first established: Richard Hunt, then Bodley's Keeper of Western Manuscripts, came across the Opies poring over eighteenth-century rhyme books in Duke Humphrey's Library, where so much of their research was carried out; he encouraged them to approach the Oxford University Press and personally effected the crucial introductions. From their encounter with Dr Hunt sprang *The Oxford Dictionary of Nursery Rhymes*, and all the subsequent Opie connections with Oxford.

Oxford has been associated with children's books for more than a century. The first and greatest of them was the work of 'Lewis Carroll', the pseudonym adopted by Charles Lutwidge

Dodgson, a diffident young mathematics tutor at Christ Church, who enjoyed inventing jokily allusive stories to amuse the three daughters of the Dean, Lorina, Edith and, of course, Alice, who gave her name to the best-known children's book in the world. Roger Lancelyn Green, a generous supporter of the Opie appeal, presented a copy of the rare cancelled first edition of *Alice* to the Bodleian in 1987, just before his death. Green himself wrote books for children, as well as being a great expert on them and, as a former librarian at Merton College, he could be thought of as an Oxford author. There have been many others: Andrew Lang was once a fellow of Merton, C. S. Lewis was a fellow of Magdalen; J. R. R. Tolkien was for many years Rawlinson and Bosworth Professor of Anglo-Saxon; Kenneth Grahame, a Thames valley man who had been at school at St Edward's, left his manuscripts to the Bodleian. Since the war many other writers for children have lived in Oxford and set children's stories there. The Opies' own books have always been published by the Oxford University Press who have a notable juvenile list of their own, and who commissioned Humphrey Carpenter and Mari Prichard to compile the *Oxford Companion to Children's Literature*, the first comprehensive reference work on the subject.

But though this country has produced the greatest children's literature of any culture, it has valued that tradition so little that many of its earliest treasures have been allowed to slip away across the Atlantic: until recently Oxford University took no official interest in the subject, unlike the United States where it is recognized as suitable for study at universities and where most recent scholarly research has been carried out.

But when in 1986 Iona Opie generously offered to give the Bodleian half the value of her collection of some 20,000 books, the finest private collection in the world, provided the other half could be raised by a public appeal, Oxford University was the first to respond. Nearly all colleges contributed, though many were heavily engaged in fund-raising on their own behalf: some gave substantially and some gave who never normally contributed to appeals. They were joined by the Friends of the Bodleian both as a group and as individuals, and then by the general public who showed a touching enthusiasm. There were hundreds of private donations: Women's Institutes, Brownie packs, schools, villages, and libraries all over the country organized their own fund-raising events. The National Heritage Memorial Fund, seeing the extent of popular support for the cause, stepped in to make the really large contribution without which no appeal on this scale can reach its target.

In the summer of 1987 a selection of some of the most interesting books from the Opie collection was put on display at the Bodleian, and as a prelude to this event a series of public lectures were put on under the aegis of the Oxford English faculty; these covered topics as various as the activities of children in early modern England and the subversiveness of Beatrix Potter. It was the first time that lectures on children and children's books had been advertised in the University Gazette, and though the audiences sometimes strained to hear the speakers in the echoing spaces of the Examination Schools, they were large and enthusiastic. Those five lectures provide the nucleus of this book, and to these have been added fifteen others. The majority of the contributors are associated with Oxford, either through its colleges or its libraries, and their participation is itself further evidence of the university's growing recognition of the import-ance of the Opies' scholarship, and the unique nature of their investigations into the lives and words of children. Several contributors are members of the Oxford English faculty, some of whose graduates now undertake research into children's books, and whose undergraduates may be able to do so one day.

But the Opies' own work has never been narrowly literary—it has involved social and cultural history, anthropology, and social sciences; one aspect of their achievement has been that, in exploring the world of children past and present, they have incidentally exposed the arbitrariness of the boundaries between academic subjects. The range and variety of the essays here collected is intended to reflect something of the Opies' open-ended approach to research: they include accounts of the be-haviour of children in history and in fiction, as well as discussions of the material proffered for their consumption: fairy tales, nursery rhymes, and specially designed fiction and illustration. Two essays examine the writing, in diaries and magazines, of children themselves. Though individual contributors have chosen to take independent directions, certain links and common ideas inevitably emerge: adult attitudes to childhood activities, attempts to restrain or redirect these, and a growing acceptance of the autonomy and voice of childhood are obviously recurrent themes, as is the contribution of women in helping to create a nursery world.

This volume opens with some account of the excitement of collecting children's books by Brian Alderson, uniquely expert in the field and intimately acquainted with the Opie collection. This is followed by an essay on Peter Opie's fascinating and charmingly eccentric accession diaries in which he records the growth of his collection. Its author is Clive Hurst, who has had special responsibility for receiving the Opie collection into the Bodleian, where he is Keeper of Rare Books. Keith Thomas, President of Corpus Christi College and a supporter of the Appeal from the outset, has contributed a characteristic—that is to say, a wonderfully documented—account of the role of children in early modern society, touching in the process on some of the inadequate attempts to restrain their disruptive energy and exuberance. Nigel Smith and Gillian Avery develop this point further in looking at the role of Puritanism in the development of children's books, while Jack Zipes and Giles Barber (the Librarian of Oxford's Taylor Institution) turn to eighteenth-century France and consider the history of particular fairy tales and nursery rhymes, genres that the Opies, in *The Classic Fairy Tales* and *The Oxford Dictionary of Nursery Rhymes*, had made especially their own.

William St Clair looks in detail at the kinds of book brought out by an early publisher for children, William Godwin: as a political radical, he was often obliged to write under an assumed name, and this essay incidentally extends our knowledge of his canon significantly. Moving into the nineteenth century, John Batchelor reconsiders *Alice*, and Kate Flint, an art historian as well as a literary critic, contributes the first account of Arthur

Hughes, Pre-Raphaelite painter, as an illustrator of children's books. His work brings together a number of Victorian children's classics, including *Tom Brown's Schooldays*, *At the Back of the North Wind*, and Christina Rossetti's book of verses for children, *Sing-Song*. Julia Briggs provides a summary history of children's books from the mid-eighteenth century to the end of the nineteenth, as written by women. She ends with the work of E. Nesbit, whose early collection of stories *The Book of Dragons* is the subject of W. W. Robson's essay. The so-called 'golden age' classics, Kenneth Grahame and Beatrix Potter, are discussed by Neil Philip and Humphrey Carpenter. Instead of the usual focus on Potter's appealing drawings, Carpenter has chosen instead to analyse her curiously formal, ironic, and tough-minded prose; he finds unexpected echoes of it in the work of Graham Greene, Evelyn Waugh, and Blake Morrison.

In a pair of complementary essays, Barbara Everett and John Bayley turn away from books written for children to children in the fictions of Henry James and Walter de la Mare, authors whose incipient modernism, they would argue, expresses itself in the centrality of the child observer, whose limited vision provokes a more active participation by the adult reader. Hugh Brogan, Arthur Ransome's biographer, considers the impact of the First World War on Tolkien's fictions, while Alison Lurie reassesses the work of William Mayne, a novelist for children whose large output of fiction has, until now, remained comparatively neglected. The last two essays turn to examine the creativity of children themselves as A. O. J. Cockshut looks at some nineteenth-century children's diaries and Alan and Olivia Bell find, among the rich resources of the Bodleian Library, a number of family magazines written by children. Material of this kind has scarcely been examined before. The editors hope that this volume may provide a stimulus to the scholarly study of children and their books, and even suggest new sources and directions that such research might take.

The editors would like to thank the Oxford English faculty, especially Roger Lonsdale and Malcolm Godden for their support in mounting the lectures initially, the Bodleian Library and particularly Clive Hurst for help in preparing this book, and the Oxford University Press, especially Kim Scott Walwyn, for their part in its production.

GILLIAN AVERY
JULIA BRIGGS

1

Collecting Children's Books: Self-indulgence and Scholarship

BRIAN ALDERSON

Of multiplying books, my dear Richard, there is neither end
nor use. The CACOETHES of collecting books draws men into
ruinous extravagance. It is an itch which grows by indulgence and should be nipt in the bud . . .

(Reginald Heber to his fifteen-year-old son Richard,
15 April 1789)[1]

THAT book-collectors are self-indulgent beasts needs little argument. Testimony abounds: from the dispirited family left to its
own devices in a bleak market-town on a Monday afternoon,
while its bibliomaniac leader goes questing after backstreet
bargains, to the heroic acquisitiveness of such as Richard Heber,
subject of the above remonstrance, who began collecting before
he reached his teens and ended up by filling eight houses with his
spoils.

Books are so wily in their seductiveness. For although Peter
Opie is—as ever—right to say that no collector worthy of the
name limits himself to items that he can afford, the threshold of
the unaffordable where books are concerned can make collectors
of us all. Few minors today are likely to start in on antique clocks
or Georgian silver, but any who are so inclined could lay the
foundations of a library. Moreover they will not be long in
discovering the supplementary truth: that any one book that is
'collected' immediately needs to be supported by several more for
its full and proper justification (and so *ad infinitum* . . .).

This is not just to say—sticking with our juvenile example—
that the acquisition of *The Tale of Peter Rabbit* may forthwith
prompt the acquisition of the boxed-up uniform series of 'Beatrix

Potter Books', but rather that *Peter Rabbit* is a phenomenon that may be found to have a relationship with various apparently independent phenomena ranging from 'Uncle Remus' and the Dumpy Books edition of *The Story of Little Black Sambo* to the contemporary editorial machinations of a publisher like Ladybird Books. The one book spawns a desire for a dozen more.

Given the literary nature of their interest the book-collectors have not been short of apologists, willing to put a gloss of respectability on their obsessions. Aesthetic arguments may be adduced ('books do furnish a room'), or economic ones ('what an investment this will prove to be'), or, most familiarly, intellectual ones ('collecting in the service of scholarship')—and it is not difficult to see in this last anyway a substantial reason for approving the more ambitious flights of self-indulgence. How little we would know today of the foibles of Compositor B if Henry Folger had not collected eighty copies of the First Folio and Charlton Hinman had not fed them through his ingenious collating machine; and how much slower would the revival of interest in the Victorian novelists have been if Michael Sadleir had not assembled and so magisterially catalogued his collection of XIX Century Fiction?[2]

In all the ramifying literature on book-collecting though ('as a hobby'; 'taste and technique'; 'book-madness') there is very little said about those who have a penchant for collecting children's books. Protestations—however specious—about the virtue of buying Modern Firsts, or Old Bibles, or books on butterflies have an air of authority about them which the collector of children's books cannot so easily muster. These trivia, compiled for the immature, must surely only appeal to the immature. There is no clearly institutionalized discipline within which their study has been able to set down roots and gain respectability—and indeed the very notion that material so intellectually undemanding requires study appears to many to be a contradiction in terms. We cannot hear the tone of voice which that member of the Bodleian staff employed when he reproved Richard Gilbertson for selling the 1706 edition of the *Arabian Nights* to Peter Opie, but the account (see page 31) makes it sound somewhat denigratory.

Collectors of children's books, alas, may well be on the defensive in face of their fellow book-collectors to say nothing of the uncomprehending world outside.

Judging from reactions that I have observed myself, the most favoured explanations of this particular manifestation of self-indulgence are that the collector is hopelessly nostalgic for his vanished childhood, or that he is overcome by the 'charms' or the quaintness of the objects he pursues. For every one visitor to the Opie collection who finds his pulse-rate quickening when he sees, say, William Ronksley's *Child's Weeks-Work* of 1712 there are probably a hundred who will nod and find justification for the whole enterprise in Meggendorfer's cunningly engineered *Lebende Tierbilder*, with articulated movement of the pictures as you pull the tabs, or in the absurd 'speaking book' that emits various bleats and grunts when appropriate strings are pulled.

No doubt a recognition of this playful facet of the collection is included in Peter Opie's comment on the fun, the interest, and the love which inspired his life as a collector. Within his other notes and essays on the subject however, and superabundantly in the books that he and Iona wrote together, there is an altogether stronger and, intellectually, a far more subtle and satisfying rationale for the collecting of children's books. For here, as nowhere else, we are vouchsafed a view, not necessarily of great literature, but of the fundamental process that makes great literature possible. We are given an insight into the making (and possibly, more often, into the un-making) of readers—the experiences which authors and illustrators and publishers and educators and other didacts have thought best at any one time to place in print before the impressionable young.

By a happy coincidence, that disputed copy of the *Arabian Nights* (or, as it also calls itself, the *Arabian Winter-Evenings Entertainments*) supplies an appropriate example. Certainly it has about it an aura that should excite the cupidity of any book-collector. It contains the first translations of these stories into English, only a year or so after their previous appearance in French. It seems to be one of only two known copies with a 1706 date, and is now worth many hundred times the modest twelve guineas which Mr Gilbertson set upon it. But it is also a book of especial significance for the Opie collection because (*pace* that voice) of its central place in the making of readers.

For sure, the *Arabian Nights* was not published as a children's book—such a concept barely existed in 1706—but it quickly figured among those books which children might be expected, or might not be allowed, to read. (And for the benefit of the Bodleian commentator one needs to point out that plenty of expurgation had gone on for the adult buyers of the book. As the translated Preface remarks: 'the *Arabians* have been shew'd to the *French* with all the Circumspection that the Niceness of the *French* Tongue, and of the Time requires'; the text has been varied 'when Modesty obliged us to it'.) Throughout the eighteenth century— from at least 1711, when Alexander Pope recommended the book to Sir William Trumbull as 'proper enough for the Nursery'—the *Arabian Nights* influenced child readers and was plundered for adaptations and cheap abridgements which most certainly counted children among their consumers. And one has only to read the rapt testimony of the Romantics to see the impact that Galland's Arabia had on the young imagination.[3]

Through its character as a compendium of fantastic stories the *Arabian Nights* is a particularly pointed example of a book from which circles of influence on children's literature spread out in multifarious directions. (After all, English readers were not to meet with the more homely European fairy tales, as rehearsed by Charles Perrault, for another twenty-three years.) Similar instances though—if less significant ones—may be multiplied through the whole history of children's books and an awareness of them may help us to gain some insight into the passionate emotions that stirred Peter Opie as a collector in this neglected, and sometimes derided, quarter.

Consider, as another example, that sixteen-page chapbook from Kendrew of York, *The Cheerful Warbler* (*c*.1820).[4] In all the brouhaha over the Opie Appeal, this work has achieved a measure of journalistic fame as being the foundation of the collection (alongside that anonymous Bedfordshire ladybird who gave the impetus to the *Oxford Dictionary of Nursery Rhymes*). A closer look at *The Cheerful Warbler* however may perhaps provide a fuller realization of the repercussions that can be set going by the most insignificant of printed books.

One may certainly imagine Peter Opie's excitement when, on that momentous visit to Hatchard's in 1945, he looked into *The Cheerful Warbler, or Juvenile Song Book* and observed that the first song, 'London Bell.' [*sic*], was a reprint of the early version of 'Oranges and Lemons' beginning:

> Two sticks and an apple,
> Ring the bells at whitechaple. [*sic*]

And as he leafed through the other pages of the flimsy little book he would have seen that it was almost entirely made up of rhymes which would be part and parcel of the projected *Oxford Dictionary*. Variant versions they might be, and thus useful examples of the editorial process in operation, but *in toto* they were also symbolic of how printed rhymes were sold on the popular market. *The Cheerful Warbler* was not just a pretty acquisition, it was an artefact whose significance could only be realized by placing it alongside as many equivalent works as possible. That department of the Opie collection devoted to nursery rhymes was under way.

Thanks largely to the analytical work that Iona and Peter Opie did for this part of the collection (supplemented by work done elsewhere on books that could not be acquired) we are now able to see *The Cheerful Warbler* as one of a growing number of cheap rhyme books that were put out by the chapbook-sellers in the first decades of the nineteenth century. Of its eleven rhymes (not counting the quotation from Dr Watts's 'Against Idleness and Mischief' that forms the legend to the Frontispiece) nine were among the successful candidates for *ODNR* and one of these figures in that work with *The Cheerful Warbler* quoted as its original source:

> Wine and cakes for gentlemen,
> Hay and corn for horses,
> A cup of ale for good old wives,
> And kisses for young lasses.

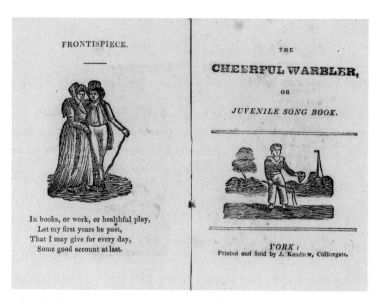

The Cheerful Warbler, an early nineteenth-century rhyme book, Peter Opie's first acquisition.

The Child's New Play-Thing. This important eighteenth-century rarity was acquired by Peter Opie in 1958.

(Why the tenth rhyme 'The Brown Cow' did not get in to *ODNR*, I do not know; it has all the characteristics needed. But the eleventh, 'Sports at the Fair' on the back cover, looks like one of John Newbery's semi-didactic effusions.)

To show how *The Cheerful Warbler* contributed to the *Dictionary* is not to exhaust its frail substance however. For it was not published by J. Kendrew of Colliergate in order that P. Opie of Hampshire could make use of it as evidence in a reference book. J. Kendrew was in the business of turning out penny booklets like this as part of his general trade as stationer and printer and *The Cheerful Warbler* offers a tiny glimpse into that large arena where so much reading-matter, for children and adults alike, was manufactured. What can be guessed about the book's inception and production?

The primary factor determining the making of the book was surely its part in this particular Kendrew series: uniform sixteen-page chapbooks, whose outer pages, acting as covers, were given a distinctive yellow wash and whose contents were cobbled up from traditional sources which might encourage a large and speedy turnover—a quick printing job that could fill in time when the presses were idle and add a mite of profit to the firm. (The success of this policy is not easily ascertainable. Judging by the numbers of Kendrew chapbooks still to be found in near-mint condition there seems to have been a largish quantity of unsold stock tucked away.)[5]

Given the printer's casual mode of procedure one may assume that *The Cheerful Warbler* was not so much edited into existence as cheerfully thrown together. Iona and Peter Opie, in their *Three Centuries of Nursery Rhymes and Poetry for Children* (2nd edn., 1977), remark that the book 'is notable for the number of references . . . to drink'—but that is probably due to accident rather than to any intention to promote Total Abstinence. The most likely mode of compilation may well have been the striking of compromises between printing rhymes that were well known, or that were to be found in other contemporary chapbooks, and matching them to woodcuts that happened to be in stock. From the Opie notes to those nine rhymes that are dealt with in *ODNR* there seems to have been no single source-text used (although Kendrew may have had to hand copies of, or books based on, *Gammer Gurton's Garland* of 1784 and Ross's *Nursery Songs* of *c*.1812—both north-country publications).

The illustrative cuts are for the most part familiar pictures, which crop up promiscuously in a variety of Kendrew chap-books. For instance, the pipe-smoking 'Drummer and Sot' ('Drunk or sober, go to bed, Tom') has also done duty as an alphabetical mariner ('S was a Sailor that plough'd the deep Sea') in *Nurse Lovechild's Golden Present*. One would need a much fuller index to the popular illustrations of the period before theories could be hazarded about the sources from which Kendrew had his pictures cut, but they belong to the common style of the period. Indeed it is not perhaps altogether fanciful to see a relationship between Taffy riding on an uncalled-for goat in 'Jolly Welchman' and a similar figure—but engraved with far greater verve—in Thomas Bewick's *General History of Quadrupeds*, Newcastle upon Tyne, 1790; and there may well be a direct connection between the Ferris Wheel in 'Sports at the Fair' and the one shown in a woodcut in John Newbery's *The Fairing* of 1765—which pro-vided source-material for other chapbook-makers.

If any sort of profit is to be derived from this heavy-handed dissection of a penny chapbook, it lies first in the recognition that, even at this elementary level, we have to do with a publication that is more than merely quaint, and second in the demonstration that diverse resources are needed if we are to advance our understanding of the book, its contents, and its *raison d'être*. Peter Opie surely discerned this when he first looked at that copy of *The Cheerful Warbler* in Hatchards in 1945, and the resolution and tenacity with which he and Iona followed up the implications is manifest in the more than 20,000 items that followed it into 'the collection'. For although the *Warbler* relates primarily to their work on nursery rhymes the inexorable law of book-collecting determined that neighbouring territories be annexed and, as Peter foresaw, the logical outcome was a library in which every aspect of children's books was represented as completely as was feasible.

As he notes in the Accession Diaries, it was a fortunate moment (although fifty years earlier would have been even more fortunate). The books were still to be found in what now can be seen as mouth-watering abundance and—largely because scholars such as Iona and Peter Opie had not yet drawn attention to the importance of the minutiae of the subject—collecting was still rather desultory and prices were not matched to the pockets of oil sheikhs and Japanese industrialists.

Even so it was an endeavour that could never be entirely converted from an experience of 'fun, interest and love' (self-indulgence in the happiest sense) to one of comprehensive scholarship. If the lesson of *The Cheerful Warbler* is that a nothing-book becomes a something-book when it is placed in its true context then how ramifying do the questions become when one is faced with the ever more frenetic activity of the publishing industry in the century and a half that followed it. When I remarked once to Iona Opie that the collection's Andersen holdings were somewhat patchy, she answered that she and Peter had not given special attention to this key-figure in children's literature because they knew of the collection that was being assembled by Dr Richard Klein. And when that collection came into the sale-room in 1980 one could see how right she was. Another Westerfield House would have been needed for Hans Christian Andersen on his own.[6]

If children's books are to be treated as objects worthy of study, therefore, there can be nothing but satisfaction that a great private self-indulgence is to be institutionalized in the Bodleian Library (and indeed the campaign that has got it there, and its aftermath, may help to bring children's literature out of the murky corners of bibliographical neglect). Collectors of the future should not despair however. For although Peter Opie was surely right to say that no one now will be able to assemble a like collection of the incunabula of the subject—or even five drawers full of its bright Regency youth—there do remain those rich years of its growth to maturity. With so much labour having been spent on the foundation bibliography of the eighteenth century we still hesitate before the labyrinthine journeyings that need to be made into the nineteenth.[7]

15

In his *Taste and Technique in Book-Collecting* (Cambridge, 1949) John Carter observes how 'the history of book-collecting is a record of service by book-collectors . . . to the republic of letters. The book-collector is in fact one of the assault troops in literature's and history's battle against the inequity of oblivion.' This chimes happily with Peter Opie's philosophy of the collector as a dynamic investigator whose curiosity may lead him into unexpected byways which the institutional intelligence will be slower to discover.

If, for instance, we recognize that, in the *Arabian Nights*, we are not just presented with questions about what is or is not a children's book but also with critical issues related to the translation, the abridgement, and the adaptation of texts—if we recognize that, in *The Cheerful Warbler*, there are still imperfectly understood chains of textual and graphic transmission, together with an exemplary display of the popular publisher at work—then we are also recognizing plots of territory within which the book-collector may work. His 'grand object' need not be on the scale set by Iona and Peter Opie, but, as Peter said, when he has settled upon it he will develop a degree of knowledge and flexibility in action which will give him the advantage over more cumbersome rivals. His energies (whether or not assisted by reluctant familial support) may indeed lead him to ruinous extravagance; they may also lead him to collocations and interpretations of facts that nobody else has reached.

And we are assured that it will not be boring.

Notes

1. Cited in A. N. L. Munby, 'Father and Son; the Rev. Reginald Heber's vain attempt to stem the rising tide of his son Richard's bibliomania', *The Library*, 5th ser., 31/3 (Sept. 1976), 183.

2. See respectively: Charlton Hinman, *The Printing and Proof-Reading of the First Folio of Shakespeare*, 2 vols. (Oxford, 1963); and Michael Sadleir, *XIX Century Fiction: A Bibliographical Record*, 2 vols. (London, 1951).

3. I have discussed the *Arabian Nights* as a children's book in my essay 'Scheherazade in the Nursery' in *The 'Arabian Nights' in English Literature*, ed. Peter Caracciolo (London, 1988).

4. A facsimile of this chapbook, with untinted covers, was published at Oxford by the Bodleian Library in 1987 in aid of the Opie Appeal.

5. See Roger Davis, *Kendrew of York and his Chapbooks for Children* (Wetherby, W. Yorks., 1988). I am very grateful to Mr Davis for his help.

6. Dr Klein did not live long enough fully to exploit his collection, and even now little attempt has been made to chart the complexities of Andersen's English translations. See my *Hans Christian Andersen and his Eventyr in England* (Wormley, Herts., 1982).

7. An immediate example comes to hand. Not the least of the treasures of the Opie collection is its run of Victorian toy-books, and especially those put out by the rival houses of Routledge and Warne (Frederick Warne having once been George Routledge's partner). Tracking the dates and the competitive relationships of these series calls for a formidable exercise in organization, which has so far never been closely attended to. Now it has been triumphantly undertaken by a Scandinavian scholar, whose interest was first aroused by seeing editions of the toy-books prepared for the Swedish market. See Göte Klingberg, *Denna Lilla Gris Går Till Torget; och andra brittiska toy books i Sverige 1869–79* (Stockholm, 1987).

2

Selections from the Accession Diaries of Peter Opie

CLIVE HURST

Introduction

PETER OPIE was an inveterate keeper of records (see the first extract below), so it is somewhat surprising to learn that he did not begin a systematic register of his book acquisitions until 1955, when he had already been an assiduous collector of children's books for ten years. On 8 March 1955 the first accession entry was made, some four-fifths of the way through a quarto notebook, hitherto used, and to be used in the future, for various notes on catchphrases and memorabilia, tongue-twisters, ideas for books (including *A Dictionary of Superstition* and *A Dictionary of the Habits, Prejudices and Homelinesses of the Opie Family*), initials, abbreviations, and synonyms. At first the entries were simply lists of titles with dates of receipt, source, and prices where appropriate. The second volume, beginning on 25 August 1962—the first devoted exclusively to books—introduces the format which Peter Opie was to follow for the next twenty years: date of acquisition, in the form 25862, followed by title, date, source, and price; and with increasing frequency a comment on the day's haul: annotations on particular books, or more general observations on the state of the market, on the nature of the Opie collection, and on his aims and intentions in collecting children's books. Together, the six notebooks, which maintain the diary until 30 January 1982, six days before Peter Opie's death, constitute a remarkable autobiography of a collector.

In making the following selection I have tried to represent as interestingly as possible the two major themes running through the diaries: the philosophy behind the relentless pursuit, 'Peter Opie's guidelines as a collector of children's books', and the sheer enjoyment, the fun, not unalloyed with disappointment, of that pursuit, 'The pleasures of the chase'. The chosen passages could often be replaced by any of a dozen others, but they should be read in the context of the daily record of books purchased, most regularly from Frank Westwood's stall in Petersfield market on Saturdays. It is important to remember too that these are not the only accession records kept by Peter Opie: his non-book acquisitions have their own separate ledger.

There is evidence in the diaries that Peter Opie was thinking of their publication in some form or another; he frequently 'improves' a word or phrase, or gives an alternative reading (usually in pencil—the original entries are in ink, first from a fountain-pen, later from a ball-point), and occasionally rewrites an entire passage. These revisions occur over the years, and it is clear that the author was constantly referring back to the record of past purchases. Nevertheless, diaries they remain, and part of their special flavour, their excitement, derives from the haste in which much of the text was written. In preparing this selection I have interfered as little as possible, silently correcting only grammatical solecisms and misspellings; where there is more than one version of a word or phrase I have adopted the later, although in one instance the four possible readings have been allowed to stand.

Each diary save the first has its epigraph; that chosen for the one begun 22 November 1973 is a quotation from an article by Sir Francis Palgrave in the *Quarterly Review* of January 1819:

The man of letters should not disdain the chap book, or the nursery story. Humble as these efforts of the human intellect may appear, they shew its secret workings, its mode and progress, and human nature must be studied in all its productions.

It is appropriate to juxtapose a note scribbled by Peter Opie and loosely inserted in the previous diary describing his and Iona Opie's approach to the 'material related to child life':

We are most interested in those books & objects which have been the most popular, or are the most ordinary, or are the most typical of their period. We prefer the trivial to the pretentious, the ephemeral to the monumental.

The Origins of the Opie Collection of Children's Literature

14 January 1969

To David Low[1] who has been recalling the day when he found a wonderful collection of children's books belonging to an 'Irish professor who lived in a decaying castle in Cork':

I can tell you (because I keep records) that it was on the 22nd November 1948 that I was walking through Cecil Court—not, if I remember rightly, looking for books—and I happened to meet you going to your shop and you said you had bought a collection of children's books. We went in together—you were still pricing the books—and I spent £40. We had been collecting for little more than two years, chiefly nursery rhymes and fairy tales. This was the first large miscellaneous collection I bought (I thought Iona would be shocked at the extravagance and she wasn't), and it was this purchase really, of the nicest of the Irish professor's books, that laid the foundations of our forming a general collection of children's books which, over the years, have pushed us out of cottage, then out of high street house, and into a mansion (almost) which the family complains is becoming too cramped.

Peter Opie's Guidelines as a Collector of Children's Books

6 November 1962

Throughout the time that I have collected books the factors which have made me resolve/determine to buy a particular volume that has been on offer have been either that, knowing the value that has been put on it elsewhere, I have felt that I was never likely to be offered it for less—in other words, that I was obtaining a nice bargain; or, secondly, that the book has been so rare, or the particular copy has been so special in itself, that I have felt it improbable, if I did not go for it now, that I would ever have a second chance of obtaining its like.

This policy (which I have never regretted) means that I have a largish number of fairly ordinary books which have been picked up cheaply when the occasion offered, either in quantity at an auction or individually from market stalls—for I dearly love a bargain; and it means that I have, I think, an unusually high proportion of rarities or special volumes. Thus fifteen years ago, when we probably had no more than a dozen 18th century children's books, we had the offer of the only other known copy of the earliest extant edition (1766) of *Goody Two-Shoes*.[2] It cost us as much as the rest of our collection put together, but it became and has remained a corner stone of the collection. With the possession of this key book few other collections of John Newbery's publications can rival us, perhaps only one. And I have often thought since that it is not a bad way to form a collection to start with the most important book in one's subject, that which will be the apex of one's collection, and then fill in the path that will lead up to it.

The drawback to my policy is that I do not so much find myself acquiring the books of medium value and scarcity. I have not yet had reasons sufficiently pressing to induce me to get the first editions of, for instance, The Water Babies, Treasure Island, The Child's Garden of Verses, The Jungle Books, and Kate Greenaway's Under the Window. Each one of them is a landmark in the history of children's literature, and is clearly essential for my collection, and yet I have never yet felt it imperative that I should buy them. Each of these volumes has been one which I have felt is going to turn up again, usually at least once in each season, consequently I have had no inducement (or felt no compulsion) to part with the £4 to £20 which was asked for them; whereas I have seized the opportunity on the, to me, wondrous occasions, when I have been offered Lear's Book of Nonsense, 1846, both vols in nice condition in original wrappers; Black Beauty, presentation copy from the author; Tom Brown's Schooldays, a fresh copy; and altho I haven't taken the plunge with Treasure Island, always believing that I will see it again, I have the story as it first appeared in a set of Little Folks which is infinitely scarcer (& to me more interesting) than its 1st appearance in book form.

THE
HISTORY
OF
Little GOODY TWO-SHOES;
Otherwise called,
Mrs. MARGERY TWO-SHOES.
WITH
The Means by which she acquired her
Learning and Wisdom, and in conse-
quence thereof her Estate; set forth
at large for the Benefit of those,

Who from a State of Rags and Care,
And having Shoes but half a Pair;
Their Fortune and their Fame would fix,
And gallop in a Coach and Six.

See the Original Manuscript in the *Vatican*
at *Rome*, and the Cuts by *Michael Angelo*.
Illustrated with the Comments of our
great modern Critics.

A New EDITION, Corrected.

LONDON:
Printed for J. NEWBERY, at the *Bible* and
Sun in St. *Paul's Church-yard*, 1766.
[Price *Six-Pence*.]

Little Goody Two-Shoe.

(*Above*) 'a corner stone of the collection',
Little Goody Two-Shoes; one of only two
known copies of the second edition.
(*Below*) inscription from Alastair
Grahame's copy of *The Wind in the
Willows*. This book, bought from a South
Kensington dealer in 1945, was one
of Peter Opie's earliest acquisitions.
(*Right*) *Jack and the Giants*, *c*.1750, 'the
best text and probably the earliest
complete printing known'.

THE
HISTORY,
OF
Jack *and the* GIANTS.
PART I.

Printed in this present Year.

To
Alastair Grahame
from his affectionate father
Kenneth Grahame

Cookham Dean,
Oct. 1908.

25 March 1964

Going thru old catalogues & putting them away with Tish,[3] I thought: I have *tried* to collect what I felt to be beautiful or fun or, most of all interesting, without reference to fashion or other people or prevailing prices. If it happens that there are now other people of like mind, then it is my bad luck when buying, my good luck when selling.

4 February 1965

A collector, to be a good collector, must believe that he appreciates the things he collects more than does anybody else. He may, even, persuade himself that it is actually more *important* that he rather than anybody else should be the possessor of these things. To this end he makes himself (or believes he makes himself) the most knowledgeable person there is on his subject—and the greater his knowledge the greater becomes his appreciation; he provides proper facilities for the arrangement, maintenance, and display of his collection (as we do here); and, most of all, he knows what the grand object is of his collection, what it is that he is trying to create with his collection, or find out, or demonstrate, with his collection.

Which is sometimes when institutions fall down, for after the original impetus of their founder, their collections may tend just to come about, & they cannot know all the purposes to which their collection will be put. The collections of the institutes almost inevitably lag behind those in the dedicated private collection in any special field in discrimination, in detail, in condition, in novelty, & in love.

25 May 1965

I sometimes feel I am mad or rare or perverted the way I collect books and pamphlets and even cards and sheets of paper. Then sitting in the lavatory, I read in the new Sotheby's catalogue[4] about the Tollemache family who, in 1510, moved from Bentley Hall, the house they had built in the 12th century, to their newly finished Hall at Helmingham. 'The manuscripts at Helmingham were collected shortly before or after 1600 by Sir Lionel Tollemache, 1st baronet, or perhaps by some scholar acting on his behalf. Only two generations had then passed since the dissolution of the monasteries and the dispersal of their libraries and it was still possible to assemble a collection of manuscripts not unlike that which would have been owned by one of the religious houses of East Anglia.' Further, one reads of successive generations, adding to, or taking care of the collection, thus a manuscript note on the fly-leaf of 'A Remedy for Sedition' 1536 by the 4th Earl of Dysart (as the family had now become):

'I found this Tract rumpled up amongst a parcel *of Waste Paper at Helmingham*. New Bound 1745. NB it never had been bound before. LTHD'

So, once again, I am reminded that people have been doing the sort of thing I am doing for centuries, and that perhaps I am not so mad nor, it is perhaps gratifying to realise, so unusual as I sometimes feel myself to be.

It has always seemed to me incredible that one can be an ordinary person, with no official standing, and can go into a shop and come out again having bought something unique.

I remember my wonder 20 yrs ago at buying, near the British Museum, an abridged edition of Robinson Crusoe, 1737, for 25/-, and then going into the BM and finding they did not possess it. Today that copy is listed in an American bibliography with my name after it as the sole possessor of a copy of this edition.

It took me some time before I realised that 'rare books are common'. I probably acquire an item or two which is unique, or almost unique, every month of the year.

A Remedy for Sedition, 1536 is cracked up by Sotheby's with a note in capitals 'Only Nine Other Copies Recorded.' And again, one of the prize items in the catalogue, The Greate Herball, 1561, is announced as 'Only Nine Other Copies Recorded: British Museum; Cambridge University Library; Edinburgh University; Harvard . . .'

Such a work is almost common compared with the items I go after. Today I ordered from a list 'Granny's Wonderful Chair, 1858,' for 8/-. This is a classic children's story which has given pleasure for over a hundred years, as may be seen from the way that it has been constantly reprinted, even in recent years: 1909, 1912, 1927, 1938, 1943, 1948, 1955. These are the eight editions that the BM possesses (or possessed in August 1961). It has, or had then, no 19th century edition whatsoever. The copy I have ordered is, I suspect, the 2nd edition. I already possess the 1st edition, which seems to be unrecorded.

So it has come about that I have in this room some of the rarest books in the world, and to me not all of them seem to be inconsequential volumes, for instance, the first editions of The Arabian Nights, Lear's Nonsense, and Smart's Hymns and special copies such as the dedication copy of The Wind in the Willows, a presentation copy of Black Beauty, and the corrected copy of Bewick's Birds. Has it then been a specially favourable period for collecting? Could such a collection have been assembled so cheaply at any other time?

Twenty years seems a long time when one is looking ahead. It even seems a long period when one is looking at it in a history book. It has not seemed a long time to me while I have been living it. When a historian of collecting comes to look at this period he will remark on how circumstances have changed. Twenty years ago one could buy 18th & early 19th century ballad sheets for 1/6 each; mint pictorial music sheets for 1/3; 19th c theatre posters for 1/6; chapbooks for 2–3 shillings from Maggs Brothers; and postcards were so cheap one did not buy them, one thought people who collected them to be juvenile. Today one seldom gets ballad sheet, music cover, poster, or chapbook under a £1. Collecting postcards has become a fashionable pursuit, and they are sold singly at 1/- each. But these figures may mislead the historian of collecting. The feel of collecting has scarcely altered. When I began buying chapbooks at 2/6 each, they were expensive trophies I could scarcely afford at these inflated prices. People reminisced about the 'thirties when they could pick these trivial pamphlets out of unsorted 6d boxes put in front of the book-sellers in the street. Collectors items have, I suspect, *always* been expensive. Possibly because no collector worthy of the name limits himself merely to items that he can afford.

20 April 1966

Boreman, Description of Gt. Variety of Animals 2nd ed. R. Ware 1744 Maggs £8-10-0

Bought for the hell of the thing. A duplicate, & as it turns out not such a good copy as the one I bought nine years ago from Heap for 7/6, but I hope to show—now that I see how to do the book on children's books[5]—that this is one of a group of highly important juveniles; I felt almost that I must have it to keep the position Roscoe says I have of topmost private collection of children's books; and I bought it in the hope that it will attract the remaining missing Boremans to me.

16 September 1966

Today came The History of England by Thomas Thumb Esq [M. Cooper] 1749 Murray Hill 12-10-0 and Sydney Roscoe's Provisional check list of Newbery books.

Mary Cooper's History looks like a more enterprising history for children than any that appeared subsequently in the century, in fact until the coloured creations of the Regency (how children's books mirror the spirit of their age). Roscoe's bibliography seems to show that the Opie collection is not inconsiderable even when set beside the Bodley, BM and the American holdings. It appears that a biblio of the Opie collection in itself could be interesting— or is it just that 'Opie' springs to my eye as I turn the pages. But oh how I wish I had known that the collection could become important in itself: how I wish I'd bought a few more of these books when I had the offer.

8 November 1966

Yesterday missed 1st ed. of Original Poems 1805 by the Taylors for £21 'one of the scarcest books in English literature'.[6] My foolishness throughout in thinking that exciting books never now turn up, & not reading some of the mish-mashy catalogues instantly and assiduously.

11 May 1968

While working on CBEL[7] I have also been wondering what kind of bibliography or catalogue or work on 18th century children's books we ourselves could best do. I would like to describe the books (that is comment on their contents, their significance, and the children who are known to have read them), & I would like to list the known editions, or anyway those in the British Museum. (This would be a book in itself.) Yet I would also like to describe in detail our own actual copies.

Each copy of a book that has been standing around for 200 years or so is liable to vary from other copies, even of the same printing, and to have acquired its own characteristics. Its binding may vary from other copies, its condition certainly does; in addition it may carry the label of its original bookseller; surprisingly often it may still have its original price marked in it. It may bear an inscription by its original owner or donor, there may be comments in it written in a contemporary hand; it may be possible to trace its change of ownership over the years (one of our children's books has come down in our family through six generations), and there may even be fascinating evidence of its extra curricula use, such as in our copy of Cato's Distiches 1712 — which a Georgian schoolboy has converted into a fortune-teller. It is always good to be reminded that the history of a book does not end with its being written and being published, but with it being read, and a catalogue of actual copies can show more vividly than can any general bibliography or history, the story of its readership.

Our Collection

Eighteenth century children's books which were often small in size and fragile in their binding are almost more items for a museum than a library. Almost inevitably national and public libraries have had to re-bind these books, and, for convenience, they have usually bound more than one together. Chapbooks, for instance, are generally bound a dozen or two dozen together, and a student who has never handled an individual chapbook in its original uncut state will be hard put to visualise exactly what the schoolboy was getting for his happenny, he will not easily think of it as a comic to be tucked in the pocket of his coattail during school. Our object has been to bring together examples of the reading-matter that the young had in the 18th c. in their original state, and, as much as possible, in their original condition.

Our aim has been to form a representative collection, to have at least one early edition of each of the best known books. We have contented ourselves with second editions where the first edition varies little from the 2nd printing, is to be found in national libraries, and, being a known highlight, commands a considerable price. Rather we have gone after volumes of which the first edition is unknown, or of which, perhaps, no edition is readily available, or of which (in our estimation) the significance is not yet fully appreciated, or of which the particular copy in itself seemed to us to be of interest.

29 January 1966 [8]

People who cannot appreciate a book as an object, as, almost holding the hand of the author who informs or entertains them, will rarely go far in understanding the author, but this can, I am aware, only be done truly by holding the original edition, which is why I would rather have the original edition,—say Bernard's Comforts of Old Age, bought today, than I would a Penguin edition of a classic (at about seven times the price). And this copy has not aged, although it is 150 years old, and was out in the rain today on the stall.

5 November 1970

One of the biggest disappointments I have ever had was last Monday when I rang Miss Atkins at 8.30 in the morning to ask for Perrault's Mother Goose, Englished by Robert Samber, 3rd edn 1741—hitherto unknown—for merely £32, and she said she had sent advance catalogues to the libraries, and the Bodleian had got it. Normally I can dismiss a disappointment quickly, especially when it is not my fault that I have missed a book. But in a way it was my fault I missed this one. Miss Atkins lives only a dozen miles away in Chichester. I have been to see her more than once, and she has said how much she wants to come here, and I have not found time for her. Had I done so I know I would now possess that book, the earliest edn of the fairy tales in this country, and, in the mysterious way that ownership has, my voice would have had that much more authority.

12 March 1971

Have been led a fascinating chase by the MS note on the cover of The Birth-Day Gift.[9] It seems the illustrations may in fact be by Princess Elizabeth. In which case this is another example of how valuable can be an individual copy compared with a facsimile. Away with facsimiles! I like 'individual' copies, copies given individuality by their binding, or association, or inscriptions, or, even, enclosures.

11 June 1980

A collector does not need to live dangerously. The secret of success lies I think more in keeping on and on and on rather than in spending beyond his means. Given that he keeps his eyes open, given that he has taste, judgement, discrimination, which cannot be taught (which apparently is something in his genes), and given that he has a third eye which is always fixed on his target, success is simply the natural result of the amount of reading, the amount of thought, and the number of years he is willing to devote to his objective. He needs endurance, plus courage in an emergency. If I had had a little more courage when something splendid was suddenly offered me my collection would now be superb. I have let opportunities slip, not realising they would never reoccur.

At the Europa Schiller tried to sell me a rather worn copy of MacDonald's Dealing with the Fairies 1867 for £235. Immediately on my return I was looking through some duplicates and was annoyed by a book that was oversmall compared with its neighbours. It was Dealing with the Fairies. I would not be surprised if we had three copies.

The Pleasures of the Chase

12 August 1960

Select Tales & Fables (Nourse, Crowder, Baldwin) c1775 Brimmell £2 2 Found, suddenly, towards end of pricey modern-books catalogue, got up in middle of breakfast and rang for, & just as well I did, becos Brimmell when sending it says: 'The Bodleian rang for this just after your call and said they were glad it was going to a good home.' How does a library get onto a thing so quickly—bet they have not also got 1st ed. 1746 like we have.[10]

22 August 1962

Arabian Nights Entertainments 4 vols 1706–1717 R. Gilbertson £12-12-0 This is the only known copy[11] of the first English translation. When Gilbertson sent the receipt he wrote: 'I think you might like to know that the Bodleian wanted the Arabian Nights. They rang up for it and when I told them you had bought it, a very disgruntled voice said: 'I thought he collected children's books; I hope you expurgated it first.'

15 October 1964

Got onto the Book Shop at Wells pretty early last Monday (12th) but haven't been sent any of the Newberys & Carnans I asked for—perhaps Roscoe got them. Mr Heap's lists are, in some respects, my favourite. Ordering books from them is like taking tickets in a lottery. One not only has little idea whether one will win anything—this is as with other booksellers; one is given little idea of the edition or condition of what one is hoping to get. The joy is that, on the whole, individual tickets are not priced high, and my usual experience is that although I may [get] a number of dud books (there were several this time), there will be one winner amongst them that will be worth what one gave for the lot. This has happened again:

The Historical Pocket Library 6 vols Roan illus Bath 1790 50/- turns out to be a perfect pristine complete set of charming little $4\frac{1}{2} \times 3\frac{1}{2}$ volumes printed by Hazard of Bath for G. Riley of Ludgate Street 1789–90 1st editions each with full page engraved frontis, and numerous woodcuts within—as fresh as the day they were bought, and as rare and exquisite as strawberries at Christmas. Worth all of the £10 the whole order cost me.

22 May 1965

Outwardly I appear to lead an unexciting life; in reality I am perpetually gambling. Book buying is much like horse racing, even placing the bets is similar. The day before yesterday I sent a telegram 'DEVA 126 368'.[12] I put 5 guineas on 126 and 15/- on 368. Of course I didn't know whether these horses would run my way. When placing money from a catalogue the items are apt to run off in somebody else's direction and never be heard of again. When they do come it is a gamble, as often as not, what one is getting for one's money.

17 June 1965

Antiquarian Book Fair and a week of book buying.

Went a bit wild at the book fair, esp. after seeing mint flowery Dutch books sold in front of my eyes within minutes of the opening of the Fair.

From Pratley:

Lessons for Children, set of 4 vols 1788-7-8-4 21-0-0 He insisted I should have them, and is probably right. [There is a further note to this purchase on the facing page of the diary:]

Lessons for Children seems, and was, pricey, tho it appears to be an earlier than any set recorded. One hundred and eighty years ago it cost 2/-, but 2/- at 5% cumulative interest would now, I think, be more than £100, so perhaps collecting is not all that profitable a hobby.

10 August 1965

To R,[13] who sent a package of ephemera including the Vendonis [*sic*] Twins in Africa, (Manufacturers Gift Books for Children is one of my favourite sub-sections. What a charming subject for a bibliography) and two catalogues containing many children's books c 1940, to which was immediately drawn, despite eyes.—

When I die my heart will be found pressed between the pages of a book catalogue.

Two observations:

(i) Where have all these books gone that were offered for sale? Presumably they must still be somewhere. There are half a dozen items in each that I would dearly like a sight of.

(ii) How erratic the prices are. The dozen gems apart—not necessarily recognised as such by their vendors—many of the books are expensive even by today's prices, and in those days would have been wholly out of reach. These pussylogues are before my time, but I don't regret it. Collecting is not just a matter of buying, or even of finding, it is, as you know, of 'recognising'—of being able to see—& thereafter make others see—what is interesting and what is rubbish.

8 November 1965

From Edward Morrill & Son, Inc. of Boston

Juvenile Trials for Robbing Orchards, Telling Fibs, and Other Heinous Offences. Printed in Boston, 1797 for twenty cents. I am paying twenty-nine dollars for it, but have the same feeling of wonder at receiving this book from Boston after a hundred and seventy years that American collectors must sometimes feel when they receive the first edition of a London-printed eighteenth century book from London. £10-13-0

5 April 1966

Another point about this [i.e. the above-mentioned book] is that I turn out to be the only person who possesses the first English edition.[14]

18 November 1967

In the market I happened to ask Westwood if he thought the Monthly Review was obtainable. I had been going thru it at the London Library, and it had a number of reports of 18th [century] children's books when they came out. He said that he did not know but he had a lot of 18th C periodicals up in his office if I liked to come and see. He showed me a large grocer's carton box in which there was a higgledy piggledy mass of variously clean and scruffy magazines, but all in their original parts as issued. He said he had bought them for the plates, but I could have any that I wanted for very little after he had taken the plates. I had a small look which was difficult becos the small room was stuffed with stuff and I knew Iona would be waiting in the car to go home. So I said I would be interested and left it at that. We worked hard all the weekend and onwards, & by Thursday I was not only exhausted but having second thoughts about those magazines. Rang up & Westwood said he had removed the plates he wanted. I could take them home, and have any I wanted at 2/- each. Iona & I went into Petersfield & brought them back. I spent the next 48 hours virtually living in the 18th century. Devaluation, the foot and mouth epidemic, the looming hostilities between Greece and Turkey, and even the games book were forgotten. Virtually every number had something of interest in it. There were more than a dozen different magazines, published between 1738 and 1775. On the flimsy blue-paper covers of these periodicals, or on tipped in pages which the binder removes before binding, were contemporary advertisements of many of the books I have in this room. There were magazines with contributions by men such as Goldsmith & Smollett. There were three or four first numbers. Magazines with Newbery adverts, & even published by Newbery. There were magazines which Boswell would have read (one with an account of Mrs Rudd) and they were in the form that Boswell would have read them. In the end I took every one that was perfect or near perfect (Westwood had removed only views or coloured plates) & some had never had plates, or had something interesting to it . . .

On 25 Nov. my 49th birthday, Iona, Bob, & I went into Petersfield. I asked Westwood if I could buy the two missing plates from the British Magazine, which seems to me an important mag; and Westwood charged 30/- for one of them and 15/- for the other. However, I scarcely minded. I was getting the 124 nos for £14-10 and was now realising I had been foolish, not being bold & offering something for the lot before he had removed the plates (I believe he would have taken £25 for the lot). Kicking myself somewhat, I asked if he had any more. He said no, but there were some pamphlets and other pieces upstairs he had got from the same source. If I liked I could look through them. I took the key and went to his cubby-hole up stairs, and found a further grocer's box stuffed full of what outwardly look very dull and dusty papers. The first thing I saw was odd numbers of the London Chronicle 1758 for which Westwood wanted 5/- a number. I realised I was not going to look through this box in five minutes, and it was already nearing eleven o'clock. I rushed back to the car, summoned Iona and Bob to Westwood's and we spent the next two hours there, unaware of time, or our cramped state, arriving back late for lunch. It appeared that these things came from a room in a house in East Meon, a room that the owner did not know he possessed. The owner had recently inherited the property; spent his time, Westwood said, drinking and watching television; and when he could not pay his gambling debts he rang Westwood and asked him to go over. The rooms were lined with books. He would pick a book off a shelf and ask Westwood how much he would give for it. Westwood would say, perhaps, £30. The man would say 'Chickenfeed, not worth selling,' and put the book back. They went on like this round the house until they came to the room, which, as the owner said, he did not know was there. In this room was a cupboard, which was stuffed with the stuff that was now in the grocery cartons. How much for this? the man asked. 'A hundred pounds' said Westwood. 'Right' he said, 'clear it out.'

Westwood, who likes angling books, oriental & Africana, fine bindings, and plates, told us he was disappointed with his purchase. He had hoped to find something special, and he doubted he was going to do more than cover what he had paid. But to Iona & Bob & I it did not look like rubbish. Here were the unbound books, magazines & ephemera that, over the course of a hundred years, a country family of landed gentry had stuffed into a cupboard instead of throwing away. They had been hoarders these people but not embellishers. Every article was in the state in which it had been issued or purchased. And, judging by the dust, it seems that nobody had looked in this cupboard for 200 years, merely shoved more things in it. The result, to me, was an exhibition of pieces 'as issued' in original state from the 1630's to 1770's and we had the first pick.

14 August 1968

Frank Westwood says that the Bodleian came and had a look round his shop the other day, 'and you know those pamphlets, and so on, you had; they took away every single one that was left. I told them you had had the pick of them, and they were rather annoyed, they said they did not know you collected that sort of thing.' It is good when one's judgement is vindicated.

3 May 1968

Rose at 6am at Godfrey Street, and caught the 8.30 at Liverpool Street Station for Norwich, not knowing whether or not I was on a wild goose chase.

A fortnight before there had been an advert for 'Marshall's Juvenile Library' 18 vols dated 1800 in box painted to simulate a bookcase £30, inserted in the Book Market by a music shop in Wisbech, Cambridgeshire. I wrote and was told it had been sold in the shop that day; I wrote again & was told it had been sold to a bookseller & he would pass on my card. On Tuesday, while Tom Todd was here, I got a postcard from Derek Gibbons of Norwich saying he had it, & [that I] could look at it, if I wished, for CBEL. When I arrived I found two things (i) that Derek Gibbons genuinely did not want to sell it, becos he wanted dollars for it to satisfy his bank manager & overdraft (ii) he was genuinely embarrassed by the offers he had already had for it, since I knew how much he had paid for it. I stayed talking with Mr & Mrs G. for eight hours continuously (they gave me lunch) and in the end I got it for four times what he had bought it for, which in fact was only the same as Pickering paid for a set of the Infant's Library at Sotheby's recently, and lacking one volume. In my favour was that they had read all my books right back to The Case of Being a Young Man and Having Held the Nettle, and that they only started dealing in children's books a year ago and came increasingly to like the idea of the bookcase coming into our collection.

There are eighteen little volumes in original boards with engraved labels stuck on back and front, each of those on the back declaring that the volume is part of 'The Juvenile or Child's Library'. All are illustrated with copper plates, all are in fine condition, and all of them interesting; including Views of London 2 vols, Copperplate views of historic houses, Geog, Grammar, Kilner's Poems, 2 vols Tales a 5 vol set of Natural History, & even a drawing book. Although the box does not seem completely full I suspect that it has all the volumes that it originally had. Nothing appears to be missing, and every volume shown on the lid appears in the case. I know of no other set. Have never heard of this box, so much larger than the Infant's Library, and so much less likely to have been kept through the years. I did not even mind forgoing the early 19th C chapbooks with which the box was stuffed. I would almost put this purchase beside my dash to Hodgson's when I got the 14 Carnans for about the same price, and with the ever-to-be-regretted purchase that I did not make of the Boremans for about the same sum. . . . Arrived home at 11.30.

20 May 1969

Finished at 3.45 [a visit to Mr E. O. Golding's book warehouse in Surbiton]. Had chatted and searched continuously since 11 am, and went off to get some tea & continue on to Waterloo arriving 4.45, too late to go anywhere; but David Drummond stays open until six, so thought I might go there for a gossip. Unfortunately—or fortunately—an American with an unpronounceable name and a fat wad of fivers was there, and as I did not want to go to Godfrey Street yet (I had said 6.30) there was nothing for me to do but finger books. Eventually I started going through some rows in a case in the window, chiefly nineteenth century keepsakes at enormous prices, £4 or £5 a time. Then I pulled out a little book called The Minor's Pocket Book for the Year 1791, and shut it up again quickly in case, if I looked more closely, it turned out to be something other than what I thought it was. However several glances at various parts of it seemed to confirm that it *was* Darton's Minor's Pocket Book, and when, eventually, the American left & David Drummond was shutting the shop I said I had found one expensive one. He looked at it (it was priced £4-10-0) and said Yes, he had had it on display in his showcase, open at the title-page & folding frontispiece, but when people had asked to look at it, they had been disappointed with the rest of it which was just a blank diary. I could have it for £4.

In his bibliography of *The Taylors of Ongar* 1965 pp. 19–20, Harris writes:

'The Minor's Pocket Book 1796(?)–1815 was for a period edited by Ann. Her first contribution to the 1799 issue was signed 'Juvenilia' ... The British Museum has no copy of any volume of this most rare periodical, Sawyer and Darton knew of a copy in America. E. V. Lucas never saw one. The Alexander Turnbull Library in New Zealand has a copy of the 1804 issue with MS notes by Ann Taylor. My own copy is 1797 probably the second volume.'

For fifteen or twenty years I have had this title in mind as one that was highly desirable and might one day be found, and when found turn up unnoticed. (But The Minor's Pocket Book is such a legend I was beginning to wonder whether it had any reality.) Incidentally this is the second 18th C children's diary to come to Westerfield from Cecil Court in ten days: both exceedingly rare.[15] Three days ago I sent off our CBEL section in which we say The Minor's Pocket Book probably started in 1795. This, if nothing else, made my visit to London worthwhile.

23 March 1971

Amongst the catalogues on Saturday had been a mimeographed typescript list of children's books from Mr Heap at the Book Shop, Wells. I began reading and there was first one treasure and then another, Marshall's History of England in Verse, The Universal Shuttlecock, Don Stephano Bunyano, books I have dreamed of possessing for more than twenty years, and not seen for sale, and here they were being offered for a pound or two each. The list had come by second-class mail, the postmark was indecipherable, I had no way of knowing how long it had been in the post. Iona kept saying 'Ring him up, ring him up.' I said 'He doesn't arrive at the shop until nine.' I remembered once I had rung before nine and there had been no reply, when I rang a second time it was just after nine, and someone had got in before me. At ten to nine Io was still saying 'I should ring him now' so I thought I would, and be able to get in the second call at nine exactly. I rang and astonishingly the phone was answered. 'I don't know how long your catalogue has been out' I said. 'You're the first to ring' he said. I ordered 17 items by number, and afterwards had awful doubts whether I had given the right numbers. 'I'll parcel them up for you,' he said. It seemed incredible that three minutes before one had been a person who didn't possess these treasures, and now one was a person, apparently, who did. I had only woken up an hour and a half before. And how tempted I have been, after the strike, to give up fetching the post. The post would not yet have arrived if I had not been down to the village on my bike to fetch it.

The books from Wells came this afternoon, a small grocer's carton with a piece of string round it. I opened it and there were Dutch paper-covered books and leather bound books and little paper books lying there naked. It was an incredible sight. Few people can have received such treasures so nonchalantly packed . . . Fourteen 18th C vols in one parcel pushed inside the door.

When I had ordered these books I felt, once again, that I now had everything a collector of 18th C children's books could possibly want, & I could do a catalogue of them, and rest content. But this morning I was writing to California, first thing, in the hope—a vain hope I'm sure—of obtaining a lovely-sounding item.[16]

12 July 1974

(Friday) On Tuesday received a catalogue from George's divided—most unusually these days—into sixteenth century books, seventeenth century books, and eighteenth century books. Naturally looked at the eighteenth century where were one or two books of moderate interest, e.g. some schoolbooks, but nothing we did not have. Toward the end of breakfast opened the catalogue at the seventeenth century, and where I opened it was startled to see Janeway (James) A Token for Children, The

Second Part ... 1672 £30. Have long looked upon A Token for Children as being just about the first book produced for the young that was likely of itself to engage a child's interest; and have also appreciated the rarity of the early editions, the first editions of the two parts 1671 and 1672 being unknown until recently when Toronto got hold of them. In fact the first edition of A Token for Children has been much in my mind this past six months after hearing the lengths Miss St John was prepared to go to obtain the copy for Toronto. She even had a national Church conference organised to which the then owner of the Janeway, who was a clergyman, could be invited, and could be made much of. I was fascinated both by the lengths a public institution was prepared to go to bring moral pressure to bear, and then by her candid admission, at a meeting, how her success had been achieved, as if it was something of which to be proud. And here, in the catalogue before me, was the first edition of a half of it, described as 'Very rare. Not in Wing', but priced at only £30. I looked at the postmark and saw, with resignation, that it had been posted on the 6th—Saturday. It was already a day old. But I went to the phone, although it was not yet nine, and stuck on the phone, letting the bell go on ringing (fortunately Bristol is now on STD) until a quarter past nine, when it was answered by—one of my worse fears—someone who said the catalogue department was engaged, but that he would give them a message. By past experience I know this means (a) that the person or persons responsible for the catalogue have not yet arrived, and (b) that when the person or persons do arrive, they start taking orders, and only learn of my order after what I wanted has been promised to someone else. My feelings, after this phone call, plunging and tossing between hope and despair, the hope that I might be becoming the possessor of one of [the] rarest and most desirable of children's books—for a sum (unlike at Sotheby's) that I could easily afford—and the fear that I might miss it by human error or tardiness or disinterestedness, were too awful for me now to look back upon. The more so as the man at the other end did say that orders for the catalogue had 'started coming in' only that morning. I even rang again, half an hour later, on the pretext of ordering another book; and had the same reply as for the first call, which almost made the situation worse. This morning both books arrived. The Token is a drab little book, and already it seems of no special consequence to possess it. Perhaps this is as it should be. Most of today we have been recording an interview for the World this Weekend.

17 October 1975

Iona came back from her night in London with three notable volumes. She had tea with Justin Schiller, and he had acquired them for us at the Oppenheimer sale:

  1118 A Guide for the Child and Youth 1723 £160 a bid over the University of California

  1188 Jack and the Giants 2 pts Newcastle, Printed in the Present Year [*c.* 1750] £55

  1249 The Celebrated Nanny Goose 1813 £35

Much money, but a tale is attached to each of these volumes. The *Guide for the Child and Youth*, 1723, to begin with, has haunted me for twenty-five years. I was first aware of this actual copy from one of Rosenthal's catalogues. Dr Ettinghausen dealt chiefly in Continental books, and he was almost apologetic about including some children's books, amongst them this item, priced at £4, which was already sold before the catalogue came out. Dr E told me he had bought it from some refugees from the Nazis, that he had found it in a cupboard under the stairs, that he believed there were other children's books there, and he gave me the address in South Kensington; but the few other books he himself had brought away were of little interest, and I did not follow up the introduction. Nevertheless I was actually given a chance to buy the volume. In December 1949 another expatriate——Romer, held a little exhibition or book fair, so called, in South Molton Street, and when I went to it on the first day there was this book, and it was for sale. His pencil marking can still be seen at the back '£v 11/49 AR 8gns. for sale.' It was, and is, a lovely book, specially bound in morocco gilt for the little girl to whom it was presented, with her initials in gilt in the centre of the rich ornate gilt tooling. It was the earliest book for the young I had ever seen—from the beginning of my collecting priority and age have been important—and it was of the size of a Newbery book, although pre-dating Newbery's publications by almost a generation. There was one snag to it; although it was a lovely copy it lacked one leaf. I was resolved to buy it, however, and had it in my hand, when in walked Roland.[17] (We were the first people at the fair. There was no one else.) Immediately I went on the defensive. This is an interesting book, I said, but unfortunately it is imperfect, and I put it down. I did not want Roland to see me pay so vast a sum for a book lacking a leaf. He himself always insisted on the importance of condition. But ever since that day, 8 December 1949, I have regretted the way I played safe, and pretended to be grown-up by disparaging the book, and the high price being asked for it, and did not allow myself to act on my natural inclination which was to have it. I now have it but I have had to pay twenty times over to rectify my mistake. But in my experience one is very seldom given the chance to rectify a mistake at any price. Of course I now know the book to be more important than I had then thought it—I believe the original edition of 1667 to have been the inspiration of The New England Primer—and my income too is probably twenty times that of 1949.

Of the second item, Jack and the Giants, I have written on a separate slip for insertion in the copy. Suffice to say that it appears to be the best text and probably the earliest complete printing known of Jack and the Giants, and would have saved us a world of trouble if we had possessed it two or three years ago.

And having rectified one mistake of long ago, and made good a deficiency that became worrisome three years ago, we have, with the third item, looked to the future. It contains the earliest known version of 'The Three Little Pigs' and will become invaluable if we do The Nursery Mythology.

Notes

1. This entry was copied into the diary from a letter of the same date to David Low.

2. The British Library has since acquired the only known copy of the first edition of 1765. The Opie copy of the 1766 edition, enlarged from the 1765 text, is of an earlier state than the only other one known. Roscoe J167(2).

3. Peter Opie's daughter Letitia.

4. Sotheby's sale of 14 June 1965.

5. 'I have seen, at last, how to do my book on 18th c children's books. I was adding another literary reference to my file on the Arabian Nights, and noticed that I had now quotations on it by Wordsworth, Coleridge, & Southey, and realised what a splendid miniature essay could be written on the Arabian Nights. I realised how one might take as one's subject a hundred 18th C books, authors, or themes. Have a reproduction and bibliographical description of a selected item, & then write about it, as an example of its type, listing later editions or other vols by same author. "Children's Books in the Eighteenth Century. An examination (exemplification/social and literary resume/Some observations) principally based on the collection at Westerfield House."' (From the diary entry for 11 Apr. 1966.)

6. Quoted from the catalogue *The Festival of Britain Exhibition of Books, arranged by the National Book League at the Victoria & Albert Museum* (1951), exhibit 53.

7. Peter and Iona Opie compiled the section on children's books for G. Watson, ed., *The New Cambridge Bibliography of English Literature*, vol. ii, 1660–1880 (Cambridge, 1971).

8. This passage was actually written some years later, facing the entry for 29 Jan. 1966 which records the purchase of *Comforts of Old Age* from Westwood's stall in Petersfield market for 6d.

9. *The Birthday Gift or The Joy of a New Doll, from Papers Cut by a Lady* (1796). Bought two days earlier from Mrs Leeming of Boyle's of Worcester.

10. The Bodleian had no edition of this selection.

11. One other copy is now known, in the library of Princeton University.

12. To The Abbots Bookshop Ltd, Shepton Mallet.

13. This entry was copied into the diary from a letter to his son Robert.

14. Published in 1772. Roscoe J229(1) cites Opie as the only location.

15. The other book (not a diary) was *The Virtuous Novelist; or, Little Polite Court Tales* (1750), bought from 'H. M. Fletcher, or, rather, his son. The first really special and really early children's book of the classic type and era that I have acquired for many a long month—and the young Fletcher bought it last Easter Monday when in Connecticut.' (From the diary entry for 13 May 1969.)

16. 'It was an 18th century edn of William Rusher's Reading Made Most Easy of which Alston was unable to locate even one copy of any date, and knew only by a reference in a contemporary review. . . . It is a superb copy.' (From the diary entry for 7 Apr. 1971.)
17. Roland Marcus Ignatius Julius Knaster (1892–1972), Peter Opie's mentor and friend, built up a collection of children's books described by the latter as 'fabulous'; it was eventually incorporated into the Opie collection.

3

Children in Early Modern England

KEITH THOMAS

OVER the past twenty-five years, historians have devoted an increasing amount of attention to the study of children. The initial stimulus was Philippe Ariès's *Centuries of Childhood*, which was translated into English in 1962 and which attracted a good deal of attention because of its claim that before the early modern period, 'the idea of childhood did not exist'. In the Middle Ages, said Ariès, children were dressed and treated as miniature adults; and they were not segregated from adult activities. The 'discovery' of childhood as a distinctive phase of life with its own emotional and intellectual characteristics was, he thought, a gradual process, with faint beginnings in the thirteenth century but not fully accomplished until the seventeenth century or later. Only then were older children shunted off into educational institutions and protected from the harsher facts of life. And this segregation involved a new severity; early modern children were harshly disciplined and regularly beaten. Not until the eighteenth century did attitudes soften.[1]

This theme was taken up with relish by other historians. According to Lawrence Stone, Tudor and Stuart parents were reluctant to invest much emotional capital in their offspring because of the high rate of infant mortality. Childhood was thought to epitomize original sin. Infants were imprisoned in swaddling bands and, whenever possible, put out to wet nurses. Older children were severely repressed.[2] Sir John Plumb agreed: 'For the majority of families in the seventeenth century,' he wrote, 'there was a coldness, almost a callousness, in the relationship between parents and children which we find very hard to believe.' Only in what he called the 'new world' of the eighteenth century did people start to take pleasure in children, to buy them toys, books and games, and to dress them distinctively. Only then were children perceived as innocent and good and made into a focal point of attention.[3]

These accounts had the attraction of making modern readers feel infinitely superior to the brutal parents of the past, but only a little of the picture drawn by Ariès, Stone, and Plumb has survived more recent research and reflection. Far from there having been no medieval conception of childhood, we now know that doctors, lawyers, and religious writers in the Middle Ages all recognized infancy and youth as a vulnerable, fragile period of diminished responsibility.[4] Far from infant mortality deadening parents' sensibilities, we know that the loss of young children frequently drove them distraught.[5] Far from there being no affection between early modern parents and their offspring, we know that most of the moralists who urged the strict treatment of children did so because they thought that their contemporaries were spoiling them by coddling them unduly, calling them pet names, dandling them on their knees, feeding them with sweets, dressing them in pretty clothes and rushing for the doctor at the slightest upset; as a preacher complained in 1558, they 'dandill him and didill hym and pamper hym and stroke his hedd . . . and gyve him the swetyst soppe in the dish' and make him say, 'I am father's boy' or 'I am mother's boy'.[6] Far from the market in toys being an eighteenth-century novelty, we know that children's dolls had been imported from abroad since at least the mid-Tudor period.[7] Far from John Locke at the end of the seventeenth century being the first to urge that children should be encouraged to learn for pleasure, rather than out of fear, he was merely the most influential of a long series of such writers: 'too much threatning and over many strokes' did children no good, thought the Welsh paediatrician John Jones in 1579; instead they should be 'enticed' by 'good examples, fair allurement and fine behest'.[8]

Ralph Houlbrooke's recent book on *The English Family 1450–1700* (1984) accordingly gives a totally different picture of the relations between parents and children from that offered by Lawrence Stone and others. Similarly Linda Pollock concludes in her work *Forgotten Children* (1983) that there were no great differences in the nature of parental care for children between the sixteenth and nineteenth centuries. More often than not, the parent–child relationship was one which today would be thought of as natural and normal.

Of course, the older picture was not entirely without foundation. In early modern England the poverty of the lower sections of the population meant that childhood was not something which many parents could afford to prolong; they put their children out to earn their living as soon as possible; small children might be coddled but older ones had to work. Since adults in a servile condition were often beaten, so were children, for that was how discipline was customarily enforced, particularly in the grammar schools, whose methods were much more severe than those of parents at home; and so long as original sin was emphasized by Calvinist theologians, it was inevitable that young children should be thought to exemplify it as much as everyone else. Nevertheless, recent work confirms the view that although the *methods* of early modern parents may have been different from ours, their affection and concern for their children were no less great.

Yet the modern writers who have revised the earlier picture drawn by Ariès and Stone have in one fundamental respect continued to follow their example. For whether they take an optimistic or a pessimistic view of early modern child-care, whether they think the concept of childhood was always there or had to wait to be discovered in the eighteenth century, they persist in seeking to write, *not* the history of children, but the history of adult attitudes *to* children. Indeed Lawrence Stone actually says that 'the history of childhood is . . . the history of how parents treated children'.[9]

Now the treatment of children is a vital subject and there is still a lot more to be found out about it. But it is not to be confused with the history of children proper, any more than the history of attitudes to women should be taken for the history *of* women. For children, like women, are what anthropologists like to call a 'muted group'.[10] That is to say, their own values, attitudes, and feelings are largely excluded from the official record and can only be discovered if they are excavated by the historian. A true history of childhood must tell us how children themselves saw the world, what *they* did and what *they* felt.

Some historians might very reasonably say that it is impossible, because the evidence is not there. 'These myriads of children,' writes Peter Laslett, 'have left nothing much material behind them . . . We do not know very much about what they played or even about what they were encouraged to play or do.'[11] This is unduly pessimistic, for a good deal can in fact be found out about what children did and about what they played, though only by using literary sources of a kind which Dr Laslett does not much like because they do not lend themselves to statistical analysis. In the early modern period, roughly 1500–1800, the imaginative literature of the time is less revealing than might have been expected, because most contemporaries did not regard the experiences of children as intrinsically interesting, leave alone formative of character. For example, when the realistic novel appeared in the eighteenth century, the novelist seldom thought it worth lingering on the childhood of the central character. 'The things of my childhood are not worth setting down, and therefore I commence my life from the first month of the seventeenth year of my age.' So begins Thomas Amory's *John Buncle*. For Fielding's Jonathan Wild, 'nothing very remarkable passed in his years of infancy', while during the first years of Tom Jones's life 'nothing happened worthy of being recorded'.[12] Much the same is true of most of the autobiographies of the period, in which the years of childhood are normally passed over very quickly. 'My first ten years', says the seventeenth-century astronomer John Flamsteed, 'were spent in such employments as children use to pass away their time with, affording little observable in them.'[13] Even a relatively informative work, like the unpublished memoirs of the eighteenth-century exciseman John Cannon, omits what the author calls 'a Multitude of Childish and Youthfull follies and extravagances . . . incident to puberty or juvenality, which if . . . remembered and recorded would swell a volume to a vast bulk . . . not very pertinent to my purpose and no way edifying to the reader'.[14]

Nevertheless such works can be illuminating and so can

schoolboy diaries and letters by children, of which there are quite a few. Admittedly not much is to be gleaned from the first effort at the age of seven of the great letter-writer, Horace Walpole:

Dear mama I hop you are wall and I am very wall and I hop papa is wall and I begin to slaap and I hop al was wall and my cosans like thers pla things vary wall and I hop Doly phillips is wall and pray give my Duty to papa

HORACE WALPOLE

and I am very glad to hear by Tom that all my cruataurs are all wall . . .[15]

But sometimes these letters strike an authentic note, as in this mid-eighteenth-century letter by Frederick Reynolds on his second day at Westminster School:

My dear, dear Mother,
    If you don't let me come home, I die—I am all over ink, and my fine clothes have been spoilt—I have been tost in a blanket, and seen a ghost.

I remain, my dear, dear mother,
Your dutiful and most unhappy son,
Freddy

P.S.   Remember me to my father.[16]

   There are also a number of miniature biographies of children who were too good to live. Of course, in such works children are depicted spending much time in the company of adults, and displaying largely adult thoughts and emotions. Grown-ups, as a modern critic remarks, find it easiest to portray childhood in the way they themselves think and feel, so we get little of the child's 'discontinuous logic, free-floating anxiety, fantasy games or extended, desultory conversations with other children'.[17] Yet biographers of children do tell us something, occasionally at considerable length. Thomas Williams Malkin, born in 1795, at the very end of the period, died at the age of six. But he was commemorated in a 172-page volume containing his life and letters. He was, however, a prodigy, capable of writing sententious poems on the mental weaknesses of infancy.[18]

   Above all, there are the contemporary perceptions by adults of children's behaviour. Incidental remarks about children abound in the sermons, treatises, letters, and diaries of the period; and some people observed children very closely. For example, the work of John Hall of Richmond, a minor political writer of the mid-seventeenth century, is full of acute vignettes of small children learning to walk and talk, playing in the mud and grappling with lessons at school.[19]

So someone seeking to reconstruct the world of children in early modern England is not totally starved of evidence. He is, however, confronted by the major difficulty that there was not one single world of children, any more than there was of women. Even if we concentrate on children between roughly six and fourteen, we are faced by differences in age which seemed vast to the children themselves, and even more by huge variations in class, wealth, and locality which it is impossible to exaggerate. Poverty, bereavement, or the idiosyncrasies of parental temperament could make spectacular differences to children's experience. Some children were at school; others were at work; others were unemployed. The children of great men, thought the Puritan William Gouge, were commonly of more understanding at the age of twelve or fourteen than were the children of the poor at seventeen or eighteen. Conversely, the children of gypsies and the vagrant poor were notoriously more capable of taking care of themselves at the age of three than were well-to-do children at six.[20] Differences of gender were even more fundamental, for after the first few years of life the experience of girls diverged quite sharply from that of boys. Their world was in many ways a different one and one about which we know much less.

Nevertheless, it is possible to say something about the mental attitudes and values of early modern children as a whole. For guidance on how to do so I must acknowledge two separate sources of inspiration. The first are the folklorists, starting with the compilers of the regional glossaries and dialect dictionaries of the early nineteenth century, a marvellous and under-exploited source for children's lore, and culminating in the magnificent studies by Iona and Peter Opie of modern schoolchildren's games, rhymes, tricks, and stories.[21] The Opies' work has considerable historical relevance, for they argue for the relative continuity of children's culture and demonstrate that many of the jokes, riddles, and conventions of modern children have a long pedigree. They suggest by implication that there was in the sixteenth and seventeenth centuries a children's subculture which has yet to be reconstructed.

The second stimulus comes from those anthropologists, most recently Charlotte Hardman, who have pursued the theory that 'muted groups' have their own separate view of the world, quite different from the official one. On the basis of observing children in the playground of an Oxford primary school, Miss Hardman argues that children have their own model of reality, largely independent of that of adults. They inhabit a separate society with its own system of order and classification, its own perceptions and values. Children are not just passive or assimilative recipients of grown-up instruction: they have a specific model of the world both linked to and different from the dominant adult model.[22] Of course, it is hard for a member of the adult culture to cast off his or her own categories in order to apprehend those of children. But such an act of empathetic understanding or translation is in principle no different from that of any other form of historical or anthropological endeavour. Even if historians cannot, like Iona Opie, stand in some bygone playground and let the children swarm around her while she searches for order in their apparent chaos, we can do something with the historical evidence available.

What then can be said about the children of early modern England? The first point to make is that they were ubiquitous; and the second that they tended to behave in a way which was inconsistent with the values of adult society. At the end of the seventeenth century the under-fifteens were over 30 per cent of the population.[23] Some were at school and some were at work, but a great many were daily to be seen playing in the streets, shouting, swearing, throwing stones, and abusing passers-by. In Tudor Exeter 'troupes . . . of children' were observed 'loytering and floistering in every corner of the citie'. In Stuart Gloucester the 'poorer sort of children' were found 'playing in the streets the better part of the day'. In Portsmouth in the reign of Anne there was an 'incessant din' caused by the cries of children in the street.[24] 'Even when Jerusalem is a City of Truth, a Holy Mountain,' thought a preacher, 'it shall be full of boys and girls playing in the streets.'[25]

For the children themselves this kind of unsupervised life had obvious hazards. Medieval coroners' inquests suggest that girls were more likely to stay at home and get involved in accidents with pots and cauldrons, while boys tended to wander out and fall into water.[26] The diary of William Coe, a Suffolk yeoman farmer at the turn of the seventeenth century, records literally scores of accidents to his small children, through falling into ditches, being run over by wagons, injured by cows and horses, or bitten by dogs, cutting themselves when playing with dangerous tools, swallowing pins, or overturning boiling water.[27]

But though such misfortunes greatly worried anxious parents, the most common adult reaction was that children were tiresome creatures who played in the wrong way, at the wrong time, and in the wrong places.

For example, they frequently disturbed church services. Salisbury cathedral suffered in the 1630s from 'the ordinarie ... clamours of children'. At St Paul's in the 1590s schoolboys played in the yard, broke the windows, and disturbed the people at service time. At Wells, children had to be prevented from playing games in the cloisters. At Stratford-on-Avon in 1629 they had to pay a man an annual salary 'for lookinge to the scollers in the churche'. In Exeter in 1658 a cage was erected in the cathedral yard to hold boys who disturbed the minister in service-time.[28] Everywhere there were complaints of choirboys, pouring noisily into church, jostling among themselves, fighting and arguing, pushing the elderly out of their seats, running round the church during the sermon, and trooping out before the service was finished. Yet, in the words of a Tudor preacher, if you looked in a chorister's face, 'yow wold think that butter wold not melt in his mouth'.[29]

In the later seventeenth century, Quaker meetings suffered incessantly from disturbances created by the children of their own members, playing noisily outside or causing disorder within. At Bristol, for example, two or three of the Friends had to be appointed as guards, one at the door and the others in the gallery, where the children sat; when the boys in front of the gallery became rude and boisterous, it was decided to raise the bench to make it high enough for men to sit there as well, 'hopeing thereby the boys may be kept the better in order'.[30]

When the churches were not being used for services, there would be children playing around them, leaping over the graves, relieving themselves against the walls and throwing stones at the windows. At Wimborne in 1629 the churchwardens lamented that 'our church and the seats thereof have often been beastly abused and profaned by uncivil children'. At Durham cathedral in 1681 children were found frolicking in the cloisters and playing cards on the communion table.[31]

Children thus showed no reverence for buildings and occasions which adults regarded with solemnity. They desecrated the sabbath by playing games in the street; and when they went on the annual perambulation of the parish they turned it into 'rather a businesse of divertisement than devotion'.[32] They regarded the highway as a playground rather than as a thoroughfare and consequently got into conflicts with the municipal authorities, similar to the late Victorian battles between police constables and small boys playing street football. In 1651 the London Grocers' Company complained of the 'resort and confluence of boyes and children to play, wherefore the windowes are broken, and other prejudice and damage about the Hall and Garden'; and in 1691 the Stationers' Company had to put up a wall 'to keep out boys from breaking the windows'.[33] There is little doubt that the spread of glass windows in this period brought with it a new form of juvenile pleasure. It is hard to find a church, town hall, or public building which did not suffer from boys throwing sticks and stones in anticipation of the sound of broken glass.

They threw other things too. In 1735 there were said to be 'a number of idle disorderly Boys that plays before the gates of [Emanuel] Hospital [London] in a very disturbing manner, to the great indangering of the Hospital's being set on fire by frequent throwing in of Squibs'.[34] It was quite easy to obtain gunpowder, and the manufacture of fireworks was common, often with catastrophic results to the children themselves. In 1621, when he was about twelve, Marmaduke Rawdon of York 'had a minde to show [a girl he admired] what fine crackinge squibs he could make; so he and three or four boyes more . . . had gott some quantitie of powder, and putt itt in one of the boyes' hatts: Mr. Rawdon goinge to give fire to the crackinge squib, itt would not att first goe of; soe Mr. Rawdon fell a blowinge of itt, and the boy with the hatt of powder came nere Mr. Rawdon to see what was the matter thatt it would not goe of, when, of a sudden, itt went of . . . [He was carried home], his head sweld as big as tow heades, and his eielids seemingly burnt up, to the great griefe of his parents, who presently sent for the most eminent doctors and surgeons of the cittie, who, consultinge togeather, did apply thosse things that were most convenient for him . . . He lay nine dayes blinde without anie sight att all.'[35]

In the streets, gangs of children were a recognized threat to passers-by. In later Stuart London one could find 'whole companies' of them at play, wrangling, cheating, swearing, whipping horses, endangering riders, and throwing dirt or stones at coaches; and it was the opinion of one political theorist that, but for the fear of the resulting punishment, 'the boys and youths as we passed the streets might be inclined, even for sport['s] sake, to abuse us with dirt or stones or the like'.[36] 'It must needs pity any Christian heart,' thought one observer in 1663, 'to see the little dirty Infantry, which swarms up and down in Alleys and Lanes, with curses and ribaldry in their mouths, and other ill rude behavior.'[37] Scores of preachers commented on the oaths and imprecations which dropped from the lips of even very little children.

Young people were also thought to be persistent mischief-makers, undeterred by adult notions of gravity and responsibility. Schoolboys were proverbially associated with stereotyped anti-social activities, notably robbing orchards and stealing fruit. They did not usually do this out of hunger, for, as was often remarked, they climbed crab-apple trees with great difficulty after fruit which even pigs would disdain.[38] Their motive was bravado, competition with each other, and defiance of adult claims to property. At Durham school in the Elizabethan period, the boys 'in the winter evenings ... enacted many a lewde stratageme about the shoppes in their way to the Schoole, as bursting glasen windowes, overthrowing Milkemaides pailes, pulling downe stalles and crushing out the linckes which were hung foorth to give light to the Passengers in the streetes'.[39]

There is a long pre-history to the adult-baiting pranks which the Opies have noted in more recent times: knocking at the door and running away, setting booby traps, putting candles inside turnips cut out to look like deaths' heads, throwing sticky burrs and misdirecting pedestrians. The yeoman William Coe recalled that, when he was a schoolboy at Bardwell, Suffolk, around 1680, he 'ledd a poor blind man out of his way into the water'; and even Sir Isaac Newton was capable as a child of such juvenile misdeeds as 'stealing cherry cobs', squirting water on Sunday and 'putting a pin in John Keys hat ... to pick him'.[40]

At certain times of the year this juvenile misbehaviour was officially permitted, for virtually every small community or institution in early modern England had its annual 'mischief night' or occasion of customary misrule, when all forms of childish licence were permitted. Twelfth Night, Plough Monday, St Valentine's Day, Shrove Tuesday, May Day, Oak Apple Day, Hallowe'en, and the Fifth of November were all accepted times for youthful pranks; and so were fairs, weddings, sheep-shearings, and mayoral elections. On these dates one might expect bells to be rung and horns blown. There would be knocking at doors, putting dirt in the keyhole, nailing people's clothes to the wall, bonfires, cock-throwing, and football. Some of these occasions involved apprentices and rather older juveniles, as on Shrove Tuesday in London, where in the seventeenth century there was usually a violent raid against brothels. But often it was the younger children who played the crucial part; and such occasions were key dates in the youthful calendar.

Frequently these acts of misrule were accompanied by demands for food or money as protection against further acts of depredation. Children in Stuart Oxfordshire went around the houses demanding bacon and eggs to mark the breaking-up of school and becoming abusive if they did not get them. In Plymouth on 'Freedom Day' the boys had liberty to help themselves to anything eatable which they encountered.[41]

The trouble was that such demands were not always confined to privileged times of the year. In some of the cathedrals, for example, the choristers claimed a customary right to extract 'spur money' from anyone coming into church without taking off his spurs. In Elizabethan St Paul's these children used to abuse those who would not give them anything, while if a rich visitor drew forth 'a perfumed embroidered purse', the choirboys would swarm around him 'like so many white butterflies'. In Durham some people were too frightened to come to the cathedral at all, because of 'their insolent importunity'.[42] Children had all sorts of ways of soliciting money. They dived for coins in the Roman baths at Bath. They held up the bridegroom after weddings and demanded a ransom. They went into taverns 'to shew their writing or sing'; and they troubled visitors at fairgrounds 'under pretence of cleaning shoes'.[43] As a boy, the future Clive of India is said to have run a protection racket in Market Drayton, demanding payment from shopkeepers for not breaking their windows.[44]

It is easy to see how such activities could shade into more serious forms of delinquency. Shop-lifting, pick-pocketing and stealing chickens and pigeons came easily to young people who were habituated in so many contexts to claim a prescriptive right to help themselves to adult property. As Charles Dickens would write later of the destitute children of London, they 'hop about like wild birds, pilfering the crumbs which fall from the table of the country's wealth . . . They . . . have no more idea of what we call justice than . . . blackbirds . . . have of nets, scarecrows and guns'. The records of early modern England contain many references to vagabond children who lived by their wits, hiding in barns, milking cows, and stealing food.[45]

There has been a tendency among historians studying similar manifestations of childish disorder in more recent times to dramatize it as the symptom of an enduring 'war against adults', paralleling, in Dr Paul Thompson's opinion, 'the wars between the classes and the sexes'. These acts of mischief and delinquency, he thinks, were 'symbolic (and perhaps hopeless) protests against the entire system of adult control of society'.[46] A similar interpretation is offered by Stephen Humphries in his *Hooligans or Rebels?* (1981), where he argues that the persistent rule-breaking and opposition to authority so characteristic of many working-class boys in the period 1889–1939 were not signs of indiscipline or delinquency but deliberate resistance to the hegemonic dominant culture of the state and the middle classes.

In the early modern period, at least, there was no such war against adults, certainly not in any self-conscious form. Rather there were periodic collisions between children and grown-ups because many children had their own values and priorities to which adults were either indifferent or positively hostile.

We have already seen that the essential attributes of juvenile subculture included a casual attitude to private property, an addiction to mischief, and a predilection for what most adults regarded as noise and dirt. Young children were notoriously indifferent to grown-up standards of cleanliness: as a contemporary remarked, they 'made pies of dirt and ran after gay bubbles made from froth and slime'.[47] They splashed in filthy puddles, made houses of mud and threw dirt at each other; and they relieved themselves in unacceptable places. In 1595 the choristers of St Paul's were even accused of 'pissing upon stones in the Churche . . . to slide upon, as uppon ysse'. 'See . . . how they make choice of the basest [of places]!' exclaimed a Jacobean bishop, 'the sinke, the channell, the chymnie, wallowing in the mire, all daubed on with durt.'[48] Children had a different sense of values, collecting objects which adults despised, like shells or pebbles: 'things most worthye,' remarked a medieval commentator, 'they repute least worthy and least worthy most worthye.'[49] Children had a different sense of time, resenting a regular routine and crying when it was time to go to bed. And the food they liked most was not that which adults recommended.

But in no way did they more obviously reverse adult priorities than in the value they set on play. Sir Thomas More recognized this when he wrote

I am called chyldhod; in play is all my mynde,
To cast a coyte, a cokstele, and a ball.
A toppe can I set, and dryve it in his kynde,
But would to god these hatefull bookes all
Were in a fyre brent to pouder small.
Than myght I lede my lyfe always in play.

So did the Boy in John Heywood's *Play of the Wether* (1533):

All my pleasure is in catchynge of byrdes
And makynge of snow ballys, and throwying the same.

.   .   .   .

O to se my snow ballys lyght on my felowes heddys,
And to here the byrdes how they flycker ther wynges
In the pytfale! I say yt passeth all thynges.[50]

Of course, when we say that children preferred play to work we mean only that they liked to spend their time doing serious things which adults regarded as trivial and frivolous. As a modern student of child psychology puts it, 'play is merely the name we give to the child's activities.' It is not trivial to the child. In Montaigne's words, 'children's playes are not sports and should be deemed as their most serious actions.'[51] Conversely, it could be held that adults spent most of their time playing too, though their games were different. But that is not how most contemporaries saw it; and since in early modern England, as today, it was the grown-ups who decided what was or wasn't frivolous, 'play' was officially what children did, not adults.[52]

There is room for only a few general remarks about children's play in this period. First, there was no shortage of toys to play with. Toys are ephemeral things; they soon get lost or thrown away, which is why it is often assumed that they were uncommon before the eighteenth century. But literary sources make it clear that Tudor and Stuart children had a very wide range of them: tops, hoops, rattles, balls, trumpets, hobby horses, toy soldiers, marbles, paint boxes, alphabetical bricks, and kites with paper streamers. An Elizabethan guide to horse training casually refers to 'a whurlguigge as children run withal against the winde'; in 1659 Henry More mentions the 'Jack-in-a-box that Schoolboyes play with . . . held in by the cover pressing against it'; and another writer tells us that at Bartholomew Fair in Jacobean times children could buy a 'bauble' out of which they could 'shoot a Snake to scare their fellowes'.[53] By the eighteenth century such playthings had grown quite elaborate. A mother sends a shopping list to her husband in 1714: 'Jonny requires the huntssman hunting the Hair; they turn about in a Box and make a noise; and a Barking Doggy too you must bring him.'[54]

But much more important than these manufactured toys were the natural objects which children converted to their own uses. They played conkers with cob nuts or snail shells; they smoked clematis and made pop guns out of elder twigs or stalks or cow parsley. The herbalist John Gerard tells us that many children poisoned themselves through 'playing or piping with quils or kexes of Hemlockes'. The Tudor botanist William Turner remarks that catstail was also called reed mace, 'because boyes use it in theyr handes in the stede of a mace'.[55]

Turner's picture of little boys in Northumberland parading with imaginary maces held before them (or did he mean that they used them as mock weapons?) reminds us that if we wish to divide children's games into their main categories we must begin with those which were essentially imitative of adult activities. Before the Reformation Sir Thomas Elyot saw children 'knelynge in theyr game before images, and holdyng up theyr lytell whyte handes . . . as they were prayeing; other[s] goynge and syngynge as hit were in procession.' In 1583 John Dee's son Arthur and Mary Herbert 'being but three years old . . . did make as it wer a shew of childish marriage, of calling ech other husband and wife'; and Nicholas Blundell's children in 1712 buried a doll 'with a great deale of Formallity, they had a Garland of Flowers Carried before it, and at least twenty of their Playfellows & others that they invited were at the Buriall'.[56] Girls played at cooking and keeping house; boys imitated hunting and war. In 1654 John Hall thought that 'bigger children's most eager sports are usually made in imitation of what they see men do; and the end of them [is] to aim at victory and pre-excellence one above another'. Drums, rattles, and hobby horses, agreed John Earle, were 'but the emblems and mocking of man's businesse'.[57] This was why the reformer Thomas Tryon in the 1680s wanted all children's war games to be prohibited because they fostered aggressive instincts.[58] The enlightened parents of the late twentieth century were not the first to disapprove of children playing with guns.

For girls, the vital imitative activity was playing with dolls, either bought commercially or, more often, made for themselves in clay, wood, or wax. (Many Tudor writers refer to 'the babies that children make'.) These dolls were carefully dressed up, given miniature houses in which to live and buried at the end of their lives. The emotional relationship between a child and her doll could be very intense. As John Hall remarked, 'we shall finde girls . . . providing apparel and food for their Babies, with most high and great indulgence: as supposing they do hereby as really pleasure and benefit these as their parents do them.'[59] A similar affection was bestowed on 'dogs, birds, monkeys and the like'. Girls, remarked John Milton, 'are wont to invent games of weddings and births, striving to catch and hold the shadows of those things for which they long and yearn'.[60]

After these imitative activities came all the competitive games (running, hiding, chasing, and catching), and all the musical games which involved singing and dancing. The pioneer work of Alice Gomme and other collectors of folklore makes it possible to compile a list of hundreds of children's games which we know to have been played in the early modern period; and the total can be augmented further from contemporary sources. It is likely, however, that most children spent more time engaged in less formal kinds of play. They went running, swimming, and sliding, and they had innumerable less sophisticated ways of testing their physical dexterity and exploring their own bodily awareness. As a child, William Cobbett used to roll downhill like a barrel; and there were many games which involved standing on one leg or otherwise testing the limits of endurance and bursting out of the conventions of 'normal' posture and movement which adults inculcated. Children, 'by way of sport,' remarked John Hall, 'turn [. . .] themselves often around, not only for pride and affection['s] sake, to see who can turn oftenest, but on purpose also that they may then stand delighted with those transient and giddy figures and apprehensions which are then made in their brain.'[61] They had contests to see who could say the same word most often in one breath; and, as Francis Bacon casually remarks, it was already a familiar child's sport to see whether one could rub one's chest and pat one's forehead simultaneously.[62]

There were also all the pursuits which could be engaged in by children in the countryside, which was where most of them lived. First came bird's-nesting—taking home eggs, young ones, nest and all; and after that chasing small animals: squirrels, rats, weasels, rabbits, and hedgehogs. In the eighteenth century, when urban middle-class attitudes to animals were changing, this was the aspect of children's play which excited most unfavourable comment from enlightened adults. For children had for centuries tortured insects, birds, frogs, toads, and any other accessible small creatures; and it was hard to get them to relinquish such activities.

Finally, there were all the private reveries and fantasies in which small children spent much of their waking thoughts. The egregious Thomas Williams Malkin, subject of the 172-page life and letters, had an imaginary country, of which he drew maps and wrote a history and detailed description of the topography, language, and inhabitants.[63] Other children were less systematic than this six-year-old prodigy, but they too challenged adult assumptions about the existence of a firm distinction between fact and fiction, fantasy and reality.

Implicit in many of the collective activities of children were elaborate rules, codes of honour, forfeits, and punishments. There were words and ceremonies, for the assertion of ownership, for sealing irrevocable bargains, for choosing teams and deciding who went first. The Opies, who have done most to codify this lore for modern times, assert that much of it goes back to the early modern period; and they quote John Arbuthnot, who declared in the reign of Queen Anne that the games and plays of schoolboys were 'delivered down invariably from one generation to another'.[64] In fact, most of the earlier precedents for modern children's usage cited by the Opies go back no further than the early nineteenth century; and a large proportion of those which are older prove on closer examination to refer, not to the usage of children, but to that of adults: for example, the truce terms 'barley' (parlay) and 'fainites' (fains I) were used by medieval warriors; and many modern children's insults, jokes, and riddles began as quips exchanged by Tudor adults.[65] Nevertheless, we have enough casual evidence to suggest that by the sixteenth century, and probably much earlier, there was a well-developed specifically juvenile code of behaviour. Borrowing and swapping, for example, were common among Elizabethan schoolboys and were regulated by unwritten conventions. John Wheeler wrote in 1601 that 'children, assoone as ever their tongues are at libertie, doe season their sportes with some merchandise or other; and when they goe to schoole, nothing is so common among them as to change and rechange, buy and sell of that which they bring from home with them.' And a preacher remarked in 1624 that 'it is a proverb among our children' that something once given cannot be taken back.[66] There is no doubt that seventeenth-century children shouted 'halves' when they wanted to claim a share in something they had found, or that they chanted rhymes when they played with ladybirds urging them to fly home.[67]

Underlying what seemed to be the disorderly play of children, therefore, were rules, codes, and conventions not much less rigorous than those which defined adult society. Children shared some games with adults, for even Samuel Pepys played blind man's buff at Christmas,[68] but they also had a range of sports which were distinctively theirs. They had their own calendar, for then as now many games were strictly seasonal and there were different times of the year for different activities: entertainments in Venice, remarked the English envoy there in 1614, came about in their seasons, 'like our children's sports in schools'.[69] They had their own vocabulary, for they gave childish names to many plants and flowers, and the regional glossaries reveal a huge range of terms used only by children, for example 'bunny', the Suffolk name for the swelling on the head caused by a rap of the schoolmaster's ruler.[70] They had their own values and codes of honour: the infant daughter of the godly Margaret Corbet (mid-seventeenth century) is on record for saying that 'she had rather dye than tell a Fibb'.[71] And they had their own ritual punishments for dealing with those who infringed the code. Of course, these rules did not constitute a single moral universe. There were innumerable regional differences; and the conventions of children varied according to the particular social and institutional milieu. But, wherever they lived, their activities had more underlying structure than was always apparent to those adults who saw them only as a source of noise and disorder.

The process of social reproduction requires that children be turned into adults. Today we are prepared to wait for that to happen. We accept that playing is a natural stage in a child's development and are not usually in a hurry to accelerate the process of growing up. But in the early modern period it was more usual to feel that children's play was at best a waste of time and at worst a very bad preparation for adult life. Protestant culture was particularly hostile to the notion of play for playing's sake. Children, as one Tudor preacher put it, should 'avoid . . . too much childish pastimes'; while at the end of the seventeenth century Thomas Tryon declared there to be 'nothing more pernicious, nor promotes Idleness and Vanity more, than Children's Playing promiscuously one amongst another'.[72]

There were two ways of converting rowdy, disrespectful, anarchic children into sober, respectable, hardworking citizens. They could be sent to school or they could be put to work. The school kept children off the streets and forced them to apply themselves in a systematic manner, disciplined by the rod and regulated by the clock. It was not claimed that by going to school children would necessarily learn very much, but it was agreed that the experience of school discipline was intrinsically valuable: 'the confinement of them betimes to sit two or three hours still in a place will be of mighty advantage to them because it inures them betimes to business, and puts a check to their desires after pleasure.'[73] In 1682 George Townsend left money to found schools in four Gloucestershire towns, prescribing that the pupils should attend every day, including Easter, Whitsun, and Christmas, 'to avoid their being offensive at home or elsewhere'.[74] A grammar-school education, thought a mid-seventeenth-century

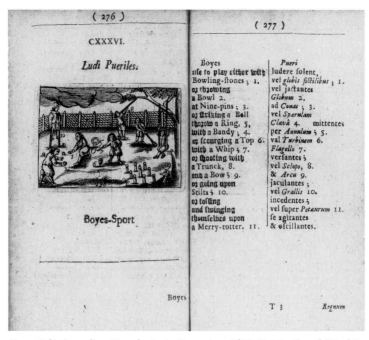

From *Orbis Sensualium Pictus* by J. A. Comenius, 1672. Originally published in Nuremberg in 1658, this illustrated school-book was translated by Charles Hoole, schoolmaster and author of several educational works, and appeared in England the following year.

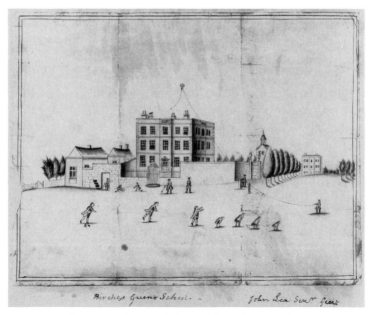

Sketch of a school made by an eighteenth-century boy.

schoolmaster, was the best preventive for 'all loose kinde of behaviour . . . as it is too commonly to be seen, especially with the poorer sort, taken from the Schoole and permitted to run wildeing up and down without any control'.[75]

The alternative to schooling was to put children to work; and this was the only option for most parents. In Jacobean Norwich children of six years and upwards knitted fine jersey stockings. In Gloucestershire they made pins when they were eight. In the Birmingham button industry they worked from the age of six. In Westmorland four-year-olds made stockings. When Defoe visited Taunton at the beginning of the eighteenth century he found 'that there was not a child in the town, or in the villages round it, of above five years old, but, if it was not neglected by its parents, and untaught, could earn its own bread'.[76] In agriculture, particularly, child labour was universal, for even tiny infants could scare crows and pick stones. The young Thomas Shepard, later a famous New England preacher, who at the age of three was put 'to keepe geese and other such cuntry worke', is representative of tens of thousands of his contemporaries who were similarly employed.[77] Here too, the argument was not that children's labour was necessarily very productive, but that it inculcated the right habits for later life. One authority thought it a good idea to keep children employed at least twelve hours a day so as to habituate the rising generation to the notion of regular work.[78]

Yet neither work nor school could wholly curb youthful spirits. We know very little about how child labour worked in practice, but some of it must have been highly inefficient: 'something between a hindrance and a help', as Wordsworth put it. At Dunbar, where children customarily spent three or four days each summer cutting rushes for the school, it was found that 'often tymes they fall a-wrestleing with hooks in their hands, that sometymes they wrong themselves, other tymes their neighbours'.[79] The boys who worked as chimney sweeps in London were notorious for cheating their masters by filling their sacks with dirt and rubbish, covering them at the top with soot, to give the impression of a hard day's work. In the opinion of the agriculturalist Arthur Young, boys were 'never to be trusted at any work whatever', unless in the company of men. As the proverb had it: one boy, one day's work; two boys, half a day's work; three boys, no work at all.[80]

The reluctance with which many children submitted to school is much better documented. 'Divers Scholers of Eaton be runne awaie from the Schole for feare of beating' is the beginning of Roger Ascham's Tudor dialogue on *The Scholemaster*. And there is plenty of evidence to suggest that the reaction of many children on first being beaten at school was to set out at once for home, like Widow Wilby's son, who was whipped three times on his first day at Batley free school in 1694 for not bringing an entrance penny and could never be prevailed upon to go there again.[81] Many of those who stayed engaged in more indirect forms of resistance, throwing stones at the windows—as is revealed by almost every extant set of school accounts—carving their names on the walls and desks, or taking every opportunity to leave the classroom on 'necessary occasions, reall or pretended'. 'As sone on as I am cum into the schole,' laments a fifteenth-century schoolmaster, 'this felow goith to make water.' (Many schools regulated the exodus by forbidding more than two children to go at a time and requiring them to carry a club which had to be brought back before the next one could leave; rather like the engine-driver on the old single-line railway from Oxford to Cambridge.)[82] Boys doodled on their textbooks: 'Alexander Meason can write better nor Robert Barclay, but he is a blockhead at countins,' runs an inscription of 1710.[83] They asserted their ownership ('This book is mine and none of thine and so let it alone. If thou it take, this hand I'll break and send thee crying home') and they drew pictures of their master. In 1622 Henry Peacham tells us that his teacher caught him drawing a copy of the picture in his Latin grammar of boys throwing stones at a pear tree; and many tattered schoolbooks survive with inscriptions and graffiti by their long-dead schoolboy owners, well worth collecting in an anthology one day.[84]

Above all, children devoted their energy to securing extra holidays, when they could apply themselves to the real business of life: play. In the North and the Midlands most grammar schools had an elaborate ritual of 'barring-out', by which schoolchildren ceremonially locked out their teacher at a recognized time of the year and denied him readmission until he had negotiated the holiday arrangements for the ensuing session. Sometimes this was done amiably, with light refreshments provided; sometimes it was a violent business, with guns and broken furniture.[85] Other methods of getting holidays involved soliciting visitors and parents of new boys to ask for one, or engaging in deliberate deception. The schoolboy diary kept by Daniel Walters in the Vale of Glamorgan in 1777-8 remarks that the day of return to Cowbridge Grammar School at the end of the holidays was known as Black Monday, for 'Boys, when they have been long absent, conceive a Dislike to their Book'. However, not more than half the pupils were there when term reopened: 'it is a very bad Practice of theirs', remarks the priggish Daniel Walters, 'to tell their parents that the Holidays are of five Weeks duration; they are in reality but a Month.'[86] In short, it was not just literary convention which portrayed children creeping like snail unwilling to school, but bounding out in an animated way when they were released, to return to their natural habitat. The school meant sitting still, attention, obedience, and the constant threat of punishment. Some children liked the work and enjoyed the competition. But schoolboy culture, then as now, was hostile to swots and preferred the playground, where there was movement, noise, and no rules save those created by the children themselves. For not until the nineteenth century did the schools set about controlling children's leisure time through the invention of compulsory games.

We can thus form some impression of the conventions governing the various children's subcultures of early modern England. But we know little of the inward thoughts and emotions of the young people themselves. We do, however, have some idea of what they were most afraid of. Infants were usually brought up to fear supernatural beings: elves, ghosts, and hobgoblins. A seventeenth-century writer remarks that 'Children hide their heads within their bed-clothes, though they see nothing, when they have affrighted themselves with the shapes of Devils pourtray'd only in their Phancies.'[87] Anything black was also to be feared, whether chimney sweepers or blackamoors or dark rooms or Black Parr, the Northamptonshire bogey man, or 'the low black sow that carries away children'. 'He smered his face with soote to fraye [frighten] chyldren,' says an early Tudor textbook.[88] Adults had a great range of other bogeys and boggarts which they invented in order to intimidate the young: the Old Man; Raw Head and Bloody Bones; Nelly Long-Arms; Awd Goggie. As the first duke of Newcastle remarked, 'a litle childe dreames howe Jack a Dandye followed him and frightened him.'[89]

As children got older there were the more realistic agonies of everyday life. 'Your master shall hear of it,' was the standard threat of Elizabethan parents to children who were at school. The young John Evelyn would not go to Eton because he was 'unreasonably terrified with the report of the severe discipline there'; and John Cannon never forgot that on his first day at school he was whipped for fouling his breeches because he did not know how to undo them and could not get anybody to do it for him.[90] Bullying and initiation rites were universal. A writer remarks of someone in 1712 that he 'always came in so dirty, as if he had been dragg'd thro' the Kennel [gutter] at a Boarding-School'.[91] The tyrannical subjection of junior boys to seniors was a feature of all the grammar schools.

There were also the terrors of judicial punishment. An early Tudor textbook informs its schoolboy readers that on London Bridge could be seen the heads of executed traitors, adding that 'it is a straunge sight to se the heere [hair] ... fale [fall] or moole [moulder] away and the gristell of the nose consumed ... It is a spectacle for ever to all yonge people to beware.' A Jacobean divine comments that 'When theeves are hanged, or whoores carted, we shew them to our children.'[92]

Another fear was that of hell-fire, for it was essential, as one cleric put it, to teach everyone 'whither good children go when they dye, and whither naughty children go'.[93] The effect of such teachings can be seen in some late seventeenth-century biographies of godly children. There was Sarah Howley, for instance, who was 'awakened' by a sermon at the age of eight which left her weeping bitterly. When she died six years later, she was still desperately worried about her lack of assurance of salvation. Other tots of four, five, and six were piously praised for their fear of hell and frequent weepings at the thought of what might happen to them in another world.[94] Against the stark background of high infant mortality this concern had a real immediacy. The young John Sudlow was permanently affected by the death of his little brother. 'When he saw him without breath, and not able to speak or stir, and then carried out of doors and put into a pit-hole, he was greatly concerned, and asked notable questions about him, but that which was most affecting ... was whether he must die too, which being answered, it made such a deep impression upon him, that from that time forward he was exceeding serious, and this when he was four years old.'[95]

Along with death the other inevitable preoccupation of growing children was sex. For this there is no lack of evidence, whether in the remarkably obscene drawings which decorate the margins of some Tudor books or in the confessions of John Cannon (b. 1684) of how, after a lesson on the subject by an older boy, he secured a copy of *Aristotle's Masterpiece*, the popular sex manual, so as to learn about the female anatomy, and later bored holes through the wall of the 'necessary house', so that he could secretly observe his master's maidservant at closer quarters.[96] Although seventeenth-century children were customarily told that babies were found at the bottom of the garden in the parsley bed, there was enough evidence around them to make them doubt it. By the 1750s, when there was more sexual concealment than there had been previously, Thomas Scott, who was at school in Bolton, tells us that his schoolfellows would 'often procure the vilest publications; and, by the help of indexes and other means ... sometimes become better acquainted with the most indecent passages of the classic authors than with their daily lessons'.[97]

The world of the children of early modern England is therefore not totally inaccessible; and their history can, up to a point, be written, no less than the history of adult attitudes *to* children. Nevertheless, these remarks have inevitably been impressionistic and it is not really possible to reconstruct the world of any specific group of children with any great rigour. The evidence is too sparse and too heavily weighted in the direction of the children of the well-to-do and of the children who were segregated from adult life by being sent to school. We know far less about the experience and attitudes of the poor children who were speedily put to work and plunged into adult life.

The subject as a whole poses some very difficult but interesting methodological problems, similar to those raised by any other investigation of popular culture, but rather more perplexing. How was children's lore transmitted—by older children or by adults? What relationship did it bear to the literary and verbal culture of adult society at large? Why was it slower-changing than adult culture? (For the Opies are surely right when they remark that 'if a present-day schoolchild was wafted back to any previous century, he would probably find himself more at home with the games being played than with any other social custom'; and it is hard to quarrel with Philippe Ariès when he describes the world of childhood as 'a sort of islet of archaism'.)[98]

Indeed the most serious question to raise about the whole subject is that of how, if children's lore is so constant, it can be said to have any history at all. It could be argued that children's games do not lead into an understanding of historical particularities, but rather provide more universal evidence for the natural predispositions of the human mind. For it is not only the games of children of the *past* which are so similar to those of modern times. It is also the play of children in other cultures. As an early twentieth-century anthropologist in Africa naïvely remarks, 'Nothing makes the European feel his kinship with the Kafirs more than watching the games of the children.'[99]

Since the development of the child's mind and body is essentially a biological constant, it is not surprising that there should be great similarities between the ways of children in early modern England and their ways today, even though the attitude of adults to children has changed so much. We seem to have in them yet another instance of that history of abiding structures and the *longue durée* to which the *Annales* school of historians in France attach so much importance and which some of the unconverted dismiss as not proper history at all. But if it should turn out on closer investigation that the experiences, values, attitudes, and mental categories of early modern children were not very different from those of their modern counterparts, that would not have made them any less worth studying. For history cannot be exclusively concerned with change. Enduring structures determine the nature of experience as much as do shifting circumstances; and it is as important to know the ways in which the past was the same as the present as to know the ways in which it was different.

It is also necessary to remember that, at all times in history, society has been pluralistic, made up of a number of semi-autonomous subcultures, of which the ruling culture is only one. As historians nowadays we do not feel it necessary to endorse any of the values of the Tudor or Stuart ruling classes, leave alone accept their verdict as to what was important about their society and what was trivial. If we did, we would never shift our attention from courts, councils, and parliaments. Instead, we must readily accept the need to explore, however imperfectly, the mental worlds of all subordinate groups, whether women, children or the poor, regardless of whether they were at the time disparaged as 'ignorant' or 'childish'. For it was within the confines of these subordinate groups that all the people of the past spent some of their lives and the majority spent all of them.

Notes

An earlier version of this essay was given as the A. H. Dodd Memorial Lecture at the University College of North Wales, Bangor, in 1986.

1. Philippe Ariès, *Centuries of Childhood*, trans. Robert Baldick (London, 1962), esp. p. 128.
2. Lawrence Stone, *The Family, Sex and Marriage in England 1500–1800* (London, 1977), esp. pp. 70, 159–78.
3. J. H. Plumb, 'The New World of Children', *The Listener*, 95 (1976), 232 (more fully in *Past and Present*, 67 (1975)).
4. Jerome L. Krull, 'The Concept of Childhood: the Middle Ages', *Journal of the History of the Behavioral Sciences*, xiii (1977).
5. e.g. Linda A. Pollock, *Forgotten Children* (Cambridge, 1983), 134–9; Ralph A.

Houlbrooke, *The English Family 1450–1700* (London, 1984), 137; Paul Seaver, *Wallington's World, A Puritan Artisan in Seventeenth-Century London* (London, 1985), 87–91, 229.

6. 'Two Sermons preached by the Boy Bishop', ed. John Gough Nichols, p. 26, in *The Camden Miscellany*, vii (Camden Soc., 1875).

7. *A Tudor Book of Rates*, ed. T. S. Willan (Manchester, 1962), 48; Joan Thirsk, *Economic Policies and Projects* (Oxford, 1978), 182.

8. John Jones, *The Arte and Science of Preserving Bodie and Soule in Healthe, Wisedome and Catholike Religion* (London, 1579), 63 (citing, in turn, the views of Quintilian, Plutarch, and Boethius).

9. Lawrence Stone, *The Past and the Present* (London, 1981), 229.

10. For this term see Shirley Ardener, 'Introduction' to *Perceiving Women*, ed. Shirley Ardener (London, 1975), xii.

11. Peter Laslett, *The World We Have Lost—Further Explored* (London, 1983), 121.

12. F. Lamar Janney, *Childhood in English Non-Dramatic Literature* (Greifswald, 1925), 79–80.

13. Paul Delany, *British Autobiography in the Seventeenth Century* (London, 1969), 155 and n. 44.

14. Ἀρρονεχα [*sic*] seu Annales: or Memoirs of the Birth, Education, Life and Death of Mr. John Cannon, Sometime Officer of the Excise and Writing Master at Mere, Glastonbury & West Lydford in the County of Somersett . . . written by himselfe' (MS in Somerset County Record Office), 70.

15. *Horace Walpole's Correspondence with the Walpole Family*, ed. W. S. Lewis and Joseph W. Reed Jr. (Yale Edition of Horace Walpole's Correspondence, vol. 36) (London, 1973), 1.

16. *The Life and Times of Frederick Reynolds Written by Himself* (London, 1826), i. 59. The highly coloured tone of this autobiography of a popular dramatist suggests that this letter, if it ever existed, may have been improved upon in recollection.

17. Nicholas Tucker in *Times Literary Supplement*, 12 Aug. 1983, 868.

18. Benj. Heath Malkin, *A Father's Memories of his Child* (London, 1806).

19. John Hall of Richmond, *Of Government and Obedience* (London, 1654).

20. William Gouge, *Of Domesticall Duties* (3rd edn., London, 1634), 553; A. Hunter, *Georgical Essays* vi (York, 1804), 291–2.

21. There is a Select Bibliographical List of regional glossaries at the beginning of Joseph Wright, *The English Dialect Dictionary* (Oxford, 1898–1905). Some idea of their resources is given by Elizabeth Mary Wright, *Rustic Speech and Folk-Lore* (London, 1913). Two pioneering studies are William Wells Newell, *Games and Songs of American Children* (New York, 1883), and Alice Bertha Gomme, *The Traditional Games of England, Scotland, and Ireland* (London, 1894–8; reissued 1984). The most relevant of the books by Iona and Peter Opie are *The Lore and Language of Schoolchildren* (Oxford, 1959);

Children's Games in Street and Playground (Oxford, 1969); and *The Singing Game* (Oxford, 1985).

22. Charlotte Hardman, 'The Study of Children in Social Anthropology' (Oxford University, B.Litt. thesis, 1974); 'Can there be an Anthropology of Children?', *Journal of the Anthropological Society of Oxford*, iv (1973); 'Children in the Playground', ibid. v (1974).

23. E. A. Wrigley and R. S. Schofield, *The Population History of England, 1541–1871* (London, 1981), 218.

24. W. K. Jordan, *Philanthropy in England 1480–1660* (London, 1959), 174; Samuel Harmar, *Vox Populi, or, Glostersheres Desire* (1642), sig. A3ᵛ; *The Works of Mr. Henry Needler* (2nd edn., London, 1728), 105.

25. *Children and Youth in America. A Documentary History*, ed. Robert H. Bremner (Cambridge, Mass., 1970), 110 (echoing Zechariah 8: 5).

26. Barbara A. Hanawalt, 'Childrearing in the Lower Classes of Late Medieval England', *Journal of Interdisciplinary History*, viii (1977), 16.

27. 'The Diary of William Coe of Mildenhall, Suffolk, A. D. 1680–1729', *East Anglian*, new ser., xi–xii (1906–8), *passim*.

28. Dora H. Robertson, *Sarum Close* (London, 1938), 193; Reavley Gair, *The Children of Paul's: the Story of a Theatre Company* (Cambridge, 1982), 40; *Historical Manuscripts Commission. Calendar of the Manuscript of the Dean and Chapter of Wells* (1914), ii. 351; *The Vestry Minute-Book of the Parish of Stratford-on-Avon from 1617 to 1699 A.D.*, ed. George Arbuthnot (n.d.), 36; W. Cotton and Henry Woollcombe, *Gleanings from the Municipal and Cathedral Records relative to the History of the City of Exeter* (Exeter, 1877), 167.

29. 'Two Sermons preached by the Boy Bishop', 25.

30. *Minute Book of the Men's Meeting of the Society of Friends in Bristol, 1667–1686*, ed. Russell Mortimer (Bristol Record Society, 1971), pp. xx, 160 *et passim*. Cf. Stanley Henry Glass Fitch, *Colchester Quakers* (Colchester, n.d.), 88, 93.

31. A. Lindsay Clegg, *A History of Wimborne Minster and District* (London, 1960), 94; *The Remains of Denis Granville*, ed. George Ornsby (Surtees Society, 1865), 70.

32. *Remains of Denis Granville*, 18.

33. Brigid Mary Urswick Boardman, 'The Gardens of the London Livery Companies', *Journal of Garden History*, 2 (1982), 95, 98.

34. C. Wilfrid Scott-Giles, *The History of Emanuel School 1594–1964* (London, 1966), 44.

35. *The Life of Marmaduke Rawdon of York*, ed. Robert Davies (Camden Soc., 1863), 2–3.

36. Tho. Firmin, *Some Proposals for the Imployment of the Poor* (London, 1681), 4; John Hall of Richmond, *Of Government and Obedience*, 451.

37. M. N(eedham), *A Discourse concerning Schools and School-Masters* (London, 1663), 2.

38. *The Letters of John Wilmot, Earl of Rochester*, ed. Jeremy Treglown (Oxford, 1980), 119.

39. *Dobsons Drie Bobbes*, ed. E. A. Horsman (London, 1955), 14.

40. 'The Diary of William Coe', *East Anglian*, new ser., xi (1905–6), 290; Richard S. Westfall, 'Short-Writing and the State of Newton's Conscience, 1662', *Notes and Records of the Royal Society*, 18 (1963), 13. Cf. Opies, *Lore and Language of Schoolchildren*, ch. 18.

41. John Aubrey, *Remaines of Gentilisme and Judaisme*, ed. James Britten (Folk-Lore Society, 1881), 161–2; James Yonge, *Plymouth Memoirs*, ed. John J. Beckerlegge (London, 1951), 79.

42. Gair, *Children of Paul's*, 28–9; *Remains of Denis Granville*, 162.

43. P. Rowland James, *The Baths of Bath in the Sixteenth and Early Seventeenth Century* (Bristol, 1938), 29; J. S. Purvis, *Educational Records* (York, 1959), 107; *John Lucas's History of Warton Parish*, ed. J. Rawlinson Ford and J. A. Fuller-Maitland (Kendal, 1931), 36; Violet A. Rowe, *The Bluecoat Children in Ware 1564–1761* (Ware, 1983), 16; *Middlesex County Records, Reports of the late W. J. Hardy and W. Le Hardy* (Fakenham, 1928), 11.

44. *Dictionary of National Biography*, s.n., 'Clive, Robert, Lord Clive'.

45. Jo Manton, *Mary Carpenter and the Children of the Streets* (London, 1976), 6; Seaver, *Wallington's World*, 28; *Tudor Economic Documents*, ed. R. H. Tawney and Eileen Power (London, 1924), ii. 337–8; A. L. Beier, *Masterless Men* (London, 1985), 55; *The Diary of Samuel Pepys*, ed. Robert Latham and William Matthews (London, 1970–83), viii. 319.

46. Paul Thompson, 'The War with Adults', *Oral History*, 3 (1975) 29, 37.

47. *The Morning Exercises at Cripplegate, St. Giles in the Fields, and in Southwark*, 5th edn. by James Nichols, n.d., iii. 571.

48. *The Pilgrimage of Man* (1612), sig. B1; Gair, *The Children of Paul's*, 26; Godfrey Goodman, *The Fall of Man* (London, 1616), 329.

49. *Batman uppon Bartholome his Booke De Proprietatibus Rerum* (1582), fo. 73.

50. *The Workes of Sir T. More* (1557), sig. Ciii; *Tudor Interludes*, ed. Peter Happé (Harmondsworth, 1972), 172–3.

51. G. T. W. Patrick, quoted in Mrs S. Herbert, *Child-Lore* (London, 1925), 175; Michel de Montaigne, *Essays*, trans. John Florio (1603: 1893 edn.), i. 106, echoing St Augustine, *Confessions*, I. ix. 3.

52. Cf. Orest Ranum, 'Jeux de Cartes, Pédagogie et Enfance de Louis XIV', in *Les Jeux à la Renaissance*, ed. Philippe Ariès and Jean-Claude Margolin (Actes du xxiiie Colloque International d'Etudes Humanistes, Tours, juillet 1980) (Paris, 1982), 561.

53. Thomas Blundeville, *A Newe Booke containing the Arte of Ryding*, n.d. (?1561), iii. sig. Dii^v; Henry More, *The Immortality of the Soul* (London, 1659), 124; Helkiah Crooke. *ΜΙΚΡΟΚΟΣΜΟΓΡΑΦΙΑ. A Description of the Body of Man* (2nd edn., London, 1631), ii. 4.

54. *Memoirs of a Royal Chaplain, 1729–1763. The Correspondence of Edmund Pyle*, ed. Albert Hartshorne (London, 1905), 33.

55. John Ray, *A Collection of English Words not Generally Used* (2nd edn., London, 1691), 131; John Gerard, *The Herball*, enlarged by Thomas Johnson (1633; New York, 1975), 750; *The Seconde Parte of William Turners Herball* (Cologne, 1562), fo. 159ᵛ.

56. Sir Thomas Elyot, *The Boke named the Governour*, ed. Henry Herbert Stephen Croft (London, 1883), i. 30; *The Private Diary of Dr. John Dee*, ed. James Orchard Halliwell (Camden Soc., 1841), 14; *The Great Diurnall of Nicholas Blundell*, ed. Frank Tyrer (Record Society of Lancashire and Cheshire), n.d., ii. 29.

57. Hall of Richmond, *Of Government and Obedience*, 440; John Earle, *Micro-Cosmographie*, ed. Edward Arber (London, 1895), 22.

58. Tho. Tryon, *A New Method of Educating Children* (London, 1695), 57–9.

59. Hall of Richmond, *Of Government and Obedience*, 300.

60. *Complete Prose Works of John Milton* (New Haven, 1953–), i. 283.

61. William Cobbett, *Rural Rides* (Everyman edn., n.d.), i. 101; Hall of Richmond, *Of Government and Obedience*, 438.

62. Ibid. 40; *The Works of Francis Bacon*, ed. James Spedding, Robert Leslie Ellis, and Douglas Denon Heath (London, 1857–9), ii. 367.

63. Malkin, *A Father's Memories*, 93–129.

64. Opies, *Lore and Language of Schoolchildren*, v.

65. Ibid. 42, 57, 148, 151, 167, 193.

66. John Wheeler, *A Treatise of Commerce* (London, 1601: 1931 edn.), 6; Opies, *Lore and Language of Schoolchildren*, 133 n. Cf. Margaret Spufford, *Small Books and Pleasant Histories* (London, 1981), 73.

67. Opies, *Lore and Language*, 137; William Turner, *A Compleat History of the Most Remarkable Providences* (London, 1697), iv. 51.

68. *Diary of Samuel Pepys*, ed. Latham and Matthews, v. 357.

69. *Dudley Carleton to John Chamberlain 1603–1624: Jacobean Letters*, ed. Maurice Lee, Jr. (New Brunswick, NJ, 1972), 154. Cf. Richard Mulcaster, *Positions* (London, 1888), 80.

70. Edward Moor, *Suffolk Words and Phrases* (1823: Newton Abbot, 1970), 55.

71. Ralph A. Houlbrooke, *The English Family 1450–1700* (London, 1984), 148.

72. Thomas Becon, *Prayers*, ed. John Ayre (Parker Society), (Cambridge, 1844), 132; Tho. Tryon, *Tryon's Letters upon Several Occasions* (London, 1700), 115–16.

73. (John Mortimer), *Advice to Parents: or Rules for the Education of Children* (London, 1704), 10.

74. A. Platts and G. H. Hainton, *Education in Gloucestershire. A Short History* (Gloucester, 1954), 24.

75. Charles Hoole, *A New Discovery of the Old Art of Teaching Schoole* (London, 1660), i. 25.

76. Thomas Wilson, 'The State of England Anno Dom. 1600', ed. F. J. Fisher, 20, in *Camden Miscellany*, xvi (Camden Series, 1936); William Bradford Willcox, *Gloucestershire. A Study in Local Government 1590–1640* (New Haven, 1940), 252; W. H. B. Court, *The Rise of the Midland Industries 1600–1838* (London, 1953), 240; E. Lipson, *The History of the Woollen and Worsted Industries* (London, 1921), 70; Daniel Defoe, *A Tour through England and Wales* (Everyman edn., 1928), i. 266.

77. Carl Bridenbaugh, *Vexed and Troubled Englishmen 1590–1642* (Oxford, 1968), 37.

78. Edgar S. Furniss, *The Position of the Laborer in a System of Nationalism* (Boston and New York, 1920), 114–15.

79. William Wordsworth, 'Michael' (1800); James Miller, *The History of Dunbar* (Dunbar, 1830), 213.

80. William Ellis, *The Modern Husbandman* (1750), i. 86; (Arthur Young), *Rural Oeconomy: or, Essays on the Practical Parts of Husbandry* (Dublin, 1770), 32.

81. Roger Ascham, *English Works*, ed. William Aldis Wright (Cambridge, 1904), 175; D. N. R. Lester, *The History of Batley Grammar School 1612–1962* (Batley, n.d.), 34.

82. *A Fifteenth Century School Book*, ed. William Nelson (Oxford, 1956), 39; John Brinsley, *Ludus Literarius or the Grammar Schoole*, ed. E. T. Campagnac (Liverpool, 1917), 299; *The Life of Adam Martindale*, ed. Richard Parkinson (Chetham Society, 1845), 15; Aubrey, *Remaines of Gentilisme*, 41.

83. *Notes and Queries*, 9th ser., xi (1903), 145.

84. Henry Peacham, *The Complete Gentleman*, ed. Virgil B. Heltzel (Ithaca, NY, 1962), 129–30; for the picture see [William Lily], *A Short Introduction of Grammar* (1606), sig. E8ᵛ. For examples of book inscriptions see G. F. Northall, *English Folk-Rhymes* (London, 1892), 102–7; Clifton Johnson, *Old-Time Schools and School-Books* (London, 1904: New York, 1963), ch. vi; and J. G. Milne, *The Early History of Corpus Christi College, Oxford* (Oxford, 1946), 49.

85. Keith Thomas, *Rule and Misrule in the Schools of Early Modern England* (Stenton Lecture) (Reading, 1976), 20–34.

86. Iolo Davies, *'A Certaine Schoole'. A History of the Grammar School at Cowbridge, Glamorgan* (Cowbridge, 1967), 371–2.

87. Nathanael Ingelo, *Bentivolio and Urania in Six Books* (3rd edn., London, 1673), ii. 175.

88. Thomas Sternberg, *The Dialect and Folk-Lore of Northamptonshire* (London, 1851), 10; B. Dew Roberts, *Mr. Bulkeley and the Pirate* (London, 1936), 41; William Horman, *Vulgaria* (1519), fo. '278' (actually 280).

89. Daniel Defoe ['Andrew Moreton'], *The Protestant Monastery* (London, 1727), 2–3; Hall of Richmond, *Of Government and Obedience*, 450; Wright, *Rustic Speech and Folk-Lore*, 197–9; S. Arthur Strong (compiler), *A Catalogue of*

Letters and Other Historical Documents exhibited in the Library at Welbeck (London, 1903), 232.

90. [William Kempe], *The Education of Children in Learning*, 1588, sig. F1ᵛ; *The Diary of John Evelyn*, ed. E. S. de Beer (London, 1959), 6; 'Memoirs of . . . John Cannon', 26.

91. John Arbuthnot, *The History of John Bull*, ed. Alan W. Bower and Robert A. Erickson (Oxford, 1976), 29.

92. *The Vulgaria of John Stanbridge and the Vulgaria of Robert Whittinton*, ed. Beatrice White (Early English Text Society, 1932), 69–70, 138–9; *The Overthrow of Stage-Playes, by the Way of Controversie betwixt D. Gager and D. Rainoldes* (2nd edn., Oxford, 1629), 116.

93. 'A Divine of the Church of England' (?James Kirkwood), *The True Interest of Families* (London, 1692), 8.

94. James Janeway, *A Token for Children* (London, 1676), i. 1–18.

95. Ibid. ii. 2–3.

96. 'Memoirs of . . . John Cannon', 41.

97. John Scott, *The Life of the Rev. Thomas Scott* (5th edn., London, 1823), 10.

98. Opies, *Children's Games in Street and Playground*, p. 7; Ariès, *Centuries of Childhood*, 315.

99. Dudley Kidd, *Savage Childhood. A Study of Kafir Children* (London, 1906), 161.

Booklist

Most historical writing about children in early modern England relates to the attitudes of adults to children rather than to the world of children themselves. There is, nevertheless, a great deal of relevant material in Philippe Ariès, *Centuries of Childhood*, trans. Robert Baldick (London, 1962); Lawrence Stone, *The Family, Sex and Marriage in England 1500–1800* (London, 1977); J. H. Plumb, 'The New World of Children in Eighteenth-Century England', *Past and Present*, 67 (1975); Ralph A. Houlbrooke, *The English Family 1450–1700* (London, 1984); Linda Pollock, *Forgotten Children. Parent–Child Relations from 1500 to 1900* (Cambridge, 1983); and the same author's *A Lasting Relationship. Parents and Children over Three Centuries* (London, 1987).

Although their focus is not primarily historical, the books of Iona and Peter Opie listed in note 21 above make an excellent introduction to the subject-matter of this essay. Also helpful is Alice B. Gomme, *The Traditional Games of England, Scotland, and Ireland* (1894–8; reissued 1984). The writings of the anthropologist Charlotte Hardman (see note 22 above) provide an exemplary model for historians of childhood. The notes to this chapter give some idea of the wide range of contemporary sources from which the evidence has to be gleaned.

4

A Child Prophet: Martha Hatfield as The Wise Virgin

NIGEL SMITH

CHILDREN's literature emerged in part within Puritan culture. It was an extension of the educational and edifying aims of godly publication: a consequence of the catechism. To say this is to acknowledge the essentially responsive nature of Puritan education—the answer given to each question in the catechism was a help towards the realization within each believer of a godly conscience, an authentic reaction to circumstances based upon a successful integration of godly knowledge with personal experience. Ideally, the heart should speak the language of grace. That this should be so, that the godly of the seventeenth century should expect so much of their children, troubles us today, as much as it was a cause for concern in their day. In special cases, the concern became a vital issue in the life of a community. In this essay, I want to show how a Puritan life led not only to words for children, but words by children, as both ideals and circumstances raised children to the status of authors, even prophets. One particular, well-documented, and well-publicized episode enables us to see how the Puritan child raised questions concerning the relationship between illness and inspiration, the passage from childhood to adulthood, the comparison between youthful innocence and maturity, and the matter of conversion to the godly way itself.

In 1653, the Sheffield Congregational minister James Fisher published an octavo tract of some 170 pages entitled *The Wise Virgin*. The title-page carried a description of the contents: 'A wonderfull Narration of the various dispensations of God towards a Childe of eleven years of age: wherein as his severity hath appeared in afflicting, so also his goodness both in enabling her

79

(when stricken dumb, deaf, and blind, through the prevalency of her disease) at several times to utter many glorious Truths concerning *Christ, Faith*, and other subjects; and also in Recovering her without the use of any external means, lest the glory should be given to any other'. The child was Martha Hatfield, daughter of Anthony Hatfield, a gentleman from Laughton in Yorkshire. Fisher, who was her uncle, produced a narrative which told of Martha's physical weakness, her illness, and the trance-like states in which she spoke as a prophet, from 19 May to 8 December 1652, when, as the narrative relates, she was gradually restored to life and union with her family through God's power.

Though Martha is always referred to as a child in the narrative, she does in fact play the part, or rather, occupy the space, of a very different personality within the Puritan movement. Fisher's representation of her is that of a woman prophet. Within Puritanism, prophesying was generally understood to be the interpretation of Scripture, though during the seventeenth century, especially in the turbulent decades of the 1640s and 1650s, prophesying became associated with a kind of emotional outpouring, sometimes sung, which was regarded as a manifestation of inspiration by the Holy Spirit. A number of women prophets emerged during these years, some of them associated with extreme millenarian groups.[1] Like Martha Hatfield, they delivered prophetic speeches while in trance-like states, which, so the reports tell us, are usually the result of prolonged fasting and physical weakness.

James Fisher was at pains to separate his niece from any overt connection with prophetic personality (he calls her utterances 'speeches', not prophecies), but the force of his narrative cannot but suggest that Martha was so gifted. He strives to dissociate Martha from the kind of prophecy which foretold the future or which worked miracles. None the less, if a prophet is a mouthpiece of God, Martha certainly was one: 'God was with her mouth, adapting her speeches to their necessities.'[2] Fisher says that some of her speeches were the result of confused and perturbed 'intellectuals', but most were made through the Spirit's

The Portraiture of
Mrs MARTHA HATFEILD

assistance, and when Martha returned to health, this itself was the 'miracle' for her family.[3]

Prophets played an important role in the Fifth Monarchist movement of the 1650s. Fisher was at one point accused of preaching the ideas of the Fifth Monarchists, a militant collection of soldiers, clergy, and lay people, expecting the bodily return of Christ, whose thousand-year reign would begin in their own lifetimes.[4] The constitutional, ecclesiastical, and social reforms which they demanded would, they hoped, help to bring on this Second Coming. Anna Trapnel, the daughter of a Hackney shipwright, became a key figure for the Fifth Monarchists when her prophesyings in London and Cornwall appeared to many to justify the veracity of the millenarian cause, and the authorities were sufficiently worried to imprison her and put her on trial.

Both Anna Trapnel, and her major predecessor, Sarah Wight, were members of Independent (that is, Congregational) or Baptist churches, and their prophetic activities—both what they said and the sufferings of their physical bodies—were interpreted as signs which revealed the relationship between the church, community, or nation and God. While their speech told of glorious things to come, their bodies, often immobilized through fasting, and bereft of apparent sensory activity, became maps upon which the congregation and the nation might see the divine dispensation set forth.[5]

Martha Hatfield was understood in just such terms by her family and her congregation. Out of Martha's mouth come 'things' which 'should prove instrumentall for the promoting of some part at least of that glorious Gospell', the 'Composition of Wonders'. That Martha was a child allows Fisher to find a new description of prophecy. He takes the familiar Pauline metaphor for the Bible, the 'sword of the spirit' (Ephesians 6: 17) with the reference to babies in Psalm 8: 2. In a striking apocalyptic picture of Martha, the child becomes an agent of divine vengeance as well as divine grace: 'He hath not chosen armes, or armes of the Mighty Ones, nor the mouth of the Sword, but the Sword of the Mouth; for *out of the mouths of Babes and Sucklings he hath ordained strength*, whereby he effecteth wonderful things here in the World. That which comes out of the mouths of these Babes shall accomplish his Royall Will.'[6]

The modern reader has to try to imagine the Hatfield family holding this elevated image of Martha in their heads while also seeing in front of them a very frail creature who had lost the use of her legs, who had become blind, at times deaf and dumb, and who could take little or no food. The sword of the mouth contrasts sharply with the picture of the frozen girl, teeth tightly locked together, with her mother and sisters trying to drip liquid through a crack made by a broken tooth. Like the women prophets, Martha was able to keep very little food down and incessant vomiting was the result of most attempts to sustain her with food. For Fisher, the fact that his niece was able to live on without nourishment ('her flesh [was] very firm and solid, and she did look very fair and fresh') was clear proof of the text (Luke 4: 4) that man does not live by bread alone.[7] The spectacle presented to the Hatfields was one of extremes: a child who gave forth what appeared to be prophetic speech and who threw up anything she ingested from this world. It was seen as a clear indication that the child was moving out of her earthly existence and closer to her final resting-place in heaven. At the same time, her family were able to read her physical afflictions as signs of her battle with Satan. She was seen to distort her face in order to dismiss Satan, though in her struggle with the demonic, she gnashed her teeth until she broke them.[8] Rigidity in convulsions, when Satan was fought, was complemented by periods when Martha became 'limber', flexible, and so less involved in some transcendental turmoil.[9] Around her bed sat relatives who prayed for her: such a vigil brought the family into the battleground for salvation (and life) which her body enacts, and which is understood to occupy her inner life: at one point the vigilant onlookers record nearly one hundred 'actions and postures in her right hand in one night'.[10] The postures are never interpreted but the narrative implies that they are to be regarded as signs of supernatural workings.

In so far as the whole episode enables us to understand how the Hatfields responded to Martha's plight, it is clear that Martha was expected to die: 'She hath been from her birth a Child of Wonders, being so little when shee was brought out of her Mothers Wombe, that it was thought she would speedily have return'd to the common wombe.'[11] Her prophesyings are a clear indication to her parents that she is about to depart from this world. The family and community involvement in the process of her bedridden prophesying begins as a ritual involvement in the act of dying (*ars moriendi*) and ends with a retrieval of the child from the threshold of the afterlife. Barbara Dailey has shown how the circumstances of Sarah Wight's prophesying fascinated not only Puritan ministers but also godly physicians, anxious to understand the relationship between physiology and the life of the spirit, between which they saw no division.[12] Sarah's return to a normal state was greeted as a triumph of Providence from which the excited godly doctors could learn much. This took place in the excitable and fashionable Puritan circles of 1640s London, where millennial religious beliefs were closely linked to the cause of medical reform. But in secluded Yorkshire, Martha apparently refused all medical assistance because she knew that God would protect her, a feature which Fisher later interprets as an indication of the primacy of the doctrine of justification by faith alone. For one Yorkshire doctor, a compromise diagnosis was possible: her speech was supernatural, her disease natural.[13] The sense of joy, relief, recognition, and fulfilment in the repeated greetings exchanged when Martha's illness ends stands as an example of the conjoining of physical and spiritual destinies for these seventeenth-century Puritans.[14] Lazarus-like, Martha returns from the grave quite literally: she was at one point given up for dead, and a cloth was put over her; only her breathing revealed that she continued to live.[15]

The most sensible way to describe this combination of illness and prophecy is to imagine a process by which the religious codes prevalent in the community afforded an interpretation of the phenomena witnessed in terms that provided consolation for the community as well as an affirmation of its sanctified nature. Illnesses or unusual conditions manifested by the women prophets look to us like some form of anorexia, except that they were understood entirely differently by the communities in which these conditions appeared. Behind this we may also see prophecy functioning as the manifestation of transition from one stage in a person's life to another, from childhood to adulthood, for instance. Both Sarah Wight and Anna Trapnel were young women, and their prophetic crises might be seen as registering the transition into full womanhood. Trapnel's prophetic powers were such that she had an authority almost superior to that of the male ministers. Sarah Wight's subsequent return to accepted practices of worship, appearing in church wearing a veil, is an example of how the religious community contained the energy generated by the crisis in the female prophet's life, and reinstated her in a subservient role in the congregation.[16]

Perhaps because Martha Hatfield was not at the point of

transition from child to woman, it was easier and even unprob-
lematic for James Fisher to describe her as a '*Child-Preacher*' even
though, in seventeenth-century professional terms, such a
description is in fact a contradiction. Eleven is a relatively
advanced age for a child, but Martha probably looked considera-
bly younger and less developed because she had been repeatedly
ill as a child. She seems to have been prematurely born, was not
expected to survive, and her smallness was much noted by her
family. Here, it is possible to see an early Puritan version of the
later and more widespread attitude that the innocence of children
gives them a special insight into reality, which is often more
truthful than the insights of adults, tainted as they are by worldly
experience. Martha was always regarded as somewhat special by
her family in this respect: '*Even while she spelled words and syllables,
she spelled out Christ: for if she met with a free promise, or some good
sentence, holding out Gods love to man, she would say*, Mother, this is a
sweet place, *and usually read it over again.*'[17] Another minister, John
Firth, describes Martha's closeness to God as a kind of Enochian
journey (Gen. 5: 22, 24): 'God seemed to take her out of the
crowd into his Chamber above, where hee sweetly whispered his
minde unto her; and now he hath sent her back again, that shee
may live over her own Sermons.'[18]

Her inspiration raises the question of the degree to which
Martha might have understood and even been responsible for the
things which she said. Coming to consciousness after her illness,
'*she replyed thus in her childish speech*, Have I? me cannot tell, I can
doe nothing in my self, it was not me, it was the spirit of God in
me; I am nothing but a poor earth-worm, and me have nothing
but what God giveth me; for me is nothing but what God giveth
me; for me is nothing but dust and ashes.'[19] Fisher's representation of her speech is a good example of the pious dissimulation
visible in Puritan confessions. Martha's innocence is signified by
her incorrect grammar, but what she says is a perfectly proper
statement of a prophet's responsibility for his or her inspired
speech—it all comes from the divine source. Where did Martha
learn this? Did it come by inspiration? If she was as well trained in
Bible and catechism reading as the text suggests, then her

humility in the prophetic act is a good example of the efficacy of such a godly education. For Fisher, it is a perfect marriage of training or discipline and inspiration. Moreover, Martha describes herself in exactly the same words here as those used by the women prophets, a '*nothing-creature*', a play on the regenerate 'new creature' of 2 Cor. 5: 17 and Gal. 6: 15.[20]

Despite this cultivated yet also inspired innocence, Martha had a sense of her own will, which was apparently respected by her family and friends: 'This childe being acquainted with some intentions of some of her Friends to print her Speeches, answered, I wish they may aim at a right end; a most seasonable *Item*; and if we do not endeavor to have them first printed in our hearts, and to publish them in our lives, we shall give but a poor account of them to the world.'[21] She did not just have pious intentions, but as this quotation reveals, she was also adept enough in preaching techniques to use a rather sophisticated if well-known metaphor for inner self-education, taken from the printing press.[22] Perhaps our credulity should cease here. Could a child of eleven so readily have laid hold of such an apt and deliberate image, which of itself, suggests the continuity between inspiration and publication? Or is James Fisher speaking here? Has he, in his extensive and detailed effort to interpret for a mass readership the significance of Martha's experiences, made her words entirely his own? After all, at this point in the pamphlet, Fisher is telling the reader Martha's story, rather than the speeches which come later on. This being the case, there could be no greater example of the way in which Martha's speeches suggested in themselves the very aims of Puritan educational thinking. The saving of souls, soteriology, found in a child prophet clear evidence of its own success, though it took the higher presence of God in the ailing Martha to make this apparent. Indeed, as a prophet, Martha carried more authority with a large readership, something amply testified by the five editions of *The Wise Virgin* published between 1653 and 1664.

Martha was believable not only because she spoke prophetically. Congregational worship was distinctive among other forms of Puritanism for the importance of the confession of experience, a (usually) short account of how the individual believer had come

to be converted, read out to the congregation when that individual was admitted to the gathered church. 'Experiential' theology
then permitted an authentic verbal expression of God's dealings
with each believer. Such authenticity was judged not only by
particular representational conventions—for instance, reworked
biblical dreams and visions—but also by the particular social
roots of the believer, in so far as they could be reflected in
language.[23] Martha is singled out not only for her childish speech,
but also for the rustic nature of that speech. There is a sense
almost of embarrassment in Fisher's description of his community's 'Countrey-Dialects'.[24] For some Nonconformists, notably the Quakers, rusticity was approved: a godly countryman
was a clear sign that the spirit or inner light could be present
without the false trappings of university education and established churches.[25] The Independent ministers were usually formally educated, however, so Fisher regards rustic language not as
a sign of virtue in itself but as a resource which should ideally be
reformed and made to reflect godliness. Martha was therefore a
double testimony to her sincerity: the innocence of childhood and
the authenticity of the rustic. Traces of Yorkshire dialect pervade
Martha's speech and Fisher's narrative account. In a moment of
guilt, she laments 'What a naughty, naughty Lasse was I', while
Fisher talks of the 'short Dorms' (northern dialect for 'dozing')
into which Martha falls after vomiting gall, soot, and blood.[26] The
expectation of 'experiential' truthfulness is transposed on to the
child's words, thereby creating another generic condition for a
child author.

Moreover, by means of the dialect and the strong presence of
family and local ties, the tract takes the reader into the world of
provincial Puritanism in the early 1650s. Martha Hatfield's case
represents a document in the domestication of millennial zeal
during the early, optimistic years of the Commonwealth. If the
triumph of the godly in the army and Parliament during the late
1640s was to be consolidated, the signs of a regenerate community, and the imminent Second Coming, would have to be seen
nationally, in the cities and in the localities. Some of the well-
known urban Independent churches published large collections

of experiential narratives as a manifestation of their own grace.[27] The writings of the women prophets and *The Wise Virgin* were part of this movement. All these publications reflect the inherent social hierarchies which the gathered churches sustained, to such an extent that they almost reflect angelic hierarchies. While the London churches had many merchant members, the Hatfield family were godly gentry at the top of their local community: *'a Branch of a family of good Note in the West of* Yorkshire, *as to externalls, having wherein they might glory'*.[28] The two males who take down Martha's speech are Edward and William Rhodes, the sons of Sir Edward Rhodes.[29] She herself becomes a living example of the child figures who populate the dream visions which many of the experiential narratives recall. In these inner worlds, children appear, often identified with the Christ-child, to provide a message of assurance and certainty to the dreamer. Martha becomes a living dream child, as she is carried around by the other members of her family, a prophetic vessel and figure of Christ, in an exact parallel to the contents of one particular Puritan dream.[30] In this way, the reader comes to see how Martha can stand alongside God's 'Gallant and Heroick Commanders' (the ministers and politicians of the Commonwealth) in importance.[31]

'Family-Duties' are never far from Fisher's immediate focus. For Martha, these included not only domestic service but also reading edifying books. Fisher mentions the presence of the catechisms of John Ball and the treatises of Jeremiah Burroughes.[32] *The Wise Virgin* itself conforms to the kind of strict order and definitions that characterize Puritan soteriological reading matter. Fisher divides his narrative into three parts. Martha's sufferings, her speeches, and her recovery. Among the speeches are dialogues, and much of the content of the speeches corresponds to the language of the catechism, except that Martha asks and answers her own questions: *'What did God create man* [for]*? For his glory.'*[33] Catechism and prophecy are elided: 'My Christ is come again, Oh, how sweet my Christ is! Oh, how sweet he is! those that feel the sweetnes of Christ, they will trust in him.'[34] Each day's record of her speeches is presented as if it were a daily reading in a devotional book. Fortunately for Fisher,

Martha's speeches never threaten to do anything but justify Congregational ecclesiology. She is visited at one point by a Quaker, but she is afterwards very careful to distance herself from what most Independents, especially the less enthusiastic, like Fisher, regarded as a false form of worship. Quakers, she correctly observes, are 'above Onances' (child language for Ordinances), and for such errors, Martha will not wear shoes made by them.[35] It was in the very early 1650s that the first Quakers became active in the north of England, so Fisher's account of Martha's opinions functions incidentally as a valuable piece of sectarian propaganda. Indeed, it is claimed at one point that Martha had been responsible for the conversions of many in the local community, possibly some of those strangers who came to visit her.[36]

Most important of all these formalizing interpretations by Fisher are the various allegorizations he offers of the prophetic and the experiential. The narrative of Martha's sufferings is a series of 'Providences', particular instances of God's dealings with mankind, in which the very concept of the child plays a symbolic role: 'there will be much use of a submitting frame of heart, to submit our selves, children and all, to the Will of the Father of our spirits, Heb. 12.9 and we should improve this Providence (in raising up this Child) by faith for the raising up of the Church from under all her Convulsions and prevailing Diseases.'[37] The child becomes the church, her body, rent with suffering, the temple of the spirit. The significance of Fisher's interpretation is that a kind of didactic abstraction is being implicitly associated with the experience of children, though he makes no distinction between the edification of adults and children here. Bunyan wrote his allegory *The Pilgrim's Progress* (1678) not primarily for children. None the less, it is possible to detect in Fisher's thinking about this particular child's traumatic experience, the association of childhood innocence and the special scope it afforded for insight with edification by allegorical means. *The Pilgrim's Progress* is an abstraction of Bunyan's earlier experiential account of his conversion and calling to the ministry, *Grace Abounding* (1666). Martha's struggle, though in one sense an example of a Puritan Saint's life, like a martyrological portrait, also contains within itself the hint that children are able to profit from an allegorical account of experience. *The Pilgrim's Progress* caused some controversy among Bunyan's fellow Dissenters in Bedford because it was felt that the popular heroic and military allegory was unsuitable for godly teaching. Though this attitude to the education of Puritan children did not begin to change until at least the mid-eighteenth century, Martha's speeches and the narrative describing her experiences contain a degree of heroism, instanced in her denunciating speeches: '*They are Bastards and not Sons, whom the Lord correcteth not.*'[38] Heroic or holy violence for Puritans was acceptable when it was located not primarily in allegory but in experience. In a Yorkshire child, a quasi-military courage was clearly present.

Her prophesying speeches themselves, which were subject to close examination by local ministers and lay people, engage directly with parental relations. She sees her own afflictions as the result of God's paternal punishment: 'As the father calleth his child when he hath done amiss, and asks why he doth so? & gives him correction: so God gives his children correction, but it is for their good & comfort'.[39] Maternal figures, however, she sees in need of protection and help: 'O Mother, love God, love him; O get faith, get faith; her Mother said, so I have need.'[40] But with these statements are mingled a few extraordinary sentences that point to a final release from worldly constraints: 'Come, let us flye unto the Throne of grace, as a Bird doth into the air.'[41] This kind of utterance, together with figures like the much repeated roaring lion (another psychic envisaging of Satan), make up an authentic and expressive landscape for the child prophet. Her speeches not only suggest that they should be read as catechisms, but also reveal Martha's habitual thinking in terms of parent–child relationships. And this at the very point where she reveals her prophetic identity: Matt. 23: 37 is referred to more than once— Martha seeks consolation in the image of the hen gathering her chickens together under her wings. But in the verse, not quoted in full in *The Wise Virgin*, the hen (Jerusalem) is asked to gather up her *prophets* in a hen-like way.[42] Martha's speech becomes almost a cry for help, even while it is offering divine truth, and it certainly reveals her to be exactly what she is, a sick child in need of care and protection.

When Martha came back to consciousness and to the possibility of a fuller physical recovery, she was no pleasant sight: 'her sinews were drawn all upon knots in the flesh; and at her first Recovery her flesh was blackish, red and white (as they compared it) like Marble.'[43] None the less, there was evidence of God-provided natural sustenance: 'shee had the benefit of nature; but her stools were such as all that beheld them admired: they are round, of the quality of a Nutmeg, very hard and like a piece of earth rolled in lime, and they have no smell.'[44] She had undergone a fantastic transformation: it is no surprise that some would call her a witch, an accusation often made against women prophets. In *The Wise Virgin*, however, such charges are not taken seriously. Instead, a final coda records that Martha survived as an exemplary godly woman, and married, while her significance as a holy instrument within her family grew with the death of her sister Hannah.[45]

Lives of godly children were not unusual in the mid-seventeenth century, though the nature of Martha Hatfield's experiences was uncommon. At the heart of millennial religious culture, a child had seemed to have God speaking through her. Without any other appropriate authorial category, she was likened to a prophet, and was presented as an apocalyptic figure. Given the popularity of *The Wise Virgin*, it is not unlikely that godly children read this narrative: the contents of the speeches are simple enough for the young to understand. It is perhaps only fitting that, as the revolutionary moment of Puritanism passed, the exciting and powerful figure of the prophet should be made to function as a sober catechizer, the innocence of an afflicted yet gifted child the most effective mover of human hearts.

Notes

1. See Keith Thomas, 'Women and the Civil War Sects', *Past and Present*, 13 (1958), 42–62; Nigel Smith, *Perfection Proclaimed. Language and Literature in English Radical Religion, 1640–1660* (Oxford, 1989), 45–53.

2. James Fisher, *The Wise Virgin* (1653, all quotations taken from 3rd edn., 1656), 123.

3. Ibid. 137.

4. See B. S. Capp, *The Fifth Monarchy Men. A Study in Seventeenth-Century English Millenarianism* (London, 1972).

5. Smith, *Perfection Proclaimed.*

6. Fisher, *The Wise Virgin*, sig. A3$^{r\,v}$.

7. Ibid., sig. B3^v, 73.

8. Ibid. 7–8.

9. Ibid. 14.

10. Ibid. 18.

11. Ibid. 1.

12. Barbara Ritter Dailey, 'The Visitation of Sarah Wight: Holy Carnival and the Revolution of the Saints in Civil War London', *Church History*, 55 (1986), 438–55.

13. Fisher, *The Wise Virgin*, sig. B5^v–B6^r, 72.

14. Ibid. 135.

15. Ibid. 13.

16. Smith, *Perfection Proclaimed*, 16.

17. Fisher, *The Wise Virgin*, sig. B3^r.

18. Ibid., sig. A8^v.

19. Ibid., sig. B5^v.

20. Ibid., sig. B2^v. See also Ian Green, '"For Children in Yeeres and Children in Understanding": The Emergence of the Catechism under Elizabeth and the Early Stuarts', *Journal of Ecclesiastical History*, 37 (1986), 397–425.

21. Fisher, *The Wise Virgin*, sig. A4^v.

22. Smith, *Perfection Proclaimed*, 273.

23. Ibid. 23–45, 78–84.

24. Fisher, *The Wise Virgin*, 2.

25. See, for instance, Samuel Fisher, *Rusticus Ad Academicos* (1660).

26. Fisher, *The Wise Virgin*, 8–9.

27. See John Rogers, *Ohel or Bethshemesh. A Tabernacle for the Sun* (1653); Henry Walker, ed., *Spirituall Experiences, Of sundry Beleevers* (1653); Samuel Petto, 'Roses from Sharon' in *The Voice of the Spirit* (1654).

28. Fisher, *The Wise Virgin*, sig. B2^v.

29. Ibid. 17.

30. '*Experiences of* T.M.' in Henry Walker, ed., *Spirituall Experiences*, 270.

31. Fisher, *The Wise Virgin*, sig. A5^v.

32. Ibid. 13.

33. Ibid. 11.

34. Ibid. 23.

35. Ibid. 52, 149.

36. Ibid.

37. Ibid.
38. Ibid. 140.
39. Ibid. 33.
40. Ibid. 135.
41. Ibid. 19.
42. Ibid. 30.
43. Ibid. 139.
44. Ibid. 73.
45. In fact, Martha had begun to speak as an agent of God when her brother Jonathan died. This in itself was a comfort for her father: ibid. 166.

5

The Puritans and their Heirs

GILLIAN AVERY

CHILDREN'S books have always been particularly vulnerable to the ideologies of the age. Since there is in most of them, if not a didactic element then a reflection of the social rules and ethic of the period, and since few children have the ability or the experience to make the necessary allowances for a viewpoint different from their own, inevitably their books have a lower survival rate than almost any other sort of literature. But it makes these books of particular interest to the historian, for in them at any given period you find what parents and teachers desired for children, their concept of the ideal child, and the faults they sought to correct. Even spelling lists from reading primers are revealing. Take a random sample from *The Protestant Tutor* of 1683, a seventeenth-century compilation of aggressive matter concerning the grievous errors of Rome.[1] The lists of words here provide a fascinating insight into the vocabulary, mostly scriptural and theological, that Protestant parents apparently felt should be on the tip of their children's tongues: Beautiful, Benjamin, Bountifully, Beelzebub, Beneficial, Baalperazim [this being a place where David smote the Philistines. See 2 Samuel 5: 11], Beatification. Candle, Caleb, Chastising, Canaan, Catechising, Canterbury, Christianity, Chederlaomer [a king of Elam mentioned in Genesis], Consideration, Consubstantiation.

Children's books as a separate category of literature can be said to have made a tentative beginning in the seventeenth century. Before that there were school books and books of courtesy, but we do not find a substantial body of child-slanted books before the middle years of the seventeenth century, and these were almost exclusively religious. It was not until the middle years of the eighteenth century that children were given recreational books of their own. They undoubtedly had recreational reading—but they shared it with adults, for the stories of the marvellous, of knightly deeds, and fabulous creatures, and talking animals and magic, the ballads of Robin Hood and his like, which we now have relegated to children, were then enjoyed by everyone with simple tastes. Stories such as these were available in the broadsides and ballads which were peddled by chapmen. The children whose fathers had libraries had access to books of history, natural history, travels, as well as the traditional stories which were part of a well-established oral tradition.

But the books marketed for children were almost all designed for their religious education. 'Nothing in our more diffuse civilisation', William Sloane wrote in his account of English and American children's books of the seventeenth century, 'quite holds the pivotal position, the centrality, which religion held in seventeenth century England and America. To man's relation with God all the other circumstances of his life were peripheral ... This centrality of religion, which gave the period its peculiar hue and makes it for us at once remote and strangely fascinating, gave it also an extraordinary singleness of purpose.'[2] In England there were of course many cultural strands, but it was the Puritan one that dominated such books as there were then for children. The range of juvenile publications in Old England indeed differed very little from the books published in New England where the Puritans had a stranglehold on literary culture that lasted well into the eighteenth century. Of 261 books that William Sloane, after exhaustive consideration of some thousands, considered were written for children, all were religious with the exception of two books of riddles, one or two on sport, and a few more on polite manners. Not all of these were written from the Calvinist point of view, but most were because that was the position held by the average Protestant Englishman in the seventeenth century. And it always does seem that those who write for children in any age meekly tend to range themselves with the most dominant and vociferous moralists among their contemporaries, paying lip service at any rate to a code they may not necessarily feel strongly about themselves.

For instance, since we find no element of fantasy in children's books before the nineteenth century, it would be possible to draw a conclusion that they read none, that responsible adults all agreed that works of the imagination were unsuitable for children. But in a book of advice which an unnamed parent wrote for his family in 1678, we find this:

Beside the true, there is also a fabulous History, which is that of Romance; the reading of which I do not forbid you. ... True History represents to us only things as they are, with all their faults, their events depend more on Fortune than Reason, and the narration becomes very often tedious, because it gives account of no extraordinary success; when on the contrary every thing in a Romance is great, there Virtues and Vices are extream, and always recorded according to the measure of merit. A thousand rare and unforeseen Adventures there, surprise the Reader, and keep him always in breath, in expectation of some other novelty which may prove still more wonderful. In fine, the Soul elevates itself by this reading, and it comes often to pass, that being instructed by the excellent qualities of some imaginary Hero, it regains in effect some real impression of them; or some horror of Vice, from the borrowed shape of the villainous.[3]

It is an eloquent and, one would have thought, convincing defence of the traditional popular romance of the day, but though many privately might have agreed with the writer, nobody was bold enough to act upon it by publishing these stories in versions suitable for children, and the educationalists and moralists appeared to be united in assuming that children were only to be given didactic reading. 'When thou canst read,' Thomas White, a Nonconformist divine, told children,[4] 'read no Ballads and foolish Books, but a Bible, and the *Plain mans pathway to Heaven*,[5] a very plain holy book for you; get the *Practice of Piety*;[6] Mr Baxter's *Call to the Unconverted*;[7] Allen's *Allarum to the Unconverted*;[8] read the Histories of the Martyrs that dyed for Christ ... Read also often treatises of Death, and Hell and Judgement, and of the Love and Passion of Christ.' He is apparently addressing children who are not yet old enough to read by themselves, but he is directing them towards devotional books and theological works written for adults. In the list there is nothing written for children, and no recreational books at all. And he condemns outright all imaginative tales. Puritan views on the evils associated with imagination were to affect the books provided for children for many generations. 'Imagination is the wombe, and Sathan the father of all monstrous conceptions,' Richard Sibbs had said in 1635.[9] The products of the imagination were inevitably suspect. Fiction was not only a lie; it was also unprofitable. *The School of Good Manners* (1715), one of the earliest New England publications for children, devotes a chapter to the sin of lying, and following customary Puritan teaching divides it into three categories: the officious lie (intended to prevent some danger or procure some good); the sporting lie 'which is to make one merry, or to pass away Precious Time', and the pernicious lie 'which is made for some evil, hurtful, dangerous intent against our Neighbour. All these sorts of Lying are Sinful. A Lying Tongue is one of the things that are an Abomination to the Lord. Prov. 6. 16, 17.' And it goes on to muster other scriptural denunciations of lying and the fearful fate of all liars.[10]

No difference is made in the weight of the sin attached to the three very different categories of lying, and in this respect it is perhaps interesting to tell a story of the youth of Frank Stockton, a distinguished nineteenth-century American writer for children. The Puritan ethic lingered for a long time in the United States, and in Stockton's boyhood in Pennsylvania in the 1840s it was still dominant. He and his friends had a secret society, and when a candidate presented himself for admission he was asked: 'If your mother was being chased by an Indian who wanted to tomahawk her, and she hid herself in some place that only you knew about, what would you say to the Indian if he asked where she was?' If the boy said he would brace himself to tell a lie to the Indian in those very testing circumstances then he would be admitted; if he said that his regard for truth would compel him to say where she was hidden then he was rejected.[11] It is made quite clear that this was not to test the boy's love for his mother or his feelings about Indians with tomahawks, but whether he could bring himself in these extreme circumstances to discard ingrained teaching about the fearful sin of lying. A real tearaway could, and would therefore be a suitable candidate for the secret society.

All the Puritan moralists took the same view about lying, and the lying incurred by writing that was not strictly true, and they censured the popular tales and ballads of the time, very often by name. 'A Sporting Lye, or a Lye in jest, is that which is meerly to make one merry, to pass away time, with the like, such are old Wives tales of Robin-hood, Fortunatus, and the like,' said Thomas Gouge,[12] adding that it was a sin against truth, that lying was a mark of the devil's children, and that such reading was an unwarrantable misspending of precious time. The story of Fortunatus, his wishing cap and magic purse, frequently came in for stricture, as did the exploits of the knight, Guy of Warwick who slew giants and dragons and who finished his life as a poor pilgrim to atone for his sins. Most censured of all was Tom Thumb, there apparently being something about the pranks of this little creature that preachers found particularly subversive. This deep distrust of fiction long persisted among evangelicals, particularly in America. 'Is it a true book, John?' a grandmother of the 1840s asked. 'Because if it isn't true, it is the worst thing that a boy can read.'[13]

The thought of the precious time misspent on such frivolity grieved the mercantile mind as much as the lies involved, for there was always much Puritan uneasiness about leisure and much emphasis on material gain. 'Without doubt those recreations are best, which mix pleasure and profit together,' said a popular book of advice of 1671.[14] It was addressed to apprentices, whom it wished to groom for a comfortable middle age as masters. Those who study their markets have always been able to derive profit from purveying godly books, and Anglo-Saxons derive a peculiar pleasure (and material profit) from godly disapproval of moral turpitude in others, particularly if there are salacious details. There is the example of Nathaniel Crouch, for instance. He was a literary hack of the Restoration period who published under the name of Richard Burton (posthumously this was changed to Robert Burton). No Puritan zealot himself, he nevertheless saw that his books, to sell, would have to have a Puritan cast to them. He was not an original writer; rather, a reaper of other men's fields, a ransacker of houses not his own, who retold stories and

99

assembled marvels and curiosities and furnished them with
suitable morals. He also demonstrated what could be done to
make sensational if not pornographic material out of the holy
Scriptures. The title page of *Youths Divine Pastime*[15] states that it is
'Very Delightful for the Virtuous imploying the Vacant Hours of
young Persons, and preventing vain and vicious Divertisements,'
and Crouch adds a self-congratulatory couplet which summarizes
his attitude to publishing:

> He certainly doth hit the White
> Who mingles Profit with Delight.

He selected almost exclusively Old Testament stories of the
more spectacular sort, many distinctly unedifying. Part I has the
story of Jezebel, with a woodcut of her being eaten by dogs; we
have David seducing Bathsheba; the assault by Potiphar's wife on
the virtue of Joseph; Elisha's bears devouring the children. Part
II contains the story of the Levite and the concubine, illustrated
by a dismembered corpse, with the Levite holding a severed leg.

> The Levite into twelve parts cut
> Her Body; and with speed
> Sends them through Israel to proclaim
> This execrable deed.

There is the story of the ravishing of Dinah, also illustrated, and
the story of Lot and his two daughters, who in the woodcut
repose languidly beside him, naked-breasted, Lot, the doggerel
says severely, being guilty of

> That great and Heinous Sin
> Of Incest with his Daughters who
> Were both with Child by him.

One gathers that Crouch did hit the white with this lubricious
material as the book went into several editions.

The compilation that he called *Several Excellent Young Persons*[16]
is less original, being the memoirs (taken from other men's
books) of godly young people on whom Protestant youth should
model themselves. Some were from the Old Testament such as
Isaac and Joseph, others were early martyrs; there were also the

traditional youthful upholders of the faith such as Edward VI and Lady Jane Grey. The one that is of most interest is Lord Harrington, Baron of Exton who died in 1613 aged twenty-two, since this gives an idea of the model youth of the time.

He spent not his time in Courting of Ladies, and Contemplating the Beauty of Women, which are the bellows of Lust and the baits of Uncleanness, but preferred his Books before their Beauty ... He was also very temperate in his Diet, avoiding Feasting, and was frequent in Fasting, hating Idleness and much Sleep, the two Nurses of Uncleanness. . . . As soon as he was awake his constant Care was to put his Soul in order . . . Being ready, he read a Chapter and then went to Prayer with his Servants in his Chamber; and afterwards commonly spent an hour in reading some Divine Treatise to enliven his Affections and increase his knowledge. Before Dinner he read a Chapter, sung a Psalm, and went to Prayer with his Family and after Supper he also sung a Psalm and Prayed with them; and beside these publick Duties he Prayed privately, in his Closet every morning, and then retired for some hours to some serious study. The residue of the morning he spent in conversing with his Friends, riding the great Horse, or some other noble and honest Recreation till Dinner.

This young man also studied sermons, read history and mathematics and military discipline, kept a diary of his thoughts and wrong-doings, and would ride miles to hear a sermon. It was an ideal of youth that was constantly held up for imitation. Even in New England where conditions demanded that its inhabitants should necessarily be active and hardy and practical if they were to survive, it was the studious, contemplative type of young man who was commended by the preachers. Nathanael Mather came from a line of Puritan divines distinguished both in Old and New England; he was the son of Increase, brother of Cotton Mather, and died in 1688 aged nineteen. In the style of the time, Cotton, then a young man of twenty-five, turned his brother's death to good use in a sermon. (He was to do the same some years later when his own very wayward son, young Increase, died in a shipwreck; this being perhaps the only occasion when young Cresy's unsatisfactory life was of benefit to others.) Nathanael was a learned youth who was admitted to Harvard when he was

twelve and had taken his third degree by the time of his death. On
his brother's admission he had so devoured books that 'it came to
pass that Books devoured him. His weak Body could not bear the
Toils and Hours, which he used himself unto,' and his neglect of
exercise ruined his health 'by that time sixteen Winters had
snow'd upon him'. He was a melancholy youth, given to fits of
terrifying despair, full of self-loathing. He had said that 'of the
manifold Sins which I was guilty of, none so stick upon me, as
that being very young, I was whittling on the Sabbath-day; and
for fear of being seen, I did it behind the door.' Cotton Mather
presented this paragon to the young people of New England as a
'Mirrour, wherein you may see the Exercises of a Virtuous Youth
. . . you shall see as what should be done, so what may be done by
a Young Person.'[17] It was very remote from the lives led by New
Englanders, even the clergy who were often six-day farmers,
outdoor men, but also versed in medicine and in law, pioneers
who might well have to organize resistance to the Indians.
Nathanael was old beyond his years, 'a sign of ninety at nineteen',
his brother said of him—this being a sign of great grace in a
young person. Of another child who died of 'bladders in the
windpipe' [diphtheria] aged 'upwards of five years and a half'
Cotton Mather said that she fulfilled the prophecy that a 'child
should dye an hundred years old'.[18]

The ideal child was certainly not a playful child. It was grave
and serious, and indeed the first indications of that early piety
which parents watched so anxiously for might be when it turned
from childish diversions. In the life of the truly godly child there
was no room for play. We get a picture of how the good child
should conduct himself in a book addressed to children in the last
decade of the seventeenth century.[19]

A good Child is one that loves his Book, and if his Father and Mother
send him to School, then up he gets in the morning betimes, he dresses
himself, and then as soon as he is drest, he goes into some corner to
Prayers, and having done, he goes to his Father and Mother, and makes
obedience, to them, and then he prays his Mother to give him his
Breakfast that he may be gone, then away he hies to School, and strives
to be there before any of the rest of the Schollars; and those two hours at

Noon, which are alowed to Schollars to play, if his School-fellows are rude and wanton, he will not go to play amongst them, but will seek about the Town, or Street, to find out such Children as are good and civil, and will spend the time in Discoursing with them about God and Christ, and the matters of another World; and so will keep them company until one of the clock, that it is time to go to School again; and whilst he is in School, let the other Schollars play and do what they will, this Good Child will be careful to mind his Book, and to learn his Lesson; and then towards Night, as soon as he comes home, having made obedience to his Father and Mother, he asketh his Mother if she have anything for him to do, if she say no, then he takes his Bible and reads a Chapter, and then he tells his Father and Mother what he has learn'd at School, and then he goes by himself into some corner to Prayers.

This same book shows readers how children ought not to behave. The account of the good child is an unconvincing ideal, but here are the voices of recognizable children, a very rare glimpse of seventeenth-century children that we can believe in.

All the time his Father is a Reading, or at Prayers, he sits laughing and giggling, and playing with his Brothers and Sisters, not minding anything that is said. Then another time, his Father and Mother being in the Shop at work, and leaving him and his Brothers and Sisters within, charging every one of them to read their Books; and his Brothers and Sisters being almost as bad as he, instead of reading their Books they play and rude with each other: and, oh! there is such a frolic and flutter amongst them as if none was to be heard but themselves. Then they play so long, until at last they fall out and quarrel with one another, and call one another all to nought; one is called Dog, another is called Bitch, and another is called Rogue, and another is called Bastard; then it may be they go to fighting, and fling one another down in the House. Then John goes with a Story to his Mother that Mary hit him in the face. Then Mary and Betty go with a story to their Mother that the Boys do nothing but tear them about, and will not let them alone. Then Tom goes with a story to his Mother, saying, Mother, William flung me aground and hurt my Arm. Then William goeth with a story to his Mother, saying Mother, Tom hit me with his Batt. Then Tom crys out, But you lye, I did not touch you, you flung me aground first. But you lye: And you lye: And you lye: and you lye.

What Robert Russel deplored in these children was that they played when they should have been minding their book; all the subsequent squabbling stemmed from that. In John Locke's treatise on child-rearing in 1693[20] we find the first acknowledgement that play was necessary for children. It was to have far-reaching effects, though not at once, and the strictest resisted it. Indeed the notion that children could and should exist without play lingered among evangelicals for years to come. At Kingswood, the school founded by Wesley, for instance, there was no recreation for the boys; they were either working or praying, and were never free from adult supervision. Puritan parents had no wish to see playfulness or carefree high spirits in their children; what they earnestly desired was signs of early piety.

What was this early piety so much stressed in all the sermons and books addressed to seventeenth-century children? Calvinists held that since the Fall the whole creation was depraved, vile, and utterly corrupt; that God had made a covenant with the faithful, the Covenant of Grace, whereby the elect would be saved provided they had experienced conversion. The first step towards this was conviction of sin, an overpowering sense of one's depravity that brought the soul to the depths of despair, a sense that one was utterly lost and helpless. Inevitably the person thus aware of his lost condition asked himself what he must do to be saved. The terrifying answer was, there was nothing, he was utterly helpless in his sin; God had mercy on whom He would have mercy. Only when the human soul accepted this unquestioningly could redemption come.

Preachers toiled, struggled, wrestled to bring about the necessary change of heart, labouring the point not only with children but their parents, for the parents had unique responsibility in the matter. Their office was held directly from heaven. 'Thy father and mother are next and immediately under God the instrumental authors of thy being,' a Boston minister reminded the children in his congregation in 1721,[21] and the concept of the parents as God's viceroys was a familiar one, still to be found among evangelicals in the nineteenth century. '"I stand in place of God to you, whilst you are a child,"' Mr Fairchild told his little son

Henry in that famous nineteenth-century evangelical classic, *The History of the Fairchild Family*.[22] It was the solemn duty of parents to instruct their children, catechize them, worship with them, pray with them, and keep them out of the reach of bad influence, safe within the sanctity of the family circle.

The family unit was assuming an importance it had never had before. Puritan preachers and writers of books on family government described it again and again as a church and a commonwealth in which the father was priest and governor, responsible for the spiritual welfare of each member. The severity towards children might seem to arise partly from guilt about the manner of their begetting. Puritans felt considerable unease about their sexuality. There was no place for celibacy in their ethic. It was better to marry than to burn, and marriage increased the numbers of God's people. But it was for this purpose only, not to satisfy carnal lust. 'Remember that the sins of the children may be due to the sin involved in the conceiving of them,' one of the most popular books of household government warned parents, telling them to examine their hearts and they would recognize the too carnal conception of their children. 'Thou euen by breeding thy children hast helped them into corruption, and a damnable estate: how oughtest thou then, by all holy care and pains taken with them in teaching them the knowledge of God in Christ, to helpe them out of it, that they may not be firebrands of hell?'[23]

Life was so short, eternity yawned beyond the grave; responsible adults must strive to find ways of impressing upon the young the sense of their mortal nature, and the message was repeated over and over again, with an urgent eloquence. 'Man's Life is the Shadow of Smoak, the Dream of a Shadow; one doubteth whether to call it a dying Life, or a living Death,' a preacher of a funeral sermon told his young congregation: 'I am now Young, and in the Flower of my Days; but who knows what a Day may bring forth? The greatest Weight hangs upon the smallest Wires, and Eternity depends upon those few Hours I am to breathe in the World.'[24] It is a patchwork of quotations, the first one from Sophocles, but strung together with that resonance that all seventeenth-century preachers apparently could command. In actual fact, in spite of the stress laid upon early piety whenever preachers addressed children, most Puritan conversions seemed to take place in late adolescence, and those experienced earlier were often realized by the subjects of them to be false conversions; the child might go through a religious phase only to backslide.

The greatest desideratum was that all children should be prepared for death, and if they died during a religious phase then they were felt to be safe. It is perhaps not unfair to say that the Puritans expressed more pleasure in their dead and dying children than in their living ones. Cotton Mather gave three pages of his diary[25] to the triumphant dying of his daughter Katherine, otherwise his references to his children only convey anxiety about their spiritual well-being, concern whether he is doing all that he might to effect their salvation. If the children died in a state of grace, then the parent had no more to fear for them, for the records that we have suggest that there was far more anxiety in Puritan parenthood than there was pleasure, that even if children appeared godly and dutiful the parents might expect lapses. And if we are to believe the accounts, dying was often by far the most joyful moment of a lifetime. Increase Mather described the triumphal death in childbirth of his daughter Jerusha—Cotton's sister. She had been a studious and deeply pious child and young woman, so scrupulous and so fearful of telling a lie that she used to qualify everything she said with 'I think', or 'It may be' or ' 'Tis likely'. But her deathbed transcended sober duty; it can only be described as glorious:

It is not the Portion of all the Children of God, to Dy with Triumphant Joyes ... On the other side, it is the Portion of Some, to go away Triumphing unto the Heavenly World. So did our Great Ames, unto the Astonishment of a Popish Physician; who asked, Whether Protestants did use to Dy after that manner? ... And so our Dying Jerusha, when she certainly knew that she was to Dy, she said unto those about her; Here is a Strange Thing! when I was in Health, Death was a Terror to me. But now I know, I shall Dy, I am not at all afraid of it. She said, This is a Wonderful Work of God! I know, that I am going to Christ: that I shall shortly be in the Heavenly Jerusalem, with an Innumerable

Company of Angels, and among the Spirit of Just Men made Perfect. Said she, I see things that are Unutterable! Then she Sang for Joy.[26]

Death in a state of grace was what every parent wished for a child, and if it died young it had been put beyond the reach of the evils of this world which Puritans knew were so many and so insidious. Children encountered death frequently then, in their own family, among their schoolfellows. A father began his book of parental advice in 1694 by saying, 'My dear Children, if ever you live to Maturity of Age, and I happen to die before you do so . . .'[27]. And Cotton Mather wrote: ''Tis now upon Computation found, that more than half the Children of men Dy before they come to Seventeen years of age.' He urged children: 'Go unto the Burying-Place; there you will see many a Grave shorter than your selves.'[28] He himself lost thirteen of his own children, and his diary records the deaths of scores if not hundreds of others. The image of graves shorter than oneself became indelibly printed on the minds of American children for a hundred and fifty years or more from the famous verse in the New England Primer.

> In the burying place may see
> Graves shorter there than I.
> From Death's arrest no age is free,
> Young children too may die.
> My God, may such an awful sight
> Awakening be to me!
> Oh! that by early grace I might
> For Death prepared be.

Thomas White had told children to read 'treatises of death', and the obvious place to find these would have been in Foxe's *Book of Martyrs*, which with its splendidly explicit illustrations must have been pored over by most young Protestants. Apart from the Bible and *The Pilgrim's Progress* it would have been one of the very few books allowed that had narrative. Samuel Clarke had included children in a compilation of biographies in 1646.[29] There is for instance a description of the martyrdom of a seven-year-old, whose mother watched with dry cheeks and rebuked him for asking for water, charging him to 'thirst after the cup which the infants of Bethlehem once drank of'. And there is also a description of a godly youth at Cambridge (one suspects this to be the author himself) who when he is upbraided by his tutor, waits for him to be calm, and then tells him that his father had placed him in the tutor's charge to be brought up in the fear of God, but 'you giving way to your passion this last night, gave me a very evil example'. The tutor is so contrite that he buys the undergraduate a suit of new clothes. In 1660 Thomas White had included a few examples of early piety in *A Little Book for Little Children*. This compilation throws an interesting light on contemporary attitudes to children. Thomas White is unusually tender with them. He begins:

My Dear Pretty Children, let me shew you how dear you are to God, O let God be as dear to you; do you but love God as God loves you. . . . God hath appointed his Holy Angels to wait upon you, when you are at Prayer. God and his Holy Angels stand by thee; how dear are your Praises and Prayers to God! . . . When thou art, or wast a Child, and first began'st to speak when thou wert not able to speak plain, thy Father and Mother loved to hear thee speak in thy broken language; and know that God doth so likewise.

At a time when fear was mentioned far more often than love in theological discourses, to suggest to children that God loved them rather than regarded them as young vipers was something out of the ordinary, as was Thomas White's conclusion: 'My dear Children, remember me in your Prayers, for I much desire and value your Prayers.' But after the gentle opening and the advice adapted to the capacities of young children, to pray, tell the truth, love their parents, comes the reading list mentioned earlier—of theological works well beyond their capacities, followed by a horrifying story from Maccabees, about how a Syrian king tortures seven brothers, the tortures in each case being described in great detail. Children of course encountered horrors in Foxe's *Martyrs*, but views about what is appropriate in their own books have changed so much that we inevitably are startled at Thomas White's choice of subject-matter when he is specifically addressing very young children.

But he also included a few accounts of early piety. We have the boy who died at the age of fourteen, who exhorts his companions to 'put off the Old Man Adam', and 'to prepare your self for Death, for it knocks at the doors of Young ones as soon as the Old; there are many Young Sculls in Golgotha as old; the Sythe of Mortality mows down Lilies as well as Grass.' (To exhort one's companions was a required part of every Puritan's duty, for the sake of one's own soul rather than for the benefit the rebuked might derive.)

More attractive are his accounts of younger children. There is the tender story of the little child who 'when he died was in Coats' (that is, he was not yet wearing breeches, and presumably was under five), with its tiny home-like details of the mother taking the child in her lap and asking him why he cried. On his deathbed he names his sins: he whetted his knife upon the Lord's Day; he did not reprove one that he heard swear; he once omitted prayer to go to play; he found his heart dead and therefore omitted prayer; he omitted prayer because he thought God was angry; when his mother called him he answered Yes, and not Forsooth. There is another story of a five-year-old who was whipping a top one day, and flung away his whip and his top and said, 'O Mother, I must go to God, will you go with me?' A month later he sickened and died, repeating these words.

And these are the sort of narratives that we find in James Janeway's far more famous compilation, *A Token for Children*,[30] published about twelve years later. Janeway was a Nonconformist, educated at Christ Church, Oxford. He became a preacher in London, and eventually had his own meeting-house in Rotherhithe. He lived through the Plague and the Great Fire and died of consumption in 1674, not yet forty. The full title of *A Token* is *A Token for Children, being an Exact Account of the Conversion, Holy and Exemplary Lives, and Joyful Deaths, of several young Children*. It was published in two parts between 1671 and 1672, and gives an account of thirteen children who died young. He claimed no sort of originality for his work and may well have been influenced by Thomas White. 'Get your Father to buy you Mr White's little book for Children,' he says in the introduction. He admits that the story of Charles Bridgman who died when he was twelve, was taken from 'Mr Ambrose His Life's Lease'. And if we turn up *Life's Lease* in the works of the Puritan divine, Isaac Ambrose, we find an account of this 'sweet rose, cropt in its blossom, no sooner budded but blasted'. Perhaps in the twentieth century with different concepts of the ideal child we would not find this rose so sweet as Isaac Ambrose and Janeway did; Charles Bridgman was a very upright youth who made a point of 'teaching them their duty that waited upon him', and rebuking his brothers and sisters. 'His sentences were wise and weighty,' Ambrose and Janeway said, 'and well might become some ancient Christian.' But his dying words are moving.

God is the best Physitian; into his hands I commend my spirit, O Lord Jesus receive my soul: Now close mine eyes: Forgive me Father, Mother, Brother, Sister, all the World. Now I am well, my pain is almost gone, my joy is at hand, Lord have mercy on me. O Lord receive my Soul unto thee. And thus he yielded his Spirit up unto the Lord, when he was about twelve years old.

None of the children seems to have been personally known to Janeway; some of them died when he himself was a child, two of them lived in Holland. Twice he acknowledges that friends of the child had told him the story, and in the preface to the second part of *A Token* he speaks with indignation of the people who disbelieved his account of 'a child that began to be serious between two and three years old'. He had it, he said, from 'Mrs Jeofries in Long-Lane in Mary Magdalen Parish, in the County of Surry . . . and as a reverend Divine said, Such a Mother in Israel, her single Testimony about London is of as much Authority almost as any one single Minister'.

In the twentieth century Janeway has been called morbid, chilling, gloomy, soul-battering. The Victorian writer of his biography in the *DNB* referred to the compilation with evident distaste as 'extraordinary'. But as has been seen, the theme was by no means extraordinary in the seventeenth century; the sole innovatory feature of *A Token* was that the deaths recorded were only of children, and not early martyrs or biblical characters but

CXX.

Societas Parentalis.

120

The Society betwixt Parents, and Children.

Married Persons,
(by the blessing of God)
have issue,
and become Parents.
The Father 1. begetteth, and the Mother 2.
beareth Sons, 3.
and Daughters, 4.
(sometimes Twins.)
The Infant 5.
is wrapped in
Swadling-clothes, 6.
is laid in a Cradle, 7,
is suckled by the Mother with her breasts, 8.
and fed with Pap. 9.
Afterwards
it learneth to go by
a Standing stool, 10.
playeth with Rattles, 11
& beginneth to speak.
As it beginneth to
grow older, it is accustomed to Piety 12.
and Labour, 13.
and is chastised 14.
if it be not dutiful.
Children owe to Parents Reverence,
and Service.
The Father maintaineth his Children
by taking Pains. 15.

Conjuges, suscipiunt
(ex benedictione Dei)
Sobolem (Prolem)
& fiunt *Parentes.*
Pater 1. generat,
& *Mater* 2.
parit *Filios* 3.
& *Filias,* 4.
(aliquando *Gemellos.*)
Infans 5.
involvitur *Fasciis,* 6.
reponitur in *Cunas.* 7.
à matre
lactatur *Uberibus,* 8.
& nutritur *Pappis.* 9.
Deinde,
incedere discit
Serperastro, 10.
ludit *Crepundiis,* 11.
& fari incipit.
Crescente ætate,

Pietati 12.
& *Labori* 13. adsuefit,
& castigatur 14.
si non sit morigerus.
Liberi debent
Parentibus
Cultum & Officium.
Pater,
sustentat Liberos,
laborando, 15.   *Socie-*

The

(*Above*) the nurture of children in the seventeenth century, from *Orbis Sensualium Pictus* by J. A. Comenius, 1672. This book illustrating Latin and vernacular vocabulary (first published in Nuremberg in 1658) is usually credited with being the first picture book designed specially for children. (*Left*) the death of a young Quaker, from *Examples for Youth in Remarkable Instances of Early Piety in Children and Young Persons, Members of the Society of Friends,* a late imitation of Janeway published by the Quaker firm of Darton in 1822.

children of Janeway's own time. And far from being a gloomy book it is triumphant. These are *good* children going to their heavenly reward, and it shows them enjoying the sort of dignity and esteem that few of their contemporaries could have experienced and all must envy. Moreover, Janeway forbears to sermonize during his narratives, to point out the difference between good and bad children. Certainly in the preface he addresses his readers and asks them which sort they are, but he does it with tenderness. In this he was following Thomas White, but it was a tone lacking in most Puritan exhortations to the young. 'I would fain have you one of those little ones, which Christ will take into his Arms and bless,' Janeway says, and he finishes:

And now dear Children, I have done. I have written to you, I have prayed for you; but what you will do, I can't tell. O children, if you love me, if you love your Parents, if you love your Souls; if you would escape Hell fire, and if you would live in Heaven when you dye, do you go and do as these good Children; and that you may be your Parents joy, your Countreys honour, and live in Gods fear, and dye in his love, is the prayer of your dear Friend, J. Janeway.

The thirteen narratives are set down with the same sweet artless simplicity. No doubt Janeway invented the dialogue in many places since, as has been said, he had not known any of the children personally. But the most conscientious parent could not take exception, and *A Token* was read in families where fiction was anathema. Yet it was one of the most powerful pieces of writing ever produced for children, all the more so since it stimulated their own imaginings. There is the dying child, lying in his chamber, surrounded by marvelling spectators whom he is rebuking and exhorting, his words treasured and remembered; his immortality assured. 'I felt as if I were willing to die with them if I could with equal success, engage the admiration of my friends and mankind,' wrote William Godwin.[31] (Born into a dissenting family in 1756, he had been reared on the traditional Puritan books.) And in a little story in a nineteenth-century periodical we get a glimpse of the way Janeway could grip a boy who probably found any reading difficult, and would have had no other book but the Bible. The Sunday school teacher calls at Tom's cottage home, and finds him reading *A Token* and tells him that he hopes Tom too will become like the children in it. At this Tom's mother becomes tearful.

'Ah sir! that's what I am afraid of; for the best seem always to go first, and now my poor boy is become so good, I sometimes fear I shall lose him too, and I can't bear the thought of it:—but to be sure it is the most entertaining book that can be. Night after night, as soon as ever Tom comes home from work, he helps me turn the mangle, and then gets to his book; we be never tired of it.'[32]

'The most entertaining book that can be'—this gives some idea of what Janeway must have meant to the starved imagination of children in Puritan families, and to those strict evangelicals who forbade fiction. It is probably the most influential children's book ever written. It seized its readers, and the impact it made can be seen in generations of later books for children. There were of course hundreds of direct imitations, the pious lives and deaths of children, written as a memorial by a sorrowing family and used by preachers to try to inspire the living. But few if any of them have the poignancy and directness of Janeway; the nineteenth-century examples are particularly leaden. One American example, *A Legacy for Children, being some of the last expressions and dying sayings of Hannah Hill, Jnr, of the city of Philadelphia* was published in 1714 'at the ardent desire of the deceased' whom one suspects of having been stirred by Janeway as William Godwin was later to be. Some Sunday school publications had to warn children that sickness was not the time to prepare for death—no doubt many children in health felt they could atone for all their misdeeds by a glorious death in the Janeway manner.

But the influence of Janeway—derived maybe second or even third hand—shows in far less obvious ways than in factual examples of early piety. It spreads out like the ripples on a pool. No doubt it was Janeway, at several removes, who was responsible for the mawkish and by now purposeless deaths that clogged third-rate Victorian fiction and stories for children, written by people who had experienced in childhood a heady emotion from reading about pious deaths. Juliana Horatia Ewing who herself took pride in her ability to draw tears from her readers, and who like many of her contemporaries put much thought and literary expertise into contriving pathetic situations involving children, remembered exactly how she used to feel.

'But nurse never thinks of my feelings, any more than the cruel nurse
   in the story about the little girl who was so good.
And if I die early as she did, perhaps then people will be sorry I've
   been misunderstood.
I shouldn't like to die early, but I should like people to be sorry for
   me and to praise me when I was dead.
If I could only come to life again when they had missed me very
   much, and I'd heard what they said.[33]

The Puritan influence on children's books lasted long beyond the seventeenth century. In the eighteenth century it took the form of a robust preoccupation with material gain—prosperity was always a strong Puritan theme—which went with a contempt for the irrational and an emphasis on fact. The publications of John Newbery's firm provide an illustration of the temper of the times. Newbery, who was also a purveyor of patent medicines, was the first British publisher to create a permanent and profitable market for children's books, to establish them as a genre of their own. He had arrived in London in the early 1740s, and his first publication was *A Little Pretty Pocket Book*, a hotch-potch of miscellaneous advice, much of it taken from John Locke's treatise on education and child-rearing. There are fables and rhymes and an alphabet. The child is told how to behave, and the carrot dangled in front of boys is the prospect of driving in a coach and six. The good girl gets a gold watch and the promise of a coach ride. 'This ingratiating cant', says a recent angry commentator, 'invites the child to offer a precocious attention to the dubious matter of "How to Win Friends and Influence People"; in its fake-Lilliputian tones, it speaks for a mercantile knowingness ... designed to yield a due return of social and business success.'[34] And he quotes Newbery's rhymes about sports and pastimes. Newbery moralizes about Chuck-farthing, for instance:

Chuck-Farthing, like Trade,
Requires great Care;
The more you observe,
The better you'll fare.

But what must interest us is the acceptance of play as part of childhood; we have moved a long way in fifty years, from a time when the moralists made no room for it, or mentioned it only as something to be cast behind one.

It has to be said that in America where the Protestant work-ethic had a far greater force, play was suppressed for much longer. European visitors to the United States marvelled at the precocity of the young, and the absence of childhood. We find allusions to it from the seventeenth century until the mid-nineteenth century — the cigar-smoking small boys who studied the financial news and talked politics, the little girls who wore grown-up dress and prinked and minced and aped their elders' conversation. The nineteenth-century juvenile periodicals, at least up till the Civil War, were full of advice about how to succeed in business, on marriage and how to break oneself of the habit of dram-drinking, and news items about the latest murder, execution, massacre, or European coup. One of the most chilling of these publications for the juvenile business man was *The Juvenile Key*, issued from Maine. The first number appeared in 1830 and bore the names of two children, aged seven and nine respectively, sons of the proprietor. Not only had they done most of the typographical work, said their father, they were also involved in the make-up, promotion, and distribution of the initial two hundred copies. The ideal of *The Juvenile Key* was the child dedicated to usefulness. Little boys were told to eschew such trivialities as driving hoops, flying kites, playing ball, and girls to stop jumping with skipping ropes, for 'as soon as the little boy is strong enough to lift a hammer, hatchet, hoe or shovel he should be taught to use these implements', while the girl should of course be employed usefully at home. As for reading and writing they should limit themselves to practical matters which would make them good farmers or mechanics. And a contemporary but very different person, Mrs Lydia Child, the

Massachusetts Abolitionist, told mothers that it was a great deal better for children to pick blackberries at six cents a quarter than to wear out their clothes in senseless play. Even a child of six could be useful, and she deplored the practice of allowing children 'to romp away their existence till they get to thirteen or fourteen'.[35]

If one holds that in fantasy children's books reach their highest literary point, then undoubtedly children had to wait until the Puritan influence had spent itself before they got good reading. And the American moralists took a long time to reconcile themselves to works of high imagination; all through the nineteenth century there was anxious American debate about the validity of fairy stories, and publishers who wanted to elude the denunciations of the zealous tended to put out books containing fairy stories under such titles as *Wonder-World Stories* or *Tales of Adventure*.

But Puritans can be said to have made a positive though indirect contribution to children's books—the stories of tightly-knit families characteristic of the mid-Victorian period, a type perhaps seen at its best in Louisa Alcott's *Little Women* of 1868. For it was the Puritans who attached high importance to the family unit. Parents were severe with their children because they were so deeply concerned for their spiritual well-being; it was they and not the church who had the responsibility for their souls. Again and again preachers referred to the household as a church; the family with the father as priest figure took over the functions that before had been the responsibility of the church—daily worship, religious instruction, catechizing. 'Family teaching, Worship and Discipline hath many advantages which Churches have not,' said Richard Baxter in a book much used in the later seventeenth century. 'A Holy Family is a place of Comfort: a Church of God. What a joy will it be to you, to live together daily in this Hope, that you shall meet and live together in Heaven! to think that Wife, Children and Servants shall shortly be fellow Citizens with you of the Heavenly Jerusalem.'[36] It was an ideal that took root in Protestant culture, and we have only to look at

the seventeenth-century books on family government to find the
origins of so much that we think of as characteristically Victorian.

Notes

1. Benjamin Harris, *The Protestant Tutor* (London, 1683).
2. William Sloane, *Children's Books In England and America in the Seventeenth Century* (New York, 1955), 11.
3. *The Father's Legacy, or Counsels to his Children* (London, 1678).
4. [Thomas White], *A Little Book for Little Children* by T.W. (London, 1660).
5. Arthur Dent, *The Plaine Mans Path-way to Heaven* (London, 1601).
6. Lewis Bayly, *The Practise of Pietie* (London, 1613).
7. Richard Baxter, *Call to the Unconverted* (London, 1657).
8. Joseph Alleine, *An Allarum to the Unconverted*. The date given by the *DNB* is 1672, four years after Alleine's death, but it was clearly regarded as a classic by Thomas White in 1660.
9. Richard Sibbs, *The Soules Conflict* (London, 1635), 27.
10. Eleazar Moody, *The School of Good Manners* (New London, Conn., and Boston, 1715), 35–8.
11. William H. Rideing, *The Boyhood of Famous Authors* (New York, 1897).
12. Thomas Gouge, *The Young Man's Guide* in *Works* (London, 1706), 396.
13. Charles Dudley Warner, *Being a Boy* (Boston, 1877).
14. Caleb Trenchfield, *A Cap of Grey Hairs for a Green Head* (London, 1671).
15. [Nathaniel Crouch], *Youths Divine Pastime* by R.B. (3rd edn., London, 1691).
16. [Nathaniel Crouch], *Remarks upon the Lives of Several Excellent Young Persons of Both Sexes* (London, 1678).
17. Cotton Mather, *Early Piety Exemplified in the Life and Death of Mr Nathanael Mather* (London, 1689), 21.
18. Cotton Mather, *Magnalia Christi Americana*, ed. Thomas Robbins (Hartford, Conn., 1853), ii. 64.
19. Robert Russel, *A Little Book for Children* (London, c. 1696).
20. John Locke, *Some Thoughts Concerning Education* (London, 1693).
21. Benjamin Colman, 'The Nature of Early Piety as it Respects Men', in *A Course of Sermons on Early Piety* (Boston, 1721), 8.
22. Mary Martha Sherwood, *The History of the Fairchild Family*, part I, (London, 1818). This episode occurs in 'Story on Absence of God'.
23. Robert Cawdrey, *A Godly Forme of Household Government*, ed. John Dod and Robert Cleaver (London, 1614).
24. Thomas Brooks, *Apples of God for Young Men and Women* (London, 1657).
25. Cotton Mather, *Diary* (Massachusetts Historical Society, Boston, 1911).
26. Increase Mather, *Memorials of Early Piety, occurring in the Holy Life and Joyful Death of Mrs Jerusha Oliver* (Boston, 1711).

27. John Norris, *Spiritual Counsel, or The Fathers Advice to his Children* (London, 1694).
28. Cotton Mather, *Corderius Americanus* (Boston, 1708).
29. Samuel Clarke, *A Mirrour or Looking Glass both for Saints and Sinners* (London, 1646).
30. James Janeway, *A Token for Children* (London, 1672).
31. C. Kegan Paul, *William Godwin, his Friends and Contemporaries* (London, 1875).
32. *The Sunday Scholars' Magazine or Monthly Reward Book* (Oxford, 1821).
33. Juliana Horatia Ewing, 'A Sweet Little Dear', *Verses for Children* (SPCK collected edn., London, 1895).
34. Geoffrey Summerfield, *Fantasy and Reason: Children's Literature in the Eighteenth Century* (London, 1984), 83.
35. [Lydia Child], *The Frugal Housewife* (3rd edn., Boston, 1830).
36. Richard Baxter, *The Poor Mans Family Book* (London, 1684).

6

The Origins of the Fairy Tale for Children
or, How Script Was Used to Tame the
Beast in Us

JACK ZIPES

In his endeavour to establish the origins of the fairy tale for children, Peter Brooks stated that 'when at the end of the seventeenth century Perrault writes down and publishes tales which had been told for indeterminate centuries—and would continue to be told, and would be collected in varying versions by the Grimm Brothers and other modern folklorists—he seems to be performing for children's literature what must have been effected for *literature* long before: that is, he is creating a literature where before there had been myth and folklore. The act of transcription, both creative and destructive, takes us from the primitive to the modern, makes the stories and their themes enter into literacy, into civilization, into history.'[1] Indeed, almost all literary historians tend to agree with Brooks that the point of origin of the literary fairy tale for children is with Perrault's *Contes du temps passé* (1697),[2] yet they never adequately explain why this came about in relation to the development of *civilité*[3] and place too much emphasis on Perrault and his one volume of tales.

In order to comprehend the historical origin of the literary fairy tale for children in France towards the end of the eighteenth century, we must shift the focus away from one author and try to grasp how many authors contributed to the formation of the literary fairy tale as an institution. It was not Perrault but groups of writers, particularly aristocratic women, who gathered in salons during the eighteenth century and created the conditions for the rise of the fairy tale. They set the groundwork for the institutionalization of the fairy tale as a 'proper' genre to be used with children who were to be educated according to a code of *civilité* that was being elaborated in the seventeenth and eighteenth centuries. But what does institutionalization of the fairy tale mean? What were the conditions during the seventeenth century that led these aristocratic women to give birth, so to speak, to the literary fairy tale? These questions are important to address, if we want to understand our contemporary attitudes toward fairy tales for children. In the course of this essay I shall use the notion of the literary fairy tale as institution in an endeavour to clarify the historical origins of the literary fairy tale for children, and I shall turn to the evolution of *Beauty and the Beast* as a concrete example of how the fairy tale as genre can best be grasped if we understand its social function.

The importance of the term 'institutionalization' for studying the origins of the literary fairy tale can best be understood if we turn to Peter Bürger's *Theory of the Avant-Garde*.[4] Bürger argues that 'works of art are not received as single entities, but within institutional frameworks and conditions that largely determine the function of the works. When one refers to the function of an individual work, one generally speaks figuratively; for the consequences that one may observe or infer are not primarily a function of its special qualities but rather of the manner which regulates the commerce with works of this kind in a given society or in certain strata or classes of a society. I have chosen the term "institution of art" to characterize such framing conditions.'

The framing conditions that constitute the institution of art (which includes literature in the broad sense) are the purpose or function, production, and reception. For instance, Bürger divides the development of art from the late Middle Ages to the present into the following phases:[6]

	Sacral Art	*Courtly Art*	*Bourgeois Art*
Function or purpose:	cult object	representational object	portrayal of bourgeois self-understanding

Production:	collective craft	individual	individual
Reception:	collective (sacral)	collective (sociable)	individual

In the period that concerns us, art at the court of Louis XIV, Bürger maintains that art is 'representational and serves the glory of the prince and the self-portrayal of courtly society. Courtly art is part of the life praxis of courtly society, just as sacral art is part of the life praxis of the faithful. Yet the detachment from the sacral tie is a first step in the emancipation of art. ("Emancipation" is being used here as a descriptive term, as referring to the process by which art constitutes itself as a distinct social subsystem.) The difference from sacral art becomes particularly apparent in the realm of production: the artist produces as an individual and develops a consciousness of the uniqueness of his activity. Reception, on the other hand, remains collective. But the content of the collective performance is no longer sacral, it is social.'[7]

If we examine the rise of the literary fairy tale during the eighteenth century in light of Bürger's notion of institution, we can make the following observations. The literary fairy tale was first developed in salons by aristocratic women as a type of parlour game by the middle of the eighteenth century.[8] It was within the aristocratic salons that women were able to demonstrate their intelligence and education through different types of conversational games. In fact, the linguistic games often served as models for literary genres such as the occasional lyric or the serial novel. Both women and men participated in these games and were constantly challenged to invent new ones or to refine the games. Such challenges led the women, in particular, to improve the quality of their dialogues, remarks, and ideas about morals, manners, and education and at times to oppose male standards that had been set to govern their lives. The subject-matter of the conversations consisted of literature, mores, taste, and etiquette, whereby the speakers all endeavoured to portray ideal situations in the most effective oratory style that would gradually have a major effect on literary forms.

In the case of the literary fairy tale, though one cannot fix the exact date that it became an acceptable game, we know that there are various references to it towards the end of the eighteenth century and that it emanated out of the *jeux d'esprit* in the salons. The women would refer to folk tales and use certain motifs spontaneously in their conversations. Eventually, women began telling the tales as a literary divertimento, intermezzo, or as a kind of dessert that one would invent to amuse other listeners. This social function of amusement was complemented by another purpose, namely, that of self-portrayal and representation of proper aristocratic manners. The telling of fairy tales enabled women to picture themselves, social manners, and relations in a manner that represented their interests and those of the aristocracy. Thus, they placed great emphasis on certain rules of oration such as naturalness and formlessness. The teller of the tale was to make it 'seem' as though the tale were made up on the spot and as though it did not follow prescribed rules. Embellishment, improvisation, and experimentation with known folk or literary motifs were stressed. The procedure of telling a tale as 'bagatelle' would work as follows: the narrator would be requested to think up a tale based on a particular motif; the adroitness of the narrator would be measured by the degree with which she/he was inventive and natural; the audience would respond politely with a compliment; then another member of the audience would be requested to tell a tale, not in direct competition with the other teller, but in order to continue the game and vary the possibilities for linguistic expression.

By the 1690s the salon fairy tale became so acceptable that women and men began writing their tales down to publish them. The most notable writers gathered in the salons or homes of Mme D'Aulnoy, Perrault, Mme de Murat, Mlle Lhéritier, or Rose Caumont de La Force, all of whom were in some part responsible for the great mode of literary fairy tales that developed between 1697 and 1789 in France.[9] The aesthetics developed in the conversational games and in the written tales had a serious side: though differing in style and content, these writers were all anti-classical, and their tales were implicitly told and written in opposition to Boileau, who was championing Greek and Roman literature as the models for French writers to follow at that time. In addition, since the majority of the writers and tellers of fairy tales were women, there is a definite distinction to be made between their tales and those written and told by men. As Renate Baader has commented: 'While Perrault's bourgeois and male tales with happy ends had pledged themselves to a moral that called for Griseldas to serve as a model for women, the women writers had to make an effort to defend the insights that had been gained in the past decades. Mlle Scudéry's novels and novellas stood as examples for them and taught them how to redeem their own wish reality in the fairy tale. They probably remembered how feminine faults had been revalorized by men and how the aristocratic women had responded to this in their self-portraits. Those aristocratic women had commonly refused to place themselves in the service of social mobility. Instead they put forward their demand for moral, intellectual, and psychological self-determination. As an analogy to this, the fairy tales of the women made it expected that the imagination in the tales was truly to be let loose in any kind of arbitrary way that had been considered a female danger up until that time. After the utopia of the "royaume de tendre", which had tied fairy-tale salvation of the sexes to a previous ascetic and enlightened practice of virtues and the guidance of feelings, there was now an unleashed imagination that could invent a fairy-tale realm and embellish it so that reason and will were set out of commission.'[10]

If we were to take the major literary fairy tales produced at the end of the seventeenth century—Mme D'Aulnoy, *Les Contes des fées* (1697–8), Mme La Force, *Les Contes des contes* (1697), Mlle Lhéritier, *Œuvres meslées* (1696), Chevalier de Mailly, *Les Illustres Féés* (1698), Mme de Murat, *Contes de fées* (1698), Charles Perrault, *Histoires ou contes du temps passé* (1697), and Jean de Prechac, *Contes moins contes que les autres* (1698)—one can ascertain remarkable differences in their social attitudes, especially in terms of gender and class differences. However, they all have one thing in common that literary historians have really failed to take into account: they were *not* told or written for children. Even the tales of Perrault. In other words, it is absurd to date the origin of the literary fairy tale for children with the publication of Perrault's tales. Certainly, his tales were popularized and used with children later in the eighteenth century, but it was not because of his tales themselves as individual works of art. Rather, it was due to certain changes in the institution of the literary fairy tale itself.

Up until 1700, there was no literary fairy tale for children. On the contrary, children like their parents *heard* oral tales from their governesses, servants, and peers. The institutionalizing of the literary fairy tale, begun in the salons during the eighteenth century, was for adults and arose out of a need by aristocratic women to elaborate and conceive other alternatives in society than those prescribed for them by men. The fairy tale was used in refined discourse as a means through which women imagined their lives might be improved. As this discourse became regularized and accepted among women and slowly by men, it served as the basis for a literary mode that was received largely by members of the aristocracy and haute bourgeoisie. This reception was collective and social, and gradually the tales were changed to introduce morals to children that emphasized the enforcement of a patriarchal code of *civilité* to the detriment of women, even though women were originally the major writers of the tales. This code was also intended to be learned first and foremost by children of the upper classes, for the literary fairy tale's function excluded the majority of children who could not read and were dependent on oral transmission of tales. Let us examine the development of *Beauty and the Beast* as an example of how the literary fairy tale evolved in France, bearing in mind that France set the cultural standards in the seventeenth and eighteenth centuries throughout Europe.

Most scholars generally agree that the *literary* development of the children's fairy tale *Beauty and the Beast*, conceived by Madame Le Prince de Beaumont in 1756 as part of *Le Magasin des Enfans*, translated into English in 1761 as *The Young Misses Magazine Containing Dialogues between a Governess and Several Young Ladies of Quality, Her Scholars*, owes its origins to the Roman writer

Beauty and the Beast, illustration by Eleanor Vere Boyle, 1875.

Apuleius, who published the tale of *Cupid and Psyche* in *The Golden Ass* in the middle of the second century AD.[11] It is also clear that the oral folktale type 425A, the beast bridegroom, played a role in the literary development. By the middle of the eighteenth century, the Cupid and Psyche tradition was revived in France with a separate publication of Apuleius' tale in 1648 and led La Fontaine to write his long story *Amours de Psyche et de Cupidon* (1669) and Corneille and Molière to produce their tragédie-ballet *Psyché* (1671). The focus in La Fontaine's narrative and the play by Molière and Corneille is on the mistaken curiosity of Psyche. Her desire to know who her lover is almost destroys Cupid, and she must pay for her 'crime' before she is reunited with Cupid. These two versions do not alter the main plot of Apuleius' tale and project an image of women that are either too curious (Psyche) or too vengeful (Venus), and their lives must ultimately be ordered by Jove.

All this was changed by Madame D'Aulnoy, who was deeply obsessed by the theme of Psyche and Cupid and reworked it or mentioned it in several fairy tales: *Le Mouton* (*The Ram*, 1697), *La Grenouille bienfaisante* (*The Beneficent Frog*, 1698), *Serpentin vert* (*The Green Serpent*, 1697), *Gracieuse et Percinet* (*Gracieuse and Percinet*, 1697), *Le Prince Lutin* (*Prince Lutin*, 1697), and *La Princesse Félicité et le Prince Adolphe* (*Princess Felicity and Prince Adolph*, 1690). The two most important versions are *The Ram* and *The Green Serpent*, and it is worth while examining some of the basic changes in the motifs and plot that break radically from the male tradition of Psyche and Cupid. But before doing this, I want to emphasize that it was Madame D'Aulnoy who prepared the way for the literary version of *Beauty and the Beast*, not Perrault. Though her versions were contrived and simplistic, it was she who initiated changes in the literary fairy tale as an institution that have had a far-reaching effect. Madame D'Aulnoy wanted to make the fairy tale part of the living practice of the aristocratic salon, and her tales were elaborated in the parlour games that she and her contemporaries (mainly females) played before they were composed. In the conscious composition of the tales she clearly intended to present a woman's viewpoint with regard to such topics as tender love, fidelity, courtship, honour, and arranged marriages. As a representative artwork, the fairy tale was D'Aulnoy's contribution to a discourse on manners that was to be shared by an intimate group of people, whom she hoped would embrace her ideals. Thus, the fairy tale was not separated from the aristocratic life-style of her time but played a representative role indicating her female preferences with regard to the code of civility, preferences that were shared and enunciated in fairy tales by other women.

What were these preferences? Madame D'Aulnoy was by no means a rebel, although she had been in some difficulty at King Louis XIV's court. That is, one must be cautious about labelling her an outspoken critic of patriarchal values or to see feminist leanings in her writings. Nevertheless, as a member of the aristocratic class, who had experienced the benefits of changes in education and social roles for upper-class women, Madame D'Aulnoy created a setting in her tales that placed women in greater control of their destinies than in fairy tales by men, and it is obvious that the narrative strategies of her tales, like those she learned in the salon, were meant to expose decadent practices and behaviour among the people of her class, particularly those that degraded independent women.

The Ram and *The Green Serpent* are D'Aulnoy's two most interesting commentaries on what manners a young woman should cultivate in determining her own destiny—and I should like to point out that the power in all her tales is held by fairies, wise or wicked women, who ultimately judge whether a young woman deserves to be rewarded. In *The Ram*, the heroine is actually punished. Based on the King Lear motif, this tale has Merveilleuse, the youngest daughter of a king, compelled to flee the court because her father believes mistakenly that she has insulted him. She eventually encounters a prince who has been transformed into a ram by a wicked fairy, and she is gradually charmed by his courteous manners and decides to wait five years until his enchantment will be over to marry him. However, she misses her father and two sisters, and through the ram's kind intervention she is able to visit them twice. The second time, however, she forgets about returning to the ram, who dies because of her neglect.

In *The Green Serpent*, the heroine Laidronette acts differently. She runs away from home because she is ashamed of her ugliness. Upon encountering a prince, who, as usual, has been transformed into a serpent by a wicked fairy, she is at first horrified. Gradually, after spending some time in his kingdom of the pagodes, who are exquisite little people that attend to her every wish, she becomes enamoured of him and promises not to see him and to marry him in two years when his bewitchment will end. However, even though she reads the story of Psyche and Cupid, she breaks her promise and gazes upon him. This breach of promise enables the wicked fairy Magotine to punish her, and only after she performs three near-impossible tasks helped by the Fairy Protectrice is she able to transform herself into the beautiful Princess Discrète and the green serpent back into a handsome prince. Their love for each other eventually persuades the wicked fairy to mend her ways and reward them with the kingdom of Pagodaland.

The issue on hand in both fairy tales is fidelity and sincerity, or the qualities that make for tenderness, a topic of interest to women at that time. Interestingly, in Madame D'Aulnoy's two tales, the focus of the discourse is on the two princesses, who break their promises and learn that they will cause havoc and destruction if they do not keep their word. On the other hand, the men have been punished because they refused to marry old and ugly fairies and seek a more natural love. In other words, Madame D'Aulnoy sets conditions for both men and women that demand sincerity of feeling and constancy, if they are to achieve true and happy love. Nothing short of obedience to the rule of 'fairy' civility will be tolerated in D'Aulnoy's tales. The tenderness of feeling was definitely a goal that women sought more than men during D'Aulnoy's times, and her two tales that discuss the proper behaviour of young aristocrats have an ambivalent quality to them that makes for interesting reading. D'Aulnoy projects the necessity for women to decide their own destiny, but it is a destiny that calls for women to obey men and actively submit themselves to a rational code that is not really of their making.

Thus, while D'Aulnoy wants the fairy tale to have the social function of serving women's interests, there is a dubious side to the manner in which she represents these interests. Active submission to a male code qualified by tenderness does not lead to autonomy, and in fact, though there is this call for female autonomy throughout most of her tales, it is the prescribed taming of female desire according to virtues associated with male industriousness and fairness that marks the morals attached to the end of each narrative. Of course, it should not be forgotten that D'Aulnoy makes young men toe the 'fairy' line of civility. That is, she is extremely critical of forced marriages and makes all her male heroes obey a code of decorum that demands great respect for the tender feelings of the aristocratic woman.

In short, the aesthetic composition and structure of all of D'Aulnoy's fairy tales depended on their social function as game and discourse. Plot is secondary to the discussion of manners and the enactment of proper behaviour that serves a moral, and each one of D'Aulnoy's tales ends with a verse *moralité*. Her tales were generally long (35 to 45 pages), complicated, filled with references to literary works (correct reading), proper dress and manners, and folklore. Though her own writing was not as elegant and subtle as some of the other fairy-tale writers of her time, she set models that they followed.

Madame Gabrielle de Villeneuve was one of her 'followers'. She published her unique version of 'Beauty and the Beast' in *La Jeune Amériquaine et les contes marins* in 1740, and it became the classic model for most of the Beauty and the Beast versions that followed in the eighteenth century. Not only did it serve as the basis for Madame Le Prince de Beaumont's tale in 1756, but it also provided the material for Genlis's dramatic adaptation in 1785 and for the opera by Marmontel and Gretry in 1788. Most significant by this time is the fact that de Villeneuve wrote a tale of over 200 pages (the length depends on which edition one reads) and was addressing a mixed audience of bourgeois and aristocratic adult readers. The social function of the fairy tale had changed: its basis was no longer the salon and the games that had been played there. Rather, the literary fairy tale's major reference point was another literary tale or an oral tale and was intended to amuse and instruct the isolated reader, or perhaps a reader who read aloud in a social situation. Whatever the case may have been, it is clear from the length of de Villeneuve's tale, which is more like a small novel, that it was intended for private reading.

Like Madame D'Aulnoy, de Villeneuve was concerned with the self-realization of a young woman, and like Madame D'Aulnoy, the message for women is ambivalent. While all the rules and codes are set by women—there are numerous parallel stories that involve a fairy kingdom and the laws of the fairies—Beauty is praised most for her submissiveness, docility, and earnestness. In de Villeneuve's version, she does not break her vow to the Beast. Rather she is steadfast and sees through the machinations of her five sisters in time for her to return to her beloved Beast. Then, after she saves him, and he is transformed into a charming prince, she is ready to sacrifice herself again by giving up her claim to him because she is bourgeois and he an aristocrat. Her fairy protector, however, debates with the prince's mother, who has arrived on the scene, and argues that her virtues are worth more than her class rank. Eventually, though the fairy wins the debate, we learn that Beauty is really a princess, who had been raised by her supposed merchant-father to escape death by enemies of her real father, a king.

The justification of Beauty's right to marry is part of a series of discourses on manners that constitute the major theme of the tale: virtuous behaviour is true beauty, and only true beauty will be rewarded, no matter what class you are. Beauty (and other characters as well) are tested throughout the tale to determine whether they can tame their unruly feelings (desire, greed, envy, etc.) and become civilized. For instance, once Beauty arrives at the Beast's castle, she has a series of dreams about an unknown admirer, who is actually the prince, and about a wise fairy, and in these dreams she carries on conversations about responsibility and correct courtship with regard to natural love and obligations. Beauty *always but always* chooses to fulfil her obligations rather than follow her heart. Although it does turn out that, by fulfilling her obligations, her heart is rewarded, it is plain to see that her destiny depends on her self-denial which she comes to believe is wish-fulfilment.

With de Villeneuve's projection of Beauty, the person as an embodiment of the virtue 'self-denial', the ground was prepared for a children's version of the Beauty and the Beast tale, and de Beaumont did an excellent job of condensing and altering the tale to address a group of young misses, who were supposed to learn how to become ladies and that virtue meant denying themselves. In effect, the code of the tale was to delude them into believing that they would be realizing their goals in life by denying themselves.

This theme of self-denial that had very little to do with the female autonomy that aristocratic women had sought in the seventeenth century is closely connected to the *changing* social function of the fairy tale and its transformation into an institution for children. First of all, it should be noted that the origins of the fairy tale for children cannot be associated with Perrault but with the change in the institution of the fairy tale created by women. As we have seen, the fairy tale served the social function of representation in aristocratic circles in the latter half of the seventeenth century. During the first part of the eighteenth century, the fairy tale was separated from its representative function and became more an artwork that depicted the possibilities for self-realization and was intended mainly for reading audiences of the aristocracy and bourgeoisie. At the same time, writers began to introduce didactic tales and fairy tales with a strong message for children in primers and collections intended for young audiences of the aristocracy and bourgeoisie.

With regard to the 'origins' of the fairy tale for children, it is practically impossible to give an exact date, but it is more than likely that, given the shifts in the institution of the fairy tale itself, the fairy tale for children arose in the 1720s and 1730s. De Beaumont's tale was thus one of the first fairy tales written expressly for children, and we must not forget that it was first published within a book where a governess tells different kinds of lessons and tales to a group of girls in her charge. Madame de Beaumont herself was a governess in England during the time she wrote her book, and it is quite conceivable that she based the structure of her book on the way she structured the day that she spent with her wards.

Clearly, the social function for the literary fairy tale was to instruct in an amusing way. It was received by children of the upper classes in the home where lessons were taught by private tutors or by governesses. Moreover, some of the fairy tales were evidently used in schools or in schooling the children of the upper classes. That boys were to be treated differently from girls is apparent from the title of de Beaumont's book, or in other words, *Beauty and the Beast* originated as a sex-specific tale intended to inculcate good sense and good manners in little girls.

What is this good sense? The sense to: (i) sacrifice one's life for the mistakes of one's father; (ii) learn to love an ugly beast-man if he is kind and has manners; (iii) keep one's pledge to a beast, no matter what the consequences may be. When confronted by her sisters, who accuse her of not being concerned about her father when they learn he may have to die for picking a rose, Beauty responds: 'Why should I . . . it would be very needless, for my father shall not suffer upon my account, since the monster will accept of one of his daughters, I will deliver myself up to all his fury, and I am very happy in thinking that my death will save my father's life, and be a proof of my tender love for him.'[12]

Beauty is selfless, and perhaps that is why she has no name. She is nameless. Are all girls supposed to become 'beauties', i.e., nameless? There is a false power attributed to beauty as a virtue. By sacrificing oneself, it is demonstrated, the powers that be, here the fairies, will reward her with a perfect husband. The most important thing is to learn to obey and worship one's father (authority) and to fulfil one's promises even though they are made under duress. Ugliness is associated with bad manners like those of her sisters. The beast is not ugly because his manners are perfect. Beauty and the Beast are suited for one another because they live according to the code of civility. They subscribe to prescriptions that maintain the power of class.

De Beaumont's classic fairy tale enables us to see key features of how the fairy tale was institutionalized for children. The framing conditions of this institutionalization are: (i) the social function of the fairy tale must be didactic and teach a lesson that corroborates the code of civility as it was being developed at that time; (ii) it must be short so that children can remember and memorize it and so that both adults and children can repeat it orally; this was the way that many written tales worked their way back into the oral tradition; (iii) it must pass the censorship of adults so that it can be easily circulated; (iv) it must address social issues such as obligation, sex roles, class differences, power, decorum, etc., so that it will appeal to adults, especially those who publish and publicize the tales; (v) it must be able to be used with children in a schooling situation; (vi) it must reinforce a notion of power within the children of the upper classes and suggest ways for them to maintain power.

Both *Beauty and the Beast* and the fairy tale for children function very differently today. However, the 'difference' can only be understood if we grasp the fairy tale's origins. We claim *not* to use the fairy tale to socialize children and breed manners in them, but I suspect that the way manners were first scripted in fairy tales to tame the beast in us has been developed in remarkably sophisticated ways through literature so that the so-called imagination that the fairy tale supposedly wants to stimulate and free is still bombarded with coded messages about civil behaviour and good sense. Fortunately, the institution of the fairy tale now includes fairy tales that are intended to provoke and challenge our sense of decorum and good sense, and it is the contemporary fairy tale as *institution* that deserves our attention if we are to learn whether the fairy tale continues to minimize the value of self-realization as in the case of *Beauty and the Beast*, or whether the framing conditions allow for tales to free the imagination and reassess the scripted taming of all the beasts that are lurking within us.

Notes

1. *Yale French Studies*, 43 (1969), 11.
2. See also Philippe Ariès, 'At the Point of Origin', *Yale French Studies*, 43 (1969), 15–23.
3. In my book *Fairy Tales and the Art of Subversion* (London, 1983), I endeavoured to trace the origins in relation to the civilizing process, and the present essay is an amplification of the ideas developed in my book.
4. Trans. Michael Shaw (Minneapolis, 1984).

5. Ibid. 12.
6. Ibid. 48.
7. Ibid. 47.
· 8. The following remarks are based to a large extent on Renate Baader's excellent study, *Dames de lettres: Autorinnen des preziösen, hocharistokratischen und 'modernen' Salons (1649–1698): Mlle de Scudéry—Mlle de Montpensier—Mme D'Aulnoy* (Stuttgart, 1686). In particular, see 'Mme D'Aulnoy und das feminine Salonmärchen (1697–1698)', 226–77.
9. Cf. Jacques Barchilon, *Le Conte merveilleux français de 1690 à 1790* (Paris, 1975) and Raymonde Robert, *Le Conte de fées littéraire en France de la fin du XVIIe à la fin du XVIIIe siècle* (Nancy, 1981).
10. *Dames de Lettres*, 239.
11. For the most complete history of this development, see Betsy Hearne, 'Beauty and the Beast': A Study of Aesthetic Survival (University of Chicago thesis, 1987). I have also commented on this development in my book *Fairy Tales and the Art of Subversion* (London, 1983), 32–44.
12. 'Beauty and the Beast' in *The Classic Fairy Tales*, ed. Iona and Peter Opie (London, 1974), 143.

Further Reading

Philippe Ariès, 'At the Point of Origin', *Yale French Studies*, 43 (1969), 15–23.

Renate Baader, *Dames de lettres: Autorinnen des preziösen, hocharistokratischen und 'modernen' Salons (1649–1698): Mme de Scudéry—Mlle de Montpensier—Mme D'Aulnoy* (Stuttgart, 1986).

André Bay, *La Belle et la Bête et autres contes du Cabinet des fées* (Paris, 1965). This volume contains different versions of *Beauty and the Beast* by Mme de Villeneuve, Mme D'Aulnoy, Mme Fagnan, Mme Le Prince de Beaumont, and Duclos.

Jacques Barchilon, *Le Conte merveilleux français de 1690 à 1790* (Paris, 1975).

Peter Brooks, 'Toward Supreme Fictions', *Yale French Studies*, 43 (1969), 5–14.

Peter Bürger, *Theory of the Avant-garde*, trans. Michael Shaw (Mineapolis, 1984).

Betsy Hearne, 'Beauty and the Beast': A Study of Aesthetic Survival (University of Chicago, 1987 Ph.D. thesis). This study will soon be published in book form by the University of Chicago Press.

Iona and Peter Opie, eds., *The Classic Fairy Tales* (London, 1974).

Raymonde Robert, *Le Conte de fées littéraire en France de la fin du XVIIe à la fin du XVIIIe siècle* (Nancy, 1981).

Mary Elizabeth Storer, *La Mode des contes de fées (1685–1700)* (Paris, 1928).

Jack Zipes, *Breaking the Magic Spell: Radical Theories of Folk and Fairy Tales* (London, 1979).

—— *Fairy Tales and the Art of Subversion: The Classical Genre for Children and the Process of Civilization* (London, 1983).

7

'Malbrouck s'en va-t-en guerre' or, How History Reaches the Nursery

GILES BARBER

FOR many in the Anglo-Saxon world the legendary phrase 'la plume de ma tante' will evoke elementary stages in the learning of French. More sophisticated instructors, especially in private schools or lessons, have, for a century at least, made use of traditional French children's songs so that for others 'Frère Jacques', 'Sur le pont d'Avignon', and 'Au clair de la lune' will bring back childhood, if not Proustian, memories. 'Chansons et rondes' are to French children in many ways what nursery rhymes, a very Anglo-Saxon concept and corpus, are to British ones. Some of the tunes are traditional and surface with a variety of words but all are easy, catchy, and doubtless a good educational medium so that, starting with the classics listed above, the English pupil too can go on to others and people his French world with characters such as 'le roi Dagobert' (with his absent-minded vestimentary habits) and Cadet Rousselle, not forgetting the cat-loving Mère Michel and her cruel and rapacious tormenter, Compère Lustucru.

Historical evidence for the antiquity of popular songs, and especially that for those now considered principally as children's songs, is of course hard to find. Tunes and words may have different origins and date from different periods while the words themselves may well combine parts of more than one original song. Both texts and tunes of many songs were in some form of print by the seventeenth century, and represent widely differing fields, some being church music or the popular 'Noëls', others theatrical, drinking, or love songs. The number in print increased in the eighteenth century and some literary writers from Madame de Sévigné to Rousseau began to express an interest in them. In the last two decades of the century operatic arias as well as revolutionary and military songs began to affect the traditional base. The Romantics and the nineteenth century generally took the subject up with fervour, beginning to collect and publish songs on a regional basis although scholars were divided as to whether such songs were, thematically at least, initially based on liturgical models or whether they were created (or made use of) by the people and, if so, whether there were different traditions in town and countryside. Early twentieth-century writers were agreed on the importance of folksongs as a reflection of the regional or national soul but an increasingly historical approach has led to attempts, by no means all on the same lines, to trace the origins or at least the social background of such songs.

Those now well known to a certain English public evidently reflect a further selection process during the very late nineteenth and early twentieth centuries, but the songs mentioned earlier do in fact illustrate fairly well some of the evolutionary history of such songs generally.[1]

> Au clair de la lune,
> Mon ami Pierrot,
> Prête-moi ta plume
> Pour écrire un mot

may be one of the best known of French nursery songs generally and the one first learnt by many French children. It seems to have surfaced in the 1790s in Paris although the tune has been ascribed, without much evidence, to Lully but seems, more firmly, to have been known as a popular dance tune in the second half of the eighteenth century. 'Sur le pont d'Avignon' is in some ways older, being known from 1503 and taking its point of reference from the famous twelfth-century Pont de Saint-Bénezet over the Rhône, only the chapel and four of the original arches of which survive. Avignon was the site of one of the most famous French fairs, became of course Papal territory, and was legally separate from France until 1791. The song is recorded in a number of variant forms but all follow the opening, locational, line. The baiting of cats and cat owners was an old sport and led to another popular song:

> C'est la mère Michel
> Qui a perdu son chat,
> Qui crie par la fenêtre
> A qui le lui rendra,

the present words of which are only attested however from the 1820s and which is clearly for an urban climate. It takes its tune nevertheless from a seventeenth-century song, 'Ah! si vous aviez vu Monsieur de Catinat', which concerns the exploits of Nicholas de Catinat (1637–1712), one of Louis XIV's most modest generals, and which was used for a number of songs in the mid-eighteenth century.

'Cadet Rousselle' is based on a dance tune of the 1780s and the words appear to have been written about 1792, becoming immediately remarkably popular so that the actor Jean Joseph Mira *dit* Brunet, 'le roi de la Bêtise', made Cadet Rousselle the hero of a series of plays. The song became the theme tune of the Royalist party in Provence and therefore had ominous overtones for republicans during the White Terror. It has presumably owed its survival into the nursery repertoire both to its tune and to its surrealist/nonsense words. Another song to move from the late eighteenth-century political field to the elementary school is

> Le bon roi Dagobert
> A mis sa culotte à l'envers.
> Le grand Saint Eloi
> Lui dit: 'O mon roi,
> Votre Majesté
> Est mal culottée.'
> 'C'est vrai,' lui dit le roi,
> 'Je vais la remettre à l'endroit.'

The Merovingian king Dagobert (600–38) had indeed such a saintly minister but the song only came to fame in 1814, being viewed as a satire on Napoleon, later verses for example referring to the king who 'se battait à tort et à travers' or 'voulait conquérir l'univers'. As such it was prohibited after Napoleon's return but achieved great popularity immediately after the battle of Waterloo. Thus it can be seen that while such songs reuse traditional themes or tunes they often only reach their recognizable modern shape, or become recorded, in the late eighteenth century, being picked up generically as 'popular traditional songs' early in the following century.

Among these essentially French subjects French children will, at an early age, suddenly come up against England and one aspect of their own history with a classic which has as its main character an English general: John Churchill, first duke of Marlborough. 'Malbrouck s'en va-t-en guerre' has a far-ranging and complex history, aspects of which will be summarized and discussed here since they involve a now familiar mixture of history, popular song, and misapprehension.

A song concerning a well-known historical character of the early modern period would appear to have, or to be able to have, a firm basis in fact and to be more easily dateable. Before attempting to see if this is the case it may be helpful first to recall and establish certain facts about him. John Churchill was born in 1650, the son of Sir Winston Churchill of Ashe in Devonshire. In 1672 he became a captain in a foot regiment and served under Monmouth with the English contingent in the French army, subduing the Dutch in Flanders under the command of the noted French general, Henri de La Tour d'Auvergne, viscount Turenne (1611–75). The latter noted that Churchill was a soldier of considerable promise and that he was also distinguished for his gallantry. In 1674 Churchill received a commission from Louis XIV as colonel of the English regiment. In 1678 he married Sarah Jennings, the favourite attendant of the Princess Anne, younger daughter of the duke of York. The Churchills, changing political grouping not infrequently, prospered on the accession of James II, during the duke of Monmouth's rising and on the arrival of William II, always managing to be on the winning side. In 1689 John Churchill became earl of Marlborough but three years later his very opportunism put him briefly into the Tower. Nevertheless he prospered again during William's later years and even more after the accession of Queen Anne in 1702 when he became captain-general of the English troops both at home and abroad. The War of Spanish Succession started in the same year and Marlborough became commander-in-chief of the united armies of England and Holland. His immediate successes led to his advancement to a dukedom in December 1702. After some subsequent reverses Marlborough and Prince Eugene led their armies into Bavaria and on 13 August 1704 met the notably larger French forces under Marshal Tallard at Blenheim. Despite some early uncertainty as to the outcome, they finally won a resounding victory for which Marlborough was much acclaimed and richly rewarded at home, Blenheim Palace being to this day the visible monument of this regal and national favour and gratitude. In another victorious encounter, at Ramillies on 23 May 1706, Marlborough's horse was shot from under him and his aide-de-camp, standing close by, was killed by a cannonball. The last major battle of this war took place at Malplaquet on 11 September 1709. This encounter has been described as the bloodiest carnage before Borodino or the great battles of the First World War. Both sides claimed victory while admitting heavy casualties. On the French side these even included their commander-in-chief, the Maréchal de Villars, who was wounded half-way through the battle and carried off unconscious, 'so that I remember no more of the proceedings' as he recorded in his memoirs. However Britain had achieved much through the war, both in Europe and elsewhere. The Whigs fell out of power through the war and the Churchills finally lost the favour of Queen Anne. The duchess was dismissed from her offices and even Marlborough, the leading 'hawk', had finally to relinquish his command at the end of 1711. After a period abroad and an old age affected by senility, he eventually died at Cranbourne Lodge, Windsor on 16 June 1722. He was buried in Henry VII's chapel in Westminster Abbey, eight dukes and the Knights of the Garter taking part in the ceremony. Later the body was removed to Blenheim Palace.

It is time to turn to the song commemorating him: the standard modern French text runs as follows:

1

Malbrouck s'en va-t-en guerre,
(refrain: Mironton, mironton, mirontaine)
Malbrouck s'en va-t-en guerre.
Ne sait quand reviendra. (bis)

2

Il reviendra-z-à Pâques,
Ou à la Trinité.

3

La Trinité se passe,
Malbrouck ne revient pas

4

Madame à sa tour monte,
Si haut qu'elle peut monter.

5

Elle aperçoit son page
Tout de noir habillé:

6

'Beau page, ah! mon beau page,
Quelles nouvelles apportez?'

7

'—Aux nouvelles que j'apporte,
Vos beaux yeux vont pleurer:

8

Quittez vos habits roses
Et vos satins brochés;

9

Monsieur Malbrouck est mort,
Est mort et enterré.

10

Je l'ai vu porté-z-en terre
Par quatre-z-officiers:

Hand-coloured popular print by Gangel of Metz, *c.* 1840; the text of the song was printed on either side.

11

L'un portait sa cuirasse,
L'autre son bouclier;

12

L'un portait son grand sabre,
Et l'autre rien portait.

13

Alentour de sa tombe,
Romarin l'on planta.

14

Sur la plus haute branche,
Le rossignol chanta.

15

On vit voler son âme
A travers les lauriers.

16

Chacun mit ventre à terre,
Et puis se releva,

17

Pour chanter les victoires
Que Malbrouck remporta.

18

La cérémonie faite
Chacun s'en fut coucher

19

Les uns avec leur femme
Et les autres tout seuls.

20

Ce n'est pas qu'il en manque,
Car j'en connais beaucoup:

21

Des brunes et des blondes,
Et des châtaignes aussi.

22

Je n'en dis pas davantage,
Car en voilà-z-assez!'

As will be seen, this version is short on historical facts and establishes only that (a) Marlborough died while on campaign away from home, and (b) that he was buried with ceremony. The first of these is notably untrue and the second, while true, would probably have been so of any person of his rank and importance. The contents of the song giving little guidance, it is necessary to consider how the song arose and when it was composed, although here again there is little hard evidence.[2]

Two undated sources have been used to prove the existence of the song in the 1760s and 1770s. The first sign seems to be the appearance of the music, headed 'Marlbroug', in a collection of 758 songs in MS 34 at the Maatschappij tot bevordering der toonkunst in Amsterdam, the manuscript volume being dated to about 1770.[3] Equally the text of the song features in an undated twelve-page gathering of street songs, part of a collection *Chansons choisies et chantées par Duchemin*, published in Paris by Valleyre, neighbouring gatherings having official approbations dating between 1762 and 1778. This later date suggests that the Valleyre in question can not have been either Gabriel or the widow of Guillaume Amable II Valleyre, each of whom died in or before 1772.[4] The publisher could therefore have been either Jean Baptiste Paul or Nicolas François Valleyre since these were active from 1749 and 1763 respectively and both were still active in 1788, the earliest of the approbation dates probably favouring the former publisher. What this slightly complex dating argument does suggest however is that this songbook could date from as late as the 1780s.

This paucity of evidence in the mid-eighteenth century suggests that although the song evidently existed it was far from being well known or popular. The years around 1780 were however to change the situation radically. In August 1778 a scandal sheet, written anonymously by M. F. Pidansat de Mairobert and called *L'Espion Anglois, ou Correspondance secrète entre Milord All'Eye et Milord All'Ear*, gives a lead-in to the Marlborough story. The occasion for this was notable in itself and is worth recording. On 27 July of that year a naval engagement threatened between the British fleet under Viscount Keppel, then off Ouessant on the Breton coast, and the French among whom Marie Antoinette's pet hate, the duc de Chartres ('Philippe Egalité', 1747–93, duc d'Orléans from 1785, who voted for the death of Louis XVI but was himself executed the same year), was prominent. The engagement was inconclusive, resulted in a *cause célèbre* in England, and, despite evidence very much to the contrary, was seen in France as proof of the duke's courage. Through the queen's influence he was received coldly at Versailles but greeted ecstatically by the Parisian mob in a scene which foreshadows the more sinister power of that element a few years later. Mairobert describes the scene thus:

Among all the mad things to which the enthusiasm of the crowd gave rise, particular mention must be made of the pantomime put on about Admiral Keppel, the commander of the English fleet. A stuffed dummy had been dressed to represent the admiral; a complaint concerning his defeat was sung in the presence of their serene highnesses; he was taken in procession on a bier, and, after being pelted, he was thrown into the water with all the curses and maledictions which the crudest elements of the crowd allow themselves at the height of their frenzy. There was some surprise that the august couple in no way checked such public licence and indeed seemed to sanction it by their very presence.

However that may be, t'was thus that, more than half a century ago, the famous Marlborough being dead, a France which still remembered the ills caused her by that warrior, rejoiced indecently, all in peacetime, and that he was ridiculed by the riffraff in song where insulting verses accompanied burlesque ceremonies.[5]

This first clearly dated reference to songs accompanying Marlborough's death is closely followed by another, this time associating his name with a tune. C. S. Favart's vaudeville, *Les Rêveries renouvellées des Grecs*, first performed on 26 June 1779 and printed within the same year by Lormel in Paris, contains a duo in Act II, scene x, which is directed to be sung to the 'Air de Marlborough'.

Two years later the queen, Marie Antoinette, became pregnant and, on 22 October 1781, gave birth to a dauphin, Louis Joseph Xavier François (who died in June 1789, his younger brother Louis, born 1785, becoming dauphin and, although he died at the age of ten, being viewed as Louis XVII). The tradition runs that a countrywoman had arrived at Versailles some months previously and had insisted that she should be appointed as royal wet-nurse. She was installed at court and became universally known as 'Madame Poitrine'. Marie Antoinette is said to have picked up the Marlborough song from her and thus to have ensured its popularity at Versailles.

At much the same time Beaumarchais was writing his play, *La Folle Journée, ou Le Mariage de Figaro*. He seems to have finished a first draft in 1778 and this certainly circulated, in manuscript form, in the social world in the following year. From the start the text includes references to a *romance* to be sung by Chérubin but it is not clear at exactly what date this became the lines in Act II, scene iv:

> Auprès d'une fontaine,
> Que mon cœur, que mon cœur à de peine!
> Pensant à ma Marraine,
> Sentis mes pleurs couler.
> Sentis mes pleurs couler. (bis)

There are three known manuscripts of the play: one is in the Comédie-Française, one is in the Bibliothèque Nationale, and one belongs to the Beaumarchais family.[6] The first was probably the one accepted by the *comédiens* on 29 September 1781 and that approved for acting and printing in 1784, the first formal performance being on 27 April of that year. However the romance (Air: Malbrouck s'en va-t-en guerre) is written in a different hand from the rest of the text and on separate, inserted, sheets. It could thus be a later addition or substitution but must have formed part of a publicly known, if still clandestine, text by March 1783 since on the ninth of that month Bachaumont, in his

Mémoires secrets, speaks of 'la fortune incroyable de la romance de Beaumarchais'.[7] In fact, despite readings and even semi-public rehearsals and a false start in June 1783, the play was first performed publicly only on 27 April 1784. Two years later the song was transformed into the equally famous arietta 'Voi che sapete che cosa è amor' in the Da Ponte/Mozart *Le nozze di Figaro*, first performed in Vienna in May 1786.

Clearly the song achieved incredible popularity by the early months of 1783 and it was not clear even to contemporaries who had set it on its way. Bachaumont's report, given on 9 March and referred to above, is however probably the best account not only of the song's resurgence but also of its origin. He wrote:

In 1722, at the death of Marlborough, that English general whose victories at Hochstet and Ramillies were so fatal to France, the event was marked by the composition of one of those foolish songs with which the police ceaselessly amuse the riffraff of the capital as a matter of course. The song had a notable popularity in its day. We have seen that Monsieur de Beaumarchais revived the tune on which it was composed. By an odd chance no one at court knew this ridiculous and dull tune. The Dauphin's wet nurse, Madame Poitrine, alone had picked it up in her native village and was humming it one day when the king and queen overheard her and forced her to sing it. They found it amusing. They wished to learn it, and their courtiers did not fail to copy their masters: this was the source of the incredible success of Beaumarchais's song.

The police songsters seized the occasion and refurbished the original song which was thus chanted in every street. Mr Audinot fleshed out the song with a sexy pantomime entitled *Mal'broug s'en va-t-en guerre* and Nicolet did the same with an even more burlesque one. Lastly the Carnival set-pieces copied it everywhere so that there were to be seen nothing but Marlborough biers with a hundred similar types of joke which gave rise to a desire to go back to the origin of the scene and to follow that through.

This account of how the song received royal support and therefore court popularity is persuasive and doubtless accounts for the start of its revival in the 1780s, but the light it casts on the police role both in its original composition and in its popular diffusion later on is equally worthy of note.

Writing three months later, in June 1783, Meister refers to the tune

—about which France has been so enthusiastic for three months. It is not easy to guess how this old song has come so strongly back into fashion but what is sure is that this lunacy is no less to the fore than that of the puppets: our boots, our hats, our ribbons, our curls, our clothes, everything, even our processions, are in the Marlborough style. I have just seen the procession recalling the Swiss soldier in Bear Street, where the huge dummy was dressed in the Marlborough style; one would hardly be surprised if our judges gave their verdicts to the tune of Marlborough. Does the honour of having introduced such a loony fashion go to the page's song written by Monsieur de Beaumarchais or to Madame Poitrine's predilection for rocking His Royal Highness to this clever tune? This is something we must look into at once and with all the attention such a subject deserves.[8]

In fact however he then gives no more than a detailed synopsis of *Le Mariage de Figaro*, which he must have seen in rehearsal, and makes no further comment on the song.

The earliest recorded event of the Marlborough 'season' seems to have been the production of J. F. Arnould-Mussot's one act comedy-pantomime, *Marbrough s'en va-t-en guerre*, performed at the Ambigu-Comique on 24 February 1783. This was followed but a few days later by F. M. Mayer de Saint-Paul's *Monsieur de Marlborough ou L'Enchanteur Rossignolet*, a pantomine tragi-parade in two acts given at the Théâtre des Grands-Danseurs on 2 March. Mardi Gras or Shrove Tuesday fell that year on 4 March when, as Métra recorded on the 19th,

We saw them taking around in the town . . . the dummy of the famous duke of Marlborough, accompanied by others of each sex, representing the deceased's pages and the attendants of his wife, whose pretences at grief caused the crowd much mirth. The tune now in fashion, that written about General Marlborough long ago, enlivened the whole procession. It all ended in the burial of the dummy and in the general carousal and drunkenness of the actors.[9]

At a meeting at the Musée de Paris on 6 March, when Benjamin Franklin was present, the musical part of the programme included a song rendered by a quartet to the air of *Malbrough*.

Although the king had expressly forbidden the performance of *Le Mariage de Figaro*, considered too revolutionary, Beaumarchais endeavoured to have it performed on the royal stage at Versailles: the performance was only countermanded on 13 June 1783, the eve of the opening night, when the tickets, 'les plus jolis du monde, car c'étaient des billets rayés à la Marlborough', had already been distributed. The fashion persisted and four days later Bachaumont wrote:

Due to the song Marlborough has become the centre of every fashion: everything is nowadays done in the Marlborough style. There are ribbons, hair styles, waistcoats, and above all hats in the Marlborough style, and one sees all the women going about in the streets, on the promenades, at the theatre, crowned with this grotesque head cover under which they enjoy hiding their charms, such is the empire that fashion has over them.[10]

An anonymous lyric pantomime entitled *Le Combat, la mort, les funerailles et le reveil de Marborough* was performed at one of the fairs and a one-act ballet, *Les Bilboquets, les pantins, Bacchus et Marborough* tried to cram all the popular themes into one, being produced on 15 July. August saw C. J. Guillemain's *Churchill amoureux ou la Jeunesse de Marborough*, a two-act comedy performed at the Variétés-Amusantes on the seventh of that month.

News of the fashion was spreading abroad and on 14 August Bachaumont recorded:

Her Grace the Duchess of Marlborough, the granddaughter of the famous general of that name, and who made her husband take this name, when informed of the goings-on here since last year and that the memory of a man so detrimental to the fortunes of France had been recalled to mind, has asked that a collection should be made for her of all the songs, pieces, pantomimes, the jokes and stories about him. At the same time she has instructed Miss Bertin to send her a sample of all the fashions invented in the 'Marlborough' style, whether they are for women or for men.[11]

This lady must in fact have been Caroline Russell (1743–1811), daughter of the duke of Bedford, who married George Spencer, the fourth duke of Marlborough (1739–1817). His father, the third duke, had inherited the title through his mother, Anne Churchill (wife of Charles Spencer, third earl of Sunderland), after the death of his elder aunt, Henrietta, the second duchess; both Henrietta and Anne being daughters of the first duke. Bachaumont is correct in that the title had passed to the Spencer family but it was only in 1817 that the fifth duke was authorized to take and use the name of Churchill, in addition to and after that of Spencer, in order to perpetuate in his family 'a surname to which his illustrious ancestor, the first duke, had added such imperishable lustre'.

By the end of 1783 the song had travelled all round Europe: in December it was printed in the Berlin paper, the *Vossische Zeitung*, and it appeared in the 1784 issue of the Leipzig *Frauenzimmeralmanach*. Its universality was recorded by Goethe who wrote from Verona in 1786 'Das Liedchen von Marlborough hört man auf allen Strassen' and, a year later in his *Elegien*:

Thus it was that the 'Marlborough' song pursued the British traveller, first from Paris to Leghorn, then from Leghorn to Rome, and then on down to Naples, and if he had sailed to Madras, even there the ditty, even there 'Marlborough' would have greeted him in the harbour.

The fame of the song was such that it was reproduced in the following years both as music and as an illustrated broadsheet, most of these popular forms being undated. It seems likely however that those which make mention in their title of the 'petit page' are associating themselves with Beaumarchais's play since the page in the song is never referred to as 'petit' and indeed only plays a minor part in it. These songs date therefore presumably from the later 1780s or the earlier 1790s. The song sheets include:[12]

Malbroug s'en va-t-en guerre. Chanson de Mr D'Malbroug ou le Petit page. [? Paris], 8°. [British Library B. 362. 3. (40)]

Malbrough s'en va-t-en guerre. Chanson de Mr D'Malbroug ou le Petit page. [London], J. F[entu]m, fol. [British Library H. 346. (20)]

Malbrouck s'en va-t-en guerre. Couplet, sur la mort de Mr

Malbrouck. [Paris], chez Bignon, 8°. [British Library B. 362. (205)]

Air de Malbroug. Pour Nanine de cinq ans à jouer sur le clavecin de sa sœur. [British Library B. 362. (215)]

In: [James] Aird's Selection of Scotch, English, Irish and foreign Airs. Adapted to the fife, violin, or German-flute. Glasgow, J. McFadyen, obl. 8°. [British Library a. 27. c]

At the same time the text of the song was reproduced for popular consumption printed around a coloured woodcut illustration, the top usually being reserved for a heading.[13] The earliest of these is probably *La Mort de M. de Malbroug. Ou le Petit Page. Air connu*, and was printed for Perdoux, a well-known popular printmaker active at Orléans from 1773 to 1805. This print shows in the centre a large swashbuckling character with, to the right, a lady on a tower complete with outsize hat and telescope, while to the left are angels, the messenger on horseback (carefully labelled 'le page'), a catafalque tomb bearing the hero's name, and attendants carrying sword, breastplate etc. The tomb discreetly bears the artist's initials, J. D., so far unidentified. This design was copied by another Orléans printmaker, Letourmi, and a legal battle ensued.

In the early years of the nineteenth century other print firms produced their versions, all naturally incorporating the standard items taken from the song, the messenger, the duchess, the tomb, and the carrying of divers items of the duke's apparel. The Beauvais version by the Diot-Feltrappe firm is said to be before 1826. Later versions tend to shift the emphasis of the title, possibly significantly. Thus the Chartres version, to be found only in a unique copy pasted to the sacristy doors at St Jean Pierrefixte, near Nogent le Rotrou, is entitled *Convoi du duc de Malbroug*, that by Pellerin of Epinal, *Mort et convoi de l'invincible Malborough*, and that by Gangel of Metz, *Convoi du grand et invincible Malborough*.

There were probably literary reasons (as will be argued below) for shifting from the page and the death of the hero to his state burial and for underlining his military successes. Undoubtedly the song continued to be incredibly popular in the early years of the nineteenth century. The preface to a French life of Marlborough, printed in the Imprimerie impériale in 1808, notes: 'His name, nevertheless, resounds among us daily, repeated endlessly by children and their nannies, who shout in our ears that quite absurd song which comes nevertheless and despite its ridiculous nature, from the lips of Fame itself.'[14] At the same date however the tune appears to have been on the lips of the Emperor himself, for Las Cases, his faithful Boswell on St Helena, is said to have recorded that he hummed it whenever he rode into battle and that, in his last years, having evoked and praised Marlborough, Napoleon thought of the song, smiled, and commented, 'Voila pourtant ce que c'est que le ridicule; il stigmatise tout, jusqu'à la victoire!', whereupon he whistled two verses.[15]

Following on after the interest of the Romantics in popular songs, the mid-nineteenth century saw the more systematic collection of such material and some attempt to trace its origins. The first major anthology was T. M. Dumersan and Noel Ségur's *Chansons nationales et populaires de la France*, published in 1851–2. The note appended to the song recalls the dauphin's wet-nurse as the source of its modern popularity but mentions that anti-Marlborough songs were current from 1706 onwards and that 'les paroles burlesques avaient probablement été rapportées dans plusieurs provinces après la bataille de Malplaquet, en 1709, par quelques soldats de Villars et de Boufflers.'[16]

From this time on the words of the Marlborough song seem, without further evidence, to have been dated back to on-the-spot innovations at Malplaquet in 1709. This bland assertion, repeated by every commentator however critical, requires some brief consideration and refutation. Malplaquet was notoriously the bloodiest battle of the early eighteenth century and if, technically, the Allies won, the losses on both sides were so considerable that all parties became revolted with the proceedings. England had achieved much both in Europe and elsewhere and henceforth the peace party could put pressure on Queen Anne both to bring about Marlborough's downfall and to end the War of Spanish Succession. No account of the battle suggests at any stage however that Marlborough's life was particularly in danger: at

Ramillies (23 May 1706) his horse had been shot under him and, as he mounted another, the aide-de-camp holding it was killed by a cannonball, but Marlborough remained unscathed. At Malplaquet Villars, the opposing general who was indeed wounded and had to be carried off, makes no mention in his memoirs of any rumour of Marlborough's death. Nor is it hinted at by Saint-Simon or Voltaire in their accounts of the battle.[17]

Voltaire's passage in *Le Siècle de Louis XIV* concerning Marlborough is however important and evidently used by the editors of the nineteenth-century prints. He describes John Churchill as

. . . the man most detrimental to the prestige of France to have appeared for several centuries. . . . As soon as Marlborough took command of the confederate armies in Flanders, it was evident that he had learnt the art of war from Turenne: he had indeed served his earliest campaigns as a volunteer under that general. He was then known in the army as 'the handsome Englishman'—but viscount Turenne had already seen that the handsome Englishman would be a great man one day . . . outstanding among the generals of his time he had that tranquil courage in battle and that inner serenity when in danger which the English call 'cold head'.

The Epinal and Metz prints each bear an identical historical note reading:

The famous Marlborough was born in England in 1650. He first bore arms for France, under Marshal Turenne, and was universally known to the army as the handsome Englishman. Voltaire records that the French general predicted that Marlborough would become a famous leader since he remained unruffled in the heat of combat for which the English called him 'cold head'. He was killed at the battle of Malplaquet, in 1723, at the age of 73.

This note, so historically inaccurate at the end, is of interest in that it makes no mention whatever of Marlborough's successes over the French. Voltaire's generous estimate of the latter's responsibility for breaking the French dominance is nowhere present, and indeed the Turenne association could be read as totally claiming him as French! He is shown wearing French uniform and sometimes even holding a French field marshal's baton with its imperial bee insignia. This approach is taken further in referring to him in the title of the song as the 'grand et invincible Malborough'. Clearly historically aware Frenchmen know his military role but it is arguable that most French children, and indeed less cultured adults, have, since the mid-nineteenth century, seen 'Malbrouck' as one of their own successful generals! The parts of hostile ridicule and of chauvinism are hard to unravel.

The continuing popularity of the song from the 1780s naturally prompted some other, more academic, reflections on it. These surface particularly in the 1840s. As we have seen Théophile Dumersan and Noel Ségur's anthology, *Chansons nationales et populaires de la France* (1851–2, reprinted 1858, 1866) established their conjecture of a possible origin for the song arising from the battle of Malplaquet. Others however suggested that this occasion saw no more than the adaptation of an older literary form to a traditional tune with contemporary reference. Thus Leroux de Lincy, in his *Recueil de chants historiques français* (vol. ii, 1842, p. 287) recalls an older funeral song which many verbal parallels suggest as a possible source for the verses nine to twelve of the Marlborough song. This song, the 'Convoi du duc de Guise', was first published by De La Place whose *Pièces intéressantes et peu connues pour servir à l'histoire de la littérature* appeared in 1785, precisely at the height of the Marlborough fashion.[18] La Place introduces the song by saying:

Here is another, on the funeral of François de Lorraine, duke of Guise, who was assassinated by Poltrot de Méré in 1563. The song was probably written by the Huguenots, a party which he had always persecuted. We include it in this anthology out of interest since it has more than one trait in common with the song on Marlborough, from which one can conclude that one of the two is the source of the other. But as to knowing which is the original . . . Alas, how far, even today, does plagiarism not stretch?

The song runs:

> Qui veut ouïr chanson? (bis)
> C'est du grand Duc de Guise
> Et bon, bon, bon, bon, di, dan, di, dan, bon:

C'est du grand Duc de Guise,
Qui est mort, & enterré [etc.]

Aux quatre coins du Poêle,
Quatre gentilshom's y avait,

Dont l'un portait son casque
Et l'autre ses pistolets,

Et l'autre son epée,
Qui tant d'Hug'nots a tués.

Venait le quatrième,
Qui était le plus dolent;

Après venaient les pages
Et les Valets de pied,

Avecque de grands crêpes,
Et des souliers cirés,

Et des beaux bas d'Estame,
Et des culottes de piau.

La cérémonie faite,
Chacun s'alla coucher,

Les uns avec leurs femmes,
Et les autres tout seuls.

The similarities between the two songs in relation to the burlesque funeral: the line 'Est mort et enterré', the four officers of whom three are carrying personal accoutrements and the fourth nothing, not to mention the identical final lines, all have been taken as suggesting that the *Duc de Guise* must be at least a part source for *Marlborough*.

This theory of a composite nature for the song which would therefore have been an early eighteenth-century adaptation of traditional elements is supported by the survival of another song, *L'Annonce de la mort du Prince d'Orange*, first reported by P. Coirault in 1927. Although this song, in its turn, has been said to stem from an early twelfth-century one ('Belle Doette as fenestres se siet'),[19] its immediate reference is to the death in July 1544 of René de Nassau, prince of Orange, at the siege of Saint-Dizier.[20]

The opening verses are clearly reminiscent of those of verses one
to seven of the Marlborough song:

Le beau prince d'Orange
  s'est un peu trop pressé;

Il fit son équipage,
  à cheval est monté:

'Où allez-vous, mon prince?'
  demanda l'écuyer.

'—Je vais aller en guerre,
  tout droit à Saint-Dizier.'

Sa femme lui demande:
  'Prince, quand reviendrez?'

'—Je reviendrai à Pâques,
  à Pâques ou â Noë.

Voici Pâques venue,
  et la Noë passée,

Le beau prince d'Orange
  n'y est point arrivé.

Sa femme en est en peine
  et ne fait rien que pleurer.

Elle entra dans sa chambre
  pour son corps y parer;

Regarde à la fenêtre
  et voit un messager:

'Messager, porte-lettres,
  quelles nouvelles apportez?'

'—J'apporte des nouvelles
  qui vous feront pleurer:

Le beau prince d'Orange
  est mort et enterré:

L'ai vu porter en terre
par quatre Cordeliers.'

Together these two songs, although recorded in various versions at different dates, contain enough common ground with the two major parts of the Marlborough song to make it likely that they were being used by the compiler of that version. Other single verses (verse 13 and onwards) such as those referring to the nightingale, the flight of the hero's soul and the final couplets on blonde and brunette couples are also known from other traditional songs and reinforce the composite construction theory.

Does this assist in any way in learning more about the date of composition and the author? We have seen that there is a lack of evidence to support Dumersan's guess that the song arose after Malplaquet. In 1778 Mairobert, commenting on the Keppel incident wrote:

Over half a century ago, when the well-known Marlborough died, France was still conscious of the harm this warrior had caused her and, even in peacetime, rejoiced indecently at his death which became the subject of song for the populace, accompanied by insulting verses and burlesque ceremonies.[21]

If this passage is taken at face value it suggests that the death of Marlborough, which took place fifty-six years earlier, was greeted in France with acclamation and popular demonstration. Such an event would seem the most likely occasion for a mock commemorative funeral. Marlborough died on 16 June 1722 (27 June NS as in France) and his death was reported in the July number of the *Mercure de France* which recorded that while in his will Marlborough had expressed the desire to be buried at Blenheim, the king of England, 'pour honorer la mémoire de ce général, veut que son corps soit inhumé dans l'Abbaie de Westminster, avec une pompe extraordinaire, qui se fera aux dépens de l'Etat.'[22] This indeed duly took place and an *Order of the Procession at the Funeral of the Duke of Marlborough* (5 pp.) was printed in London that year by J. Roberts. The *Mercure de France* devoted seven pages of its September issue to a full description of the proceedings, noting finally that 'le Canon de la Tour tiroit incessament pendant cette longue & pompeuse marche.' Marlborough's death therefore certainly did not pass by unnoticed in France. Hard on its heels however, on 25 October 1722, Louis XV was at last crowned in Rheims cathedral and popular attention was doubtless held by this major national event. The first opportunity for other popular celebration would therefore have been the Shrove Tuesday and Carnival processions of 1723 and, it is suggested, these are the events which Mairobert and Bachaumont had in mind. Bachaumont, it will be remembered, considered the song to be work of 'chansonniers de la police', presumably paid songsters set to keep the crowd occupied with appropriate, as against inappropriate, subjects in part of a traditional policy of *panem et circenses*. The parading of a stuffed dummy was common on these occasions and a mock funeral with special attendants would have fitted in perfectly, a combination of traditional songs supporting the theme. Sadly no contemporary evidence for this has been found, although it should be noted that the survival of any evidence of these relatively unscripted popular activities is very rare. One strange coincidence might however just be relevant. Several early nineteenth-century prints give the tomb the date 1723 — could this in some way recall the French beginning of the Marlborough song?

A brief word must be said about the tune, but although this evidently played an important part in the success of the song little has been found out about it. Some scholars write it off as an eighteenth-century hunting song, while others feel it must have older origins. W. Chappell, in his *Old English popular music* (1893) suggested that it had affinities with the tune 'Calino Custurame' found in the seventeenth-century Fitzwilliam Virginal Book.[23] The words associated with this, 'When as I view your comely grace, Caleno Custure me: Your golden haires, your angel's face', come from *A Handfull of Pleasant Delites* (1584) and it is possible that this song is referred to obliquely by Shakespeare when, in *Henry V*, Act IV, scene iv, the French knight says 'Je pense que vous êtes le gentilhomme de bonne qualité' which Pistol picks up mistakenly, retorting 'Cality! Calen o custure me!' In such a world, however, words appear to survive better than tunes, and the origins of this one seem lost before its mid-eighteenth-century vogue.

However it arose, 'Malbrouck s'en va-t-en guerre' became a nationally, and even internationally, known song in the 1780s and was recorded as part of the French heritage of popular songs in the 1840s. Dumersan's anthology was clearly the basis for John Oxenford's *The illustrated Book of French Songs from the sixteenth to the nineteenth century* (London, 1855). The melody forms the basis of the English song 'We won't go home till morning', referred to by F. Mahoney in 1836, the song version by Charles Blondel being first printed in London in the early 1840s by C. W. Manby and in America in 1842. The words beginning 'For he's a jolly good fellow' date from the mid 1850s but are first recorded in print in *The Old Clown's 'W-H-O-A January' Songster* (New York, 1870) where the tune is, given as 'We won't go home ...'. Another American song to use the tune, 'The bear went over the mountain' is first found in *Twice 55 community songs* (Boston, 1920).

The fame of 'Malbrouck', in more original dress, goes however much further afield. Numerous versions with minor variations are known in the French provinces, Switzerland, and Canada.[24] An early Dutch translation is recorded as well as German and even Russian ones. Several older Italian and Piedmontese versions have been noted and several pre-1939 English translations exist, but in none of these languages does the song seem to have survived to the present day. This however is not the case with Spanish: George Borrow (1803–81), a soldier's son and brought up in the lines, knew the song from his childhood and refers in *Lavengro* (1851) to his brother, then a child, marching out with 'single drum and fife playing the inspiring old melody,

> Marlbrouk is gone to the wars,
> He'll never return no more!'[25]

This experience doubtless allowed him later in life to recognize the Andalusian gipsy version he recorded in *The Zincali*:

> 'Chalá Malbum chinguerar,
> Birandón, birandón, birandera,
> Chalá Malbum chinguerar,
> No sé bus trutera, (*ter*)
> La romi que la camela,
> Birandón, birandón, birandera.'

The 'Malbrouck' song clearly reached Spain as well as every other part of Europe on the crest of its 1780s popularity. Marlborough appeared in several *tonadillas* or brief sung narrative scenes composed to fill intervals in plays.[26] The most successful of these was Jacinto Valledor y La Calle's *La cantada vida y muerte del General Malbrú* (1785). Tonadillas were often nationalistic burlesque protests against the dominance of French culture and in Valledor's it is interesting to note that Malbrú is a French general of whom much fun is made. He speaks pidgin Spanish with an absurd French accent. During the performance the Marlborough song seems to have been sung, together with another sung by the hero's wife and starting:

> Malbrú se fue a la guerra a pelear.
> Su ausencia me mata contaato fardar.

More usually in Spain 'Malbrouck' became Mambrú and the standard version runs:

> Mambrú se fue a la guerra,
> ¡Qué dolor, qué dolor, qué pena!
> Mambrú se fue a la guerra,
> No sé cuándo vendrá.
>
> Si vendrá por la Pascua
> O por la Trinidad.
> La Trinidad se acaba
> Mambrú no viene ya.
> Me he subido a la torre.
> Para ver si aún vendra.
> Alli viene su paje,
> ¿Qué noticias traerá?
> —Las noticias que traigo,
> Dan ganas de llorar.
> Que Mambrú ya se ha muerto.
> Lo llevan a enterrar,
> Como le pertenece,
> Con pompa y majestad.
> La caja es de terciopelo,
> Con tapa de cristal.
> Y encima de la tumba

Dos pajaritos van,
Cantando el pío, pa,
Y un pajarito dice
Que ya descansa en paz.

Here the funeral procession element has not come through though, delightfully, the refrain from Beaumarchais's romance has been adopted for the second line, a testimony perhaps to the early date at which this version must have started. In contrast one of the Catalan versions uses the 'Birondón, birondón, birondera' refrain, similarly omits the procession, explains Marlborough's death by adding:

Malmés d'un cop de llansa
Lo veram espira'

but stays fractionally closer to the French tradition with regard to the birdsong at the end (verse 14) which suggests that its origins are probably in a nineteenth-century French version incorporating this extraneous element.

In his lifetime John Churchill, first duke of Marlborough, attracted considerable attention through his political and military roles, his achievements were extolled, and his actions equally often interpreted as the result of turncoat opportunism, ambition, and avarice.[27] From the date of his fall from power to the present day historians have attempted to evaluate his career and influence at what was not only an important turning-point in British history but also a notable moment in European affairs. One of the finest of these studies, if not the most impartial, is of course that by the duke's great descendant, Sir Winston Churchill. None of these however even mentions the satirical song which, we have here suggested, arose in France, made up from traditional elements, at the time of his death. For the great nineteenth-century historian Jules Michelet this song, 'une dérision de la guerre, une ironie innocente par laquelle le pauvre peuple français de Louis XIV se vengeait de ses revers', was one of the memorable, lasting souvenirs of the Ancien Régime.[28] Somehow its composite nature manages to combine a medieval romanticism with an evocation of the wars and military pageantry of early modern Europe and still

to be redolent of those last days of the Ancien Régime of which
Talleyrand said 'Qui n'a pas vécu dans les années voisines de 1780
ne sait pas ce que c'est que le plaisir de vivre.'[29] Yet too this song,
through its amazing success in the popularity charts of the 1780s,
spread across Europe and even to the New World, its very
historical inaccuracy allowing for its easy adoption in many
countries as a classic. Its traditional form as a lament detaches it
from historical fact and with the passage of time and thanks to
popular presentation the English general responsible for breaking
the power of the Sun King becomes, in the minds of many French
children, not only a Frenchman but even a popular hero. And as a
further twist of irony, he is viewed as a caricatural French general
by Spanish ones. More people have heard of 'Malbrouck' through
this song than ever knew of him in his lifetime. A legendary
character is perhaps always remote from his historical prototype.
Here the divorce is particularly blatant. Satire alone could not
achieve such afterlife which, in this case, owes much to a series of
factors: to the nature of the themes combined to mark Marlborough's death, to the catchy nature of the melody used, to the
immense success of Beaumarchais's play, to the development of
popular imagery and to the Romantics' interest in popular song.
All these put 'Malbrouck' into the repertoire of children's songs
where its tune and dramatic and processional content were bound
to ensure its permanent presence. Through, on this occasion, no
virtue or vice of his own, Marlborough became, well after his
death, a European figure, one of the stalwarts of the nursery, and
a household name in many lands. Marlborough lives! Perhaps one
might conclude that 'Nothing in his life / Became him like the
leaving it'!

Notes

1. The standard modern critical anthology is Henri Davenson (= H. I.
   Marrou), *Le Livre des chansons* (Paris, 1955, 4th edn., 1977).
2. The major modern contributions to the study of 'Malbrouck s'en va-t-en
   guerre' are: G. Doncieux, *Le Romancéro populaire de la France* (Paris, 1904),
   455–61; M. Friedländer, 'Das Lied von Marlborough', *Zeitschrift für Musik-
   wissenschaft*, vi (1918), Sonderdruck, 28 pp.; P. Coirault, *Recherches sur notre
   ancienne chanson populaire traditionnelle* (Paris, 1927), 223–32; C. D. Brenner,

'The eighteenth-century vogue of "Malbrough" and Marlborough', *Modern Language Review*, xlv (1950), 177–80; J. Urbain, *La Chanson populaire en Suisse romande*, ii (Yverdon, 1978), 113–30; J. J. Fuld, *The Book of World-famous Music* (3rd edn., New York, 1985), 231. Mrs Catherine Hilliard kindly drew the Friedländer article to my attention.

3. J. Bolte, 'Niederdeutsche und niederländische Volksweisen', *Jahrbuch des Vereins für niederdeutsche Sprachforschung*, 18, 17.

4. A. M. Lottin, *Catalogue chronologique des libraires et libraires-imprimeurs de Paris* (Paris, 1789), 167–8.

5. [M. F. Pidansat de Mairobert], *L'Espion anglais* (London, 1785), ix. 255–6.

6. P. A. C. Beaumarchais, *La Folle Journée*, publiée par J. B. Ratermanis, *Studies on Voltaire*, 63 (Geneva, 1968), avant-propos.

7. [L. P. de Bachaumont], *Mémoires secrets pour servir à l'histoire de la république des lettres en France* (London, 1777–89) xxii. 130 (9 Mar. 1783).

8. M. Grimm and D. Diderot, *Mémoires historiques, littéraires et anecdotiques*, (London, 1814) iii. 50–1.

9. F. Métra, *Correspondance secrète, politique et littéraire* (London, 1787) xiv. 188. An annual ceremony commemorating the sacrilege committed on a statue of the Virgin Mary by a Swiss on 30 June 1418. The festivity continued until 1789 although Rousseau, writing in 1776, suggests that it was falling out of favour. See *Rousseau juge de Jean-Jacques*: 'L'usage annuel de bruler en cérémonie un Suisse de paille dans la rue aux Ours. Cette fête populaire paroissoit si barbare et si ridicule en ce siècle philosophe que, déjà négligée, on alloit la supprimer tout à fait' (*Œuvres*, Paris, Pléiade, i. 44 and n. 2, 1644). I am indebted to Professor J. Garagnon for this reference.

10. Bachaumont, *Mémoires secrets*, xxiii. 12 (17 June 1783).

11. Ibid. xxiii. 103–4 (14 Aug. 1783).

12. These items are recorded in *The Catalogue of Printed Music in the British Library*, 37 (London, 1985). None of them are dated and it is not clear that there are any strong reasons to assume that any of them are in fact earlier than the year the song reached high popularity, i.e. 1785.

13. For 'Malbrouck' and popular imagery see P. L. Duchartre and R. Saulnier, *L'Imagerie populaire* (Paris, 1925), 70; L. Crick, 'Monsieur de Marlborough', *Bulletin des musées royaux d'art et d'histoire de Bruxelles*, 3ᵉ sér., 4 (1931), 117–22 (I am indebted to Monsieur Georges Colin for access to this text); J. Mistler (and others), *Epinal et l'imagerie populaire* (Paris, 1961), 183 and pl. vi; and J. Adhémar, *L'Imagerie populaire française* (Paris, 1968) 90, 96, 172 and pl. 70.

14. [—, Madgett, ed. J. F. H. Dutems], *Histoire de Jean Churchill, duc de Marlborough* (Paris, Imprimerie impériale, 1808), vol. i, iii. I am indebted to Mr M. Dunworth for allowing me access to this reference.

15. This story is reported by several modern writers but I have not been able to trace it in E. Las Cases, *Mémorial de Sainte-Hélène* (1823) although it rings true

to that work where the author does recall Napoleon discussing Marlborough in relation to Alexander.

16. T. M. Dumersan and N. Ségur, *Chansons nationales et populaires de la France* (Paris, 1851–2), i. 18.

17. L. de Rouvroy, duc de Saint-Simon, *Mémoires* (Paris, 1854) iii, ch. xx; C. L. H. Villars, duc de, *Vie du maréchal duc de Villars* (Paris, 1784); F. M. Voltaire, *Le Siècle de Louis XIV*, ch. xxi.

18. A. J. V. Leroux de Lincy, *Recueil de chants historiques français* ii (Paris, 1842), 287 and [P. A. De La Place], *Pièces intéressantes et peu connues pour servir à l'histoire de la littérature* (Brussels and Paris, 1785) iii. 243–9.

19. C. Bartsch, *Altfranzösische Romanzen und Pasturellen* (Leipzig 1870), i. 5, n. 3.

20. See Coirault, *Recherches*, 226–8.

21. Mairobert, *L'Espion anglais*, 256.

22. *Mercure de France* (July 1722), 147 and (Sep. 1722), 103–9 for the account of the funeral.

23. W. Chappell, *Old English popular music* (London, 1893), 84.

24. For these and other translations see the items cited in n. 2 *supra*, also A. Godet, *Chansons de nos grand-mères* (Paris, 1879), and M. E. Marriage, 'Marlbruck', *Modern Language Quarterly*, iii (1900), 128–31.

25. G. Borrow, *Lavengro* (London, 1906), 72. The Romany version is from *The Zincali* (London, 1907), 270, this text having been published first in 1841.

26. I am indebted to Dr J. Rutherford for the following information on the *tonadillas*. The Spanish translation comes from C. Bravo-Villasante, *Antología de la literatura infantil en lengua española* (Madrid, 1966), ii. 96, and the Catalan one from (Espasa), *Enciclopedia universal ilustrada*, xxxii (Madrid, n.d.), 625. These references I owe to my colleague, Mr John Wainwright.

27. See R. D. Horn, *Marlborough: A Survey of Panegyrics, Satires, and Biographical Writings 1688–1788* (Folkestone, 1975), which however makes virtually no reference to any material other than in English.

28. J. Michelet, *Histoire de la France au dix-septième siècle, Henri IV et Richelieu* (Paris, 1857), 2.

29. Quoted in P. Guizot, *Mémoires pour servir à l'histoire de mon temps*, i. (1858), 6.

8

William Godwin as Children's Bookseller

WILLIAM ST CLAIR

WILLIAM GODWIN's decision to write books for children was a neat solution to a number of problems. When he published his most famous works, *Political Justice* in 1793 and *Caleb Williams* in 1794, he had been a bachelor, and although he was never rich, the proceeds of his writing comfortably supplied his modest needs. After he married Mary Wollstonecraft, author of *A Vindication of the Rights of Woman*, and she brought her daughter Fanny, money was more tight, but the two famous authors confidently expected that they would manage on their joint literary earnings. By the end of 1797 however Mary was dead, struck down by a fatal infection shortly after giving birth to a daughter. Suddenly the forty-one-year-old philosopher found himself with responsibility for two motherless children.

When in 1801 Godwin married Mary Jane Clairmont, she brought two further children, Charles and Mary Jane (later known as Claire), and before long she bore Godwin a son, William Godwin Junior. By 1803 Godwin had a family which included five children under the age of eight. Fanny was the half-sister of Mary, who was the half-sister of William, who was the half-brother of Claire, who was the half-sister of Charles. Somehow he had to find the means to feed and clothe and educate them, and the only trade he knew was writing.

When Mary Wollstonecraft lay dying, Godwin had discussed with her the upbringing of her children. After her death he read the books for children she had written earlier in her career and published the fragments of another which she had left unfinished. He consulted Lady Mountcashel who had been educated by Mary Wollstonecraft when Mary was a governess in Ireland, and who saw herself as her successor. He also looked over the books for children which were available in the shops although he found few that matched his ideas.

Mary Jane, the second Mrs Godwin, was also a writer of children's books, although her name never appeared on any title-page. When Godwin met her, she was employed by Benjamin Tabart as editor of his series of nursery stories. Although she had to give up her position when she married Godwin, she was still able to write at home and so to make a contribution to the family finances. What could be more appropriate therefore than that Godwin and she should combine to write the books their own children would need?

Godwin would have preferred, no doubt, to have continued writing more serious works, philosophy and novels, but they took years to complete and the situation was pressing. It is not easy to concentrate for long with children romping and babies crying in the next room of an overcrowded cottage. But the decision was in no way a compromise with his previous aspirations. The plan was a new way of advancing the principles to which he had devoted his life, and the only one available in his new circumstances.

Political Justice is a theory of progress, both an explanation of how it occurs and a recipe for accelerating it. Human beings, Godwin argues, are for the most part the creatures of earlier events, no more capable of changing direction than a struck billiard ball can decide on its own route across the table. Behaviour is determined by opinion, and opinion by the cultural environment, by the political, social, and economic system under which individuals live, by the knowledge, values, prejudices, and myths which they pick up and adopt, without much discrimination, from earliest infancy, and by the innumerable influences which they encounter in daily life. Godwin was fascinated by what might be called the operation of the moral economy. History, he believed, offers empirical proof that progress does occur although slowly and irregularly. The amount of knowledge in the moral economy is normally increasing and with it the total of true opinion and correct choice.

Godwin's recipe for progress is very different from that of

socialists who have later claimed him among their intellectual ancestors. If the underlying moral growth rate is to be improved, Godwin believed, the process has to start with individuals not with institutions. It is useless for those in authority, whether governments, teachers, or parents, to prescribe and enforce values for others to follow. They are trying to change behaviour before they have changed opinion. The only lasting way in which individuals can be influenced is to secure their intellectual commitment by sincere discourse and just dealing.

In his earliest philosophical writings, Godwin had accepted the view advanced by John Locke that children at birth are equal in their capabilities and that experience then writes its varied impressions on the clean white paper of their minds. Within his own family he now had five refutations. Fanny suffered from the same intermittent depressions as had afflicted Mary Wollstonecraft. Mary was calm, intelligent, and earnest like her father. Charles was restless like his father, the Swiss businessman whom he had never known. Claire and William shared the unpredictable temper of Mary Jane.

But if Godwin was obliged to admit genetic factors to a place in his theory of progress, this did not alter his approach to education. Only if children genuinely share and adopt the insights which lie behind the recommended morality will they give it their commitment. They must therefore be treated with affection and respect, listened to, argued with, and convinced. As soon as they are old enough, they should be taught to read widely, particularly in literature and history, so that they can learn more about the variety of human character and human experience.

Godwin's views on education were still new. They were also widely feared and hated. Since 1793, with one brief interval, Britain had been at war with Revolutionary France. At home all signs of political dissent were ruthlessly crushed by a Government determined to uphold the values of church and king. Only if the philosophical ideas which led to the French Revolution were extirpated, so it was believed, could order be restored in Europe, in the country, and in the family.

Children, according to the prevailing orthodoxy, are conspicuous inheritors of original sin, and the sooner their rebelliousness is crushed, the sooner they will become reconciled to the place which society has allotted them. Education, according to this view, is an activity like the training of horses, dependent for its success on breaking the animal spirits, instilling a sense of fear, and flogging down any sign of deviation. The same fathers who forbade their womenfolk to read novels—on the grounds that such literature made dangerous emotions seem legitimate—were equally fearful that books for children would introduce them to the notion of choice.

Every month since 1798, the officially subsidized *Anti-Jacobin Review* had poured out its warnings against books and writers who infringed traditional deferential values. William Godwin and Mary Wollstonecraft were high on the list of those held responsible for the tide of atheism, political sedition, and sexual immorality which was believed to have swept the country. In 1802 the *Anti-Jacobin* was joined by the *Guardian of Education*, edited by Mrs Trimmer, founded to perform the same service for children's books. Since such books had only recently become widely available, most of the people who condemned them had never read one during their own childhood.

It is not surprising therefore that William Godwin's books for children all had to be written under pseudonyms. His first essay in the genre has only now been identified. *Bible Stories, Memorable Acts of the Ancient Patriarchs, Judges, and Kings ...* by William Scolfield, was first published in two small volumes in August 1802.[1] It contained engraved illustrations, perhaps by Mulready. The book was evidently a commercial success. A new edition was issued the following year and there were at least two pirated editions in the United States. It was still being advertised in London in 1828 and appears in the London Catalogue of Books as still in print in 1831. But no copy has been found in any library in Britain nor any copy of the original edition. There is no copy in the Opie collection, and when I wrote to Peter Opie some years ago, he said he could not recollect ever having seen one. The only examples known are in the United States, one copy of the 'New edition' of 1803, first volume only, and single copies of two

American reprints. Like many children's books which were once plentiful, its thread of survival was as tenuous as that of an ancient classic.

Godwin was proud of his little book. When in later years he was asked for his views on education he would refer inquirers to the preface where it was all explained. When in 1828, at the age of seventy-two, he drew up instructions for his literary executors, he asked that this preface should be reprinted among his collected works, a privilege he did not seek for any of his other lesser writings. It is therefore appropriate to quote a substantial extract.

The works lately written for the perusal of children are very different from those which they were accustomed to read twenty years ago; but are they better or worse? In the following respects they are worse.

1. They are much more incumbered with abstract and general propositions. The meanest narratives formerly written for the use of children, had at least the merit of going straight forward, and of stating in every sentence some fact to keep alive attention, or some picture to engage the imagination. They did not stop at every turn to moralize, in language which no child's understanding can comprehend, and no child's temper will relish.

2. The old books described the real tempers and passions of human beings. Their scenes were often supernatural and impossible, but their personages were of our own species. The modern books on the other hand abound in real scenes, but impossible personages. They would not for the world astonish the child's mind with a giant, a dragon or a fairy, but their young people are all so good, and their old people so sober, so demure, and so rational, that no genuine interest can be felt for their adventures. No two things can be more unlike, than the real inhabitants of the world, and these wonderful personages; their proceedings are destitute of the firmness and vigour of a healthful mind, and their records are artificial, repulsive and insipid.

3. These modern improvers have left out of their system that most essential branch of human nature the imagination. Our youth, according to the most approved recent systems of education, will be excellent geographers, natural historians and mechanics; they will be able to tell you from what part of the globe you receive every article of your furniture; and will explain the process in manufacturing a

carpet, converting metals into the utensils of life, and clay into the cups of your tea-table, and the ornaments of your chimney: in a word, they are exactly informed about all those things, which if a man or woman were to live and die without knowing, neither man nor woman would be an atom the worse. Everything is studied and attended to, except those things which open the heart, which insensibly initiate the learner in the relations and generous offices of society, and enable him to put himself in imagination into the place of his neighbour, to feel his feelings, and to wish his wishes. Imagination is the ground-plot upon which the edifice of a sound morality must be erected. Without imagination we may have a certain cold and arid circle of principles, but we cannot have sentiments: we may learn by rote a catalogue of rules, and repeat our lesson with the exactness of a parrot, or play over our tricks with the docility of a monkey; but we can neither ourselves love, nor be fitted to excite the love of others.

Imagination is the characteristic of man. The dexterities of logic or of mathematical deduction belong rather to a well-regulated machine; they do not contain in them the living principle of our nature. It is the heart which most deserves to be cultivated: not the rules which may serve us in the nature of a compass to steer through the difficulties of life; but the pulses which beat with sympathy, and qualify us for the habits of charity, reverence and attachment. The intellectual faculty in the mind of youth is fully entitled to the attention of parents and instructors; but parents and instructors will perform their offices amiss, if they assign the first place to that which is only entitled to the second.

In emphasizing the imagination, Godwin is modifying the description of the passive mind which underpinned the theory described in *Political Justice*. During the previous few years he had become friends with Samuel Taylor Coleridge and he was much influenced by his ideas. The mind, according to the emerging view, is not merely a recipient of impressions but an active creative force. It is a lamp which illuminates life, not a mirror which can only reflect it, and the imagination is the source of light. Imagination was to become one of the key concepts of the romantic movement, but to the *Guardian of Education* it was merely a modern term for the hated liberalism. *Bible Stories* was condemned out of hand as 'an engine of mischief'.

In 1805 Godwin and Mrs Godwin decided to set up in business

on their own. A number of rich friends who admired Godwin's writing were invited to subscribe to enable him to start. A shop was rented in Hanway Street off Oxford Street and fitted out as a 'Juvenile Library' to sell children's books. To preserve secrecy, it was established in the name of Thomas Hodgkins, who served in the shop but who was only the nominal owner. The main stock was to be books written by Godwin, by his wife, and by his friends; but they also sold books produced by other publishers and a wide range of stationery.

Over the next few years Godwin was to write seven substantial books besides a number of shorter works and abridgements. All were published under pseudonyms. 'Theophilus Marcliffe' sounds and writes like an earnest lay preacher of the dissenting tradition, advocating the Protestant virtues of persistence, thrift, and early rising. 'Edward Baldwin', who appeared on title-pages as 'Edward Baldwin, Esq', could have been taken as a retired schoolmaster from one of the more respectable schools. One of Theophilus Marcliffe's books, *The Life of Lady Jane Grey*, was later reprinted as the work of Edward Baldwin, but nobody noticed. Godwin was careful not to give offence and his pseudonyms were never publicly exposed. Advertisements for books by Edward Baldwin were able to quote favourable reviews from the *Anti-Jacobin Review* to the effect that they could safely be given to any child; and they were. In the Opie collection is a copy of Baldwin's *Fables* inscribed by his mother to Augustus Frederick, grandson of King George III.

Fables Ancient and Modern, Edward Baldwin's first book, is based on Aesop, but Godwin updated the stories and added others of his own. As he told them to his own children, he noticed that they were often puzzled by the abruptness of the punchline, and were inclined to ask 'what happened then?' In such old favourites as *The Fox and the Grapes*, therefore, Godwin patiently spelled out the moral:

From this fable it has come to be a proverb, when a man pretends not to wish for what he cannot have, to say to him, the grapes are sour. If you ask a poor haymaker, whether he would not like that the parsonage-house were his, perhaps he will answer, no, indeed, he likes his mud-

FABLES
ANCIENT AND MODERN.

Adapted for the Use of Children from Three to Eight
Years of Age.

BY EDWARD BALDWIN, ESQ.

VOL. I.

ADORNED WITH THIRTY-SIX COPPER-PLATES.

Published by Thoˢ Hodgkins Hanway Street, Octʳ 6ᵗʰ 1805.

LONDON: PRINTED FOR THOMAS HODGKINS,
AT THE JUVENILE LIBRARY, HANWAY STREET
(OPPOSITE SOHO SQUARE), OXFORD STREET;
AND TO BE HAD OF ALL BOOKSELLERS.

Title-page from *Fables Ancient and Modern*. The engraving was based on the
statue of Aesop over the door at 41 Skinner Street.

cottage as well. The fox was not wrong to endeavour contentedly to go without what he could not get, but he need not have told an untruth.

Baldwin's *Pantheon*, first published in 1806, was Godwin's attempt to displace the *Pantheon* by 'Andrew Tooke', then the standard school book on Greek mythology, which is full of sneers and suppresses all reference to sexuality. Godwin's simple and unpretentious little book by contrast shows a deep understanding of the symbolic and psychological meaning of the ancient myths, and, although it was sufficiently discreet to be reviewed and advertised as 'proper' for both boys and girls, it catches something of the liberating joy of Greece.

In 1810, in order to secure an order from Dr Burney's school at Greenwich, Godwin agreed to the re-engraving of four of the illustrations which were thought to be too explicit, and in all subsequent editions the nudity of Venus, Apollo, Mercury, and Mars was modestly covered over.[2] One schoolboy who owned a copy was John Keats, who was to treasure it all his life, taking it with him to Italy on his final journey, although it is not known whether his was a draped or an undraped version. The story of the titans which he used in *Hyperion* was taken from the unusual version adopted in Godwin's book. If, as his friends used to tease him, Keats could not look out at Hampstead Heath without seeking a dryad, Godwin's unpretentious little book was partly responsible.[3]

Edward Baldwin was also known for his three history books, the *History of England*, 1806, the *History of Rome*, 1809, and the *History of Greece*, 1822. They too were based on his experience of teaching his own children and reflected his own ideas, bestowing, for example, more admiration on the republican virtues than was normally acceptable at the time. They were to be adopted for the curriculum by a number of schools, including Charterhouse and Christ's Hospital, and were reprinted many times.

Godwin was unlucky from the first. Thomas Hodgkins was discovered to be stealing money and since he was nominal owner of the business, there was no redress. In 1806 there was a financial crisis which was only brought to an end by a further large advance of money from wealthy well-wishers. Shortly afterwards Godwin moved to new premises at 41 Skinner Street in the City.

Five storeys high, the house stood on a corner site with wide windows on two sides. The upper storeys were accommodation for the family and the ground floor was fitted out as a shop. Over the door Godwin installed a statue of Aesop telling stories to the children, and had an engraving made as a kind of trademark for his books. In Mrs Godwin's *Dramas for Children* the reward for good children is to be taken there and allowed to choose a book by the famous Mr Baldwin.

Skinner Street had been built as recently as 1801, during the brief peace with France, but with the renewal of the war, the ambitious development of which it formed a part was abandoned. With every passing year it became more run down. Since Smithfield was nearby, flocks of animals regularly passed through on their way to slaughter, and since the adjoining area had been a centre for the leather trade, vacant sites were diverted to this foul-smelling activity. Three prisons stood in the locality and crowds often gathered for the frequent public executions which took place at the new drop at Newgate, just out of sight from Number 41 but probably within earshot. They were not good customers.

The City Juvenile Library was to stay in business at 41 Skinner Street until 1822. To prevent a repetition of the difficulties with Hodgkins, Godwin and Mary Jane named it 'M. J. Godwin and Company', the name which appears on their publications. Several people seem however to have read the sign on the door 'Mr J. Godwin' and since there was a well-established bookshop in nearby Holborn owned by a John Godwin (no relation) some obfuscation may have been intended. Godwin himself worked upstairs and never appeared in the shop.

Although the ferocity of the anti-Jacobin reaction gradually abated, it was still wise to be discreet. In the Public Record Office is a report sent to the Home Office in 1813 by one of the informers whom the government encouraged with financial rewards. The true owner of the City Juvenile Library, the spy disclosed, was William Godwin, author of *Political Justice*, and his purpose was to infiltrate his subversive democratic ideas into schools. The spy saw evidence of Godwin's conspiracy both in his secrecy and in his openness. One showed that he needed to conceal what he was doing, the other was the flagrancy of success. The books, it was alleged, were kept cheap to inveigle the poorer classes; Baldwin's *Pantheon* condoned sexual immorality.

By these different publications it is evident there is an intention . . . to give an opportunity for every principle professed by the infidels and republicans of these days to be introduced to their notice. By such means did Voltaire and his brethren for twenty years before the Revolution in France spread infidelity and disloyalty through the remotest provinces of that country . . .

A few remarks were offered on each of Godwin's main books for children, but the spy evidently did not read them all—he offers a criticism of the *History of Greece* which although advertised at the time he wrote was not published until 1822. There is no record that the authorities took any action.[4]

M. J. Godwin and Company soon had a list that any publisher would envy. Godwin commissioned works from Charles and Mary Lamb including *Ulysses*, *Mrs Leicester's School*, and *Tales from Shakespear*. Lady Mountcashel, who had adopted the name 'Mrs Mason' in memory of the kind lady in Mary Wollstonecraft's *Original Stories from Real Life*, wrote a number of stories on the same model.[5] William Hazlitt contributed an excellent English grammar. Wordsworth was invited to contribute a verse version of *Beauty and the Beast* but declined. Coleridge eagerly offered to write books, but never delivered.

Godwin's daughter Mary, later Mary Shelley, is known to have composed *Mounseer Nongtongpaw* when she was only ten. Iona and Peter Opie published a full fascimile reprint of the plain version in *A Nursery Companion* (1980). She may have written others, notably the new version of *Monsieur Tonson* which was published simultaneously in identical format.

The greatest of all children's books is *Robinson Crusoe*. Rousseau had made it the centre of his whole education theory as the only book that children need be given during their middle years. During the late eighteenth century there was a flood of imitations, some offering an alternative morality to the patient accumulating individualism of the original. Godwin started to write his own contribution and Coleridge promised another, although neither was taken far. M. J. Godwin and Company does however have the dubious honour of having been the first to publish the *Family Robinson Crusoe* in English. It came out in two successive volumes, translated, it was said, from the original German, but more probably from a French translation. The piety of the Swiss family is a far cry from the philosophy of *Political Justice*—at one point the children are told that God has populated the world with animals in order to stimulate the international fur trade—but under its new name of *Swiss Family Robinson* it soon became a commercial favourite.

Godwin deserved to succeed. But, although the business made satisfactory profits in the early years, its capital structure was weak from the start, being financed entirely by loans. When in 1809 a number of the backers withdrew their advances Godwin found himself having to borrow large sums for short periods just to keep going. Soon he was locked in a vicious circle, borrowing increasing amounts with increasing difficulty just to replace and service other short-term borrowing. At the end of each year when accounts had to be settled he had to sell his books at knock-down discounts.

As a believer in his own principles, Godwin felt no sense of guilt or shame at accepting money from men to whom the accidents of birth had given a plentiful income. Percy Bysshe Shelley, who was heir to a huge fortune, funded Godwin's losses on the bookshop for many years. It was after visiting Skinner Street to discuss money that he ran off with Godwin's daughter Mary and his step-daughter Claire. In the summer of 1822, however, shortly before Shelley was drowned, Godwin was obliged to give up 41 Skinner Street, and although the business continued for a time at 195 Strand, it finally collapsed in the crash of 1825 which brought down a number of better-known publishing houses.

The stock and other assets were sold to the firm of Baldwin, Cradock, and Joy—the name is coincidence—and they reissued many of the books over their own imprint. Lamb's *Tales* and the *Swiss Family Robinson* have been in print continuously ever since. Several of Edward Baldwin's books were also reprinted and even when the copyrights passed into other hands, they were still in demand. Some were being reprinted as late as the 1860s still under their pseudonym. If numbers of readers are a measure of influence Edward Baldwin did more to promote human progress than William Godwin.

Notes

This essay is taken from a chapter of William St Clair's *The Godwins and the Shelleys: the Biography of a Family* (London, 1989). Full source references are given there.

1. That Godwin wrote a book called *Scripture Histories* has long been known. In *Letter of Advice to a Young American* (1818), 4, he recommends his readers to 'the preface to a small book for children, entitled "Scripture Histories given in the words of the original in two volumes 18mo."' In a manuscript note dated 2 Jan. 1828 intended for his literary executors (Abinger papers c 604/2, Bodleian Library), he makes a reference to what is evidently the same book, although he gives it a different name, 'also the Preface to a book entitled Bible Stories'. No book with either name has hitherto been identified, and it is listed in Pollin's *Godwin Criticism: a Synoptic Bibliography* (Toronto, 1967) as a lost work, along with *Rural Walks*, which is known only from a manuscript reference.

There can be little doubt that *Bible Stories* by 'William Scolfield' is the book referred to. Godwin's journal (Abinger papers, Bodleian) shows him researching and writing a book called *Jewish Histories* during 1801 and 1802. By 25 April 1802 he is revising, normally a sign that publication is imminent. The *English Catalogue of Books* reports publication in August 1802 of 'Bible Stories: Scolfield W. 2 vols 4s.' The preface is, as one would expect from the reference in *Letter of Advice to a Young American*, an essay on the theory of education. The text, which treats the people of the Old and New Testaments as interesting but non-supernatural historical figures, accords fully with what is known of Godwin's beliefs. The book was published by Richard Phillips who had recently become Godwin's publisher.

Despite extensive searches I have been unable to locate a copy of the original edition. The Library of Smith College, Massachusetts, contains a copy of volume one only of *Bible Stories, Memorable Acts of the Ancient Patriarchs, Judges, and Kings: extracted from their original historians for the use of children*. By William Scolfield. In two volumes. A New edition. London. Printed for R. Phillips ... 1803. Price 4s. Half Bound. The quoted extract is taken from this version. This book contains interesting illustrations which were presumably also included in the first edition of the previous year.

Besides the review in the *Guardian of Education*, there are plentiful references to the book under differing titles in publishers' advertisements. For example the anonymous *Rustic Excursions* published by Phillips in 1811, which has some claim to be regarded as Godwin's lost *Rural Walks*, advertises among Elementary Books Recently Published '*Scripture Histories or Bible Stories*' with no mention of Scolfield (only known from a copy in the author's collection). An advertisement dated 1 Jan. 1828 by Baldwin, Cradock and Joy, who took over Phillips's stock and copyrights, in *Stories of Old Daniel* (author's collection) lists *Sacred Histories . . . in the words of the original*, by William Scolfield. The *London Catalogue of Books* (1831) lists 'Scholefield's *Sacred Histories*, 2 vols, Baldwin'. The full text is known from two American copies of what are evidently pirated editions: one in the Andover–Harvard Theological Library with the imprint 'London, Printed: Albany. Reprinted by Charles R. and George Webster at their Bookstore, 1803'; the other in the Huntington Library is imprinted 'Wilmington, Printed for Matthew and Lockerman. Robert Porter *Printer*, 1812'.

With so many printings, copies of the book must have been plentiful at one time, but school books are not loved and are thrown away without regret when no longer needed. In Godwin's day they were not regarded as worth acquiring even by the major libraries. In the case of *Bible Stories*, I wonder too if there may not have been some element of deliberate destruction by schoolmasters and others who feared its message.

2. *Shelley and His Circle, documents in the Carl H. Pforzheimer Library* (Cambridge, Mass., 1961), ii. 563. A manuscript note among the Abinger papers makes clear that the footnotes to *The Pantheon* were supplied by Dr Raine.

3. Keats's copy of Baldwin's *Pantheon* is listed among his possessions in *Keats Circle: Letters and Papers* ed. Hyder E. Rollins (Cambridge, Mass., 1948), i. 258. Charles and Mary Cowden Clarke in *Recollections of writers* (n.d. [1878]), 124, refer to his reading Tooke's *Pantheon*, but this is probably an error. That the reconciliation theme of *Hyperion* was taken from Godwin's version of the myth has also been noted by Aileen Ward, *John Keats* (New York, 1963), 429. Godwin is known from his journal to have read *Endymion* on 13 and 14 March 1818, a day or so after Keats finished fair-copying the manuscript, and it seems likely that Godwin was asked to read it by the publisher John Taylor whom he was seeing frequently at this time. Other connections between Keats and Godwin are noted in *The Godwins and the Shelleys*.

4. Quoted in Denis Florence MacCarthy, *Shelley's Early Life* (London, 1872), 161, from a document TS11/951/3494 in the Public Record Office.

5. Notably *Stories of Old Daniel* and *Continuation of Stories of Old Daniel* which were frequently reprinted. Since their attribution to Lady Mountcashel has been questioned (by Eleanor Flexner, *Mary Wollstonecraft* (New York, 1972),

272), it may be worth noting that *The Sisters of Nansfield* (1824), which is undoubtedly by her, is described on the title-page as 'by the author of . . . Old Daniel'. Lady Mountcashel's most interesting work is *Advice to Young Mothers . . . by a Grandmother* (1823) which in some ways can be regarded as the book Mary Wollstonecraft did not live to write.

William Godwin's Books for Children

[William Scolfield], *Bible Stories: Memorable Acts of the Ancient Patriarchs, Judges, and Kings . . . for the use of children*. Printed for Richard Phillips and sold by Benj. Tabart, 2 vols. illustrated (1803).

[Edward Baldwin], *Fables Ancient and Modern, adapted for the use of children*. (Printed for Thomas Hodgkins, 2 vols. 1805).

[Theophilus Marcliffe], *The Looking Glass. A True History of the Early Years of an Artist: Calculated to awaken the emulation of young persons of both sexes in the cultivation of the fine arts* (Thomas Hodgkins, 1805).

[Edward Baldwin], *The Pantheon, History of the Gods of Greece and Rome* (Thomas Hodgkins, 1806).

[Edward Baldwin], *The History of England* (Thomas Hodgkins, 1806).

[Theophilus Marcliffe], *The Life of Lady Jane Grey* (Thomas Hodgkins, 1806).

[Edward Baldwin], *The History of Rome from the Building of the City to the Rise of the Republic* (M. J. Godwin, 1809).

Edward Baldwin, *Mylius's School Dictionary . . . to which is prefixed a New Guide to the English Tongue* by Edward Baldwin (M. J. Godwin, 1809).

[Edward Baldwin], *Outlines of English Grammar* (M. J. Godwin, 1810).

Mrs [Eliza] Fenwick, *Rays of the Rainbow* (M. J. Godwin, 1812). Godwin wrote the preface.

[Edward Baldwin], *Outlines of English History . . . For the Use of Children from Four to Eight Years of Age* (M. J. Godwin, 1814).

[Edward Baldwin], *The History of Greece* (M. J. Godwin, 1822).

The anonymous *Dramas for Children*, which was written by Mary Jane Godwin, is described on the title-page as by the 'editor of Tabart's Popular Stories'. The editors of the Osborne Catalogue, mistakenly attributing the book to William Godwin, have also as a result misattributed the Tabart stories, and their error has been followed by others.

9

Dodgson, Carroll, and the Emancipation of Alice

JOHN BATCHELOR

A CENTRAL truth about Alice was observed in Jonathan Miller's celebrated film of *Alice in Wonderland*, made in the 1960s, and that truth is this: that Alice is a child in a world of mystifying adult behaviour. Miller reinvented Wonderland so that John Gielgud's Mock Turtle, Leo McKern's Duchess, and Michael Redgrave's Caterpillar were 'types' whom the Victorian child might have encountered in Oxford; figures which to an adult audience belonged to a recognizable gallery of English comic eccentrics and which were at the same time mysteries to the child herself. Miller spoilt his film, though, by having Alice played by a large and almost pubescent girl called Anne Marie Mallik: he thus made a point which is also made in Empson's famous essay about the Alice books in *Some Versions of Pastoral*, and which seems to me to be clearly wrong, which is that they are about growing up. Malcolm Muggeridge, who played the Gryphon, emphasized, and praised, what I regard as the worst feature of Miller's interpretation: Miller, he says, sees *Alice* as 'one more sick Victorian cry in the night against the monstrous encroachment of adolescence on the purity and innocence of childhood'.[1] Alice is not pubescent, she is a sharp, intelligent seven-year-old, and *Alice in Wonderland* cannot be turned into a *Bildungsroman* with a female protagonist: it is neither fruitful nor appropriate to compare her with Jane Eyre and Maggie Tulliver and to contrast her with Little Dorrit and Little Nell.[2] 'Does it go too far to connect the mouth that presides over Alice's story to a looking-glass vagina?'[3] Yes, it does, it is a crass and loathsome idea, and the emphasis of discussion, even—as I have said—in great critics like Empson, is far too often on the notion that Alice is growing and becoming sexual. She is *not* 'adolescent'.[4] The Alice books are about learning, not about sexual growth: the person engaged in power-struggles in the two books, and who grows intellectually and socially—very fast—remains a seven-year-old girl. In *Alice in Wonderland* the problem for Alice throughout is 'by what *rules* do these beings live? How is one to engage with them; what is the point of entry into their discourse?' And as this clever child—aged seven in *Alice in Wonderland*, 'seven years and six months' in *Through the Looking-Glass*—seeks to break into the codes used by the representatives of adulthood so she finds that she is engaging in a sequence of power-struggles. The problem is particularly acute in *Alice in Wonderland*. The mechanism of size change fulfils one of the simplest child-fantasies in which one *becomes big enough to get one's own way*. Although she is imprisoned in the White Rabbit's house, gigantic Alice has no difficulty imposing her will over the Rabbit and Bill the Lizard. (The scene is balanced immediately by its obverse, in which tiny Alice beats a retreat from the gigantic puppy.) In *Alice's Adventures Under Ground* the story moved immediately from the end of the Caterpillar chapter to the Queen of Hearts chapter. The Queen is the most powerful member of the cast and the one who, though a playing-card, most closely approximates to the human (the 'real' humans, the Duchess, the Cook, and the Hatter, were added later to *Alice in Wonderland*). She is the immediate rival to Alice and—of course—the victim whose authority is completely routed by Alice's last and most spectacular size-change. The additional episodes written for *Wonderland* change the emphasis, since in the contests with (first) the Frog Footman, the cook, the Duchess, and the Pig baby (and the friendly but competitive relationship with the Cheshire Cat) and (second) the Mad Hatter, the March Hare, and the Dormouse, the ability to change size is an inappropriate weapon. Instead, Alice needs skills: social training (including upper-class social aggression and self-control), verbal and reasoning skills, memory, agility, stamina. She will need these things more urgently in her contests with the Red Queen, Tweedledum and Tweedledee, and (especially) Humpty-Dumpty in *Through the Looking-Glass*; and then, strangely, in her scenes with the White

Alice in the White Rabbit's house, drawing by Lewis Carroll for *Alice's Adventures Underground*.

Alice in the White Rabbit's house, drawing by Tenniel.

Knight, she does not need them at all. The competitive mode in which a child engages in a power-struggle with an adult figure in order to grasp that adult's code is replaced by a perfect affinity between the two figures, the child and the eccentric man, an affinity which a proleptic paragraph insists upon as the keystone of the work:

Of all the strange things that Alice saw in her journey Through the Looking-Glass, this was the one that she always remembered most clearly. Years afterwards she could bring the whole scene back again, as if it had been only yesterday—the mild blue eyes and kindly smile of the Knight—the setting sun gleaming through his hair, and shining on his armour in a blaze of light that quite dazzled her—the horse quietly moving about, with the reins hanging loose on his neck, cropping the grass at her feet—and the black shadows of the forest behind—all this she took in like a picture, as, with one hand shading her eyes, she leant against a tree, watching the strange pair, and listening, in a half-dream, to the melancholy music of the song.

One might think that the power-struggles are over and that Alice is undergoing precocious initiation into adult self-possession. But of course this is not so: Queen Alice will close the text by behaving with spectacular nursery naughtiness: 'she jumped up and seized the tablecloth with both hands: one good pull, and plates, dishes, guests, and candles came crashing down together in a heap on the floor.'

The Alice of *Wonderland* is sharp, pert, snobbish, and unlikely to pull her punches; the giantess who pushes the rabbit into the cucumber frame, kicks Bill up the chimney, and threatens to set Dinah on the assembled animals and birds has a small child's willingness to go to any lengths to get her own way. Piaget tells us that seven is the age of the dawning of moral perception and the story observes this exactly: the violent child who prevails by force shades into the social child who senses that from the Caterpillar, if she can put up with him for long enough, she will learn something that she badly needs to know (that is, how to control her growth). Before she gains that skill the Caterpillar puts her through the discipline of social self-control:

'What size do you want to be?' it asked.

'Oh, I'm not particular as to size,' Alice hastily replied; 'only one doesn't like changing so often, you know.'

'I *don't* know,' said the Caterpillar.

Alice said nothing: she had never been so much contradicted in all her life before [all seven years of it; and it is impressive in a child of this age that she should know what 'contradict' means], and she felt that she was losing her temper.

And of course by exercising self-restraint she earns her reward, tossed though it is over the Caterpillar's shoulder: 'One side will make you grow taller, and the other side will make you grow shorter.' In the final version of the story these crucial pieces of information are given in the form of a riddle from the Delphic oracle: Alice *thinks* to herself, 'One side of *what*? The other side of *what*?' And the Caterpillar replies 'Of the mushroom,' as though it had *heard* her thoughts. This weird little feature of the scene—the Caterpillar hearing Alice's unspoken question—is present in *Under Ground*, but there the riddle was less obscure: the Caterpillar says 'The top will make you grow taller, and the stalk will make you grow shorter.' The two remedies are thus clearly distinguished, and the reference to the stalk would enable Alice to work out what the Caterpillar is referring to by a process of elimination. It has been said that 'although her size changes seem arbitrary and terrifying, she in fact directs them'.[5] But in the early episodes she doesn't 'direct' them. She learns empirically that eating, drinking, and using the White Rabbit's fan cause them. But this weapon is, precisely, *un*directed (like a rogue missile) until she learns from the Caterpillar how to control her size by monitoring her intake of magic mushroom.

My word 'pert' above is taken from Empson. With his perfect nose for gentlemanly behaviour Empson compares the child with the aristocrat:

The aristocrat is essentially like the child because it is his business to make claims in advance of his immediate personal merits; the best he can do, if actually asked for his credentials, since it would be indecent to produce his pedigree, is to display charm and hope it will appear unconscious, like the good young girl.[6]

Social Alice (as against Alice the giantess) wins her victories partly because of her natural prominence in any group: social prominence as the daughter of the Dean of Christ Church, a natural aristocrat in Victorian Oxford, and biological conspicuousness as a small girl child in a society composed overwhelmingly of adult males. Mabel, who lives in a poky little house (probably in that unwelcome suburban development known as North Oxford—Hopkins's 'base and brickish skirt'—which would have been distinctly poky by contrast with the Deanery) with virtually no toys, was Alice's *cousin* (Florence) in *Alice's Adventures Under Ground*, and that fact answers Empson's surprise that Alice is allowed to know Mabel at all. Natural prominence brings responsibilities: 'Who is to give the prizes?' produces a reply from the Dodo which feels inevitable (and prompts no surprise or comment in Alice herself): 'Why, *she*, of course.'

I take it that Alice is the focus of interest and that the reader shares her perspective.[7] In *Alice in Wonderland* the learning process is Wordsworthian (the Wordsworth of 'Expostulation and Reply') in being anti-bookish (she is attracted by pictures and conversations but bored by unadorned prose text). Alice is obviously clever, quick at her lessons, eager for opportunities of showing off her knowledge and contemptuous of poor Mabel who has ever so many lessons to learn. The book mocks bookish pedagogy: Miss Prickett, the Liddells' governess, appears as the mouse quoting a history book which the Liddell girls were required to read, and the school curriculum is laboriously parodied by the Gryphon and the Mock-Turtle. In *Through the Looking-Glass* bookishness has higher standing: our interest is caught by the need to decode 'Jabberwocky' and we attend closely to Humpty Dumpty as he construes it. But Humpty Dumpty is hopelessly innumerate (he behaves like a child much smaller than Alice when confronted with arithmetic). He is an arts man as a scientist might perceive him: conceited, dangerously thin-shelled, precariously elevated, inordinately proud of his power over words: 'when *I* use a word [. . .] it means just what I choose it to mean—neither more nor less.' Alice speaks of

'Jabberwocky' in the numbly inane style in which a nicely brought up girl tries to hold her own in conversation with a don:

'It seems very pretty,' she said when she had finished it, 'but it's *rather* hard to understand!' (You see she didn't like to confess, even to herself, that she couldn't make it out at all.) 'Somehow it seems to fill my head with ideas—only I don't exactly know what they are! However, *somebody* killed *something*: that's clear, at any rate—'

'Pretty' is overworked: having insulted Humpty by calling him an egg she says 'some eggs are very pretty,' and gets smartly rebuked: 'Some people [...] have no more sense than a baby!' Alice deserves at least some of Humpty-Dumpty's scorn; yet she *is* a baby, of course, and her remarks about 'Jabberwocky' are not bad for a child of seven and a half. First-year undergraduates respond in a similar way to *Beowulf* (the first verse of 'Jabberwocky' was originally written in cod Gothic lettering as a 'Stanza of Anglo-Saxon Poetry', in *Misch-Masch*, the family magazine created by the young Dodgson to amuse his many siblings). The scene with Humpty-Dumpty has the same kind of centrality in *Through the Looking-Glass* as does the scene with the Caterpillar in *Alice in Wonderland*. The Caterpillar is equally rude and equally a teacher, but the lesson he teaches Alice is one of immediate practical value and he is not bookish at all: his subject is magic botany.

To take *Alice in Wonderland* on its own: it is not an examination of Jungian archetypes, nightmares, and the Victorian consciousness, nor is it a Modernist work comparable with Conrad and Joyce: Carroll is not about to write *Heart of Darkness*.[8] Proponents of the notion that *Alice in Wonderland* is dark and portentous emphasize the fact that its initial title was *Alice's Adventures Under Ground*, but the change of title can be used to support the opposite view: the subterranean has been replaced by the 'other', 'Wonderland' is not beneath our feet but is an alternative world. The more one contemplates its frame (the dream convention) the more sharply Wonderland insists on its separateness. And the separateness is not only from the frame. The obsessionally tidy bachelor who kept records of every letter he had received and every dinner party he had attended, with his speech impediment (seven of the eleven Dodgson children stammered),[9] his conservatism, his Anglicanism, his celibacy, writes of the Alice books (in the 'Easter Greeting to Every Child who Loves *Alice*') almost as though they are Christian allegories, written 'to add to those stores of innocent and healthy amusement that are laid up in books for the children I love so well'. In the book itself, the frame has the same quality of weirdly irrelevant inert sweetness. The prefatory poem speaks of Alice as 'the dream-child' engaged in 'friendly chat with bird or beast'. When Alice's dream is over her sister has her own dream about 'little Alice and all her wonderful adventures' and then imagines Alice as a grown woman telling the story of Wonderland to her own children: 'She would keep, through all her riper years, the simple and loving heart of her childhood', she will tell 'the dream of Wonderland of long ago' and would share her children's simple joys and sorrows 'remembering her own child-life, and the happy summer days'. If this paragraph were out of context one would assume that its author had not read the events in Wonderland (let alone written them). This radical slicing away of the frame may reflect a pathological split between Dodgson and Carroll—who can tell?—but it certainly has the effect of conferring a vertiginous freedom (a falling-down-the-rabbit-hole sensation) on the reader. Anything can happen here, and there are few appeals from Wonderland to the test of 'reality' in the normative world.

Within this closed system, Alice—Carroll's precisely observed small child—encounters challenges, and to meet them she deploys her considerable resources: intelligence (outstanding), knowledge (good for a seven-year-old), socially interactive skills (excellent), aggression and competitiveness (both well developed). One of the challenges is the question: is everybody here mad? The Cheshire Cat says 'yes' to that:

'But I don't want to go among mad people,' Alice remarked.

'Oh, you can't help that,' said the Cat: 'We're all mad here. I'm mad. You're mad.'

'How do you know I'm mad?' said Alice.

'You must be,' said the Cat, 'or you wouldn't have come here.'

But the Cat's own behaviour seems to negate its proposition. This floating head with the wise smile is a disengaged, ironically observing intelligence, the creature in Wonderland with which (as Empson noted) Alice is most at ease, least prey to passions and thus the *least* 'mad'.

Madness is a matter of unaccountability, mysteries in the speech or behaviour of others: in all our interactions we need to believe that our interlocutor has a motive for what he says or does.[10] The more conspicuous strangenesses in Wonderland are signalled often by the phrase 'out of the way'. Mysteries she encounters trigger Alice's curiosity: she has never before seen a rabbit with a watch and a waistcoat pocket (though to hear it speak English was not 'so *very* much out of the way'). Alice soon learns the rules: out of the wayness covers events as well as behaviour, and the events include falling *slowly* down a rabbit hole lined with books, maps, and pictures (and a pot of marmalade) and finding the glass table, the key, and the door into the garden, and Alice progresses readily and fearlessly to the notion that they might include (as they do) the possibility of shutting up like a telescope. Out of the wayness in *behaviour* dominates the chapters added to the revised version of the story, 'Pig and Pepper' and 'A Mad Tea-Party'. In the parts carried over from *Alice's Adventures Under Ground* there is less madness: cause and effect operate in a largely normative way in the minds of the White Rabbit, who is frightened of the Duchess and of Alice herself, and the mouse and the birds who are frightened of Dinah (the mouse's recitation from a history book is wholly explicable as a laboured pun on 'dry' and is thus not 'mad' in the sense of 'unaccountable'). But when we reach 'Pig and Pepper' rational behaviour is abandoned. Alice asks the Frog-Footman how she is to get in:

'I shall sit here,' the Footman remarked, 'till tomorrow—'

At this moment the door of the house opened, and a large plate came skimming out, straight at the Footman's head: it just grazed his nose, and broke to pieces against one of the trees behind him.

'—or next day, maybe,' the Footman continued in the same tone, exactly as if nothing had happened.

And once she is in the kitchen Alice finds, of course, that unaccountability, hidden motivation, becomes the rule:

The cook took the cauldron of soup off the fire, and at once set to work throwing everything within her reach at the Duchess and the baby—the fire-irons came first; then followed a shower of saucepans, plates, and dishes. The Duchess took no notice of them even when they hit her; and the baby was howling so much already, that it was quite impossible to say whether the blows hurt it or not.

'A Mad Tea-Party' is a more taxing version of the challenge. The unaccountability of the Hatter's and the Hare's behaviour *may* mean that they have access to yet another set of rules that Alice doesn't know and needs to learn. Their 'No room! No room!' is met by Alice's 'There's *plenty* of room!' Alice's indignation is misplaced: given a system in which they are trapped at tea-time for ever it becomes true that all the seats at the table are needed and there *is* 'No room'. On the other hand the riddle about the Raven and the Writing Desk is a different kind of challenge (no answer to it, therefore no hidden rules). The rules Alice brings to bear, since this is a tea-party, are those of social politeness and here the 'mad' figures win on points because she can be shown to break her own rules:

'Nobody asked *your* opinion,' said Alice.
   'Who's making personal remarks now?' the Hatter asked triumphantly.

And the 'mad' have access to information that Alice lacks. The Dormouse tells the story about the treacle well: 'There's no such thing!' retorts Alice. But there is, and Dodgson's young audience would have known it well: it is in Binsey churchyard. The audience must have loved the fact that they were themselves in this nonsense story (Elsie, Lacie, and Tillie are adaptations of the names of Alice and her sisters) and they would have recognized with high intellectual pleasure that the treacle well story has a heartless logic which is 'mad' in the sense that it lacks moral balance but bleakly sane in the sense that it reflects a fact about the known world, namely that there are irreversibly destructive processes at work that we can do nothing about. Alice, 'who always took a great interest in questions of eating and drinking', asks what the sisters live on. 'They lived on treacle' replies the Dormouse:

'They couldn't have done that, you know,' Alice gently remarked. 'They'd have been ill.'

'So they were,' said the Dormouse; '*very* ill.'

In Alice's dialogue with the Gnat in *Through the Looking Glass* there is a similar—bleaker—moment where the rational mind is outraged by the absence of moral balance in a chain of circumstances. The Gnat describes the Bread-and-butterfly, which lives on 'Weak tea with cream in it':

A new difficulty came into Alice's head. 'Supposing it couldn't find any?' she suggested.

'Then it would die, of course.'

'But that must happen very often,' Alice remarked thoughtfully.

'It always happens,' said the Gnat.

After this, Alice was silent for a minute or two, pondering.

The two scenes have the same structure: Alice 'gently' or 'thoughtfully' points out what she takes to be a hopeless flaw in the logic of what she has been told, to learn that there is no flaw and that the sequence really is as intolerably harsh as it appears. The process is educational: the highly intelligent small child is left 'pondering'. We're not told the outcome of her pondering, but her thoughts could go like this: the Bread-and-butterfly must live long enough to reproduce, but that need only be for a few hours. It is therefore a species which spends almost all of its life as a caterpillar. Alice asks *her* Caterpillar whether the changes involved in its existence are not disturbing to it and measures its stout denial against her own feelings: 'All I know is, it would feel very queer to *me*.'

The coherent feature of the Duchess's and the Cook's behaviour is that they both hate the baby (the cook's target, the Duchess's 'Pig'). The split between Dodgson and Carroll is felt again, momentarily, when Alice says, with Dodgson-like sickly sweetness, 'Oh there goes his *precious* nose!' But this turns out to be an adroit piece of comic planning. The nose turns into a snout and Alice closes the baby episode with satisfyingly Carroll-like astringency: 'It would have made a dreadfully ugly child: but it makes rather a handsome pig, I think.' The text wobbles into Dodgson sickliness again in the game of croquet: 'After these came the royal children: there were ten of them, and the little dears came jumping merrily along, hand in hand, in couples: they were all ornamented with hearts.' How many children had Lady Macbeth? Astringency is restored when we learn that when the playing cards lie on their faces the Queen cannot distinguish those to whom she has given suck (or the cardboard equivalent) from 'gardeners, or soldiers, or courtiers', and Alice refuses to identify them. Carroll gleefully observes the behaviour of this domineering woman:

The Queen turned crimson with fury, and, after glaring at her for a moment like a wild beast, began screaming, 'Off with her head! Off with—'
'Nonsense!' said Alice, very loudly and decidedly, and the Queen was silent.

This violent matriarch splits into two: in *Under Ground* the 'Marchioness' and the Queen were the same person, here the Duchess and the Queen are two aspects of an ageing woman with severe personality disorders. This woman can only make power relationships. She seeks to dominate: as Queen, by destroying all opponents, as Duchess, by forcing unwanted affection and instruction on a polite child:

'Tut, tut, child!' said the Duchess. 'Everything's got a moral, if only you can find it.' And she squeezed herself up closer to Alice's side as she spoke.
Alice did not much like her keeping so close to her: first, because the Duchess was *very* ugly: and secondly, because she was exactly the right height to rest her chin on Alice's shoulder, and it was an uncomfortably sharp chin. However, she did not like to be rude: so she bore it as well as she could.

How did this monstrous woman get into Carroll's imagination? Dodgson's feelings for Alice were those of a shy but happy bachelor who delighted in the friendship of an attractive, entertaining, and sharply intelligent little girl. As Humphrey Carpenter indicates, these feelings must have had some sexual component— his interest in all his girl companions faded when they reached puberty, and he experimented with photographing little girls in the nude in 1879–80—but how intense and how conscious that component was it is impossible to say.[11] Mrs Liddell discouraged the relationship and there seems to have been an open breach late in 1863: on 5 December, at the end of his account of some Christ Church undergraduate theatricals Dodgson wrote in his diary 'Mrs Liddell and the children were there—but I held aloof from them as I have done all this term.'[12] Mrs Liddell was powerful; the undergraduate joke about her and her husband reflected a perceptible truth:

> *I am the Dean and this is Mrs Liddell:*
> *She plays the first, and I the second fiddle.*[13]

Dodgson was no match for the Dean's lady in the struggle for Alice, but Carroll, I believe, both takes his revenge and covertly urges his beloved to rebel, to disentangle herself from the Duchess's stifling embrace and to say to the Queen 'Who cares for *you?*'

Another of Alice's challenges is the one I have touched on: the series of power-struggles with rude creatures who seek to dominate her socially. I take the scene with the Caterpillar to be central, the pivotal challenge. The Caterpillar can more than match Alice's social aggression—it is just as upper-class as she is and is capable of being as ruthlessly rude as she is:

The Caterpillar took the hookah out of its mouth, and addressed her in a languid, sleepy voice.
  'Who are *You?*' said the Caterpillar.

Or: 'I am a poised, bored aristocrat taking my pleasure and you are an intruder of—I take it—lower social status.' The Caterpillar is partly a don—in Miller's film it was wholly a don, played by

Michael Redgrave in a cluttered, booklined, Victorian room, so particularized that one could almost smell it. The interpretation was wonderfully apt except that, as I have said, the Caterpillar seems to me not to be an Arts man. It could also be partly based on an undergraduate: it has some experience of small children, and it might be a 'languid' (Carroll's word) Old Etonian at Christ Church, a young dandy who has recently left school and is accustomed to bullying little boys. The insolence is reminiscent of Steerforth and Flashman:

'Come back!' the Caterpillar called after her. 'I've something important to say!'
This sounded promising, certainly. Alice turned and came back again.
'Keep your temper,' said the Caterpillar.
'Is that all?' said Alice, swallowing down her anger as well as she could.
'No,' said the Caterpillar.

Alice is personally angered, and she swallows it down as well as she can, but she is also intellectually enraged—it is in part intellectual rage that saves her, she waits because 'after all it might tell her something worth hearing'. The Caterpillar resorts to a standard technique of the bully, it forces her to recite (rather as Kipling's bullies in *Stalky and Co.* force Clewer to sing). Alice takes a kind of revenge because she knows about the biological changes which will overtake the Caterpillar, and she succeeds unintentionally in insulting the creature, thus correcting the power balance so that she and it are even: 'Three inches is such a wretched height to be.' Yet the Caterpillar is, in the end, both learned and benevolent as well as crusty—a rounded portrait of a don—and Alice has made a most significant gain in her learning process: patience and the right questions can get results from the most inscrutable and unpromising adults.

Alice has a developed sense of order, and throughout *Alice in Wonderland* she seeks to impose 'order' as she understands it on the Wonderland events which have, in most cases, their own inner coherence which exists in vigorous independence of the laws of the real world. There is no suggestion of a Christian code at work in the story, in either a direct or an inverted sense. Humphrey Carpenter writes about this matter—very well—but in the end I cannot agree with his view of the split between Carroll and Dodgson, which is that the seemingly conventional Dodgson's religious beliefs were 'utterly insecure' and that Carroll has written a specifically anti-Christian book which (for example) subverts the Eucharist in the instructions 'DRINK ME' and 'EAT ME', and which is structured as a 'parody of religion'.[14] As far as references to religion are concerned there are, I think, no connections between Wonderland and the real world, between Carroll and Dodgson. With Law it is a different matter. Wonderland Law appears both in the mouse's tale and in the trial of the Knave of Hearts. In its manuscript version the mouse's tale has to do with the dangers to mice of being crushed 'underneath the mat' by a cat and a dog and there is no reference to the Law, but in its final state the verse gleefully displays a monstrous legal system, '"I'll be judge, I'll be jury," Said cunning old Fury; "I'll try the whole cause, and condemn you to death".' Alice doesn't attend to the mouse's tale, but her references to Dinah in the chapter establish a link between Wonderland Law in the mouse's tale and the law of nature in the real world (cats are violent predators) and points up the fact that Alice enthusiastically upholds the latter law: 'I wish you could see her after the birds! Why, she'll eat a little bird as soon as look at it!' The sickness of the sisters who live on treacle and the death of the Bread-and-butterfly reflect the ruthlessness of nature's law (Tennyson's 'nature red in tooth and claw') and so do the many death jokes in the story, but their use is not always consistent. The death jokes sometimes signal the *contrast* between Wonderland and reality. Alice reflects how brave she will be after falling down the rabbit hole: ' "Why, I wouldn't say anything about it, even if I fell off the top of the house!" (which was very likely true)' (she ignores, of course, the fact that normative gravity is not operating in the rabbit hole). The Queen of Hearts may be taken as having framed the legislation reflected in the mouse's tale; all opposition is to be countered by the death sentence, the Knave finds himself caught in a Kafka-like inversion of due process, sentence first and verdict afterwards.[15] Even the

King of Hearts, that cardboard titular head of the legislature, participates in the system's ruthlessness, threatening the Hatter with execution on the spot for being nervous. Throughout, as I have said, Alice has been in touch with the law of nature. She is applying one item from it, somewhat transposed, when she hurries to put the jurymen back in their box because they remind her of the gold-fish she had accidentally upset a week before. I take it that this transposition is characteristic of the dream state, and that when she begins to grow spontaneously in the court she is also beginning to wake up, and her grasp of the laws of the normative world becomes stronger: if 'Rule Forty-two' were the oldest rule in the book then it ought to be Number One, and it's natural for her, as she says to the Dormouse, to be growing. In the real world nature's law is amoral and man's law is moral: when Alice grows to full height she combines the two and is therefore irresistible. She can dominate the Queen both by virtue of being a giantess and because she can see that the Queen's behaviour violates all normative human moral (and, therefore, legal) systems:

'No, no!' said the Queen. 'Sentence first—verdict afterwards.'

'Stuff and nonsense!' said Alice loudly. 'The idea of having the sentence first!'

'Hold your tongue!' said the Queen, turning purple.

'I won't!' said Alice.

'Off with her head!' the Queen shouted at the top of her voice. Nobody moved.

'Who cares for *you?*' said Alice (she had grown to her full size by this time). 'You're nothing but a pack of cards!'

Carroll's heroine defeats the violent matriarch; Dodgson's beloved rebels against Mrs Liddell. One of the drives behind the Alice books has thus fulfilled itself, and I think this is why Alice in *Through the Looking-Glass* is a different kind of heroine, gentler and less subversive than in the previous story. Wonderland Alice herself recites the poems which mock or invert stock Victorian nursery reading, while Looking-Glass Alice has poetry recited at her and is a good deal less aggressive in her contests with the creatures she encounters. I have said that Wonderland is sharply severed from its frame. The frame tells us that Wonderland is a dream, and the story does indeed have the random particularity and wholly confident registration of unrelated material that is characteristic of dreams. The narrative voice signals the altered rules of the dream state by such phrases as 'out of the way' and by the rather more elaborate commentary that accompanies the upsetting of the jurymen ('She had a vague sort of idea that they must be collected at once and put back into the jury-box, or they would die'). But it also has a dramatic structure, of a grand and simple kind, in which Alice moves through this alternative creation engaging in conflict with animals and humans—though not in a neatly ascending order of species (the mouse and the rabbit precede the frog)—until she defeats the Queen of Hearts and the story is over. *Through the Looking-Glass* has a much more elaborate structure in that it combines the game of chess with Alice's progress towards royal estate, and it has a sophisticated relationship with its frame. The story is Alice's dream, from which she awakes to find that the Red Queen is a kitten, but Alice herself may be part of the Red King's dream:

'It's no use *your* talking about waking him,' said Tweedledum, 'when you're only one of the things in his dream. You know very well you're not real.'

'I *am* real!' said Alice, and began to cry.

'You won't make yourself a bit realler by crying,' Tweedledum remarked.

The Caterpillar's rude question, 'Who are *You?*' takes on an urgent force in this story: the Alice dramatized here has less ego-strength, less identity, than in Wonderland, and the episodes reflect and amplify this—she is unable to recall her own name in the wood where things have no names, she is regarded as a creature of myth by the Unicorn ('I always thought they [children] were fabulous monsters!' said the Unicorn. 'Is it alive?'). And she is rather easily ordered about—by the Red Queen, by the sheep, and by Humpty Dumpty. She is protective and gentle towards the White Queen and drops her pert child's subversiveness entirely in her relationship with the White Knight, though she rebels with welcome energy and force when she pulls the tablecloth from the table at the end of her own dinner party. But while Dodgson sweetness makes inroads into the story, Carroll acerbity energizes parts of the frame. One of Alice's games in the real world has to do with eating her nurse: 'Nurse! Do let's pretend that I'm a hungry hyaena, and you're a bone!' *Through the Looking-Glass* yields its own high delight but the dramatic energy at the core of Wonderland has been replaced by intellectual pleasure, as though Carroll had transformed himself into the Cheshire Cat.

Notes

1. Malcolm Muggeridge, 'Alice, Where Art Thou?', *New Statesman*, (23 Dec. 1966), 933.
2. These comparisons and contrasts are made by Nina Auerbach in 'Alice and Wonderland: A Curious Child', *Victorian Studies*, 17 (Sept. 1973), 45–7.
3. Auerbach, 'Alice', 39.
4. James R. Kincaid, 'Alice's Invasion of Wonderland', *PMLA*, 88/1 (Jan. 1973), 93. The worst treatment of Alice as an adolescent is in Mervyn Peake's illustrations to the 1946 edition, where Alice looks like a cockney nymphette.
5. Auerbach, 'Alice', 35.
6. William Empson, *Some Versions of Pastoral* (London, 1968 [1935]), 283–4.
7. This is challenged by Kincaid, 'Alice's Invasion', but supported by Empson and by most other critics of the story.
8. These approaches are expressed in Judith Bloomingdale, 'Alice as Anima: The Image of Woman in Carroll's Classics', *Aspects of Alice*, ed. Robert Phillips (London, 1972), 378–90, and in two articles by David Rackin, 'Alice's Journey to the End of Night', *Aspects of Alice*, 391–416 and 'Blessed Rage: Lewis Carroll and the Modern Quest for Order', *Lewis Carroll: A Celebration*, ed. Edward Guiliano (New York, 1982), 15–25.
9. It is said that Dodgson did not stammer when he was with children. Six of his sisters stammered to different degrees; a letter survives in which Dodgson sought treatment for them, and for himself. See Joseph Sigman and Richard Slobodin, 'Stammering in the Dodgson Family: An Unpublished Letter by "Lewis Carroll"', *The Victorian Newsletter*, 49 (Spring, 1976), 26–7.
10. I take this definition from Neilson Graham, 'Sanity, Madness and Alice', *Ariel*, 4/1 (Jan. 1973), 80–9.

11. Humphrey Carpenter, 'Alice and the Mockery of God', *Secret Gardens* (London, 1985), 54–5.
12. R. L. Green, ed., *The Diaries of Lewis Carroll*, i (London, 1953), 208.
13. Ibid. 169.
14. Humphrey Carpenter, 'Alice and the Mockery of God', 64, 65.
15. A. D. Nuttall has pointed out to me that much of Kafka's *The Trial* resembles Wonderland Law and that the assessors in *The Castle*, both of whom are called 'Arthur', closely resemble Tweedledum and Tweedledee.

10

Arthur Hughes as Illustrator for Children

KATE FLINT

ARTHUR HUGHES'S fondness for children, and sympathy with their imagination, is unmistakable. He entered readily into their games—Greville MacDonald believed that he could remember the artist playing the Mother Bear in his family's re-enactment of *The Three Bears*[1] and, like Charles Dodgson and Burne-Jones, he corresponded with them in nonsense rhymes.[2] Throughout his life, children figure in his paintings: griefstricken by their mother's grave in *Home from Sea* (1856–62); happily crowding together in a group portrait of the musical Leathart family in *A Christmas Carol at Bracken Dene* (1879). They are placed in sentimentally affecting situations, sometimes in contemporary settings, as with the sleepy little girl swept into her thankful father's arms in *L'enfant perdu* (1867), sometimes employing a stylized medievalism, as with the two companion pieces *The Rescue* (1890–5), the first showing a curly-haired small boy in the fat coils of a snake, the second depicting him sitting safely before an armoured knight on horseback. Hughes's affinity with children as a subject for portraiture was doubtless accentuated by his sense of the transience of this period of their lives: he wrote to Frederick Stephens in the early 1870s asking if he might paint Stephens's son Holly, for 'Time wont spare the picturesqueness of childhood for very much longer'.[3]

It is not, however, Hughes's career as a painter of children, but as an illustrator for them with which this essay is concerned. Nearly six hundred of his wood engravings and line drawings appear in publications intended for them. From the first of these, George MacDonald's *Dealings with the Fairies* (1867), to the last, by MacDonald's son Greville, *Trystie's Quest or Kit King of the Pigwidgeons* (1913), Hughes was connected with the MacDonald family, to whom he had been introduced by the sculptor Alexander Munro in about 1859, when he was twenty-seven. He had already made a beginning as an illustrator, following his training in the Royal Academy Schools: William Allingham's *The Music Master* (1855) contains six rather weak drawings by him. The best of these, 'Under the Abbey-Wall' and 'The Boy's Grave' hint at his later aptitude for melancholy, but they have none of the technical ability of Millais's 'The Fireside Story' or Rossetti's 'The Maids of Elfen-Mere' in the same volume. Hughes's proximity here with Millais and Rossetti reminds one of his closeness to the Pre-Raphaelites: he was one of the contributors to the Oxford Union fresco project, in sympathy with their ideals, on the one hand an accurate observer of natural effects and on the other demonstrating an enthusiasm for medieval subjects. As William Michael Rossetti wrote in *Some Reminiscences* (1906): 'his style conformed pretty faithfully (not servilely) to theirs; if the organization had been kept up a little longer, and if new members had ever been admitted ... Mr Hughes would doubtless have been invited to join.'[4] In the event, he was most closely linked to the group at a personal level through the Allingham volume, and through his illustrations for Christina Rossetti's *Sing-Song: A Nursery Rhyme Book* (1872) and her Christmas book of linked stories, *Speaking Likenesses* (1874).

Dealings with the Fairies—a collection of fairy tales by Mac-Donald—gives the first indication of Hughes's strengths. In Greville MacDonald's introduction to a reprint of this work, he observed that his father understood that 'The imagination of the child shows itself chiefly in the recognition of the wonders that lie behind phenomena',[5] and it is in giving form to these wonders, sometimes shadowy, sometimes grotesquely clear, that Hughes's illustrations add to, rather than merely accompany, the stories. Throughout his career, he felt free to amend the specific visual instructions that a written text might give. We see this in relation to his painting: he wrote to F. G. Stephens on 1 June 1899, of *Endymion* '. . . *it is from Keats*; that is it does not illustrate any actual scene, but grew out of it somehow';[6] similarly, *The King's Orchard* (1859) is based on some lines from *Pippa Passes*, but has nothing to do with the plot of the poem. In the case of MacDonald's stories, the writer gives a very clear description of 'The Shadows', the creatures who haunt the room of Ralph Rinkelmann, a writer who has been elected mortal king of the fairies, in the short story which bears their name:

> ... tall and solemn; rather awful, indeed, in their appearance, notwithstanding many remarkable traits of grotesqueness, for they looked just like the pictures of Puritans drawn by Cavaliers, with long arms, and very long, thin legs, from which hung large, loose feet.[7]

But Hughes's illustration, on p. 187, ignores these suggestions of ugly, dangling puppets, and substitutes a far more genuinely shadowy indistinctness, showing massed figures pressing down a mountainside, the space occupied by their bodies indicated through blotchy cross-hatching, but with no definite and bounding line delineating precisely where they stop and air begins. This method of indicating the supernatural was, as we shall see, to become a favourite technique of Hughes's: indeed, the whole volume represents a testing ground for graphic ideas. Whilst the medieval fair background in the first illustration to 'Cross Purposes' (p. 271) is weakly drawn—Hughes was never happy with crowded genre scenes nor with architectural details—the foreground shows a magical metamorphosis rendered the stranger through being treated in an utterly matter of fact way. Richard, the youthful hero, is trying to buy an umbrella, and Hughes depicts how the umbrellas on sale revealed themselves to have the legs of geese, getting up and waddling, fast, out of the drawing. The engravings for a revolting story, 'The Giant's Heart', about a bulbous giant who kept children to fatten them up, emphasize his bloated contours not just by juxtaposing his head with a vast cauldron, but by having him, and his wife, bulging up against the sides of the picture space. The depiction of this giantess, indeed, was enough to stick in the mind of the young Annabel Huth Jackson, who—in one of the rare contemporary accounts of how children were affected by Hughes's work—describes how this giantess resembled one of her parents' friends, Lady Mallet, 'and I always believed that she was quite up to eating small children. I never much liked being alone with her.'[8]

Illustrations to books by George MacDonald: (*left*) the Shadows, from *Dealings with the Fairies*, 1867; (*right*) the North Wind, from *At the Back of the North Wind*, 1871.

Another writer who looked back to the impact Hughes's illustrations had on him as a child was the influential art critic D. S. MacColl. Reviewing *Babies' Classics* in 1904—a volume of poems for children chosen by Lilian Scott MacDonald and illustrated by Hughes—MacColl was moved by its appearance to wonder:

How many readers of the *Saturday Review* remember the first appearance, when they were children, of 'Good Words for the Young', and the illustrations in it by Arthur Hughes to Henry Kingsley's 'Boy in Grey' and George MacDonald's 'At the Back of the North Wind'. The present reviewer, at least, has very tender memories of that appearance [he would have been a boy in Glasgow at the time], and of the first wave of Preraphaelite romance that came with the dark coils of the North Wind's hair and the strangeness of that world of imagery.[9]

MacDonald's story ran in *Good Words for the Young* from November 1868 to April 1869, and was continued from June to September of the same year, and then from November 1869 to October 1870. The magazine, started by the Scottish evangelical and populist publisher, Alexander Strahan, aimed to provide 'wholesome' reading material for children. Norman Macleod was its nominal editor for a year, before MacDonald took over in November 1869 at a salary of £600, a post which he gave up at the end of two further unsalaried years in 1871 and 72.[10] Whatever his personal frustrations with the post, MacDonald's connection with the magazine enabled him to provide a considerable amount of work for his friend Hughes: thirty-eight illustrations in 1868–9 (for Henry Kingsley's *The Boy in Grey* as well as the four plates which accompanied each instalment of *At the Back of the North Wind*), ninety in 1869–70, forty-six in 1870–1, and thirty-three in 1871–2. All the numbers were well illustrated: other artists who worked for the publication included Arthur Houghton, Thomas Dalziel, J. B. Zwecker, F. A. Fraser and, producing some interesting examples of social realism, Hubert Herkomer. Whilst much of this work was technically highly proficient, at their best Hughes's designs stand out for their daringness in composition, their fascination with the supernatural, and their ability to suggest mysterious tricks of light and celestial movement.

The illustrations to *At the Back of the North Wind* have received the greatest praise of all Hughes's graphic work. Laurence Housman, writing of 'The Illustrations of Arthur Hughes' in *The Bibliophile* (July 1908) emphasizes their reliance on the artist's ability to enter into a child's imagination, breaking down the weak 'barriers dividing vision from sight ... so that you may follow with a certain conviction those strange "night-gown adventures" when the child's body and soul walk in its sleep.'[11] Thus the North Wind, half madonna, half angel, appears to Diamond first not in distinct outline, but as a face and a stream of shimmering matter—so that, as MacDonald put it, 'the darkness in the hayloft looked as if it were made of her hair'.[12] Some of the most powerful of the drawings do not show her presence at all, but indicate Diamond's susceptibility to profound darkness in a church at night (pp. 82 and 85) or lying in the densely leafy branches of a beech-tree, illuminated only by moonlight. Forrest Reid, in *Illustrators of the Sixties* (1928)—the most comprehensive study of the group of artists working with wood engravers to which Hughes belongs—similarly writes of the high degree of subjectivity in Hughes's illustrations to this story, and of his capacity both to avoid MacDonald's moralizing, and to have conceived these drawings

in a mysterious world, out of space, out of time—a world to which the artist *goes back*, so that he is not in the ordinary sense drawing for other children at all, but drawing for himself. It is true that the past to which he returns is one in which everything is created anew after the dreamer's desire ...[13]

As Reid goes on to say, that particular dreamer, Diamond, loves all that is sweet, gentle, and innocent, and the drawings reflect this informing sentiment. But, whilst he remarks on the child's 'half angelic sexlessness', he, like Housman before him, ignores the considerable eroticism in the portrayal of North Wind herself. Her elongated figure and extraordinarily thick mane of hair blend elements of Botticelli's Venus and such Rossetti portraits as *Monna Vanna* (1866). On the one hand, North Wind is maternal, protective: her voice 'more like his mother's voice than anything else in the world', MacDonald tells us (p. 67). She cradles Diamond in her capacious arms, a strong goddess to the diminutive child, highly similar in her pose to Blake's depiction of 'Pity, like a naked new-born babe|Striding the blast'. Yet, just after the words in which MacDonald describes her motherly tones, he has her exhorting Diamond, ' ". . . be a man. What is fearful to you is not the least fearful to me." ' The accompanying illustration (p. 67) has her gently coaxing Diamond through a narrow hole in the roof, into a world where 'his legs threatened to float from under him, and his head to grow dizzy' (p. 66). Whilst this magical sensation of strangeness is left in vague, abstract language in MacDonald's text, Hughes's illustrations, with North Wind's hair suggestively billowing round the actual contours of her body, her physical plenitude threatening to break out of the bounds of the picture's frame, suggests an overwhelming womanly presence which reaches far beyond the realm of the maternal, offering an as yet dimly understood sensual world developing in the imagination of the young boy.

As Housman and Reid both noted, Hughes was not at his best when drawing everyday life: the scenes of Diamond at home are remarkably wooden, and Hughes is manifestly happier drawing horses rather than humans. These preferences are borne out by the remainder of his designs for *Good Words for the Young*. There is little of the directly magical in Henry Kingsley's *The Boy in Grey* (March–May 1869)—a tale which, taking its boy hero on a tour of English dominions, is highly critical of the spirit of Empire. Hughes fails to take up some of the challenges directly posed by the text. For example, on the Boy's arrival in Canada, a land populated by all sorts of characters from English literature, from Mrs Gamp to Robinson Crusoe, Aunt Pullet to the faithful Dobbin, we are told that another personage, the Queen of Hearts, looked 'more cross than ever Tenniel made her look'—but Hughes, rather than responding to this, constructs his most inventive designs around wildlife, as when showing some of the 2,469 monkeys which the Boy encounters on his Asian trip intertwining with each other in the tree branches. MacDonald's *Gutta-Percha Willie* (1872) similarly offered few possibilities for the mysterious. Although MacDonald is at times preoccupied in the text with describing effects of light, from calm moonbeams, to stars flashing and trembling through the falling dew, to the Aurora Borealis, with all the colours of a faint rainbow, the only drawing of Hughes's which approximates to these hints is one of Willie, in his nightshirt, talking to his father with the moonlit Gothic ruins of the Priory in the background (p. 288).

In Hughes's first illustration to *Ranald Bannerman's Boyhood* (November 1869–October 1870) there is a rare example of text and artist acting in liaison. Bannerman tells of a dream he used to have when a boy, of the room in which he slept: a dream in which the ceiling turned into the sky, with moon, sun, and stars:

The sun was not a scientific sun at all, but one such as you see in penny picture-books—a round, jolly, jocund man's face, with flashes of yellow frilling it all about, just what a grand sunflower would look like if you set a countenance where the black seeds are. And the moon was just such a one as you may see the cow jumping over in the pictured nursery rhyme. She was a crescent, of course, that she might have a face drawn in the hollow, and turned towards the sun, who seemed to be her husband.[14]

Hughes obligingly replicates this celestial domesticity, the ladder of sun rays which he shows penetrating the roof of the boy's bedroom allowing him to exploit his interest in unusual lighting effects. The remainder of the engravings for this story are unexceptional—he was constrained to produce many homely vignettes of Scottish village life. Only its incidentally related folklore provided an opportunity for him to illustrate the mysterious. The beautiful sea maiden tenderly carried along the shore by a Prince—an illustration to a ballad sung by a peasant woman (opposite p. 279)—reiterates Hughes's association of abundant hair with sexuality, yet on the other hand, his inability to portray horror directly is well shown in the figure of the Kelpie, hungry to eat the shepherd's beautiful daughter, yet with an expression far too frisky and playful to be frightening. More inventive are the illustrations to *The Princess and the Goblin* (November 1870–June 1871). None the less, Hughes was again poor at rising

From *Ranald Bannerman's Boyhood*, 1871, by George MacDonald.

to MacDonald's direct invocation of the horrible. The goblins, we are told, were

not ordinarily ugly, but either absolutely hideous, or ludicrously grotesque both in face and form. There was no invention, they said, of the most lawless imagination expressed by pen or pencil, that could surpass the extravagance of their appearance.[15]

Later, we learn that the household animals owned by the goblins 'were of one sort—creatures—but so grotesque and mis-shapen as to be more like a child's drawings upon his slate than anything natural'.[16] But Hughes's depictions of the goblins' features are successful only where they can barely be discerned—as in the faces which dimly leer out of the dark trees in the illustration that shows the Princess's walk with her nurse in Chapter VI, or the black, squat shapes which are later seen silhouetted against the moonlight (p. 88). The most powerful of all the illustrations to this story is again one with no direct supernatural content at all: it shows Irene, the Princess, peering up a huge staircase drowned in mysterious silver moonlight, shining down from above with a power which emphasizes the solitary and strange nature of the girl's explorations.

The moon is the subject, too, of one of Hughes's best single engravings for *Good Words for the Young*, accompanying MacDonald's poem 'The Wind and the Moon' (vol. 4, p. 80). The wind's violent energy is personified in the curved body of the boy who tries to blow out the bright light of the moon, wisps of cloud blowing gently across his legs in a way which conceals Hughes's deficiencies in anatomical accuracy. Among his other drawings, a sense of humour is revealed in the illustrations to Matthew Browne's verse saga, *Innocent's Island* (1872), where the Traveller, a scatty scientist, is seen first in company with his Gladstone bag festooned with luggage labels—'Capricorn', 'North Pole', then being hoisted onto a rocking horse, with much energetic flailing of legs in the air, then discovered inside a cupboard, 'In his usual cap of fur,|With a pot of blackberry jam' (pp. 121, 185, and 257). None the less, his eccentricity looks tame beside that of Carroll's White Knight who, drawn by Tenniel, had appeared the previous year, and Hughes is happier when dealing with more serious matters. Three further illustrations stand out, each of them interpretations, rather than representations, of the verbal matter they accompany. The head-piece to Browne's 'A Lilliput Lecture on Science and Philosophy' is an allegorical reworking of the article's implicit message: that knowledge and wisdom will banish darkness and superstition. Hughes shows a triumphant woman with oil lamp and shining sword crushing a snake underfoot and simultaneously dispatching a plunging monster—a cross between a pig and a horse—together with a giant bat and something too dark and horrible to be made out clearly: behind her, with a tinge of the sentiment which was to cloud much of Hughes's later illustrative work, stand a thankful boy and girl ankle-deep in a field of daisies (vol. 3, December 1870, p. 72). The two illustrations to *King Arthur's Great Boar Hunt* (anonymous: vol. 3, March and April 1871, pp. 249 and 329) are more frightening. In the first, a handsome young knight displays himself—again through unsheathing a huge sword—before an ancient, long-bearded king and his beautiful, long-haired daughter, this gesture of power being underscored by a detail which appears nowhere in the text: he is standing on a large heap of untidy, grimacing severed heads. In the second, a dense, detailed drawing, a powerful boar bristles over the body of a dead knight: the medieval trapping of the knight, blowing on a curved horn and splashing his palfrey through the edge of the sea does nothing to relieve this powerful sense of natural menace.

Despite Hughes's strength in depicting the strange and supernatural, it would nevertheless be wrong to dismiss him entirely as an artist of the everyday. The illustrations to the sixth edition of Thomas Hughes's *Tom Brown's Schooldays* (1869)[17] are awkward in some of their figure drawing: Hughes was always most easy in depicting young children, as in the plate showing Tom playing happily in the 'great muck reservoir in the middle of the yard, disturbing the repose of the great pigs'. It was these early drawings in the volume which John Betjeman praised for their recognizable portrayals of Uffington, in Berkshire: its parish church, school, and brook:[18] certainly, the first plate, a vertiginous view of the White Horse Hill on the Berkshire Downs, indicates Hughes's largely unexplored potential as a landscape artist. His depiction of the limp, motionless body of Tom after the boy's first game of football at Rugby, which emphasizes his vulnerability through the towering forms of the elder boys curving over him, shows, too, that his power to represent the human form was not as feeble as has sometimes been suggested. But the best illustrations in the volume are those which investigate effects of light: the cramped cubby hole from which Old Thomas paid out money for the boys' vacation journeys home; Tom and his friend East plucking a goose by candlelight in their study, and—an engraving which combines the ordinary with the bizarre—the explosion which the 'Madman' creates in his study through an injudicious combination of ingredients in his pestle and mortar.

The illustrations to Christina Rossetti's *Sing-Song* (1872) combine all the elements which Hughes had previously shown in his graphic work. The brothers Dalziel (the leading Victorian wood-engravers), originally proposed that F. A. Fraser should illustrate the poems, and made available some of his designs to William Michael Rossetti: he, however, thought them unsuitable, and 'strongly recommended that Hughes should be invited' instead.[19] The manuscript of *Sing-Song* included, according to the Dalziels, 'a slight pen sketch, drawn by Miss Rossetti, suggesting the subject to illustrate, but of these Mr Hughes made very little use, and only in two instances actually followed the sketch'.[20] Hughes had to work under pressure—after a fairly leisurely start, the Dalziels asked him to produce ten designs per week.[21] But the final results pleased both the Rossettis and their friends: Ford Madox Brown, records W. M. Rossetti in his Diary, went 'so far as to say that the poems are about Christina's finest things, and Hughes the first of living book-illustrators'.[22]

The volume is remarkable for its variety. Hughes's engravings range from simple vignettes of maternal affection, as in 'Love me,—I love you' (p. 2) and parental loss ('A baby's cradle with no baby in it' (p. 15)) to carefully observed fragments of nature: the stiff bird in 'Dead in the cold—a song-singing thrush' (p. 10) and the detailed shell of the snail in 'Swift and sure the swallow'

'Tom is discovered: a motionless body', from *Tom Brown's Schooldays*, 1869, by
Thomas Hughes.

Illustrations to *Sing-Song*, 1872, by Christina Rossetti: (*above*) 'A baby's cradle with no baby in it'; (*below*) 'I have a Poll parrot'.

(p. 106). The grimaces of the podgy goblins in 'A toadstool comes up in a night' are embarrassingly silly, but they represent a rare failure. Hughes is on surer ground when he represents the cruelty inherent in the bizarre, as in the snarling nine-tailed tabby-cat which accompanies the line, 'A sailor's cat is not a cat' (p. 12) or the vicious bird in 'I have a Poll parrot' (p. 109), savagely dismembering a sawdust-spilling doll: a narrative touch which is not present in the poem. Elsewhere he adds to Christina Rossetti's lines. 'Clever little Willie wee' (p. 114) is a weak rhyme, strengthened by Hughes placing Willie and Margery together on a swing seat, bent over the same book. Somewhat more idiosyncratic is his interpretation of 'The rose with such a bonny blush' (p. 111), in which a very dandified negro examines a stylized sun through a pince-nez. However, it is not just the separate illustrations to poems which make the book such a success, but the sense of design which lies behind the production of each double page. Thus the simplest drawing in the volume, the disembodied handclasp above 'Goodbye in fear, goodbye in sorrow' (p. 120) is set off on the opposite page by a highly complicated composition of a birds-nesting boy. The circular composition of 'Crimson curtains round my mother's bed' (p. 126) balances the tomb-like semi-circular illustration on p. 127 to yet another of Rossetti's gloomy poems, 'Baby lies so fast asleep'. Indeed, Hughes responded well to the pervasive morbidity of the whole volume, whether it was in juxtaposing the intense black of the mother's mourning clothes with the sepulchral void of the cradle in 'A baby's cradle with no baby in it' or showing the solemnity of a girl and her younger brother by a recent grave: 'Why did baby die?' (p. 24).

Christina Rossetti intended *Speaking Likenesses* (1874) as 'a Christmas trifle, would-be in the *Alice* style with an eye to the market ...'.[23] Hughes's depiction of Flora in the first of the *Speaking Likenesses* stories similarly seems to exploit a connection with Tenniel, as do some of his little girl figures in *Sing-Song*. Following Tenniel's example, he explores, for the first time, the potential relationship between image and content in terms of the arrangement of a page, in showing the stairs to Flora's bedroom

From *Speaking Likenesses*, 1874, by Christina Rossetti.

climbing up the side of the print to the chamber above (p. 3). He lacks Tenniel's overall delicacy of line, however, with the result that the supposed eight-year-old looks remarkably sturdy for her years. Again, in this volume we see his tendency to go further than the text. Thus, at the bad-tempered birthday party with the quarrelling children who 'tossed the apple of discord to and fro as if it had been a pretty plaything' (p. 10), Hughes actually embodies this mythological suggestion in the very solid presence of a bare-breasted Medusa, naked to her waist, snakes writhing and hissing in her hair, who towers over the party-frocked, sailor-suited children as she pitches the apple in among them. But he follows the text faithfully for the volume's most memorable plate, showing the jostling of Flora at the strange birthday party which she walks into, giving physical substance to the boy with prickly quills like a porcupine, the boy hung round with hooks like fish-hooks (p. 29), providing a whirling, bristling vortex of energy around the bewildered Flora. The illustrations to the middle story—of the frog who couldn't boil a kettle—are less remarkable, like the story itself, but Hughes's visual imagination is reactivated by the adventures of Maggie on her *rite-de-passage* journey through the fringes of a dark wood. The same band of nasty children reappear, this time as swirling, edge-less shadows (frontispiece and p. 79): yet more sinister is the figure of the boy with only a mouth in his face, whom Hughes shows as a cross between a pig and a successful reworking of his earlier Kelpie. None the less, Hughes's delineation, as opposed to suggestion, of a monstrous creature lacks the graphic conviction of the biting jaws, the catching claws of Tenniel's Jabberwock.

After *Speaking Likenesses*, Hughes executed few illustrations until the early years of the twentieth century. His energy was largely taken up by portraiture—especially of pairs or groups within settings—and, less frequently, paintings with literary, particularly medieval topics. Between 1856 and 1908, he failed to exhibit only at sixteen summer Royal Academy exhibitions. Hughes returned to illustration on the request of the family of his old friend, and worked on five further volumes—*Babies' Classics* (1904); a reissue of George MacDonald's *Phantastes: A Faerie*

Romance for Men and Women (which had originally been brought out with unsanctioned pictures); and Greville MacDonald's fairy tales, *The Magic Crook or the Stolen Baby* (1911), *Jack and Jill* (1913), and *Trystie's Quest or Kit King of the Pigwidgeons* (1913—two years before Hughes's death). In these works, Hughes's inadequacy when it comes to figure drawing is more apparent than ever; so, in the form of leaping lambs and bounding rabbits, is his tendency to whimsical sentimentality. But some elements of *Babies' Classics* show his continued interest in the integration of print and design, especially in his incorporation of the poem's title into his drawing: thus the flimsy fairies of 'Come unto these yellow sands' inscribe this invitation in footprints on the shore, and the thicket of stakes and brambles in which a lamb is entangled at the head of George Herbert's version of 'The God of Love my Shepherd Is' are knotted together to read 'Psalm XXIII'. However, Hughes's talent still lay in hinting at the horrible. In *Phantastes*, a vast, claw-like hand of a spectre-like ash tree throws its shadow across the grass, paralysing the form of the young male narrator (p. 55); in *The Magic Crook*, his old abilities can be seen in the shadowy sea-fairies who pursue the narrator, lashing him with ribbons of wet seaweed (p. 27), in the wild, scrawny tabby sea-cats who fight with this narrator (p. 158), and in the entwining tentacles of the huge Kraken (p. 238). But in all these cases, he is taking his cue from the language of the texts, Greville MacDonald's prose being conspicuously more violent and full of movement than that of his father.

In his 1908 article on Hughes's illustrations, Laurence Housman lamented the demise of the illustrators of the mid-century, due, he believed, to the introduction of photography as a medium between artist and engraver, with the consequent loss of intimate relations between the two. Thus, he claimed, 'the subtle feeling for material, the racy quality of line' disappeared, to be replaced by 'a mere mechanical process'.[24] All Hughes's last illustrations were produced from photomechanical relief blocks, rather than wood engravings, but, as D. S. MacColl noted in his review of *Babies' Classics*, 'Mr Hughes has accommodated himself' to this new process 'with something that clings from the old style'.[25]

This can be seen in the use of cross-hatching, the exploration of effects of chiaroscuro. It is this adaptation of earlier technique, of course, which gives a strangely dated effect to these drawings: an effect which, in its turn, called out MacColl's own nostalgia. What remains remarkable about Hughes's best work, however, is its ability to reflect timelessness. This is not to say that it is free of mid-Victorian preoccupations: quite the reverse. In his depictions of sexuality, of sentimental melancholy, of apprehensions of undefinable, incomprehensible, and unfriendly powers, Hughes can be seen to interrelate intimately with a variety of contemporary forms of anxiety. His impact, however, is the greatest when he refuses to locate such anxiety in a recognizable exterior world, and exploits the ability of his medium to give half-definable substance to the shadowy, suggestive realm of the unconscious.

Notes

1. Greville MacDonald, *George MacDonald and his Wife* (London, 1924), 312.
2. William E. Fredeman, 'A Pre-Raphaelite Gazette: The Penkill Letters of Arthur Hughes to William Bell Scott and Alice Boyd, 1886–97', *Bulletin of the John Rylands Library*, 49 (1967), 349.
3. Arthur Hughes to F. G. Stephens, undated letter (early 1870s), Bodleian MS Don. e. 83, fo. 116.
4. William Michael Rossetti, *Some Reminiscences* (London, 1906), i. 147.
5. George MacDonald, *Fairy Tales* (London, 1904) (reprint of *Dealings With the Fairies*, London, 1867), introduction by Greville MacDonald, vi.
6. See Robin Gibson, 'Arthur Hughes: Arthurian and related subjects of the early 1860's', *Burlington Magazine*, 112 (1970), 452.
7. *Fairy Tales*, 180.
8. Annabel Huth Jackson, *A Victorian Childhood* (London, 1932), 60–1.
9. Unsigned review (identified as being by D. S. MacColl in a letter of Arthur Hughes to F. G. Stephens, 21 Dec. 1904, Bodleian MS Don. e. 83, fo. 147), *Saturday Review* (17 Dec. 1904), supplement, vi.
10. For George MacDonald's involvement with *Good Words for the Young*, see Patricia Thomas Srebrnik, *Alexander Strahan: Victorian Publisher* (Ann Arbor, 1986), 105–6, 112.
11. Laurence Housman, 'The Illustrations of Arthur Hughes', *The Bibliophile*, i (1908), 236.
12. George MacDonald, *At the Back of the North Wind* (London, 1871), 11.
13. Forrest Reid, *Illustrators of the Eighteen Sixties* (New York, 1975) (originally published as *Illustrators of the Sixties*, London, 1928), 87.

14. George MacDonald, *Ronald Bannerman's Boyhood* (London, 1871), 5.

15. George MacDonald, *The Princess and the Goblin* (London, 1872), 5.

16. *The Princess and the Goblin*, 129.

17. Arthur Hughes—no relation that I have been able to establish to Thomas Hughes—probably became acquainted with the novelist during the early years of the Working Men's College, when both taught there.

18. Sir John Betjeman, preface to John E. Little, *Thomas Hughes 1822–1896* (Uffington, 1972) (photostat of typescript), no page no.

19. William Michael Rossetti, 15 May 1871, *The Diary of William Michael Rossetti 1870–1873*, ed. Odette Bornand (Oxford, 1977), 61.

20. George and Edward Dalziel, *The Brothers Dalziel: A Record of Fifty Years' Work in Conjunction with Many of the Most Distinguished Artists of the Period 1840–1890* (London, 1901), 91–2.

21. W. M. Rossetti, 13 Nov. 1871, *Diary*, 126.

22. Ibid., 19 Oct. 1871, 116.

23. Christina Rossetti to Dante Gabriel Rossetti, 4 May 1874, *The Family Letters of Christina Georgina Rossetti*, ed. William Michael Rossetti (London, 1908), 44.

24. Housman, 'Illustrations', 231.

25. [MacColl], *Saturday Review* (17 Dec. 1904), vi.

11

Women Writers and Writing for Children: From Sarah Fielding to E. Nesbit

JULIA BRIGGS

Nister's Holiday Annual for 1896 is remembered, if at all, for the drawings of a frog who would 'a fishing go'; initialled H[elen] B[eatrix] P[otter], these drawings mark the first appearance in print of Mr Jeremy Fisher. A few pages further on is an anonymous article entitled 'The Play Times', which purports to be the efforts of a large family of children to write their own newspaper. Jack explains:

We have settled that I am to be Editor this year, because May was so cocky all last Christmas holidays, and put horrid things into the paper about us boys. She says that books are always written by ladies now, but Tom Jones, whose father belongs to a paper (so he knows best), says that nearly all Editors are HES.[1]

Almost as interesting as Jack's assertions are the voice and context in which he makes them: 'The Play Times' stands in a parodic or 'pretend' relationship to a real newspaper while focusing upon the concept of 'play', an activity acknowledged as crucial to children's development by the end of the nineteenth century, though earlier regarded with anxiety. The mode of address also implies play or simulation, since the text speaks to the child reader not from an adult standpoint but in the voice of a child, and from what is presented as a child's point of view. A background of family bickering is implied—the boys seem to be engaged in an argument with the girls concerning gender roles, and this spills over into an ironic comment on the power structures of the adult world: 'Even if all the books are written by ladies now, Editors are still HES.' These delicately barbed comments are characteristic of their author, E. Nesbit, who contributed a series of issues of 'The Play Times' to *Nister's Holiday Annuals* anonymously during the mid-1890s. She later cannibalized material from them and reworked it into her first great success, *The Story of the Treasure Seekers* (1899).

Of course, Jack overstates the ubiquity of women writers; but as writers for children, women had from the outset been at least as productive and as distinguished as men. They were responsible for some of the earliest fairy stories and fables, nursery rhymes and moral tales; yet their large contribution in this particular field has so far attracted little attention from feminist critics. One obvious explanation for this is that, until recently, children's books were regarded as marginal, less than serious as literature, and while feminist criticism was concerned to shift women and their writings away from the periphery, this scarcely looked a promising topic for exploration—indeed women writing for children seemed doubly marginalized. As long as children's books were not taken seriously, the writing of them could not be felt to advance the status of women as writers in any way. Interestingly, this assumption turns out to afford striking parallels to those held by the earliest women writers for children: they felt they must prove themselves to be serious and persuade others to take them seriously, and this mood of seriousness was reflected in what they wrote.

This collection of essays assumes that children's books are quite as serious, complex, and deserving of study as any other literary genre. Nevertheless the commitment to being taken seriously has in the long run disadvantaged some of the earliest writers for children, since their work came to seem unpalatably didactic to later generations, excluding or repressing the high spirits, free-floating imagination, and anarchic feelings so characteristic of childhood. To chart the association of women writers with children's books for the first hundred and fifty years is to record the process by which their authors progressed from giving instruction to an identification with their readers, from proving themselves responsible adults to allowing themselves to adopt the subversive tones of childhood.

While Jack's ingenuous comments look forward to some of the

liveliest of twentieth-century writing for children, for example to that of *Just William*, the child as speaker was not in itself new; indeed some of the earliest fictions for children had used children's voices and presented children as storytellers. Yet while E. Nesbit deliberately selected for Jack an appropriate voice and attitude, the use of children as speakers or storytellers did not always guarantee that they deployed the language or outlook of contemporary children. Children's books are not written by children for children but by adults for adults, since it is the adult who provides the money to buy the book and who is therefore the most immediate consumer of the product. This point was acknowledged by the early children's bookseller William Godwin, when he wrote, 'It is children who read children's books (when they are read); but it is parents that choose them.'[2] While a book's popularity (or lack of it) may depend on how strongly it appeals to its child readers, the whole process of reading is initiated and controlled by adults. That autonomous life and culture of children that Keith Thomas describes elsewhere in this book may not be recorded at all or may only impinge slightly. Its presence depends on how much the writer can remember or observe of the state of childhood, and how far the wider cultural climate accommodates a presentation of childhood based on observation.

How women writers set about writing for children was largely determined by forces other than current attitudes to children. Economic pressures, attitudes to women, and indirectly, yet equally importantly, how women writers wished to present themselves to a wider public also played a part. The connection between women writing and children's books might be thought of as originating in a coincidence yet moving beyond it—a coincidence of timing in that women began to take up writing as a profession at about the same time as books specifically written for children began to be published in any numbers; and a coincidence of interests, in that women were committed to the nursery world as mothers, nurses, or governesses in a way that few men were. During the eighteenth and nineteenth centuries, women and children shared subordinate positions in society, both groups being regarded as weaker, less capable, and less responsible than men. It was not until the later nineteenth century, and a passage like that quoted from 'The Play Times', that women writers began to make common cause with children as irresponsible and subversive of the dominant social order—and even then, only occasionally. Earlier women writers had been preoccupied with their responsibilities as guardians and educators, with efforts to promote gravity, maturity, and sound judgement among their child readers, at the same time as revealing it in themselves.

By the late nineteenth century, as May observed, 'Books are always written by ladies now': writing had come to be widely accepted as a respectable and even ladylike profession for middle-class women to follow. But the eighteenth century had found the notion of the professional woman writer more troubling. This was a society in which women were expected to fulfil themselves in relationships of service to others—as mothers, daughters, maids, governesses, nurses, etc. The self-indulgence, self-display, and egotism implicit in the profession of writer were suspect. A few women writers were prepared to ignore convention, to scandalize and even to exploit the scandal they gave, but most preferred to remain within their society's accepted boundaries. Doing so might require them, among other things, to publish anonymously and conduct their business dealings through male relatives. By writing for and about children, however, and by emphasizing the importance of education, they demonstrated that their interests were still firmly focused upon the home and their natural functions as child bearers and raisers. As such, women had special opportunities to study the behaviour of the young as well as the incentive to correct it, preparing them to become co-operative and useful members of the adult community. The earliest women writers for children adopted approaches that implied their conformity with what was more generally expected of women. They had the further incidental advantage that they could with justification omit the dangerous and difficult theme of sexuality from any consideration.

The first fiction specifically written to amuse children was the work of a woman who adopted several of these strategies of self-exoneration. She was Sarah Fielding, sister of the more famous

Henry, and it was apparently he who arranged her dealings with publishers for her. Her main motive in writing for children, like that of the great majority of her successors in the field, was essentially an economic one: in the preface to an earlier novel she had admitted, 'Perhaps the best Excuse that can be made for a woman's venturing to write at all, is that which really produced this Book; Distress in her circumstances; which she could not so well remove by any other Means in her Power.'[3]

In 1749 she published, at first anonymously, *The Governess, or, Little Female Academy*. Although this is not a book to appeal to young readers of today, it is nevertheless an original and experimental piece of writing, lively and structurally complex. It proved immediately popular, establishing a narrative framework adopted by a number of successors. One of the earliest of these was Madame Le Prince de Beaumont, who used it to introduce a version of 'Beauty and the Beast', discussed earlier by Jack Zipes.[4] In *The Governess* Sarah Fielding created a delicate balance between the familiar and the romantic by presenting nine little girls and their daily lives at school. The element of romance was provided by the school setting—while school stories and school itself are commonplaces of modern children's books, the great majority of Sarah Fielding's original readers had never been to and would never attend school. Here was a fictional setting in which they could nevertheless plausibly imagine themselves. The nine little girls are by no means paragons—they are spirited, energetic, and inclined to quarrel, but the story encourages them to be more reflective.

Both the title and plot of *The Governess* recall John Locke's emphasis on the child learning self-government through the wise instruction of a governor (i.e. tutor), as set out in his influential treatise *Some Thoughts Concerning Education* (1693). The governess of the little academy is Mrs Teachum; as the sole adult presence, she acts as the girls' mentor and adjudicator. But in practice the girls teach one another, and their real governess is not Mrs Teachum, but one of their own number—the eldest, Jenny Peace, who proposes and organizes a programme of self-improvement in response to the violent quarrel with which the narrative begins.

And, since this is a very literary text, it all begins with an apple: Mrs Teachum kindly brings the girls a little basket of apples, but unfortunately one is much bigger than all the others. When they begin to argue over who should have it, Jenny Peace throws this apple of discord over a hedge into 'another Garden, where they could not come at it', but her action is already too late to prevent a fight breaking out, in which the rest of the girls 'fell to pulling of Caps, tearing of Hair, and dragging the Cloaths of one another's Backs. Tho' they did not so much strike, as endeavour to scratch and pinch their Enemies.'[5] Even the gentlest among them is drawn in on behalf of her friend.

In what follows, fiction becomes the medium for education, in the time-honoured tradition: the girls listen to one another's life stories and these provide opportunities for a series of moral deductions to be drawn from them. Each recounts her own story, and in so doing passes judgement upon her own actions. Education is presented as an essentially moral process, derived rather from experience than acquired knowledge.

The book contains other types of inset narratives, and several of these are also designed to promote judgement or choice of one kind or another—a romance about two girls who are rivals for a man's love and how he decides between them; an animal fable about the assembly of the birds to determine which is the handsomest, and two fairy stories. Sarah Fielding seems deliberately to have included a range of genres. The framing text nevertheless expresses distrust of the most purely fictional kinds of fiction, an unease at the use of fantasy or fairy-tale elements, as if their wish-fulfilling patterns were as likely to be dangerous as valuable, to be merely entertaining rather than edifying. When Jenny Peace has read a story involving two giants, Barbarico and Benefico, the lovers Fidus and Aminta, and the dwarf Mignon, Mrs Teachum warns her against 'the supernatural Contrivances in this Story':

'But here let me observe to you (which I would have you communicate to your little Friends) that Giants, Magic, Fairies, and all Sorts of supernatural Assistances in a Story, are only introduced to amuse and divert: For a Giant is called so only to express a Man of great Power; and the magic Fillet round the Statue was intended only to shew you, that by Patience you will overcome all Difficulties. Therefore, by no means let the Notion of Giants or Magic dwell upon your Minds.'[6]

Jenny Peace duly passes this advice on to her fellows.

Mrs Teachum's glosses are at once moralizing and perhaps wide of the mark. The helplessness of Fidus and the dwarf Mignon in the face of the giant Barbarico, and their dependence upon the kindness of Benefico, seem rather to figure the child's helplessness within the adult world—the giants are simply grown-ups in all their alienness. Seen thus, Mrs Teachum's intervention reveals only her inadequacy as an interpreter, her exclusion from the closed circle of experience common to her pupils. Alternatively the giants might be regarded not as representatives of the remote and oppressive world of adults but rather as expressing a child's fantasy of power—Dr Johnson, in conversation with Mrs Thrale, perceived that this might be the meaning of giants in fairy tales: 'Babies do not want (said he) to hear about babies; they like to be told of giants and castles, and of somewhat which can stretch and stimulate their little minds.'[7] Recent criticism has also tended to interpret the power of magic in fairy tales as enacting young children's fantasies of omnipotence.

Behind Mrs Teachum's warning lies an anxiety that goes back to Plato about the nature of fiction itself and its potential to deceive or mislead. If fiction is to be a teaching medium, as it is for Jenny Peace and her creator, the wrong sorts of fiction and the wrong sorts of reading are also potentially dangerous. The eighteenth century was particularly conscious of the vulnerability of the new female reader who had helped to create a market for fiction but who was all too easily carried away with what she read, and might even let it overflow into her life and influence her actions, usually with disastrous consequences. From Lydia in Sheridan's play *The Rivals* to Catherine Morland in Jane Austen's *Northanger Abbey*, women readers were portrayed as too easily swayed by their reading:

Women subjected by ignorance to their sensations, and only taught to look for happiness in love ... are the women who are amused by the stupid novelists ... confined to trifling employments, they naturally imbibe opinions which the only kind of reading calculated to interest an innocent frivolous mind inspires.[8]

Thus Mary Wollstonecraft diagnosed the problem. In her view, women's inadequacies were in large part the result of 'a false system of education'. At the heart of the whole question of education for women was a paradox which remained unresolved, and was still being energetically discussed a hundred years later: if women were educated only to fulfil strictly limited roles, if they were not provided with the kind of intellectual ballast their brothers were supposed to receive, they would remain so many Rosamond Vincys—vain, silly, and a danger to themselves and others. Their education taught them accomplishments that were intended to charm and attract men into marrying them, but at best such assets were useful only for an extremely brief period of time. They entirely failed to prepare women for the real business of their lives. The products of such an education were, according to Mary Wollstonecraft, 'weak beings ... only fit for a seraglio! Can they be expected to govern a family with judgement, or take care of the poor babes whom they bring into the world?'[9]

As *A Vindication of the Rights of Woman* brought home, attitudes to women's education revealed underlying confusions about the roles women were expected to play. If their education could be redefined, treated as a serious issue, then women might make a more positive and responsible contribution to society as a whole. The question 'What kind of education is appropriate for girls?' is already implicitly present in Sarah Fielding's *The Governess*. Education was to remain the key question in all serious eighteenth-century books for children, all that aspired to be anything other than merely commercial, and the question was far more contentious in relation to girls than to boys.

Mary Wollstonecraft's concern with women's education is evident from her earliest published work, *Thoughts on the Education of Daughters* (1786), written after the closure of her school at Newington Green, and before she took up a post as governess to the Kingsboroughs in Ireland. Two years later she moved to London with the aim of becoming a professional writer. Here she took up several educational projects, partly from financial necessity but also from a genuine interest: in 1789 she wrote an introduction to an anthology, *A Female Reader*, and in 1790 translated Christian Salzmann's *Elements of Morality* from the German. But she began (in 1788) with a book at least partly inspired by Sarah Fielding's *Governess*, now nearly forty years old, but still unrivalled as a popular fiction for children. *Original Stories from Real Life* blends her experiences as a governess (presumably the 'real life' referred to in the title) with Sarah Fielding's formula of teaching through stories—its full title is *Original Stories from Real Life with Conversations calculated to regulate the Affections and Form the Mind to Truth and Goodness*. It has often been written off as hackwork, which it certainly was; of no interest to today's children, which is true; irrelevant to Mary Wollstonecraft's later feminism, and of negligible merit. The last two points are less self-evident: though its author was very young and inexperienced, and her style and views as yet unsettled, the story begins purposively:

One fine morning in spring, some time after Mary and Caroline were settled in their new abode, Mrs Mason proposed a walk before breakfast, a custom she wished to teach imperceptibly, by rendering it amusing.
The sun had scarcely dispelled the dew that hung on every blade of grass, and filled the half-shut flowers; every prospect smiled and the freshness of the air conveyed the most pleasing sensations to Mrs Mason's mind; but the children were regardless of the surrounding beauties, and ran eagerly after some insects to destroy them.[10]

Mary and Caroline are quickly established as thoughtless and wantonly destructive; Mrs Mason will have her work cut out to teach them that truth and goodness promised in the title. By contrast with Sarah Fielding's *The Governess*, the girls are directly instructed by an adult, not a contemporary; the events of their outings together provide the occasions for moral instruction, but the wilder fictions of fairy tale or fable are altogether avoided. Mrs Mason directs the girls' attention towards the contrasting

examples of Lady Sly and Mrs Trueman, a contrast intended to
show that money and status do not confer happiness in themselves: Lady Sly, a habitual liar, is neglected by her husband and
son, and can take no pleasure in religion, the natural world, or in
friendship—for Mary Wollstonecraft, the main sources of satisfaction open to women. Mrs Trueman, the curate's wife, lives in a
little white house overgrown with roses, close to the church; she
is adored by her children who cluster round her, and loved by the
poor. Mrs Trueman has a cultivated mind and we are left with a
picture of her sewing for her children while her husband reads
aloud, an idealized version of the protestant companionate marriage that recalls Parthenia and Argalus in Sidney's *Arcadia*, as
well as anticipating some of the happier marriages of Victorian
fiction. However cultivated a woman's mind may be, the best she
can hope for is a husband who will share, and perhaps even
stimulate her intellectual interests. Women are not yet encouraged
to expect direct access to knowledge. The woman who reads
alone has abandoned more important duties to do so.

The character of Mrs Mason has repelled many later readers,
who find her cold and harsh. Even her kisses are strictly bestowed
as rewards for the girls' improvements in virtue and understanding, and there is no suggestion that she is fond of them for their
own sakes. She is an icily rational judge of their behaviour, never
encouraging them with warmth and affection, as Victorian parents and guardians would try to do. In this respect she seems very
unlike her creator: Godwin recalled Mary as having said 'that she
never was concerned in the education of one child, who was not
personally attached to her, and earnestly concerned not to incur
her displeasure'.[11] Perhaps warmth and affection were not written
in because she assumed they could be taken for granted.

The high premium placed on rationality, and on an education
that proceeded by means of justice rather than indulgence is
reflected in Mary Wollstonecraft's *Vindication of the Rights of
Woman* (1792), as well as in many of the theoretical discussions of
education of the day. Contemporary children's books also tended
to exemplify this theme, and as a result have been derided ever
since; for such a strong emphasis on rationality seems to imply a

disregard for the imaginative needs of children themselves. But it was symptomatic of a desire felt by many women writers to free themselves, and their offspring too, from weaknesses regularly associated with their sex—being too emotional, too fickle, too affectionate, too doting. Mrs Mason's coldness, like that shown by parents or guardians in Maria Edgeworth's tales for children, reflects the author's desire to identify herself with what had previously been thought of as masculine attributes. The concern of a number of women writers with education at the end of the eighteenth century helped to define their roles, both as writers and women, as serious and important, and to characterize their concern for children as a valuable contribution to the community.

Maria Edgeworth's stories for children conducted education by means of an appeal to reason, as Mary Wollstonecraft's Mrs Mason had done, and similar kinds of criticism have also been levelled against her. In the best known of all her tales, 'The Purple Jar' (from *The Parent's Assistant*, 1796) Rosamund's mother allows her to choose between having a purple jar that she has seen in a chemist's window or the pair of shoes that she needs. Rosamund, who is seven and lives for the moment, prefers the jar, but has some difficulty in knowing on what basis to arrive at a decision. Her mother having warned her to examine the jar more attentively, advises that she should 'choose what will make you the happiest'. 'Then, mamma, if that's all, I'm sure the flower-pot would make me the happiest,' she replies. As a consequence the next month is spoilt for her by having to wear a pair of shoes in which 'she could neither run, dance, jump, nor walk'; and she is finally obliged to acknowledge her mistake.[12] Later readers have reacted to this fable with annoyance, feeling that a more loving and less rational mother would have protected her child from the unfortunate consequences of unwise choices, that parents ought in any case to ensure that their children have shoes that fit them and that the prudential view here inculcated is not desirable in childhood and is acquired only too soon. For Rosamund, the attraction of the purple jar is aesthetic or imaginative, and the reader sympathizes with her. But the story suggests that aesthetic pleasures, or the pleasures of the senses are deceptive, if not actually dangerous, for when Rosamund gets the jar home and wants to put her plants inside it, she pours out the liquid it contains, only to discover that it is made of plain glass after all—the purple colour which had attracted her so much in the first place was no more than a dark, evil-smelling liquid inside it, and so no real part of it—accidental rather than substantial: 'I am sure, if I had known that it was not really purple, I should not have wished to have it so much.' 'But didn't I tell you that you had not examined it; and that perhaps you would be disappointed?'[13] The moral, the vanity of human wishes, is at once traditional and trite.

This, Maria Edgeworth seems to imply, is the nature of all sensual pleasures. The purple jar had appealed to Rosamund's imagination as no pair of shoes could, but imagination is not a useful or stable faculty. Maria Edgeworth was by no means the first writer for children to identify the imagination as potentially dangerous—indeed the notion went back on the one hand to the Puritan writers for children who deeply distrusted fiction and thought of it as 'lies', and on the other to John Locke and a distortion of his views concerning childhood fears. Earlier in the century, Sarah Fielding had recorded a degree of unease over giants and dwarfs. Now fairy tales were to be banned from the nursery altogether. Richard Edgeworth, Maria's father, set the agenda in his preface to *The Parent's Assistant* (1796): 'Why should the mind be filled with fantastic visions, instead of useful knowledge? Why should so much valuable time be lost? Why should we vitiate their taste, and spoil their appetite, by suffering them to feed upon sweetmeats?'[14]

In setting their faces against the pleasures of the imagination, the rational moralists were identifying with some of the ideals of the Enlightenment. Children, they believed, should not be encouraged to indulge in fruitless daydreams which only promoted dissatisfactions, but should encounter and examine the world as it really was—and this applied all the more strongly to girls and to the lower classes. From one point of view, the encounter with things as they are was especially appropriate in preparing girls for their roles as women, since this normally involved taking on responsibility for the practical and immediate physical needs of a family. From another point of view it contradicted certain features traditionally regarded as essentially feminine: for the Augustans, women were a part of the non-masculine and therefore irrational world, creatures subject to imagination, mothers or nurses whose minds were stored with old folk tales and rhymes, who belonged to a dark emotive world of feelings and sensations out of which a healthy boy would hope to grow to manhood, putting behind him all childish or feminine fancies. Those women who pursued rational arguments and education policies were thus repudiating the old associations of the feminine with the irrational, and aspiring to be recognized as reasonable beings who might be permitted to join the closed circle of male discourse. Some of their contemporaries sought to dispose of these views by caricaturing or exaggerating their proponents' feminine or childish aspects, thus firmly pushing them back into precisely those categories from which they had been seeking to escape.

Between 1780 and 1800 the rational educationalists dominated the now flourishing world of children's publishing, but beyond it the cultural tides had turned against the values of the Enlightenment, and imagination was reasserting itself. Wordsworth, Coleridge, and Lamb all insisted upon the importance of their early reading, among the chapbook tales of Tom Hickathrift and Jack the Giant-Killer, the history of St George and the Seven Champions of Christendom, and the Arabian Nights. Today, when the value of fairy tales is fully recognized, it is difficult to imagine how they could ever have appeared dangerous or subversive, and so the snorts of masculine indignation from Coleridge and Lamb seem no more than the voice of common sense: '*Damn them.* I mean the cursed Barbauld Crew, those *Blights & Blasts* of all that is *Human* in man & child,' wrote Lamb, in a now famous imprecation. His sentence makes what is 'Human in man & child' close ranks against the silent third term, women—here equated with 'the cursed Barbauld Crew'.[15] In fact Anna Barbauld was a high-principled Nonconformist, the author of *Lessons for Children* (1778), *Hymns in Prose for Children* (1781), and contributor to *Evenings at Home* (1792–6)—a series of instructional dialogues covering a wide range of activities, but firmly and committedly condemning slavery, imperialism, and war in all its forms.

Lamb's dismissal of the new fashions in children's books ('Mrs. B's and Mrs. Trimmer's nonsense'[16]) was premature, granted that he and Mary were soon to write several children's books for William Godwin's Library for Children. Of these, *Mrs. Leicester's School* (1809) is yet another reworking of *The Governess*, this time with more free-ranging invention. The disturbing tale of 'The Witch Aunt', told by Maria Howe, is recognized as Mary's work and seems to be an extraordinarily unmediated account of a schizophrenic experience, in which a kindly aunt is simultaneously, and quite irrationally, perceived as an evil witch.

The indignation of Lamb's circle towards Mrs Barbauld was increased in 1803 when she was wrongly supposed to have written an unfavourable review of his book, *John Woodvil*. De Quincey recalled in his memoirs that Coleridge liked to play upon her name so that she became 'that pleonasm of nakedness, since as if it were not enough to be bare, she was also bald.'[17] His pun is confirmed in a letter from Southey to Coleridge which demands 'Why have you not made Lamb declare war upon Mrs. Bare-bald? He should singe her flaxen wig with squibs, and tie crackers to her petticoats till she leapt about like a parched pea for very torture.'[18] Wordplay here deteriorates into a kind of imaginary violence. The remarkable popularity of Mrs Barbauld, Maria Edgeworth, and others like them seems to have invited the saucy mockery of the schoolboy thumbing his nose at female authority. On other occasions their childishness became the main target, a childishness prompted by the need to find a simple language accessible to young readers. Coleridge sneered at this aspect in a lecture of 1808, preferring the old chapbooks to 'the good books in Miss Edgeworth's style':

I infinitely prefer the little books of 'The Seven Champions of Christendom,' 'Jack the Giant Killer,' etc., etc.—for at least they make the child forget himself—to your moral tales where a good little boy comes in and says 'Mama, I met a poor beggar man and gave him the sixpence you gave me yesterday. Did I do right?' 'O, yes, my dear; to be sure you did.' This is not virtue, but vanity; such books do not teach goodness, but—if I might venture such a word—goodyness.[19]

He made the same point in later lectures, though there his ostensible complaint was that such books encouraged an undesirable love of praise.

These romantic jibes cast rationalist women writers either as bossy and repressive nannies or else as little more than children themselves. Such responses implicitly rejected their claims to be taken seriously, claims apparent in their high-minded ideals and scrupulously rational tones. The romantic commitment to the values of the imagination made the rationalist disapproval of fairy tales an obvious source of criticism, but the wording of these particular attacks exploit just those reducingly sexist labels from which women writers were trying to escape. But then their mere existence seemed provocative, as Maria Edgeworth observed: '"Censure," says a celebrated writer, "is a tax which every man must pay to the public, who seeks to be eminent." Women must expect to pay it doubly.'[20]

The rationalists were attacked on one side by the romantics, anxious to establish imagination as the crucial literary faculty, and on the other by evangelical writers who disapproved of the focus on the material and the utilitarian in their educational programme. The true centre of education should be religion, argued the evangelical Mrs Trimmer in her anti-Jacobin periodical *The Guardian of Education* (1802–6): 'Even geography, writing and arithmetic may be made in some measure subservient to religious instruction.'[21] Mrs Trimmer was actively involved in the establishment of Sunday Schools at the end of the eighteenth century. Their need for suitable textbooks and their adoption of a reward system paid in improving books soon produced a whole school of writing devoted to promoting introspection and moral self-examination.

The harshest as well as the most influential exemplar of the evangelical school was Mrs Sherwood, who took it upon herself to rewrite Sarah Fielding's *The Governess*, substituting more moral tales for those of the original ('fanciful productions of this sort can never be rendered generally useful'), imposing upon it a strongly devotional content and publishing this revised version under her own name in 1820.[22] Eighteenth-century common sense here gives place to narrowly religious attitudes: Mr Teachum, 'a

FRONTISPIECE.

W. Crosse del. Thompson Sculp.

P. 94.

(Be calm, my child, remember that you must do all the good you can the present day.)

Published by J. Johnson Sept 2, 1791.

(Left) one of Blake's illustrations for Mary Wollstonecraft's *Original Stories from Real Life*, 1788. *(Right)* frontispiece to Mrs Sherwood's first revised edition of *The Governess*, 1820.

very sensible man', is now 'truly pious', and the naughtiness of the schoolgirls takes on the grim Calvinist shadow of original sin. The fight over the apple, for Sarah Fielding 'a perverse accident', is for Mrs Sherwood an exemplum of 'the evil of the heart, that deadly evil of which we have every one of us such large experience'. It affords an opportunity for the ignorant reader to have 'the subject of human depravity familiarly explained'. The explanation includes the fall of man, original sin, and the doctrine of redemption, concluding with the admonition, 'You are therefore, my dear children, unless you have already received the Holy Spirit by faith into your hearts, in no better state than these little girls of whom we have just been reading.'[23]

The majority of evangelical writers for children were women; like Mrs Sherwood, they were committed to using children's fiction as a medium for spiritual persuasion and they wrote into their narratives the kinds of conversions they hoped their books might make.[24] Mrs Sherwood's earlier tale, *Little Henry and His Bearer* (1814), had set the pattern for many of the stories that followed—Henry, a small boy left orphaned in India, undergoes a dramatic conversion effected by an English girl, and in turn converts his Indian bearer and then dies, after an edifying deathbed scene. Children's conversions of pagan or otherwise benighted adults figured largely in Victorian children's books and may occasionally have been read with pleasure by children since they suggested that a child might possess superior insights, or else might acquire this particular form of ascendancy over an adult. The authors of such stories also expressed their own aspirations to spiritual power and influence, for this was one of the few kinds of influence that women might legitimately exert in society. For many Victorian women writers, spiritual authority was a vital source of power.

Another characteristically feminine pattern of behaviour was written into children's fiction by Maria Charlesworth in her book *Ministering Children* (1854). Visiting and tending the parish poor was much practised by Victorian ladies; it contributed not only to their practical and spiritual welfare, but was also morally uplifting for the visitor who must have given silent thanks for her own well-being, while enjoying the gratitude of others. In *Ministering Children* this ladylike mode of philanthropy is adopted by a whole family, as the well-to-do children learn to help the underprivileged.

Children's fiction expanded rapidly during the early nineteenth century and stories for boys and girls now began to be sharply differentiated: boys' stories often involved travel to far-flung places and advocated the less reflective virtues—courage, endurance, loyalty, and patriotism. Stories for girls were typically set in the home and exemplified charity, kindness, patience, and self-discipline, virtues which most girls had ample opportunity to practise. Many of the women writers for girls showed themselves fully conscious of the constraints and expectations that young women laboured under, and the particular cultural and gender influences that operated on their lives can often be found as themes within their writing, although they came from quite varied backgrounds: Charlotte Tucker, who always published under the doubly delicate acronym A.L.O.E. (A Lady of England), was born into a wealthy family and was expected to participate in a round of fashionable parties and dances, which she entirely rejected after she had undergone the evangelical conversion that inspired her books. 'Hesba Stretton' (Sarah Smith) came from a comparatively poor family and took up writing in order to support herself. Elizabeth Sewell and Charlotte M. Yonge, while rejecting the evangelical movement, remained deeply committed Anglicans. All these writers in their different ways and at different social levels, were concerned with the roles of women and children as agents of spiritual good, and all of them illustrate in some detail the day-to-day dissatisfactions of young girls in their society, while trying to reconcile them to their privations; a study of what form those dissatisfactions took and how far they derived from their authors' personal experiences would be revealing.

The evangelical writers were tender and attentive observers of Victorian life, not only in the ostentatious drawing-room but also in the draughty attic slum; yet fundamentally they accepted the existing structures of society, and when they criticized, their targets were individual acts of cruelty or depravity. Though intensely alive to the evils of poverty and social injustice, they were mainly concerned with relieving particular examples of it and ensuring that charity began at home. An exception might be made for Hesba Stretton, whose accounts of slum children, like those of her master Charles Dickens, effected changes in public opinion and eventually in legislation.

Between the educationalists and the evangelicals, any sense of the child's naturally anarchic energies had been lost, for anarchic energies, especially that most anarchic of all energies, sexuality, was profoundly repressed in Victorian middle-class women in general, and in devotional writers in particular. Even a writer like Catherine Sinclair who in *Holiday House* (1839) deliberately set out to restore the balance between Art and Nature by portraying 'noisy, frolicsome, mischievous children, now almost extinct', went on to hope that her book 'might be found to inculcate a pleasing and permanent consciousness, that religion is the best resource in happier hours and the only refuge in hours of affliction'.[25] So it was that the first genuinely subversive writing for children came from men who had less to lose by a wholesale rejection of the rational, the didactic, the useful, or the high-minded, since their reasoning, moral judgement, social worth, and high principles were less regularly called in question. In the verses of Edward Lear, violent, destructive, and wholly illogical fantasies are invented and played out, while in Lewis Carroll's *Alice in Wonderland* the whole system of educating children through their reading is mocked in a series of parodic verses, quasi-improving dialogues, and self-examining monologues that simply send up the favourite techniques of a great deal of earlier children's literature; in *Through the Looking-Glass* Carroll went on to burlesque some popular writing for adults as well.

In *Alice* the parodies of Isaac Watts's hymns and of poems by Wordsworth and Southey are obvious enough, but the school-room techniques of question and answer, the extraction of trite morals, the imperatives of instruction ('Curtsy while you're thinking'), the systems of reward and punishment and the application of practical logic to problems are all characteristic features of rational moralists like Maria Edgeworth or else of schoolroom texts, and are continually mocked. In Alice herself Lewis Carroll created a little girl who refuses to become an object, who won't be intimidated by the constant stream of orders and instructions she receives, and who remains firmly in command of herself. However small she becomes physically—at one stage she is smaller than a mushroom—her spirit is undiminished. Only the recognition of her own unreality, the thought that she may only exist as part of the Red King's dream, a fiction subject to arbitrary extinction, can reduce her to tears.

Alice was an extraordinarily liberating work, not merely for its mockery of its predecessors, or its presentation of a small girl who remains cool and self-possessed under the most trying circumstances, but also in its free and cheerful use of fantasy without allegorical meaning or a coherent system of symbols or logic. Its influence was so extensive that a single illustration of it must suffice. One woman writer with a natural bent for fantasy, who translated that impulse into a children's book with the example of *Alice* before her, was Christina Rossetti. She had published the brilliant fantasy poem *Goblin Market* in 1862, three years before *Alice in Wonderland* and ten before *Through the Looking-Glass*. In 1874 she assembled a group of three stories for children and offered them to her publisher, Macmillan, as 'a Christmas trifle would-be in the *Alice* style with an eye to the market'.[26] She proposed to entitle them 'Nowhere', but her brother Gabriel objected on the grounds that it recalled Butler's recently published and dangerously free-thinking *Erewhon*. In the end her book was called *Speaking Likenesses*, because, as the author explained, its heroines 'perpetually encounter "speaking (literally *speaking*) likenesses" or embodiments or caricatures of themselves or their faults'.[27] In other words, the stories enact self-confrontation, played out in a fantasy mode.

The individual stories are untitled, but the first is the most complex: it concerns Flora's eighth birthday which she celebrates with a party for her brother and sister, her friend Emily and her favourite cousins. But somehow the lunch and everything about it fails to please, and out in the garden after the meal, a game of blindman's buff turns into a squabble—Christina Rossetti probably had in mind the fight at the outset of Sarah Fielding's *The Governess*, when she describes the children as tossing 'the apple of discord to and fro as if it had been a pretty plaything'.[28] Quarrelling and discontent never go unpunished, and the structure here is still the traditional one of sin and retribution, even though the retribution follows *Alice* in taking a bizarre, even a surreal form. During a game of hide-and-seek Flora runs down the yew alley and finds at the end of it a little door opening into a strange house. Inside all the furniture and objects seem to be alive. A birthday party is in progress—the first of the likenesses— but like Alice at the Mad Hatter's tea party, Flora never gets anything to eat. She is, however, forced to join in the games afterwards. But now the other children are not quite children any more:

One boy bristled with prickly quills like a porcupine, and raised or depressed them at pleasure; but he usually kept them pointed outwards. Another, instead of being rounded like most people, was facetted at very sharp angles. A third caught in everything he came near, for he was hung round with hooks like fishhooks. One girl exuded a sticky fluid and came off on the fingers; another, rather smaller, was slimy and slipped through the hands.[29]

The symbolism of the boys with their projecting quills or hooks and the sticky, slippery girls is disturbingly sexual. An argument quickly arises as to what games they should play. It is settled by the unnamed Queen, whose birthday party it is and who is evidently Flora's speaking likeness; she declares that they shall play Hunt the Pincushion, with Flora as the pincushion:

Quills with every quill erect tilted against her, and needed not a pin: but Angles whose corners almost cut her, Hooks who caught and slit her frock, Slime who slid against and passed her, Sticky who rubbed off on her neck and plump bare arms, the scowling Queen, and the whole laughing scolding pushing troop, all wielded longest, sharpest pins, and all by turns overtook her. Finally the Queen caught her, swung her violently round, let go suddenly,—and Flora losing her balance, dropped upon the floor. But at least that game was over.[30]

Arthur Hughes's illustration for the climax of *Speaking Likenesses*, 1874, by Christina Rossetti.

This is followed by a game of 'Self Help' in which pins are forbidden but

each boy depended exclusively on his own resources . . . every natural advantage, as a quill or fishhook might be utilized to the utmost.

[Don't look shocked, dear Ella, at my choice of words; but remember that my birthday party is being held in the land of Nowhere. Yet who knows whether something not altogether unlike it has not ere now taken place in the land of Somewhere? Look at home, children.]

The boys were players, the girls were played (if I may be allowed such a phrase) . . .[31]

Sexuality is normally a taboo area, even in children's books today, but erotic aggression is as clearly implied here as it had been in *Goblin Market*, where Lizzie, harassed by the goblins, was compared to

> a royal virgin town
> Topped with a gilded dome and spire,
> Close beleaguered by a fleet
> Mad to tug her standard down.

Whether the party rough-and-tumbles reflect an adult aware-ness of sexual threat as in *Goblin Market*, or whether they recall the erotic undercurrent in nursery romps remains uncertain. There is a great deal more of the story—supper follows the games and afterwards each of these strange non-children builds himself into a house made up of glass blocks which glow like coloured lamps or voluptuous fruit: they resembled 'illuminated peaches, apples, apricots, plums hung about with the profusion of a most fruitful orchard',[32] images further recalling the world of *Goblin Market*. The fantasy ends as abruptly as its model, *Alice*, had done, with the building blocks all flying through the air, and little Flora waking to find that she had fallen asleep in the yew alley. Though it preaches a conventional enough moral, Christina Rossetti's story displays the uninhibited violence and inverted logic of a Freudian nightmare. Several of the constraints that had formerly operated on women writers—obligations to be rational, ladylike, high-minded—are here dissolved.

In *Speaking Likenesses*, Rossetti had created a strange blend of fantasy that combined nursery experiences with a discomfiting awareness of sexual difference. The story is told by an aunt to her five nieces and there is no attempt to recreate a child's point of view or to adopt the kind of language or tone that an eight-year-old might have used. The next generation of children's writers—Mrs Ewing, Mrs Molesworth, Frances Hodgson Burnett, and E. Nesbit were all in their different ways concerned to present children's experiences as they appeared to a child or as a child might describe them. There is all the difference in the world between Christina Rossetti describing her children as tossing the apple of discord from one to another, and Jack complaining about May's cockiness in the passage from 'The Play Times' with which this essay began, or else with its revision as it appears in Nesbit's first great success, *The Story of the Treasure Seekers*:

Dora wanted to be editor and so did Oswald, but he gave way to her because she is a girl, and afterwards he knew that it is true what it says in the copybooks about Virtue being its own Reward.

Because you've no idea what a bother it is. Everybody wanted to put in everything just as they liked, no matter how much room there was on the page. It was simply awful! Dora put up with it as long as she could and then she said if she wasn't let alone she wouldn't go on being editor: they could be the editors themselves, so there.

Then Oswald said, like a good brother: 'I will help you if you like, Dora,' and she said 'You're more trouble than all the rest of them! Come and be editor and see how you like it. I give it up to you.' But she didn't and we did it together . . .

I could write a better paper on my head, but an editor is not allowed to write all the paper. It is very hard, but he is not. You just have to fill up with what you can get from other writers.[33]

This flexible, informal, colloquial tone reflects the little revolution in children's writing that *The Treasure Seekers* was to bring about, almost single-handed. The comedy is sophisticated and ironic, mocking the literary convention of the copybook heading as well as social convention: Oswald resentfully gives way to Dora because 'she is a girl', and the rules of masculine chivalry require that he should; but he cannot help being gratified when the coveted position turns out to be something of a trial. *The*

Treasure Seekers is narrated by Oswald, though he refuses to give his identity away at the outset, challenging the reader to identify him:

It is one of us that tells the story—but I shall not tell you which: only at the very end perhaps I will. While the story is going on you may be trying to guess but I bet you don't.

It was Oswald who first thought of looking for treasure. Oswald often thinks of very interesting things. And directly he had thought of it he did not keep it to himself, as some boys would have done, but he told the others . . .[34]

The device of adopting Oswald as narrator avoids the situation of an adult talking down to children, the common pattern of so much earlier writing, though one which Sarah Fielding had ingeniously avoided. The further device of Oswald's inconsistent but often aspiringly literary third-person narrative also sets him up as a target for comic irony, the complacent Victorian patriarch in embryo. E. Nesbit can thus laugh with him and at him, enjoying his child's angle on the adult world while providing a subtle critique of his comfortable male assumptions.

The style created for *The Treasure Seekers* itself represents an enormous advance on 'The Play Times', yet 'The Play Times' can be seen as a crucial stage in E. Nesbit's development as a writer since it suggested to her the possibilities of travesty as a versatile literary mode. When Jack, May, and the others settled down to write their newspaper, what they did, as might be expected, was to write feeble imitations of the children's books or magazines then in vogue. During the previous ten years or so E. Nesbit had been supporting her family by turning out hackwork for children, employing all the clichés and copybook headings then in vogue. Now she discovered a way to exploit them and make fun of them simultaneously. As a result, *The Treasure Seekers* is structured around the Bastable children's reading. The different schemes they pick up from books and newspapers provide the occasions for their different adventures as well as forming a frame-breaking self-commentary. One chapter ends, 'But that is another story. I think that is such a useful way to know when you can't think how to end up a chapter. I learnt it from another writer named Kipling.'[35]

The book's Christmas-party happy ending reverses the usual cliché of life being stranger than fiction as Oswald observes, 'I can't help it if it is like Dickens, because it happens this way. Real life is often something like books.'[36] More often the narrative emphasizes the differences between books and life: the Bastables' conception of the world, largely derived from their reading, is constantly revealed as inappropriate or even positively misleading. Much, though by no means all of that reading had been in the improving children's books of fifty or a hundred years earlier; but when the Bastables attempt to follow their recipes for success, performing acts of kindness for old gentlemen, regaling them with impromptu hymns, or paying back bent sixpences, their actions, far from being rewarded, are either ignored or misinterpreted.

Confrontations between literary expectations and the everyday world often occasion social commentary or satire. The children's treasure hunting begins as a scheme to restore the fallen family fortunes: while the secret of their poverty is kept carefully hidden from their neighbours, the children guess it for themselves by observing the unmended holes in the carpets and chairs, the departure of servants and the shortage of pocket money. Father will never admit to it, and their neighbours too are obsessively engaged in concealing their genteel poverty from one another. On the other hand, middle-class poverty is different again from the penury of city slums, as Oswald concedes:

. . . we know that we have much to be thankful for. We might be poor little children living in a crowded alley where even at summer noon hardly a ray of sunlight penetrates; clothed in rags and with bare feet— though I do not mind holes in my clothes myself, and bare feet would not be at all bad in this sort of weather.[37]

All the children's textbook notions of poverty come into play when their Indian uncle finally appears. When he is overheard refusing Father's cheap port on the grounds that he is 'a poor broken-down man who can't be too careful', he unintentionally confirms their belief that he is genuinely poor, to which Pope's line 'Lo, the poor Indian . . .' lends further support. 'Then Dora said, "Poverty is no disgrace. We should honour honest poverty." And we all agreed that that was so.'[38] Their efforts to feed him and finance him out of their own pocket money finally reveal the genuine poverty that Father has been at pains to hide, and the Indian uncle is transformed into the generous benefactor that the children had looked for elsewhere.

The use of the child's viewpoint to pierce the disguising forms of adult conventions and pretensions (here concealing inadmissible middle-class poverty) is a technique E. Nesbit learnt from Charles Dickens. She further invests her children with a sententiousness that makes them pass judgements that incidentally expose the hypocrisies of the adult world. Thus Dora's assertion 'Poverty is no disgrace. We should honour honest poverty' unconsciously comments on their Father's elaborate attempts at concealment.

On other occasions, their sententiousness does not so much expose the shams of the adult world as mimic its rhetoric:

Dicky . . . smoked the pipe of peace. It is the pipe we did bubbles with in the summer, and somehow it has not got broken yet. We put tea-leaves in it for the pipe of peace, but the girls are not allowed to have any. It is not right to let girls smoke. They get to think too much of themselves if you let them do everything the same as men.[39]

While Oswald is here very much a small boy, smoking a clay pipe full of tea-leaves, in imitation of a Red Indian rite, he also speaks for the adult males of his society. E. Nesbit delicately exposes the childish defensiveness of grown men who feel threatened by women impinging upon exclusively male rituals. Children may mock and occasionally subvert the adult world, but they also imitate it and parrot its clichés. E. Nesbit was perhaps the first woman writer to adopt a position of detachment from the prevailing values of the day in order to explore its impact on children with sharp-eyed amusement. Behind Oswald's confident assertions of his safe male superiority, we can hear the mocking laughter of his creator, herself a chain smoker and a woman who liked to 'do everything the same as men'.

To follow, necessarily selectively, a group of women writers for children from Sarah Fielding's innovative fiction *The Governess* through to E. Nesbit's first great success *The Treasure Seekers*, is to recognize their need for acceptance within the dominant male discourses of their times, and their initial problems in identifying with the child's point of view, either by voice or by attitude. Most late eighteenth-century women writers adopted deliberately didactic tones, seeing their writing for children as a way of putting into practice Enlightenment theories about the nature of education, at precisely the moment when political events across the Channel seemed to be discrediting Enlightenment ideals. The free play of imagination, the elusiveness and wonder of childhood feelings, though accessible to romantic poets, were not assimilated into children's writing for another century. The anxiety to display maturity and responsibility inhibited women writers for some time from adopting the child's voice, characterized by parodic style and pleasure in rhythmic nonsense, or the child's point of view, whose innocence of adult modes of perception often included a critique of them.

These features are not widely used until the end of the nineteenth century, when the work of E. Nesbit articulates some of the previously hidden feelings of childhood. And what enables her to do this is her creative use of child's play as a potentially critical imitation of the adult world, a device echoed at the stylistic level by her travesties of the literary techniques of her predecessors, and their aspirations to high-minded conformity — from these, she creates a web of comedy that mocks such aspirations. In adopting the voice of the child, in exposing the adult world to the child's critical gaze, E. Nesbit had, ironically, found a way of articulating her feelings of rebelliousness and subversiveness as a woman. Adopting the child's voice allowed her not only to locate her own position as a woman in a male-dominated society, but also to escape from the pressure to write like a man.

Notes

1. *Nister's Holiday Annual* (London, 1896), pages unnumbered, 'The Play Times', 1/3, introduction.
2. Godwin to Charles Lamb, 10 Mar. 1808, *The Letters of Charles and Mary Anne Lamb*, ed. Edwin W. Marrs Jr., ii, 1801–9 (Ithaca, N.Y., 1976), 223. Godwin probably recalled Dr Johnson's observation to Mrs Thrale: 'Remember always (said he) that the parents *buy* the books, and that the children never read them.' See Thrale (n.7 below), 156–7.
3. *The Adventures of David Simple* ... by a Lady, 2 vols. (London, 1744), 'Advertisement to the Reader'.
4. The influence of *The Governess* is apparent both in the title and contents of Mme Le Prince de Beaumont's *Magasin des Enfans, ou Dialogue entre un sage Gouvernante et plusieurs de ses eleves* (London, 1756, trans. 1757). Mrs Affable and her six pupils correspond to Mrs Teachum and her nine. Among the moral fairy stories here retold is an important version of 'Beauty and the Beast'. See Jill E. Grey's introduction to *The Governess* (London, 1968), 64–6.
5. *The Governess: or, Little Female Academy* (London, 1749), facsimile reprint introduced by Jill E. Grey (London, 1968), 6, 7.
6. Ibid. 68.
7. Mrs Thrale, *Anecdotes of the Late Samuel Johnson* (1786), reprinted in *Johnsonian Miscellanies*, ed. G. B. Hill, 2 vols. (London, 1897), i. 156.
8. Mary Wollstonecraft, *A Vindication of the Rights of Woman* (1792, repr. Harmondsworth, 1982), 306.
9. Ibid. 79, 83.
10. *Original Stories from Real Life* (1788, repr. London, 1906), 1.
11. William Godwin, *Memoirs of the Author of a Vindication of the Rights of Woman* (London, 1798), 43. Elsewhere he describes Mary restoring to the Kingsborough girls the liberty that their mother had restricted, undertaking 'to govern them by their affections only' (56–7).
12. 'The Purple Jar', *The Parent's Assistant* (London, 1796), II. i. 7, 9–10.
13. Ibid. II. i. 14.
14. Ibid. I. i. xi.
15. Lamb to Coleridge, 23 Oct. 1802, *The Letters of Charles and Mary Anne Lamb*, ii. 81.
16. Ibid.
17. *The Collected Writings of Thomas de Quincey*, ed. David Masson (Edinburgh, 1889), i. 127.
18. Southey to Coleridge, 14 Mar. 1804, *The Life and Correspondence of Robert Southey*, ed. Revd C. C. Southey, 6 vols. (London, 1850), ii. 275.
19. Coleridge's *Shakespearean Criticism*, ed. T. M. Raysor, 2 vols. (London, 1930), ii. 13 (the lecture is described in a letter from H. C. Robinson to Mrs Clarkson, 7 May 1808). See also lectures 5 and 7 (1811–12), ii. 109–10, 293.

20. *Letters for Literary Ladies* (3rd edn., London, 1805), 'Letter from a Gentleman to his Friend', 28.
21. *Guardian of Education* (London, 1803), ii. 403.
22. Mrs Sherwood, *The Governess: or, the Little Female Academy* (Wellington, Salop., 1820), iv.
23. Ibid. 2, 8, 11, 12.
24. On nineteenth-century evangelical writers for children, see Margaret Nancy Cutt, *Ministering Angels* (Wormley, Herts., 1979).
25. *Holiday House* (Edinburgh, 1839), preface, viii, xi.
26. Christina Rossetti to Dante Gabriel Rossetti, 4 May 1874, *The Family Letters of Christina Georgina Rossetti*, ed. W. M. Rossetti (London, 1908), 43–4.
27. Lona Mosk Packer, ed., *The Rossetti–Macmillan Letters* (Berkeley, 1963), 101; see also Packer's *Christina Rossetti* (Berkeley, 1963), 305–7.
28. *Speaking Likenesses* (London, 1874), 10.
29. Ibid. 28.
30. Ibid. 34.
31. Ibid. 35–6.
32. Ibid. 42.
33. *The Story of the Treasure Seekers* (London, 1899), 111–12.
34. Ibid. 4.
35. Ibid. 262.
36. Ibid. 293–4.
37. Ibid. 33.
38. Ibid. 268.
39. Ibid. 198–9.

12

E. Nesbit and The Book of Dragons

W. W. ROBSON

E. NESBIT (Edith Nesbit, 1858–1924) was a prolific author of the late nineteenth and early twentieth centuries. Like 'Mother' in *The Railway Children* she wrote to support her family. By 1898 she had come to enjoy a modest reputation as a readable purveyor of light fiction, some of it written in collaboration with her husband Hubert Bland. Her output included children's stories in the popular style of the day, but without the distinctive quality she was to develop later. She wrote much verse, and longed to be a poet: Philip Larkin includes her in *The Oxford Book of Twentieth Century English Verse* (1973). But her narrative poems in the manner of Tennyson (*Lays and Legends*, 1886) make little impression on modern readers. Some of her best work is in her short stories, especially the striking tales about the return of the dead, 'Mansize in Marble' and 'John Charrington's Wedding'. But it is her books for children that are remembered. These began with the stories of the treasure-seeking family, the Bastables, which were published in magazines during 1898 and collected in book form in 1899. From then on E. Nesbit was recognized as one of the leading British writers for children. The immediate stimulus to write *The Story of the Treasure Seekers* came from an invitation by *The Girl's Own Paper* to reminisce about her own childhood, but she may also have been influenced by Kenneth Grahame's *The Golden Age* (1895) and its continuation *Dream Days* (1898), which describe the doings of a family of five orphans relatively free of adult supervision.

Nesbit's books about children fall into three categories: (i) pure fantasy, as in *The Book of Dragons* (1900); (ii) non-fantastic (if often improbable) books about children seen from the children's point of view. This category includes the trilogy about the Bastables: *The Story of the Treasure Seekers* (1899), *The Wouldbegoods* (1901), and *The New Treasure Seekers* (1904). It also includes *The Railway Children* (1906). The Bastables appear, seen from an adult point of view, in her romantic novel *The Red House* (1902). (iii) Books containing a fantastic element or marvel, but otherwise realistic: a genre used by Nesbit's contemporary F. Anstey (Thomas Anstey Guthrie, 1856–1934) in *Vice Versa* (1882), *The Brass Bottle* (1900), and other books. In *The Brass Bottle* an Arabian Jinnee is let loose in Victorian London. At the end of *Five Childen and It* the children turn to Anstey's novel to find a way out of their difficulties. This category includes the trilogy about the Five Children: *Five Children and It* (1902), *The Phoenix and the Carpet* (1904), and *The Story of the Amulet* (1906). To the same category (magic in the modern world) also belong *The Enchanted Castle* (1907), and *The House of Arden* (1908).

E. Nesbit's gift is agreed to be for the depiction of children. Some of her admirers like to claim that she was the first writer to see them as real human beings, unsentimentally (but this claim, as we shall see, has been contested). She usually takes a family of children of various ages up to, perhaps, ten or twelve and involves them in adventures, sometimes brought about by magic, sometimes not. Many of the stories are about the predicaments children get into when searching for treasure in everyday surroundings. There is always some domestic trouble in the background, a parent missing, a lack of money: many of the children's adventures come about through attempts to restore the family's prosperity. In its more fantastic aspects Nesbit's writing belongs to a kind recognized as distinctively English, with its infusion of magic, its parody of logic, and its surrealistic wit and humour. Famous writers in this kind are Edward Lear and Lewis Carroll, and Nesbit has affinities with them as a writer, though as a person she was much less inhibited than they were: Noel Coward, who came to know her well, described her as the most genuine Bohemian he had ever met.

The narrator of the Bastable books is the eldest boy Oswald (not avowedly, but the reader soon realizes this). His attempts to present objectively his own abilities and good qualities result in an unintentionally amusing self-portrait. Perhaps this is merely for the benefit of the adult reader, but with Nesbit we can never be sure how many of her subtleties are taken in by children without their being fully aware of them. As with Henry Adams and Norman Mailer, Oswald's use of the third person gives him both a commanding and an irritating quality as narrator. It would be interesting to know, but hard to find out, to what extent boys (or girls) find it easy to identify with him.

In the other trilogy, about the Five Children, character interest is less prominent: though these books too are full of comedy, it does not depend so much upon this source. It would not be inaccurate to describe them as fairy stories, but there is an essential difference between them and traditional folktales, even if we encounter these, as many of us do, in the Grimms' *Household Tales* (1824–6), where, as J. M. Ellis shows in his recent book *One Fairy Story Too Many* (1983), they are partly rationalized and brought into line with conventional ideas. In folktales the magic suffuses everything. You cannot make sense of a story like 'Rumpel-stilt-skin' unless you are prepared to take it on its own terms. The world of folktales has its own laws, physical, meta-physical, and moral. In contrast, in her Anstey-type stories, Nesbit confines the magic to one marvel: everything else belongs to the ordinary world. She excels in the consistent working out of stories based on a fantasy premiss. Though a rapid and casual writer she is careful about details: she anticipates the questions children are likely to ask, even if her answers are often cleverly evasive.

Unlike some other fantasists Nesbit makes the marvel interest-ing in itself. In *Five Children and It* the Psammead has a distinct character as the small irritable strange-looking creature who grumbles all the time at having to fulfil the wishes of the children, afraid it may injure itself in the process. To add to the comedy something always goes wrong with the Psammead's miracles: we are regaled with a display of human folly. The method is different from that of the Bastable trilogy. We remember 'It' rather than the Five Children. Many readers probably cannot recall their names. They are in a sense more credible than the Bastable children, less naïve, more endowed with competence and common sense, but they are not highly individualized as the Bastable children are.

Like all good modern writers of fairy stories Nesbit uses traditional motifs and gives her own twist to them. Humphrey Carpenter (in *Secret Gardens*, 1985) and others have noted that the Psammead probably derives from the bad-tempered Cuckoo and Raven in Mrs Molesworth. It is a distinctive character all the same. In *The Phoenix and the Carpet* the magic carpet is a traditional device, but an original slant is given to it: the carpet has been repaired and parts of it begin to lose their magic (a neat emblem of the mixed genre of the whole book). The Phoenix not only has its legendary attributes but its personal ruling passion (vanity). This book apparently suggested Rudyard Kipling's stories in *Puck of Pook's Hill* (1906) and *Rewards and Fairies* (1910). (There had already been influence in the other direction: the Bastable children play games based on Kipling's *Jungle Books* (1894–5).) It has been said that the Puck books are more didactic than *The Phoenix and the Carpet*; and certainly they contain, in a form devised to please young readers, Kipling's pondered insights into English history. Nesbit merely writes to entertain. But there are lessons in *The Phoenix and the Carpet* also. A contrast in political outlook has been seen between conservative Kipling and socialist Nesbit. The children in the Puck books are always being asked to admire unusual and heroic individuals, who perform their assigned tasks in an exemplary way. Nesbit is more concerned to show children the workings of a society as a whole, and how the people of other periods differed from, and in what ways they resembled, those of the present time.

But the main difference between Kipling and Nesbit is that in the Puck books Dan and Una are mere spectators; they do not take part in the 'past' or 'future' events, as the children in the Nesbit books do, and as does the Traveller in Wells's *Time Machine* (1895), whatever logical difficulties this may entail. In Kipling the genre is that of the 'Historical Pageant': in Nesbit it is the 'Exciting Adventure'. The sense of an enjoyment shared between author and reader is more important than edification. Graham Greene in *A Sort of Life* (1971) recalled his youthful delight at the end of the book, when the magic bird has gone and a great box arrives full of everything the children have ever desired, 'toys and games and books, and chocolates and candied cherries, and paint-boxes and photographic cameras'.

The design on the reader in Kipling does not mean that the Puck stories had less appeal than the Nesbit books. It is doubtful whether their teaching was ever the source of interest. I suspect that both the Imperialist and the Fabian would have been forgotten if they had not been able to create that sense of the mysteriousness of the past which gives it its special thrill. C. S. Lewis (whose own writings for children owe much to Nesbit) said that *The Story of the Amulet* was his favourite among her books, because it first opened his eyes to 'the dark backward and abysm of time'. And Stephen Prickett in *Victorian Fantasy* (1975) shows how Nesbit uses the fantastic to illuminate history and make it 'real'. *The Story of the Amulet* displays more than routine invention in the conjuring up of the Egypt of the Pharaohs, Babylon, Caesar's Britain, and a glimpse of a future utopia which has a definitely Wellsian flavour. Not only are the particular episodes excellent: the frame story is excellent too, with the mystery of the missing half of the Amulet, lost in the past, and the surprising conclusion to the story.

But in these books the magic is merely a datum: it could be presented on television, the great enemy of the imagination. In *The Enchanted Castle* it pervades the whole atmosphere of the book. The story tells how four children encounter magic in the gardens of a great deserted house. Here the magic is not, as in Anstey, or the Five Children books, only a postulate: it suggests the co-presence of another world with our own. 'There is a curtain, thin as gossamer, clear as glass, strong as iron, that hangs forever between the world of magic and the world that seems to us real. And when once people have found one of the little weak spots in the curtain which are marked by magic rings and amulets, and the like, anything may happen' (from *The Enchanted Castle*). There is something disturbing, even nightmarish, in the scene when the statues of dinosaurs come to life in the moonlight, and in the grotesquerie Graham Greene remembered, when the Ugly

Wuglies, made of masks and umbrellas, suddenly come alive and applaud the children's play, cheering with roofless mouths, while they clap their empty gloves. *The House of Arden* belongs to the same mixed genre but does not reach so deeply into primitive fantasies and terrors. The characteristic Nesbit comedy appears in the marvel, here the Mouldiwarp, a mole that appears on the family coat of arms: it can be summoned only by poetry composed in its honour, which is difficult for Edred and his sister Elfrida, since neither of them has any vestige of poetic gift.

With or without the use of magic Nesbit wrote gripping and convincing stories of children. How she creates life on the page cannot be explained by a formula, but the secret seems to lie in her ability to use adult skills for the expression of a child's imaginings, yet without patronage or betrayal. Children are not themselves good storytellers; they 'had the experience but missed the meaning' (T. S. Eliot, 'The Dry Salvages'). Nesbit seems to be able to give the 'experience' and the 'meaning' together. As she put it: 'The reason why these children are like real children is that I was a child once myself, and by some fortunate chance I remember exactly how I used to feel and think about things,' (quoted by Naomi Lewis in her introduction to *E. Nesbit: Fairy Stories*, 1979). There is also an element of 'generation politics': Nesbit seems to be on the child's side in a way in which many writers for children are not. In 'The Cockatoucan, or Great-aunt Willoughby' (in *Nine Unlikely Tales*) a young Edwardian seems to confront an elderly Victorian:

She had been to her Great-aunt Willoughby's before, and she knew exactly what to expect. She would be asked about her lessons, and how many marks she had, and whether she had been a good girl. I can't think why grown-up people don't see how impertinent these questions are. Suppose you were to answer, 'I'm top of my class, Auntie, thank you, and I'm very good. And now let's have a little talk about you. Aunt dear, how much money have you got, and have you been scolding the servants again, or have you tried to be good and patient as a properly brought up aunt should be, eh, dear?'

In 'Whereyouwanttogoto' (also in *Nine Unlikely Tales*) there is a similar authorial dissociation from authoritarianism:

E. Nesbit and The Book of Dragons

You are intelligent children, and I will not insult you with a moral. I am not Uncle Thomas. Nor will I ask you to remember what I have said. I am not Aunt Selina.

Edith Nesbit apparently had a difficult and insecure childhood (though with periods of great happiness). She believed that her early sufferings were in many ways representative of the sufferings of children at that time, and that they should not remain for ever unarticulated but should be preserved and shown from the inside. I have suggested that her point of view represents a combination of the adult's with the child's. It might be more accurate to say that she undermines the normal contrast between adult and child: they are both alike because they are both human. Children may have more limitations, they are physically weaker, exposed to some kinds of exploitation, material and moral, that adults may be able to avoid. But they can have all the adult qualities, both admirable and unadmirable: they can be clever, witty, temperamental, greedy, naïve, ingenious, as adults can. The slang and manners have of course dated: the characterizations have not.

Does this put E. Nesbit in a class by herself? Her achievement stands up well to comparison with some of the famous texts of canonical literature: *What Maisie Knew*, or *Huckleberry Finn*. The sense that what the reader reads is 'just happening' is better preserved in the Bastable books than in these. Henry James has a design on us (to keep us convinced of the incorruptible innocence of Maisie) and in *Huckleberry Finn*, though Mark Twain disclaimed any plan or intention in his preface (and I have never seen any convincing evidence that he did not mean what he said) there are places in the novel where we feel the presence of the collusive author. But in the Bastable books there seems to be no storyteller behind Oswald. Adult moralizing is now and then introduced, but Oswald accepts it, and his acceptance of it is part of his character: he is an establishment type. Similarly in the books in which E. Nesbit herself is the narrator there is no getting beyond a humorous, kindly, maternal presence. (The relation between this and the historical Edith Nesbit is disputed by her biographers:

some regard it as an extension of her actual personality, others say she did not really like children—as has been said of some other famous writers of children's books.)

There has not been until recently much critical debate about E. Nesbit. After the 1914–18 war her work became for a time less popular, but from the interwar years onward there was a considerable and steady rise in her reputation, and nowadays Puffin editions are scattered about in many houses. She has become a comfortable literary fixture, read, but not argued about. But during the last few years a new view of her work has been put forward, chiefly by the American critic Gore Vidal. According to this view she should be seen less as a late Victorian/Edwardian entertainer and more as a radical and subversive author, anticipating trends which surfaced in the 1960s and 1970s. Biographical considerations give this a certain plausibility: we know of the unconventionality (by the standards of her time) of Edith Nesbit's domestic ménage and private life, and her close association with Wells and Shaw and other 'advanced' figures of the day.

But much in Nesbit's work, and life, can be urged against this new reading. I think Humphrey Carpenter has put cogently the objections to seeing Nesbit as a pioneer of 'children's liberation'. The friendly adult (sometimes the narrator herself) who takes the children's side in the stories can sometimes be suspected of Fifth Columnism. Carpenter thinks Nesbit's leftism only skin deep, more a matter of short hair and smoking in public than of any real understanding of socialist ideas. She may have been excited by contact with the avant-garde; but when Women's Suffrage became an issue she opposed it. It is true that the Queen of Babylon, in *The Phoenix and the Carpet*, comments adversely on the treatment of 'slaves' (i.e. the working class) in modern London; but there is no deep concern with social change or reform in her books. The children, even if afflicted by poverty, remain middle class: all the families, however reduced their circumstances, have servants, and the parlourmaids, cooks, etc. are assumed to be socially inferior. Carpenter notes that in *Five Children and It* it is assumed that servants cannot see the result of the Psammead's magic. But I think he makes too much of this point. The author has to convey to us that the Psammead is a fantasy of the children, without actually saying so. She can be accused of clumsy plot machinery here rather than of unthinking snobbery. In real life children make all sorts of concessions to reality in their shared fantasies, and do so with the utmost nonchalance.

Still, it cannot be denied that Nesbit's stories are about middle-class children and imply middle-class values. And it is also true that she had a good deal of influence (regretted by Carpenter) on later writers for children. Until the rather self-conscious revolt against them in the 1950s it was usual to choose middle-class children as protagonists. In Nesbit this can be excused as merely a period limitation, yet, as Carpenter reminds us, her forerunners, such as Charles Kingsley and Mrs Ewing, had made poor children their heroes, and they were often the centre of interest in Mark Twain.

Carpenter's most telling point seems to me the contrast he draws between her books and Grahame's *Dream Days* and *The Golden Age*. In Grahame's books the children are not patronized but are allowed to have their own point of view, firmly critical of adults, and this is given authorial support. In his books, unlike Nesbit's, it is the adults not the children who make fools of themselves. In comparison with Grahame it can be said that Nesbit's attitude to children is patronizing. Carpenter grants that the semi-fantasy books do not make this impression, but then the issues of the real world are less challenging in them than in the Bastable books.

Are these criticisms of Nesbit fair? It must be conceded at any rate that she in no sense anticipated modern feminism. E. Nesbit takes family life as the norm, and is above all motherly. Then (to make use of a formal distinction drawn elsewhere by C. S. Lewis) the realism of her books, where there is any, is of presentation rather than content. There is a safety net under the stories: the children are never in real danger, the misery and horror of the real world are kept out and many of the underlying assumptions and attitudes are gentle and reassuring. From a modern point of view this may be seen as a limitation. They are also, on the face of it, directed to boys rather than girls. Edith Nesbit herself, it seems, was boyish, and her flattery of the boy reader can be egregious: in 'The Book of Beasts', the first story in *The Book of Dragons*, when Lionel goes to be crowned 'he was a little sorry at first that he had not put on his best clothes, but he soon forgot to think about that. If he had been a girl he would very likely have bothered about it the whole time.' But we must not forget the duplicities of the humorist and ironist that were also part of E. Nesbit.

Nor can the sense that Nesbit is pro-child—pro-girl as well as pro-boy—be eliminated. No doubt her critique of the adult world is less damaging than that in *The Golden Age* and *Dream Days*. But she is not in that business. These books have not been loved as Nesbit's books are (or Grahame's own *The Wind in the Willows*). She writes books that adults and children are meant to enjoy together. But her comedy at the expense of male complacency (as in the character of Oswald) is none the less trenchant because it is affectionate.

If there really is a subversive, 'modern' E. Nesbit it is to be found less in her realistic books than in her satiric fantasies, where she is closer to Lear and Carroll. In *The Book of Dragons* we have a sense of free play, rare in her longer stories, which links it with the *Alice* books and *The Hunting of the Snark* and *The Book of Nonsense*. Victorian seriousness was relieved by a glimpse of

> Fantastic beauty, such as lurks
> In some wild Poet, when he works
> Without a conscience or an aim.
>
> (Tennyson, *In Memoriam*, § 34)

Nonsense literature has for long been a recognized field of academic study, but it remains difficult to discuss such writing without falling into the solemn absurdities satirized in F. C. Crews's *The Pooh Perplex* (1963). The popularity and survival power of fantasy suggest that it is rooted deep in the mind, but attempts to explain it destroy the means by which its effect is achieved. To analyse E. Nesbit's charm is like cutting open a rubber ball to see what makes it bounce, a feat performed by more than one of her boy protagonists, and authorially condemned. Critics who are occupationally tempted to allegorize should remember the shrewd saying of George MacDonald that fairy tales may *contain* allegories but cannot *be* allegories. The fugitive suggestion of allegory is part of the fascination of these tales, but its fugitiveness is essential.

E. Nesbit's stories in *The Book of Dragons* have something of this quality, though superficially their humour and sophistication seem remote from that of fairy tales and folktales. They were first published in the *Strand Magazine* in 1899. The *Strand* was intended primarily for adult readers, and humorists like Anstey who appeared in it did not have a child public in mind, but the magazine regularly included stories for children as well. E. Nesbit's dragon stories were collected in book form in 1900, with the exception of 'The Last of the Dragons', which appeared in *Five of Us—and Madeline*, first published posthumously in 1925. The nine stories are now most conveniently available in *The Complete Book of Dragons*, illustrated by Erik Blegvad. His illustrations show the dragons as types of dinosaur, while H. R. Millar, who illustrated the dragon stories for the *Strand*, gives them a more traditional character. In any case there is no doubt that the dragons were suggested by dinosaurs, as in *The Enchanted Castle*. The source for them was Hawkins's stone statues of dinosaurs at the Crystal Palace (transferred in *The Enchanted Castle* to a castle in the West of England). This suggestion of the Wellsian, modern world view immediately differentiates them from traditional dragon mythology, which was apparently not based on any knowledge of the gigantic prehistoric reptiles. But Nesbit uses very little popularized science about the great lizards. And she uses very little traditional dragon-lore either, though part of the attraction of *The Book of Dragons* is the variety in appearance and character of her dragons. She makes use of the European and Near Eastern connotations of the dragon as an evil power (though in those cultures there are also traditions in which it is beneficent). But she does not draw at all on the traditions of the Far East which honour dragons. Nor, on the other hand, is she interested in the dragon as a warlike emblem, as in the royal ensign of England, instituted by Uther Pendragon, father of King Arthur. What the stories communicate is no deep use of dragon lore but the

One of H. R. Millar's illustrations for E. Nesbit's *Book of Dragons*, 1900.

The Dragon Tamers

Illustration by Erik Blegvad for *The Complete Book of Dragons*, Hamish Hamilton, 1972.

presence of a writer of exuberant and carefree invention. She invents new landscapes, with an unforgettable use of light and colour, a sense of space, and lots of weather. The dragons are all different and have different fates. In 'The Book of Beasts' the Red Dragon, culpably released from the book by little King Lionel, returns to the book's pages at the end. In 'Uncle James' the dragon eventually turns into a little, crawling, purple newt with wings. In 'The Deliverers of their Country' there is a plague of dragons of various sizes, which at the end of the story are all washed away (with one exception, the size of an earwig) in the Universal Tap Room. In 'The Ice Dragon' there is a spectacular description of a great shining, winged, scaly, clawy, big-mouthed dragon, made of pure ice, with deep, clear Prussian-blueness, and rainbow-coloured glitter. (He is melted by a bonfire.) The dragon in 'The Dragon Tamers' is made almost entirely of iron armour, a sort of tawny, red-rust colour. After years of eating nothing but bread and milk his plates and wings drop off and he grows furrier and furrier, and he is the beginning of all the cats. 'The Fiery Dragon', in the story of that name, grows small at night and is eventually put into a dragon-proof bottle. In 'Kind Little Edmund' the dragon is female: immense and yellow, like a monstrous centipede. She goes down into the centre of the earth in search of her baby, the drakling. In 'The Island of the Nine Whirlpools' the dragon is hardly more than a pantomime figure. The King takes his daughter to the Lone Tower which stands on an island in the sea, a thousand miles from anywhere. He engages a competent dragon and a respectable griffin to look after her. The dragon grows old and horrible and is drowned in the whirlpool, while the griffin is killed when the eagle part and the lion part of it fight each other. 'The Last of the Dragons' is by way of being an epilogue. We emerge in the light of common day, in the post-war years. The last of the dragons lived in Cornwall, before English History began, had no interest in Princesses, liked drinking petrol, was sentimental when called 'Dear', and eventually became the first aeroplane.

The all-pervading presence of the fireside narrator prevents the creation of an enclosed world, such as that in 'The Blue Moun-

tain' (in *Nine Unlikely Tales*), in which we feel from the inside
what it would be like to live in an ant-hill:

> ... the people of Antioch ... were very black, and generally lazy. They
> scurried up and down in their rocky little city, and always they seemed
> to be driven by most urgent affairs, hurrying to keep important
> appointments. They ran about all day long, attending to their business,
> and hardly stopping even for their dinner or their tea, and no one ever
> saw any of them asleep.

In *The Book of Dragons*, in recompense for the lack of an enclosed
world, we are given a display of the varied types of literary effect
which are possible when there is a self-conscious narrator. 'The
Book of Beasts', the first story, can be seen as a manifesto of the
newly emergent art of E. Nesbit. We may see a suggestion of
allegory: the Book represents the power of literature, or the
imagination, seductive but dangerous. But this interpretation
does not operate consistently. Some of the Beasts that fly out of
the book go back in again, two (the Butterfly and the Blue Bird of
Paradise) stay out permanently, and a Beast that was not originally in the Book, the King's own Rocking-Horse, is allowed to
go into it. I cannot see how this could be decoded as a discourse
about the relation of art to life. The charm of 'The Book of
Beasts' is that it plays with two kinds of marvel, very different.
The first is an 'improbable possibility': an ordinary little boy is
made King. This is not a wish-fulfilment story: Lionel as King
seems to be even more ordered about and rebuked and slapped by
adults than he was before. The other marvel introduces the
transgression motif, as in the Garden of Eden, or *Peter Rabbit*.
Lionel opens the Book and unintentionally releases the Butterfly
and the Blue Bird of Paradise, and the next day he lets the Red
Dragon out. 'And then Lionel felt that he had indeed done it.'
The story has no clear moral. Lionel brought trouble on himself
and his people by opening the Book, but he and they are saved by
the Hippogriff (perhaps from Ariosto?) whom he also releases
from the Book. What the young reader really gets is not a moral
but an introduction to English comic style. The conversation

between Lionel and his Prime Minister anticipates the dialogue of Noel Coward or Evelyn Waugh:

'But hadn't my great-great-however much-it-is grandfather a crown?'

'Yes, but he sent it to be tinned over, for fear of vanity, and he had all the jewels taken out, and sold them to buy books. He was a strange man; a very good King he was, but he had his faults—he was fond of books. Almost with his latest breath he sent the crown to be tinned—and he never lived to pay the tinsmith's bill.'

'Uncle James' is wholly satirical. The mock-explanations for the extraordinary natural history of Rotundia sound like a parody of Victorian popular science. In 'The Fiery Dragon' we have the prettiest of the tales: it hovers gracefully on the brink of sentimentality. Princess Sabrinetta is rescued from having to marry the boorish Prince Tiresome (who hunts with hippopotamuses) by the swineherd Elfinn, but Elfinn's hands are burned by the dragon, and he can only be cured by having the burn kissed seventy-seven times and have someone willing to die for him. The allusion to Christianity here is uncharacteristic of Nesbit and may be due to the influence of Hans Andersen.

'Kind Little Edmund' is different again, a weird tale of a round cave with a hole in the middle, in which a large pale person is sitting, with a man's face and a griffin's body, and a snake's tail and a cock's comb and neck-feathers. This is the cockatrice, who lives on fire: its fire has gone out. Kind Little Edmund helps, and in return the cockatrice tells him things they don't know at school. The manœuvres of the cockatrice and the she-dragon and the drakling, crawling through holes and tunnels and caverns, invite commentary of a psychoanalytic kind. Artistically speaking all this bizarre vitality is a foil to the cruel repressive schoolmaster in the story, who treats the marvels recounted by Edmund as all lies. He canes Edmund seven times in the course of the story.

'The Dragon Tamers' has a flavour of William Morris:

Then the dragon begged them to fasten him up at once, and they did so, with the collar and chains that were made years ago—in the days when men sang at their work and made it strong enough to bear any strain.

E. *Nesbit and* The Book of Dragons

But as usual lesson and allegory are evaded. The gold that brings the happy ending is not earned through work, whether spiritualized or not, but just found.

'The Island of the Nine Whirlpools' is rich in traditional fairy-tale features: the magician King, angry because the Queen asked the witch for a *child*, not a *boy*, and got a daughter; the Queen turning to stone and coming to life again at the end (recalling *The Winter's Tale*). Yet the rescue of the Princess at the end is accomplished by 'scientific calculations':

'My Princess', he (the hero) said tenderly, 'two great powers are on our side: the power of Love, and the power of Arithmetic. These two are stronger than anything else in the world.'

The mood of romance is quietly dispelled at the end in a glance at the adult reader over the head of the child:

I have no doubt that you will wish to know what the Princess lived on during the long years when the dragon did the cooking. My dear, she lived on her income; and that is a thing which a great many people would like to be able to do.

The elusive quality of these stories is typified by the tricks Nesbit plays with what Roland Barthes terms the 'cultural' code, the information emanating directly from the author about the 'real world'. Nesbit does not (like Flann O'Brien in *At Swim-Two-Birds*) play tricks with all the story-telling codes; she has no wish to puzzle or disturb her young readers. But she loves to tease them, and at the same time gently mock the grown-ups who are supposed to tell them what they ought to know. Many examples of her ironic duplicities can be found in 'The Ice Dragon'. This tale can be seen as a brief epitome of the whole of Nesbit's writing for children. There is the everyday setting, which for readers in the 1980s has acquired an enchantment of its own; fireworks at the Crystal Palace. But there is also the finely evoked beauty of the winter night, the Aurora Borealis, and the gradual transition to a dream world as the boy and girl go up the great slide on the way to the North Pole. The Transgression motif appears: the children were told not to go on the grass, but 'They said the *lawn*', said

Jane. 'We're not going on the *lawn*.' The evil sealskin dwarfs add a touch of domestic horror. The melting-away of the dragon corresponds to the return to ordinary life. The whole story is a parody of a homiletic tale for children, with its misleading information about the North Pole etc. and its inconsequent 'moral', which is as follows: moth-eaten things are no good for anything, not even lighting fires. 'The Ice Dragon' is typical of Nesbit's unusual gift for writing satire without destroying the sense of wonder.

The best story in *The Book of Dragons* is, I think, 'The Deliverers of their Country'. As often in science fiction the story starts with a common experience: 'It all began with Effie's getting something in her eye.' Sometimes the narrative voice speaks through Effie, in 'free indirect style'; sometimes it blends with a more authoritative voice. Voices of authority in this story are strongly adult, contemptuous of children, medical and scientific:

'Dear me,' he said, 'dear dear *dear* me! Four well-developed limbs; a long caudal appendage; five toes, unequal in length, almost like one of the Lacertidae, yet there are traces of wings.'

But for all their long words the authorities are totally impotent in face of the dragon plague. This is made wonderfully vivid, a prophetic anticipation of 1940, England attacked from the air. The scientists fail, and the children succeed—with the help of St George. This unexplained saint, whom the English presumably picked up in the Crusades, was often evoked in Edwardian conservative fantasy, such as *Where the Rainbow Ends*. Nesbit gives him a characteristically deflationary treatment:

So the children told him [St George] all about it; he turned over in his marble and leaned on one elbow to listen. But when he heard that there were so many dragons he shook his head.

'It's no good,' he said, 'they would be one too many for poor old George. You should have waked me before. I was always for a fair fight—one man one dragon was my motto.'

Just then a flight of dragons passed overhead, and St George half drew his sword.

But he shook his head again, and pushed the sword back as the flight of dragons grew small in the distance.

'I can't do anything,' he said; 'things have changed since my time. St Andrew told me about it. They woke him up over the engineers' strike, and he came to talk to me. He says everything is done by machinery now; there must be some way of settling these dragons.'

The tone and meaning of the story are epitomized in the moment when St George half draws his sword. The defeat of the dragons is also unheroic, and appropriately English: the deliverance of the country is in the end due to the weather.

The reader is left in uncertainty as to whether the children have played any part at all in what happened. That there *were* 'dragons'—or something like them—is proved by the preservation of a single specimen by the professor (the doctor, Effie's father, having thrown away the one he got out of Effie's eye). But the country shows no gratitude to, or even awareness of, its 'deliverers'. Father merely regrets not having preserved his specimen. Mother scolds. It is another example of the paradox that runs through Nesbit's work: the role of the children is both everything and nothing. Perhaps this is because what children in her work ultimately symbolize is the Imagination.

Booklist

The following children's books by E. Nesbit are referred to in this essay:

The Story of the Treasure Seekers (1899).
The Book of Dragons (1900).
Nine Unlikely Tales (1901).
The Wouldbegoods (1901).
Five Children and It (1902).
The Phoenix and the Carpet (1904).
The New Treasure Seekers (1904).
The Story of the Amulet (1906).
The Railway Children (1906).
The Enchanted Castle (1907).
The House of Arden (1908).
Five of Us—and Madeline (1925).

Biographies of E. Nesbit

Doris Langley Moore, *E. Nesbit: a biography* (1933, rev. London, 1967).
Julia Briggs, *A Woman of Passion: E. Nesbit* (London, 1987).

W. W. Robson

Other Works

C. S. Lewis, *Surprised by Joy* (London, 1955).
Graham Greene, *A Sort of Life* (London, 1971).
Gore Vidal, *Collected Essays 1952–1972* (London, 1974).
C. N. Manlove, *Modern Fantasy* (Cambridge, 1975).
Stephen Prickett, *Victorian Fantasy* (Brighton, 1979).
Humphrey Carpenter, *Secret Gardens* (London, 1985).

13

Excessively Impertinent Bunnies: The Subversive Element in Beatrix Potter

HUMPHREY CARPENTER

They are holed up in some bar among the dives
of Deptford, deep in their cups, and a packet
of cashew nuts, like Chippy Hackee and cute
little Timmy Tiptoes hiding from their wives.

Any minute now they'll be talking shop
about some crony's record-breaking bender,
like that mate of Terry's banned from his own do
after sinking twenty vodkas and a cop.

Set them up again: I'm holding my tankard
so the cloudy light will set them up—
this mermaid on a forearm, that chinstrap
of a scar—though I'll try not to look hard

for fear of finding myself there, out on the piss
with a black-eyed, sulphurous misogynist.[1]

THIS sonnet by Blake Morrison was printed in the *Times Literary Supplement* in April 1987. Beatrix Potter enthusiasts will not need to have it explained that Morrison is comparing the couple of blokes he has seen in the Deptford pub with Potter's *The Tale of Tommy Tiptoes* (1911), in which a squirrel and a chipmunk hide away from their wives at the bottom of a hollow tree and stuff themselves full of nuts.

It is a bit of a jolt to find Beatrix Potter cited in such a context. We would not have been surprised if it had been *Alice in Wonderland*, for Lewis Carroll is ceaselessly plundered, to the point of cliché, by writers, poets, and speech-makers. Carroll is respectable as a literary influence; T. S. Eliot lectured on him on at least one occasion, and you can detect Carrollian influences in his poetry. But it is hard to imagine the late Dame Helen Gardner citing *The Tale of Peter Rabbit* in her *Art of T. S. Eliot*. Chroniclers of the development of the twentieth-century literary imagination are not likely to put Beatrix Potter on the map as a source for poets and novelists. Yet one modern novelist writes:

Of course there was Beatrix Potter. I have never lost my admiration for her books and I have often reread her, so that I am not surprised when I find in one of my own stories, 'Under the Garden', a pale echo of Tom Kitten being trounced up [*sic*] by the rats behind the skirting-board and the sinister Anna Maria covering him with dough, and in *Brighton Rock* the dishonest lawyer ... hungrily echoes Miss Potter's dialogue as he watches the secretaries go by carrying their little typewriters.[2]

This passage is taken from Graham Greene's autobiography. The short story he refers to, 'Under the Garden', is not just a 'pale echo' of the Beatrix Potter *Tale of Samuel Whiskers*; it is an elaborate commentary on it, and I shall come back to it later. As to the *Brighton Rock* passage, here it is:

'I married beneath me,' Mr Drewitt said. 'It was my tragic mistake. I was young. An affair of uncontrollable passion. I was a passionate man,' he said, wriggling with indigestion ... He leant forward and said in a whisper: 'I watch the little typists go by carrying their little cases. I'm quite harmless. A man may watch. My God, how neat and trim!' He broke off, his hand vibrating on the chair arm.[3]

The source of this is *The Tale of Ginger and Pickles*, the Potter book about the dog and cat who keep the village shop:

The shop was also patronized by mice—only the mice were rather afraid of Ginger [the cat].

Ginger usually requested Pickles to serve them, because he said it made his mouth water.

'I cannot bear,' said he, 'to see them going out at the door carrying their little parcels.'

'I have the same feeling about rats,' replied Pickles, 'but it would never do to eat our own customers; they would leave us and go to Tabitha Twitchit's.'

'On the contrary, they would go nowhere,' replied Ginger gloomily.

(*Top*) from *The Tale of Ginger and Pickles*. (*Middle*) Duchess and Ribby in *The Pie and the Patty-Pan*. (*Bottom*) 'They ran, and they ran, and they ran down the hill.'

Greene's revelation of his debt to Beatrix Potter, his statement that he has 'often reread her', sent me hunting in the indexes of some other twentieth-century literary autobiographies and biographies. The catch was only so-so. W. H. Auden admitted to a lifelong fondness for her books; he writes in 'Letter to Lord Byron' (1936):

> You must ask me who
> Have written just as I'd have liked to do.
> I stop to listen and the names I hear
> Are those of Firbank, Potter, Carroll, Lear.[4]

Similarly Christopher Isherwood's biographer tells us that *The Tale of Samuel Whiskers* was 'one of the first books to have left its mark'[5] on Isherwood in childhood, and points out that the more macabre elements in the Potter stories evidently contributed to the lurid 'Mortmere' fantasies which Isherwood and his friend Edward Upward concocted during undergraduate days—fantasies which themselves influenced the writings of the entire 'Auden generation'.

But such acknowledgements of the importance of the Potter stories on writers' imaginations in childhood are rare. If Evelyn Waugh or Virginia Woolf, Robert Graves or Stephen Spender ever read, cared for, and were affected by Potter, they or their biographers do not bother to tell us. (George Orwell's biographer Bernard Crick records that Orwell was still reading Potter, particularly *The Tale of Pigling Bland*, when he was at preparatory school and, as Orwell's sister said, 'far too old for it';[6] but tantalizingly Crick fails to make the obvious link with *Animal Farm*.) Beatrix Potter gets no mention at all in a 1981 encyclopaedia entitled *Makers of Modern Culture*,[7] and though she appears briefly in the 1983 *Fontana Biographical Companion to Modern Thought*, the entry for her there scarcely explains her importance to, say, Auden or Graham Greene. We are told that she wrote 'illustrated tales about rabbits, kittens, mice and other creatures', and that these were within the 'well-established tradition' of 'the anthropomorphic animal story, often with moral attitudes'. Her originality 'was in the quality of her illustrations, drawn from life, and their aptness to the text. Rarely portraying humans, she captured essentially animal characteristics and, latterly, a feeling of the Lakeland landscape. Word and picture were used in an absolutely complementary sense.'[8]

Now it is perfectly true that everyone who has opened a Beatrix Potter book remembers her pictures. Anthony Powell, another novelist of the Graham Greene generation, refers in his autobiography to the feeling that Aubrey Beardsley's drawings were 'familiar as Tenniel's Alice or Beatrix Potter's Tom Kitten'.[9] But it is not for this, not for drawings of Tom Kitten or the Lake District, that Greene, Auden, Isherwood, and Blake Morrison have admired and been affected by her. Greene has 're*read*' her; Auden wished to have written, not drawn, like her; Isherwood acquired from her books not an interest in 'tales about rabbits, kittens, mice and other creatures', nor the 'moral attitudes' of the long-established anthropomorphic animal story, but—judging from Mortmere—a sense of the way that the grotesque and unmentionable may lurk behind any domestic façade, particularly the most respectable.

This is precisely the use Graham Greene makes of her in the short story he modestly calls 'a pale echo' of *The Tale of Samuel Whiskers*. 'Under the Garden', first collected in Greene's *A Sense of Reality* (1963), describes Wilditch, an elderly man dying of cancer, returning to the country house where he was brought up. He has come for one purpose: to see if there could possibly be any truth in a vivid memory he has of one night in childhood when, wishing to hide from his family, he penetrated to the mysterious inner reaches of the garden, crossed a lake to an island, discovered a passage leading underground between the roots of a tree, and descended to a dark and sinister region. At that moment he hears a hoarse voice calling 'Maria, Maria', whereupon

An old woman appeared suddenly and noiselessly around the corner of the passage. She wore an old blue dress which came down to her ankles . . . She was every bit as surprised as I was. She stood there gaping at me and then she opened her mouth and squawked. I learned later that she had no roof to her mouth and was probably saying, 'Who are you?' . . . The hoarse voice out of sight said, 'Bring him along here, Maria.'[10]

We would not need Greene's own admission to identify the story's model. Even the woman's name comes from Beatrix Potter:

When Tom Kitten picked himself up and looked about him, he found himself in a place that he had never seen before, although he had lived all his life in the house ... Opposite to him—as far away as he could sit—was an enormous rat. ... 'Anna Maria! Anna Maria!' squeaked the rat. There was a pattering noise and an old woman rat poked her head round a rafter. All in a minute she rushed upon Tom Kitten ...

In Beatrix Potter's illustration, as in Greene's story, Anna Maria wears a long blue dress that comes down to her ankles.

In Greene's version, Samuel Whiskers, the old rat of the Potter story, becomes an ancient man permanently seated on a lavatory, 'a big old man with a white beard ... He had one good leg, but the right trouser was sewn up and looked stuffed like a bolster.'[11] This figure of nightmare tells the boy to call him Javitt—though mentioning that this is not his real name—and makes it clear that the boy will be kept prisoner, so as to read aloud to him from a bundle of ancient newspapers; a detail recalling Tony Last's imprisonment by Mr Todd in Evelyn Waugh's *A Handful of Dust*—which incidentally leads us back to Beatrix Potter, for 'Mr Tod' is the name of one of her own principal characters in her most sinister story. (Todd and Tod both occupy sinister houses in the middle of the woodland, remote from human society.)

Who and what are Javitt and his ancient Maria the Graham Greene story does not explain. Evidently Greene and his narrator do not themselves know. They appear to be immortals, personifications of all that is ugly, but also (so they claim) the parents of a beauty queen, no less than Miss Ramsgate in the upper world. Javitt, forever seated on his lavatory, imparts much coarse wisdom to the boy, and eventually leads him down a long passage to show him a treasure-hoard of jewellery, announcing that a further store of riches lies buried still deeper in the earth. The story concludes with the boy's escape, and with the adult narrator returning to search for evidence that it all really happened—evidence that he does eventually find.

'Under the Garden' does not quite come off as a story. Greene seems to be writing about the adult's effort to recover the vivid imagination of childhood—hence, perhaps, his choice of Beatrix Potter to give the story its details—and he also appears to be trying to explore the rich depths that lie in Potter's work, to open up some of her implications. What he actually manages to evoke is the work of quite a different writer, Mervyn Peake, whose *Gormenghast* trilogy is full of just such random grotesques, living amid exotic decay. The qualities of Beatrix Potter elude Greene, and Javitt lacks most of the resonance she achieved in her usual terse manner when she created Samuel Whiskers. But one values the story for Greene's tribute to the force of her imagination, the acknowledgement that she had the power of creating archetypes that remain with her readers for the rest of their lives. And if one wants an indication that the Potter influence can fit snugly into modern writing, one need only turn back the pages to the very first piece in Greene's *Collected Short Stories*. 'The Destructors', dated 1954 and anticipating the vandalism of a later generation, describes a group of teenagers breaking into an old man's house while he is away one Bank Holiday—an exceptionally fine house with a unique carved staircase—and destroying not merely the contents but the structure itself, in an orgy of pointless waste. Again there is a strong echo of Potter:

Then Tom Thumb lost his temper. He put the ham in the middle of the floor, and hit it with the tongs and with the shovel—bang, bang, smash, smash!

The ham flew all into pieces, for underneath the shiny paint it was made of nothing but plaster!

Then there was no end to the rage and disappointment of Tom Thumb and Hunca Munca. They broke up the pudding, the lobsters, the pears and the oranges . . . Tom Thumb . . . took Jane's clothes out of the chest of drawers in her bedroom, and he threw them out of the top floor window.

This is from *The Tale of Two Bad Mice* (1904), in which the mice systematically destroy and plunder the contents of a doll's house. No doubt an indefatigable researcher could find traces of Potter elsewhere in Graham Greene's work; after all, the structure of his early novels, which usually deal with a man on the run who is saved by a girl he has met in his flight, bears a distinct resemblance to *The Tale of Pigling Bland*.

Greene's Beatrix Potter, then, is not the Lakeland water-colourist who was solely concerned with 'essentially animal characteristics'. That definition of Potter would appear to be very wide of the mark. In fact anyone with a more than superficial acquaintance with the Potter books knows it to be upside down. Like any other animal fabulist from Aesop onwards,[12] she invariably uses the creatures in her stories to display human characteristics and foibles. She can heighten and underline their character-traits because she is not obliged to clutter her stories with unnecessary social background, and she can also eliminate such elements as sexuality, so as to concentrate her attention on her themes. There is no need to waste space demonstrating this: anyone who troubles to read her stories with the slightest attention can see it. The question is: what is exclusively Potterish about the way she does it? Why should it be her animal stories, rather than Aesop's or Joel Chandler Harris's or Alison Uttley's, that stuck in the imaginations of Greene, Auden, Isherwood, and maybe George Orwell too?

If we look again at what that Fontana encyclopaedia has to say about Beatrix Potter's texts, we find that she wrote in 'a well-established tradition' of 'the anthropomorphic animal story, often with moral attitudes'. Such a tradition certainly existed, though Aesop was not part of it—his animals are pragmatic, and his tales demonstrate the virtues of common sense and looking after one's own skin, rather than offering any more lofty moral fare. Nor are 'moral attitudes' found in the work of Joel Chandler Harris, the most accomplished practitioner of the animal fable for children before Potter's time. Harris's *Uncle Remus* (1880) is a hymn to cunning and ingenious trickery, and it preaches a frontier survival-ethic rather than nineteenth-century Christian morality. The 'well-established tradition' of which the author of the Fontana entry is thinking began in the mid-eighteenth century, when various lady hack-writers penned tales for children about the tribulations of animals, generally domestic pets.[13] Sometimes these animals embody human characteristics, and the stories have a faintly satirical tinge. More often, as in the late and most famous example of the genre, Anna Sewell's *Black Beauty* (1877), the creature's maltreatment at the hands of humans serves chiefly to highlight cruelty to animals and also to expose intolerable social conditions. Clearly all this has nothing to do with Beatrix Potter. Her line does go back to Aesop, and it takes in something of *Uncle Remus* on the way—it was one of her own favourite books in childhood. But there is nothing in her work that resembles the moral tale. In fact it might be argued that she is writing something pretty close to a series of immoral tales; that the voice we hear again and again in her stories is not that of the late Victorian spinster decorously instructing her nieces and child-friends in acceptable social behaviour, but of a rebel, albeit a covert one, demonstrating the rewards of nonconformity, and exhorting her young readers to question the social system into which they found themselves born.

That this should be the case is not very surprising. Her whole life was dedicated to rebellion. Born in 1866 into a Kensington house where caution ruled, a family caution that restrained her artistically-minded father from making anything out of his life, Beatrix Potter struggled not to fall victim to this same malaise. Her biographer Margaret Lane pictures her as a solitary child who kept company with her pets—rabbits, hedgehogs, rats, and the rest—as a substitute for human affection and friendship.[14] But Beatrix's journals, deciphered by Leslie Linder and published since Margaret Lane's life of her first appeared,[15] present a much more vigorous character: somebody very determined and independent-minded, unable for purely practical and economic reasons to break away from the parental home until she was middle-aged, but from her early years displaying a vigorous contempt for most of the accepted Victorian values. Again and again in the journal she is dismissive of the absurdities of all religious sects and practices (like T. S. Eliot she was brought up a Unitarian), and also of the nuances and taboos of the class system. In other words, though born into the Victorian era, she rejected two of the chief tenets of Victorian society, religion and the class structure. If she had not been so pathologically shy and therefore so bad at getting her own way, she might have become a social campaigner and reformer. If she had been brought up in a predominantly literary household, she would probably have turned novelist. As it was, her father socialized largely with artists such as Millais, so she took to painting, and drifted into making greetings cards of 'dressed animals', whence it was a short step to *Peter Rabbit* and the beginning of her children's books. To these, she brought all the unconventionality that is recorded in her journal. Significantly, the journal stops shortly before she became a children's writer; evidently the children's books were able to act as the vehicles for her feelings about the world which had previously been recorded in it.

The 'voice' in the Beatrix Potter books would seem, at first encounter, to be a Victorian one. If you ask people what they chiefly remember about the stories, apart from the pictures, the answer is likely to be 'the long words'. She is famous, perhaps even infamous, for the demands she makes on child readers. 'I am affronted,' says Mrs Tabitha Twitchit when she finds that her kittens have made a mess of their clothes; and we are told in the same story that the kittens' behaviour 'disturbed the dignity and repose of the tea party'. Jemima Puddleduck, much put out because her eggs are taken from her and given to a hen to hatch, 'complained of the superfluous hen'. Tommy Brock in *The Tale of Mr Tod* 'squeezed himself into the rabbit hole with alacrity'. In the same story, one of the rabbits complains: 'My Uncle Bouncer has displayed a lamentable want of discretion for his years'; and words like 'indolent' and 'apoplectic' are used to portray the behaviour of Tommy Brock the Badger, snoring as he lies in bed in his boots. It seems to be an orgy of Victorian vocabulary. The present-day parent, attempting to explain these words to children, vaguely supposes that the original readers, in the first decade of this century, when the books were appearing, could take it all in their stride.

But could they? The years between *The Tale of Peter Rabbit* and *The Tale of Pigling Bland*, the first and last notable Potter stories, were 1901 to 1913, years in which Kenneth Grahame, J. M.

Barrie, and E. Nesbit were writing for children in a variety of thoroughly un-Victorian styles; years when, to look at the wider world, Joyce, Eliot, and Pound were beginning their modernist experiments. Other picture-books for small children dating from the early 1900s, such as L. Leslie Brooke's *Johnny Crow's Garden* (1903) or Florence Upton's 'Golliwogg' series (1895 to 1909), are quite without the Victorianisms of the Potter books. What is going on? Was Beatrix Potter a stranded survivor of the Victorian age, unable to jettison the diction of her parents' world, or was she consciously imitating the manners of an earlier age, and if so, why?

If you look at them carefully, her so-called Victorianisms reveal themselves as not Victorian at all. Victorians did not write that way, certainly not for children and usually not for adults. Victorian English tends to be very wordy; the Potter archaisms, or what we might call antiquities of style, are strikingly crisp. They say in one word—'affronted', 'discretion', 'alacrity'—what a true Victorian would have rambled over several sentences to convey. Consider this:

It was almost too much happiness to bear. Oliver felt stunned and stupefied by the unexpected intelligence; he could not weep, or speak, or rest. He had scarcely the power of understanding anything that had passed, until, after a long ramble in the quiet evening air, a burst of tears came to his relief, and he seemed to awaken, all at once, to a full sense of the joyful change that had occurred, and the almost insupportable load of anguish which had been taken from his breast.

This passage was chosen virtually at random from *Oliver Twist*.[16] Compare Beatrix Potter describing the return home of an entire family of young children who have nearly been cooked and eaten alive:

Great was old Mr Bouncer's relief and Flopsy's joy when Peter and Benjamin arrived in triumph with the young family. The rabbit-babies were rather tumbled and very hungry; they were fed and put to bed. They soon recovered.[17]

If Beatrix Potter, writing this in 1912, is looking back stylistically, her glance seems to have travelled beyond the Victorian age, back to an earlier period when written English was an instrument capable of greater precision.

You can see why she was doing this if you look at her journal. One of the few regular diversions that family life offered when she was young was conversation with her paternal grandmother. Old Mrs Potter, née Jessie Crompton, had been born in 1801, if not quite 'In the time of swords and periwigs and full-skirted coats with flowered lappets', as Beatrix Potter has it in the opening paragraph of *The Tailor of Gloucester*, then certainly into a society that seemed as remote from late Victorian London as Beatrix Potter's own times seem from ours. Margaret Lane tells us how, in early childhood, Beatrix would delight to hide under the table in her grandmother's house and eavesdrop on the old lady's talk. Later, she made a methodical business of writing it down in her journal, like a modern researcher collecting oral history of a bygone age. Here she is at the age of twenty-one recording a 'scene, at lunch':

My grandmother disapproved, in a state of high and violent indignation and dispute with the rest of the family, as to the cautious pace at which the coachman drives the mares. . . . 'Eh—dear—I k-now,—I've been, in, gigs, with—my fa-ther—why—we were—*all*, thrown, out, of,—a gig—at once' (roars of laughter).[18]

And three years earlier, again in the journal, she describes the old lady's appearance:

How pretty she does look with her grey curls, under her muslin cap, trimmed with black lace. Her plain crêpe dress with broad grey linen collar and cuffs turned over. So erect and always on the move, with her gentle face and waken [*sic*], twinkling eyes. There is no one like grandmamma. She always seems to me as near perfect as is possible here . . .[19]

Perfection is identified with the Regency period in which her grandmother had been brought up; note how Beatrix imitates the diction of that age in the journal entries: 'a state of high and violent indignation', 'waken, twinkling eyes'. As to the costume she describes, in old age Beatrix herself adopted it—the same muslin cap can be seen in many late pictures of her—and she seemingly modelled her behaviour on her grandmother. One also notes that it was very soon after her grandmother's death that she began, in 1893, to write the picture-letters to children of her acquaintance which provided the first material for her books. They were an act of recreating her grandmother's world.

The Beatrix Potter character most resembling her grandmother is Mrs Tiggywinkle, the hedgehog washerwoman, who wears the muslin cap and has the twinkling eyes of old Mrs Potter. But the old lady's influence on the books goes much deeper. The second book that Beatrix wrote, immediately after she had begun to make a name for herself with *The Tale of Peter Rabbit*, was *The Tailor of Gloucester*, published in 1902. This is the story which Beatrix herself preferred above all the others she wrote, which may seem odd, for it bears remarkably little resemblance in theme and style to the rest of her work. She liked it so much (one guesses) because it is an exercise in recreating the speech-rhythms of her grandmother's era, the age into which Beatrix herself evidently wished she had been born:

He cut his coats without waste, according to his embroidered cloth; they were very small ends and snippets that lay about on the table—'Too narrow breadths for nought—except waistcoats for mice,' said the tailor . . . 'No breadth at all, and cut on the cross; it is no breadth at all; tippets for mice and ribbons for mobs! for mice!' said the Tailor of Gloucester.

Now, these are in fact not the rhythms of late eighteenth- and early nineteenth-century English prose; not at all. As so often when a writer sets out to recapture the style of an earlier period, what results is something quite new. One can detect all sorts of influences on *The Tailor of Gloucester*. There is a hint of Anglo-Saxon poetry in the alliteration ('He cut his coats without waste, according to his embroidered cloth'), and at times the book seems to be almost an operatic libretto: an aria by the Tailor is interrupted by a chattering chorus of mice, and the central section is made up of a sequence of Christmas rhymes, chanted by birds and beasts 'from all the roofs and gables and old wooden houses in Gloucester'. Possibly one hears an echo of Browning—the story is a kind of *Pied Piper* in reverse, set amid the alleyways of an ancient city, with the Tailor freeing the mice from imprisonment and threatened extinction. But the voice that comes through most strongly is that of the Authorized Version of the Bible.

The reiterated 'said the tailor . . . said the Tailor of Gloucester' echoes 'saith the Lord . . . saith the Lord God' so often found in the writings of the prophets, while the characteristic Beatrix Potter sentence, which first appears fully-fledged in *The Tailor of Gloucester*, is composed of two balanced halves divided by a caesura, in the manner of the Psalms. And like the psalmist, Potter often uses the second half to introduce a disarming qualification, or some nuance:

All that day he was ill, and the next day, and the next; and what should become of the cherry-coloured coat?

Out of doors the market folks went trudging through the snow to buy their geese and turkeys, and to bake their Christmas pies; but there would be no Christmas dinner for Simpkin and the poor old Tailor of Gloucester.

With which compare:

For the Lord knoweth the way of the righteous; but the way of the ungodly shall perish. (Psalm 1.)

—or indeed hundreds of other verses in the psalms. Beatrix Potter herself spoke of 'The sweet rhythm of the authorised translation', and one notes that she says 'rhythm' rather than 'language': it is the rise and fall, the biblical cadence, that she picks up and uses in her later books to fine ironical effect. For example: 'He snored peacefully and regularly; but one eye was not perfectly shut.'

The Tailor of Gloucester is not ironical. It is an idyllic re-creation of her grandmother's age, and also, in its miniaturist way, a piece of social commentary that might have been dreamt up by Ruskin or William Morris. It evokes a pre-industrial arcadia, a perfect city where the skill of the individual craftsman plays a vital part in the social system: the Tailor is making a wedding coat for the Mayor of Gloucester, who is to be married on Christmas morning, and the wedding cannot take place without the coat. The central device of the story, the mice stepping in to finish the job when the

Tailor is taken ill, is a reworking of a well-known fairy-story motif, found (for example) in the Grimms' fairy tale 'The Elves and the Shoemaker'; but Potter gives it a nice sharp social edge, for her story, though set in an ultra-hierarchical society, reverses the usual order of power. Instead of the Mayor and the rich men of the city controlling events, the Mayor is beholden to the poor Tailor, the Tailor depends upon his cat Simpkin, whom he needs to go out and buy the missing skein of cherry-coloured silk, and in the end everyone's fate hangs on the skill and good nature of the mice, the very lowest creatures of all in the city's pecking order. *The Tailor of Gloucester* thus presents a society that is in every way an opposite to the imperfections and injustices of urban industrial life in the early 1900s, when it was written.

Its companion piece, written and published three years later, is *The Tale of Mrs Tiggywinkle*, again arcadian and idyllic in character, again intended to portray a perfect society in which the lowest person in the hierarchy—in this case a washerwoman—is able to pull the controlling strings. Mrs Tiggywinkle, though constantly giving reminders of her low position in the class system—'Oh yes, if you please'm . . . Oh no, if you please'm'—is really a person of great influence, since she supplies clean clothes to all the animals—and clothes, as we shall see, are for Potter's characters the visible sign of their identity and individuality. She even has some influence over the lives of humans. The child Lucie comes all the way up the mountainside in search of her own missing handkerchiefs, which Mrs Tiggywinkle has indeed washed and ironed. But the book is one of Potter's less secure inventions. Lucie is an uncomfortable intrusion from the real world, and the animals' clothes, such as Peter Rabbit's blue jacket, become confused with their skins—Mrs Tiggywinkle's wash includes 'woolly coats belonging to the little lambs' and a 'velvety black moleskin waistcoat'. Quite apart from the whimsy, Potter seems to have lost her grip on her own scheme. Her unease is betrayed by the uncertain narrative tone throughout the book ('Lucie opened the door: and what do you think there was inside the hill?'; a questioning, condescending manner that she never uses elsewhere) and by the fact that at the end it is suggested that the entire story may have been a dream.

The Tailor of Gloucester, then, could not be successfully imitated, not even by its own author. *Mrs Tiggywinkle* is by Beatrix Potter's standards a narrative failure, memorable verbally only for its depiction of the stone-flagged kitchen, 'a nice clean kitchen with a flagged floor and wooden beams—just like any other farm kitchen'. (Throughout children's literature, kitchens like this occur again and again as Good Places, scenes of womb-like security and domestic contentment; for example Badger's superb underground kitchen in *The Wind in the Willows*.)[20] But *The Tailor of Gloucester* itself was a crucially important book for Potter, a linguistic exercise, a study in establishing what she believed to be her grandmother's voice. Once she had practised this successfully, she could use that voice in a wide range of narrative contexts.

The theme she had chosen to tackle in her earliest story, *The Tale of Peter Rabbit*, is one that recurs throughout her work, until it comes to final resolution in *The Tale of Pigling Bland*: Jack in the Giant's castle, the little fellow, the folktale hero who has nothing but his courage and his wits, struggling against an opponent of far superior physical strength. That she should choose such a theme is not very surprising—it predominates in Grimms' fairy tales and many of the other classic folktale collections, and it was perhaps a natural subject for someone congenitally shy, who viewed the prospect of any encounter with a stranger with considerable anxiety. Is it perhaps too fanciful to suppose that the oppressors in her stories—Mr MacGregor, Old Brown the owl in *Squirrel Nutkin*, Samuel Whiskers, and the others—unconsciously stood in her mind for her own parents? It was in their home that she was trapped for much of her life, like Peter Rabbit caught by the buttons of his own jacket; and certainly the flight of Pigling Bland and Pigwig from Mr Thomas Piperson in her 1913 book seems to refer to her own final escape that very year from the family fold—1913 was when she married William Heelis and at last became independent, at the age of forty-seven.

The subject, then, is not surprising. The moral attitude of the narrator in these stories is. Far from following the 'well-established tradition' of English children's stories about animals, and exhorting the reader to good and docile behaviour, the narrator of *Peter Rabbit* and its successors is definitely on the side of the transgressors. After all, Peter is a burglar, breaking into Mr MacGregor's garden to steal vegetables. More than that, he is a familiar figure from the Victorian moral tale, the disobedient child. His mother has specifically forbidden him to go into the garden, for the very good reason that 'your father had an accident there; he was put in a pie by Mrs MacGregor'. (Note the un-Victorian understatement of 'accident'.) Peter's sisters are 'good little bunnies' and they dutifully go down the lane to gather blackberries; at the end they are rewarded with 'bread and milk and blackberries for supper', while Peter is 'not very well' after his escapade and is dosed with 'camomile tea'. So far, everything is conventional: the disobedient boy meets his deserts. And yet— 'good little bunnies'—isn't there a touch of sarcasm here?

Certainly Peter has lost his 'blue jacket with brass buttons, quite new', but he has daringly got into the giant's lair, has rewarded himself with the treasure ('First he ate some lettuces and some French beans; and then he ate some radishes'); and he has escaped through his own exertions—something of which the 'good little bunnies' would be quite incapable. Strikingly, in this first of the Beatrix Potter books, the only antiquity of diction appears at the moment of crisis:

Peter gave himself up for lost, and shed big tears; but his sobs were overheard by some friendly sparrows, who flew to him in great excitement, and implored him to exert himself.

'Implored him to exert himself' is the language of the eighteenth-century moral tales which Grandmother Potter would have read in her own childhood; indeed Beatrix herself had found it in the stories of Maria Edgeworth, which she had been given to read in the nursery. People in the Edgeworth stories and the old moral tales are always being exhorted to exert themselves, to shake off slovenly ways, to raise themselves in society by their own exertions.[21] And here we have a rabbit struggling to exert himself to get out of a gooseberry net. It is surely a parody, a gentle mockery of the old-style children's story. The leg of the moral tale is being gently but quite definitely pulled.

Next comes *The Tailor of Gloucester*, and then in 1903 we are back with the little fellow in the giant's lair, this time Squirrel Nutkin taunting Old Brown the owl with his mocking riddles and only just escaping with his life, minus not just a jacket but a tail. Again, Nutkin is the transgressor—he deliberately infuriates the august personage on whose land the squirrels are gathering nuts; the rest of them, like the 'good little bunnies', are respectful to their elders and speak politely to Old Brown ('Old Mr Brown, will you favour us with your permission . . .?'), but Nutkin, we are told, 'was excessively impertinent in his manners'—an observation straight from the moral tale. And, as in *Peter Rabbit*, the narrator is undoubtedly on Nutkin's side. Nutkin may nearly come to grief, but he has certainly (in Eliot's words) dared disturb the universe, has challenged the accepted order. And he has done it, one notes, by reviving a very ancient form of taunting, the riddle-game, which belongs to a more robust age than that which spawned the moral tale. Beatrix Potter does not necessarily intend that her young readers should emulate Nutkin, but she undoubtedly prefers his spirit and enterprise to the dull conformity of the well-behaved squirrels, and this is why, when she describes his *hubris*, she does so in a voice that mocks those who disapprove of it. He is just the sort of character whom the old writers of the moral tale would have called 'excessively impertinent'. Well, she seems to be saying, good for him.

So she is evoking her grandmother's world not entirely in admiration. The grandmother herself was admired by Beatrix for her spirited diction and independence of mind—a vigorous contrast to the caution and nervousness of Beatrix's parents—but Beatrix recognized that the world in which the old lady had grown up was alarmingly repressive towards children. Or perhaps she is simply recalling her own childhood reading, for the attitudes of the moral tale persisted in children's books, up to and even beyond the late nineteenth-century revolution inaugurated by Lewis Carroll, and Beatrix would certainly have been soaked in them from her own nursery reading. Like Lewis Carroll's Alice, the narrator of *Peter Rabbit* and its successors is striking a blow for independence and a freer moral attitude towards children. The Potter mockery of the moral tale parallels Lewis Carroll's mockery of the sanctimonious religious verses of Isaac Watts in the Alice books.

This satirical element slackens off a little in the next story in the Peter Rabbit sequence. *The Tale of Benjamin Bunny* (1904) is mainly an exercise in narrative understatement. Its subject is Peter's paralysing fear on his return to the garden to rescue his jacket, and, like a Hemingway novel, the narrative constantly sidesteps specifying the emotion that is being experienced: 'They got amongst flower-pots, and frames and tubs; Peter heard noises worse than ever, his eyes were as big as lolly-pops!' (Notice the 'got' in the first half of this sentence—not 'correct writing', then or now, but frequently used by Potter to achieve another sort of biblical echo: 'The sun got round behind the wood, and it was quite late in the afternoon; but still the cat sat upon the basket.' So 'they got amongst thieves' in the Bible.) Another feature of *Benjamin Bunny* is the use of the pictures not just, as that encyclopaedia entry said, in an 'absolutely complementary sense', but actually to say more than the text. The narrator merely states that old Mr Bunny, having rescued his son and nephew from Mr MacGregor's garden, 'took out his nephew Peter', but the picture shows him whipping Peter soundly for his disobedience.

The Tale of Two Bad Mice (1904) is purely satirical. It mocks the mores of a consumer society where the rich live amid entirely useless objects. Into a doll's house come two mice, Tom Thumb and Hunca Munca, whose names—from Fielding's satirical *Tom Thumb* play—announce disruptive farce. They find that the food set out on the dining table is 'extremely beautiful', but 'it would not come off the plates', so in baffled rage they set about destruction and looting, like two skinheads confronted with a Laura Ashley drawing-room. Again it is quite clear where the narrator's sympathies lie: not with the blandly smiling, richly dressed, entirely inanimate dolls—'Jane was the Cook; but she never did any cooking, because the dinner had been bought ready-made, in a box full of shavings … Jane leant against the

kitchen dresser and smiled . . . neither of them made any remark
. . .' Like the food, they are beautiful and fake. No, the narrator is
on the side of the live mice, who unlike most of Potter's animal
protagonists are unclothed, as if to emphasize their very real
animal energy. Tom Thumb's destruction of the plaster of Paris
ham and all the other fake food goes without authorial reproof,
and though there is a token gesture of repentance towards the end
of the story—the mice 'pay' for what they have broken and stolen
with a crooked sixpence, and Hunca Munca becomes the dolls'
charlady—the mice's 'badness' earns no more disapproval from
Potter than does the cheek of Squirrel Nutkin or the daring of
Peter Rabbit.

Having virtually advocated social revolution in *Two Bad Mice*,
Beatrix Potter next shows, in *The Pie and the Patty-Pan* (1905), the
absurd consequences of taking too seriously the niceties of upper-
middle-class social behaviour. *Two Bad Mice* portrays elegant
English society viewed from outside; *The Pie and the Patty-Pan*
shows it from within, where it looks even sillier. Two elegant
personages—Ribby and Duchess, a cat and a dog—arrange to
have an elegant tea-party together. One of them is too well
brought up to tell the other of her dietary preferences, with
absurd comic consequences. These are two village spinsters
tangling themselves in their own etiquette. At the height of the
comedy, the victims' chief emotion is social embarrassment:

> It was most conspicuous. All the village could see that Ribby was
> fetching the doctor.
> 'I *knew* they would over-eat themselves!' said Cousin Tabitha Twit-
> chit.

The doctor is portrayed as a social inferior—as doctors were
regarded in the days of Beatrix Potter's childhood. Dr Maggoty, a
large magpie, has a strikingly vulgar turn of speech ('"Gammon?
ha! HA!" said he, with his head on one side'), and he offers a very
coarse remedy for Duchess supposedly having swallowed the
patty-pan—a bread pill. It appears, indeed, that the whole tea-
party, elegant as the participants have tried to make it, has
transgressed the social code:

Cousin Tabitha was disdainful afterwards in conversation—

'A little *dog* indeed! Just as if there were no CATS in Sawrey! And a *pie* for afternoon tea! The very idea!' said Cousin Tabitha Twitchit.

Again, note the antiquated terminology. Sawrey, the scene of *The Pie and the Patty-Pan*, has become another Cranford. The story is only superficially set in Near Sawrey, Beatrix Potter's Lake District village, which is just a tiny hamlet. The society she is really mocking is the genteel world of Kensington. Incidentally Hill Top, the farmhouse she bought in Near Sawrey, was altered by her in a fashion that largely evokes the Kensington of her childhood: she installed an ornate fireplace in the ground floor inner parlour, and upstairs built an elegant drawing-room to house her brother Bertram's enormous landscape paintings.

The theme of the little fellow in the Giant's castle is resumed in *The Tale of Mr Jeremy Fisher*, one of the first stories Beatrix Potter had written, though it was not published until 1906. This time the victim is not merely preyed upon by bigger creatures—an enormous trout swallows Jeremy Fisher but spits him out again because it dislikes the taste of his mackintosh, surely a prankish reference to the exploits of Jonah—but is himself a predator. Jeremy Fisher digs up worms for bait, catches minnows, and dines on 'roasted grasshopper with lady-bird sauce'. The simple Jack-and-the-Giant motif has widened into a realistic portrayal of an aggressive natural world. After his encounter with the trout, Mr Jeremy loses some of his clothes and consequently most of his dignity—'he hopped home across the meadow with his mackintosh all in tatters'—but by the end he has resumed his pretensions, donning (as the illustration shows us) a Regency waistcoat and tail-coat, breeches, spats, and pointed shoes to welcome his friends to an elegant meal. The story highlights the absurd contrast between the rough and tumble of real life and the pretensions of society.

That theme is more explicitly worked out in *The Tale of Tom Kitten* (1907), in which the social pretensions of Mrs Tabitha Twitchit—always in the Potter books a paragon, as her name might suggest, of nervously correct behaviour—come to naught when she tries to dress her kittens for a smart tea-party. Clothes are again used as symbols of social pretension—'all sorts of elegant uncomfortable clothes' the narrator calls them; whereas the kittens 'had dear little fur coats of their own; and they tumbled about the doorstep and played in the dust'. This state of nature is not suitable for the 'fine company' Mrs Twitchit has invited to call, so she forces the kittens into pinafores, bibs, and tuckers. These quickly fall off, and are put on in jest by those very farmyard creatures whom their mother has particularly warned the kittens against, as social untouchables—the Puddle-Ducks. 'I am affronted,' says Mrs Twitchit when she contemplates her children's behaviour, and once again the stilted language separates Beatrix Potter herself from the sentiment. Nor does she approve of Mrs Twitchit telling a lie to keep up appearances:

She sent them upstairs; and I am sorry to say she told her friends that they were in bed with the measles; which was not true.

Quite the contrary; they were not in bed; *not* in the least.

Somehow there were very extraordinary noises overhead, which disturbed the dignity and repose of the tea-party.

From the comic clothing of the Puddle-Ducks in the kittens' pretentious garments it is an easy step to *The Tale of Jemima Puddle-Duck* (1908), a masterly reworking of the Red Riding Hood theme, in which Jemima's folly is emphasized by her donning of clothes—'a shawl and a poke bonnet'—as she unwisely abandons the security of the farmyard (an extended family in which everyone helps each other) and attempts hubristically to hatch her eggs in seclusion. At the end, after the disastrous failure of her venture, she is back again in her natural unclothed state. A striking thing is Potter's own obvious contempt for the naïve Jemima, who surrenders herself trustingly into the hands of 'the gentleman with sandy whiskers', a fox whose manner and costume suggest the caddish seducer of a dairymaid, a veritable Alec D'Urberville. Jemima is a poor foolish thing in comparison with his elegant diction and behaviour. Similarly in *The Tale of Samuel Whiskers*, originally published in 1908 as *The Roly-Poly Pudding*, Potter's sympathies are clearly with the ingenious, unscrupulous rats rather than with the hapless Tom Kitten; though Tom's enterprise in climbing up the chimney to escape imprisonment on baking day is clearly to be preferred to his sisters' caution, to his restraining, socially-conscious mother (Tabitha Twitchit again), and to her censorious neighbour Mrs Ribby (the cat from *The Pie and the Patty-Pan*).

The Roly-Poly Pudding, to give it the original and more appropriate title, is Potter's most resonant and multi-layered story. No wonder Graham Greene wanted to explore its implications. We may see Freudian symbolism in Tom's search up the sooty chimney of his mother's house; but if his journey away from the maternal clutches has something about it of sexual exploration, the rats themselves, omnivorous, cantankerous, and lurking under the very floorboards of an ordinary room, seem to be symbols far older than Freud and his discoveries—almost Homeric in their power over the imagination. And it is to them that Potter gives her most consistently antiquarian language. They speak in the tones of the moral tale, to richly comic effect, for they are, of course, pure amorality:

'Will not the string be very indigestible, Anna Maria?' inquired Samuel Whiskers.

Anna Maria said she thought that it was of no consequence; but she wished that Tom Kitten would hold his head still, as it disarranged the pastry . . .

And a few pages later, when rescue is at hand for poor Tom:

'We are discovered and interrupted, Anna Maria; let us collect our property—and other people's,—and depart at once.'

'I fear that we shall be obliged to leave this pudding.'

'But I am persuaded that the knots would have proved indigestible, whatever you may urge to the contrary.'

And so they depart, still arguing decorously like two clerics of Dr Johnson's day.

Beatrix Potter was probably an admirer of Johnson. She was certainly an avid reader of Jane Austen, and traces of both writers' styles appear in her work. But by the time of her

And when I was going to the post, late in
the afternoon — I looked up the lane from
the corner, and I saw Samuel Whiskers
and his wife on the run, with large bundles
on a little wheel-barrow.

They were just turning in under
the gate, to Farmer Potatoes's barn.

A page of the manuscript of *The Roly-Poly Pudding*.

penultimate notable book, *The Tale of Mr Tod* (1912) she is tackling themes that seem quite foreign to the age of Johnson, Austen, and her grandmother. *Tod* is not merely a dialect English word for 'fox', but the German for 'death', and this book, which announces itself blandly as dealing with 'disagreeable' people, is a study in murderous intentions. Tommy Brock the badger intends to kill and eat the rabbit babies; Mr Tod the fox, finding Brock in his bed, is utterly delighted when he believes he has killed him; and at the conclusion Tod and Brock engage in a vicious struggle of which the conclusion (surely the death of both of them) is left for the reader to guess.

Though *Mr Tod* is the blackest of Beatrix Potter's books, it is also the funniest. Nothing else in children's literature, and very little written for adults, comes near the hilariously macabre passage where Mr Tod, finding the badger in his bed, makes elaborate preparations for revenge on this infringement of private property, carefully suspending a bucket over the head of the bed, attaching it to a rope secured to a tree outside, and then filling it, jug by jug, with cold water—all the while Tommy Brock pretending to be fast asleep, watching with one eye, snoring industriously: 'The snores were almost apoplectic.' Trying to find some comparison, one thinks not of literary parallels but of early film comedies featuring such grotesques as Mack Sennett. The Potter story, of course, is heavily illustrated, but even without the pictures (which are, uncharacteristically, mostly in black and white) it would resemble the violent comedies of the silent monochrome cinema, the sort of film that was being made at the time *Mr Tod* was published (1912).

The final Potter story into which she put all her powers as writer and illustrator, *The Tale of Pigling Bland* (1913), is equally cinematic. It takes place within a specified time-span—two and a half days—and the passing of time and the changing of the light are very precisely recorded:

He glanced wistfully along the road towards the hills, and then set off walking obediently the other way, buttoning up his coat against the rain . . .

A little later on:

After an hour's wandering he got out of the wood [note that 'got' again]; the moon shone through the clouds, and Pigling Bland saw a country that was new to him.

The road crossed a moor; below was a wide valley with a river twinkling in the moonlight, and beyond, in misty distance, lay the hills.

And towards the end of the story, when Pigling Bland and Pig-wig, the girl pig he has met at Thomas Piperson's sinister prison of a cottage, are escaping across the moors in hope of finding freedom in the next county—shades again of *Tess of the D'Urber-villes*, and an anticipation of all those thirties poems and novels about crossing the frontier—we see everything very clearly through the camera's eye:

He opened the house door quietly and shut it after them. There was no garden; the neighbourhood of Mr Piperson's was all scratched up by fowls. They slipped away hand in hand across an untidy field to the road.

The sun rose while they were crossing the moor, a dazzle of light over the tops of the hills. The sunshine crept down the slopes into the peaceful green valleys, where little white cottages nestled in gardens and orchards.

'That's Westmorland,' said Pig-wig.

We have come a long way from *The Tale of Peter Rabbit*.

The Tale of Pigling Bland—Beatrix Potter's *Persuasion*—expresses Beatrix's exhilaration at her own personal escape, in the year that it was published, from the family fold, and the freedom that her marriage granted her. (Like Anne Elliot in the Austen novel she had suffered an earlier tragic disappointment, when her fiancé Norman Warne had died abruptly of leukaemia.) Though she lived for another thirty years, she published nothing further of importance. But though her work appeared only during the first thirteen years of this century she belongs to the modern age rather than the Victorian. There are moments when her work even bears resemblances to the modernists—her use of antiquated diction for motives of parody and social comedy has touches of Eliot and Joyce. The very least claim one may make for her is that she brought a precise diction and a vigorous use of English into books for very small children, which must have been an enormous influence for the good. There is some evidence that her deliberately flat, unemotional narrative voice, the characteristic cool Potter tone in which everything is expressed by understatement, helped to create the narrative style of Graham Greene's generation of writers—possibly including Evelyn Waugh. This paragraph, for example, could almost have been written by Beatrix Potter:

Mr Sniggs, the Junior Dean, and Mr Postlethwaite, the Domestic Bursar, sat alone in Mr Snigg's room overlooking the garden quad at Scone College. From the rooms of Sir Alastair Digby-Vane-Trumpington, two staircases away, came a confused roaring and breaking of glass. They alone of the senior members of Scone were at home that evening, for it was the night of the annual dinner of the Bollinger Club. The others were all scattered over Boar's Hill and North Oxford at gay, contentious little parties, or at other senior common-rooms, or at the meetings of learned societies, for the annual Bollinger dinner is a difficult time for those in authority.

'Confused . . . contentious . . . difficult': this sort of wry understatement seemed a new voice in English fiction in 1928, when Waugh's *Decline and Fall* appeared. Is it too fanciful to trace it back to those small books for young children which were appearing year by year during Waugh's childhood?

Notes

1. *TLS*, 3 Apr. 1987. Reprinted by kind permission of Blake Morrison.
2. Graham Greene, *A Sort of Life* (Harmondsworth, 1972), 39.
3. Graham Greene, *Brighton Rock* (London, 1938), Part 7, ch. 3.
4. W. H. Auden, *The English Auden*, ed. Edward Mendelson (London, 1979), 190.
5. Brian Finney, *Christopher Isherwood: A Critical Biography* (London, 1979), 24.
6. Bernard Crick, *George Orwell, a life* (London, 1980), 43.
7. Justin Wintle, ed., *Makers of Modern Culture: A Biographical Dictionary* (London, 1981).
8. Alan Bullock and R. B. Woodings, eds., *The Fontana Biographical Companion to Modern Thought* (London, 1983), 611. The entry was written by Juliet McLean of the Hertfordshire Library Service.
9. Anthony Powell, *Infants of the Spring* (London, 1976), 48.

10. Graham Greene, *Collected Short Stories* (Harmondsworth, 1986), 188.
11. Ibid. 189.
12. See the entry for 'Fable' in Humphrey Carpenter and Mari Prichard, *The Oxford Companion to Children's Literature* (Oxford, 1984).
13. See the entry for 'Animal Stories', ibid.
14. Margaret Lane, *The Tale of Beatrix Potter* (London, 1946), chs. 1–2 *passim* ('She had made friends with rabbits and hedgehogs, mice and minnows, as a prisoner in solitary confinement will befriend a mouse.')
15. *The Journal of Beatrix Potter from 1881 to 1897*, transcribed from her code writings by Leslie Linder (London, 1966), *passim*.
16. Ch. 34, opening paragraph.
17. *The Tale of Mr Tod.*
18. *Journal* (see n. 15), 197.
19. Ibid. 94.
20. See further the present author's *Secret Gardens* (London, 1985), 161–3.
21. See the entry for 'Moral Tales' in Carpenter and Prichard (n. 12 above).

14

The Wind in the Willows: *The Vitality of a Classic*

NEIL PHILIP

'VITALITY—that is the test,' wrote Kenneth Grahame in an introduction to Aesop's Fables. It is a test *The Wind in the Willows* passes triumphantly: Grahame's best-known book possesses in abundance that quality by which Ezra Pound defined the true classic: 'a certain eternal and irrepressible freshness'. A. A. Milne called it 'a household book': one to be kept constantly at hand, referred to, quoted, read aloud.[1]

But it is also, it has to be admitted, a very strange book. Early reviewers were entirely flummoxed by it, expecting another wickedly exact portrait of childhood in the mode of Grahame's highly successful collections of stories *The Golden Age* (1895) and *Dream Days* (1898). Instead they were offered a tale of humanized animals—or animalized humans—in which the characters are at one moment life-size water rats, moles, and toads, and at another are hitching life-size horses to gipsy caravans and taking to the road where they mix on equal terms with humans; a tale with two distinct narrative threads—one of gentle celebration of simple riverside pleasures, the other of hectic farce—and with two interpolated mystical chapters that seemed to have nothing to do with the rest. To make matters worse, Grahame was at the time of publication (1908) Secretary of the Bank of England.

However the book was soon assimilated, soon taken to its readers' hearts, and it now forms Grahame's chief claim to fame. His other writings, meagre as they are, are read mainly for their relationship to *The Wind in the Willows*. It is one of the handful of books that every English child is bound to meet, and every English-speaking child should. It is also, as my account of its genesis is intended to show, a book intriguingly poised between literature for children and for adults.

Grahame's first published writings were essays for literary journals of the 1890s, including *The Yellow Book* and W. E. Henley's *National Observer*. Many of them were collected in *Pagan Papers* (1893) which also contained the earliest stories of *The Golden Age*. Other gifted writers—Arthur Ransome, for instance, and J. M. Barrie—produced similarly vapid verbal confections at this period: all, like Grahame, looked to Robert Louis Stevenson as their model. Grahame's early essays are imitations of Stevenson's; his stories of child life are a series of narrative glosses on a particular essay, 'Child's Play', included in *Virginibus Puerisque*. Elsewhere Stevenson had written: 'I am one of the few people in the world who do not forget their own lives.' This succinct and penetrating essay proves it. In it he writes:

In the child's world of dim sensation, play is all in all. 'Making believe' is the gist of his whole life, and he cannot so much as take a walk except in character. I could not learn my alphabet without some suitable *mise-en-scène*, and had to act a business man in an office before I could sit down to my book. Will you kindly question your memory, and find out how much you did, work or pleasure, in good faith and soberness, and for how much you had to cheat yourself with some invention?[2]

As an example of this child's ability to cheat himself with inventions, he recalls:

When my cousin and I took our porridge of a morning, we had a device to enliven the course of the meal. He ate his with sugar, and explained it to be a country continually buried under snow. I took mine with milk, and explained it to be a country suffering gradual inundation. You can imagine us exchanging bulletins: how here was an island still unsubmerged, here a valley not yet covered with snow: what inventions were made: how his population lived in cabins on perches and travelled on stilts, and how mine was always in boats; how the interest grew furious, as the last corner of safe ground was cut off all sides and grew smaller every moment: and how, in fine, the food was of altogether secondary importance, and might even have been nauseous, so long as we seasoned it with these dreams.[3]

Stevenson's essay provided Grahame with a key to his feeling of dispossession:

Surely [children] dwell in a mythological epoch, and are not the contemporaries of their parents. What can they think of them? what can they make of these bearded or petticoated giants who look down upon their games? who move upon a cloudy Olympus, following unknown designs apart from rational enjoyment? ... Were there ever such unthinking deities as parents?

Of the attitude of children to adults Stevenson says: 'we should be tempted to fancy they despised us outright.' Grahame frequently represents the children as feeling contempt for 'the Olympians'. But though, as I shall show, Grahame took to heart many of Stevenson's wise and perceptive comments on children's make-believe, he disregarded Stevenson's opening statement that 'the regret we have for our childhood is not wholly justifiable'. Grahame's adults—save for a few fantasy benefactors—*are* contemptible, 'without vital interests and intelligent pursuits'.[4] Grahame takes as much pleasure as Saki in constructing imaginary retrospective revenges on them.

Children's ability and willingness to cheat themselves with invention is then for Grahame an unmitigated good. But though the stories in *The Golden Age* and *Dream Days* describe the world of make-believe with vivid accuracy, they do not enter it. The narrator is at a distance; can afford, indeed, to be amused as well as envious. This is not so in *The Wind in the Willows*.

My point can perhaps best be appreciated by considering a passage in the story 'A Saga of the Seas' in *Dream Days*, in which the narrator recollects a particularly involved and involving daydream piratic escapade. The boy's method of narrative construction is to follow the desired storyline, providing and discarding incidental characters and props in an arbitrary and *ad hoc* manner, according to necessity rather than likelihood. 'As for the pirate brigantine and the man-of-war, I don't really know what became of them. They had played their part very well, for the time, but I wasn't going to bother to account for them, so I just let them evaporate quietly.'[5] This is precisely Grahame's own

Illustrations by Ernest Shepard: (*above*) for 'The Argonauts', from *The Golden Age*, Bodley Head, 1928; (*below*) Toad Hall, from *The Wind in the Willows*, Methuen, 1931.

narrative technique in *The Wind in the Willows*. He wrote in 1919 to Professor G. T. Hill who had queried Mole's domestic arrangements: 'I would ask you to observe that our author practises a sort of "character economy" which has the appearance of being deliberate. The presence of certain characters may be indicated in or required by the story, but if the author has no immediate use for them, he simply ignores their existence.'[6]

The book's famous incongruities stem from Grahame's deliberate adoption of a narrative voice rooted in the tradition of make-believe rather than fiction. In the make-believe world it does not matter if a toad brushes his hair (a source of distress to Beatrix Potter), or if a rat says to a mole: 'I like your clothes awfully, old chap . . . I'm going to get a black velvet smoking suit myself some day.' Grahame is wonderfully deft at handling the transitions of size that are such a trouble to his illustrators and stage adaptors. With one adjective, for instance, he reduces Toad from washerwoman-size to toad-size: 'One big mottled arm shot out and caught Toad by a fore-leg, while the other gripped him fast by a hind-leg.' The barge-woman's 'big' arm expels Toad from the human world. In *The Wind in the Willows* Grahame incorporates for the first time into his narrative stance the truth observed by Stevenson: 'Nothing can stagger a child's faith; he accepts the clumsiest substitutes and can swallow the most staring incongruities.'[7]

Toad, Rat, and Mole are not only characters in a narrative arranged according to the principles of make-believe; they also order their own lives in the same fashion. Here Toad—in part an affectionate mockery of aspects of the character of Grahame's son, in part perhaps a caricature of Oscar Wilde—is of chief interest.[8] To observe Toad, deprived of real transport, resort to an arrangement of chairs on which he would crouch 'bent forward and staring fixedly ahead, making uncouth and ghastly noises', is to recall Stevenson's observation that though adults can daydream while sitting quietly, a child needs 'stage properties': 'When he comes to ride with the king's pardon, he must bestride a chair,' (though I should note here that the critic Humphrey Carpenter regards this passage in *The Wind in the Willows* as

Mr Toad, illustration by John Burningham for *The Wind in the Willows*, Kestrel Books, 1983.

suggesting masturbation).[9] When Toad translates his make-believe into action, the Olympians, again in Stevenson's words, 'reach down out of their altitude and terribly vindicate the prerogatives of age': 'Mr Clerk, will you tell us, please, what is the very stiffest penalty we can impose . . .?'[10] Toad's downfall is presented as farce, not tragedy, but it is a rueful farce, shot through with Grahame's painful consciousness of the distance between his own imaginings and his reality.

Like many children's books, *The Wind in the Willows* originated as bedtime stories told to the author's son. Grahame improvised the tale for his son Alastair, and when separated from him continued it in letters which survive in the Bodleian Library and have been published as *First Whisper of 'The Wind in the Willows'* (1944) and more recently as *My Dearest Mouse* (1988). He then wrote the whole story out as a novel, and added the two mystical chapters, 'The Piper at the Gates of Dawn' and 'Wayfarers All'. 'The Piper' stands directly between the portion of the story that was told and the portion that was sent in letters.

We cannot, of course, know what relation the spoken story had to the early chapters of the book. It seems likely that the reflective, lazy, elegiac quality of these chapters, with their rounded serene prose and the uneventful evocation of the simple affections and the simple pleasures, reflect Grahame's taste more than Alastair's. Though these are the passages that linger in the mind, they are not the ones of most immediate interest and appeal to small children, to whom Mr Toad is the novel's chief character.

Whatever the need to provide entertainment for his son, there is no doubt that *The Wind in the Willows* shapes and expresses Grahame's own deepest longings. The boy in the story 'Mutabile Semper' in *Dream Days* describes the means of access to his land of Cockayne: 'You're going up a broad clear river in a sort of a boat.' Nature for Grahame is not red in tooth and claw, but a nurturing, idyllic, cosy world in which one can escape the pressure of adult responsibilities and the confines of adult behaviour. In 'The Magic Ring', also in *Dream Days*, he writes: 'To nature, as usual, I drifted by instinct,' to console a disappointment.[11] For all its rural setting, *The Wind in the Willows* is not a countryman's book, but a townsman's potent blend of recollection and fantasy: wish-fulfilment, not observation.

This is not to devalue Grahame's achievement. His River is, like its counterparts in such later books as H. R. Jukes's *Loved River* (1935), Neil Gunn's *Highland River* (1937), or Arthur Ransome's unfinished *The River Comes First*,[12] as much an imaginative symbol—and a symbol of the imagination—as a real stretch of water. Something of its meaning is captured in an early passage of H. G. Wells's *The New Machiavelli* (published in 1911, three years after *The Wind in the Willows*). The narrator remembers the river of his childhood:

The Ravensbrook of my earlier memories was a beautiful stream. It came into my world out of a mysterious Beyond, out of a garden, splashing brightly down a weir which had once been the weir of a mill ... Yellow and purple loosestrife and ordinary rushes grew in clumps along the bank, and now and then a willow. On rare occasions of rapture one might see a rat cleaning his whiskers at the water's edge.

This might be the idyllic River of Grahame's own childhood—though for Wells, significantly, the idyllic memory is a prelude to desecration. The River is no longer an escape from the sordid world but a reminder of it, after it has become 'a dump for old iron, rusty cans, abandoned boots and the like'.[13]

Mole, who escapes from underground to the fascinations of the riverbank, is a fantasy image of Grahame himself, recalling, on the very first page, the central figure of the childhood stories. The resemblance between the opening of *The Wind in the Willows* and the opening of the first story in *The Golden Age*, 'A Holiday', is very striking, though it has not as far as I know been previously remarked. In 'A Holiday' Grahame writes:

... the soft air thrilled with the germinating touch that seems to kindle something in my own small person as well as in the rash primrose already lurking in sheltered haunts. Out into the brimming sun-bathed world I sped, free of lessons, free of discipline and correction, for one day at least. My legs ran of themselves, and though I heard my name called faint and shrill behind, there was no stopping for me.[14]

The Wind in the Willows

Here is the corresponding passage in the first paragraph of *The Wind in the Willows*:

> Spring was moving in the air above and in the earth below and around him, penetrating even his dark and lowly little house with its spirit of divine discontent and longing. It was small wonder, then, that he suddenly flung down his brush on the floor, said 'Bother!' and 'O blow!' and also 'Hang spring-cleaning!' and bolted out of the house without even waiting to put on his coat. Something up above was calling him imperiously.[15]

For the first five chapters, before Toad begins his independent adventures, the narrative focus barely leaves Mole for an instant; there is a case for seeing in Grahame's sudden diversion of attention away from Mole and on to Toad, whose adventures were already set down in the letters to Alastair, a serious flaw in the book's construction, caused by the difficulty of marrying the fantasy which was a solace for Grahame with the fantasy which was an entertainment for Alastair. The existence of the exuberant farce of Toad in written form compelled Grahame to change direction, and to remove Mole from his central position. That for Grahame Mole, not Toad, was the book's protagonist is proved by one of his suggested titles, fortunately unused, *Mr Mole and his Mates*.[16]

But, willy-nilly, Toad does take over the book the moment he takes to the road. A comparison of the letters in which his story is first charted and the chapters in which it took final shape is highly instructive. The difference between the two texts is not so much that between something dashed off and something crafted, but between a story genuinely for children—or rather a child—and one with more ambiguous purposes. It is clear that Grahame kept the letters in front of him as he wrote, simply expanding and refining the existing text: but the final result is very different in flavour. To some eyes the letters may appear a sort of plot summary without the subtle resonance of the book's full cadences; to others, the simple directness of the letters, and their robust good humour, will mark them as Grahame's only true children's story. Compare:

He stepped out into the road to hail the car, when suddenly his face turned very pale, his knees trembled & shook, & he had a bad pain in his tummy. (*Letters*)

and

He stepped confidently out into the road to hail the motor-car, which came along at an easy pace, slowing down as it neared the lane; when suddenly he became very pale, his heart turned to water, his knees shook and yielded under him, and he doubled up and collapsed with a sickening pain in his interior. (*Final text*)[17]

The intimacy of the letters has given way to a more formal relationship between writer and reader. This was inevitable when Grahame sought to attach the succinctly related story of Toad's adventures to the book's early chapters written with his natural expansiveness, and without the restriction of an immediate child audience.

This task of marrying up two different stories written in two different moods caused endless problems, which can be traced in the book's textual inconsistencies. Take Badger's speech for instance. In the letters he says of the cold tongue: 'It's real good.' in the book he says: 'It's first-rate.'[18] That shows the difference between the texts in a nutshell: but Grahame, recognizing perhaps that Badger is more convincing when he says 'real good' than 'first-rate', did not completely expunge the no-nonsense speech of the letters. In the book as in the letters, Badger defends Toad's ungrammatical 'learn 'em' against Rat's strictures: 'What's the matter with his English? It's the same what I use myself.' Yet this is the same Badger who earlier in the book, in a passage written exclusively for publication, speaks like this:

'This very morning,' continued the Badger, taking an arm-chair, 'as I learnt last night from a trustworthy source, another new and exceptionally powerful motor-car will arrive at Toad Hall on approval or return. At this very moment, perhaps, Toad is busy arraying himself in those singularly hideous habiliments so dear to him, which transform him from a (comparatively) good-looking Toad into an Object which throws any decent-minded animal that comes across it into a violent fit. We must be up and doing, ere it is too late.'[19]

To say that *The Wind in the Willows* is structurally shaky is not to condemn it. It is this very 'flaw', the book's openness to being read as chiefly the story of Mole or chiefly the story of Toad, which allows such a range of response, and appeals to such a range of temperaments. And there is also of course a third strand in the narrative, the mild nature mysticism and wanderlust expressed in the two interpolated chapters, 'The Piper at the Gates of Dawn' and 'Wayfarers All'. The poetic prose of these chapers, and their pallid Edwardian paganism, are the only elements of the book with which I am entirely out of sympathy; but these chapters were important to Grahame, and have been to many of his readers. Grahame was by no means alone in his attraction to Pan—as Somerset Maugham put it: 'Poets saw him lurking in the twilight on London commons, and literary ladies in Surrey, nymphs of an industrial age, mysteriously surrendered their virginity to his rough embrace.'[20] But it was his unique achievement to reduce the savage god to a sort of woodland nanny. Again, a strand of Grahame's neo-paganism derives from Stevenson, but how bitterly resonant is Stevenson's sentence in the light of Grahame's life and work: 'Shrilly sound Pan's pipes; and behold the banker instantly concealed in the bank parlour!'[21] Some of Grahame's nature mysticism, and some too of his descriptive style, derives from the work of Richard Jefferies, whose *Wood Magic* (1880) is an important precursor of *The Wind in the Willows*. But Grahame has not Jefferies' astringent eye, and where he is most like Jefferies he is least impressive. Here is Jefferies on 'The Pageant of Summer':

It was between the may and the June roses. The may bloom had fallen, and among the hawthorn boughs were the little green bunches that would feed the redwings in autumn. High up the briars had climbed, straight and towering while there was a thorn or an ash sapling, or a yellow-green willow, to uphold them, and then curving over towards the meadow. The buds were on them, but not yet open; it was between the may and the rose.

As the wind, wandering over the sea, takes from each wave an invisible portion, and brings to those on shore the ethereal essence of ocean, so the air lingering among the woods and hedges—green waves and billows—became full of fine atoms of summer. Swept from notched hawthorn leaves, broad-topped oak-leaves, narrow ash sprays and oval willows; from vast elm cliffs and sharp-taloned brambles under; brushed from the waving grasses and stiffening corn, the dust of the sunshine was borne along and breathed.[22]

And here is Grahame in 'The Wild Wood' chapter of *The Wind in the Willows*:

The pageant of the river bank had marched steadily along, unfolding itself in scene-pictures that succeeded each other in stately procession. Purple loosestrife arrived early, shaking luxuriant tangled locks along the edge of the mirror whence its own face laughed back at it. Willow-herb, tender and wistful, like a pink sunset-cloud, was not slow to follow. Comfrey, the purple hand-in-hand with the white, crept forth to take its place in the line; and at last one morning the diffident and delaying dog-rose stepped delicately on to the stage, and one knew, as if string-music had announced it in stately chords that strayed into a gavotte, that June at last was here.[23]

Jefferies is by no means the only influence traceable in *The Wind in the Willows*. Perhaps the most interesting, bearing in mind Grahame's association with *The Yellow Book* and his horror of the Wilde trial, which his biographer Peter Green suggests contributed to the characterization and the fate of Toad, is Oscar Wilde. Wilde's story 'The Devoted Friend' (*The Happy Prince and other Tales*, 1888), opens with the words: 'One morning the old Water-rat put his head out of his hole. He had bright beady eyes and stiff grey whiskers . . .'. Wilde's Water-rat puts into words the burden of *The Wind in the Willows*: 'Love is all very well in its way, but friendship is much higher.'[24]

Grahame himself had no real friends. His first biographer Patrick Chalmers wrote that he 'never made intimate friendships with his fellows'. Whatever his relationship with Frederick Furnivall, who taught him to row, Grahame neither contributed nor subscribed to the volume of memoirs of Furnivall edited by John Munro in 1911, though his cousin Anthony Hope did both. In an essay 'The Fellow that Goes Alone' (*St Edward's School Chronicle*, 1913) Grahame dwells on the story of St Edmund being greeted by a child who says 'Hayle, Felowe that goest alone' (a quotation from Caxton that we know was twice transcribed in the now lost ledger book that contained Grahame's earliest work). Grahame writes:

But specially should we envy him his white vision in the meadow; for which he should be regarded as the patron saint of all those who of set purpose choose to walk alone, who know the special grace attaching to it, and ever feel that somewhere just ahead, round the next bend perhaps, the White Child may be waiting for them.[25]

The redemptive child waiting round the corner in this cherished notion of Grahame's is not Christ, but his own lost childhood self. He told Constance Smedley in conversation:

I feel I should never be surprised to meet myself as I was when a little chap of five, suddenly coming round a corner ... The queer thing is, I can remember everything I felt then, the part of my brain used from four till about seven can never have altered ... After that time I don't remember anything particularly.

As Barrie put it: 'Nothing that happens after we are twelve matters very much.'[26]

Despite making a virtue of 'going alone' Grahame did at least in his younger days appreciate a particular sort of easy male companionship, a society of free cheerful talk, no petticoats, no irksome responsibilities. The folklorist Edward Clodd, Secretary of the London Joint Stock Bank and an acquaintance of Grahame's, held gatherings at Aldeburgh each Whitsun which encapsulated what Peter Green has called the 'weekend myth'. George Gissing records in his diary for 6 June 1895: 'These men's parties at Whitsuntide have been an institution with Clodd for many years; he has had numbers of well-known men down at his house. Everything simple, but great geniality and heartiness.'[27] This is the atmosphere recalled for Patrick Chalmers by one of Grahame's bank colleagues, Sydney Ward, who went on rural weekends with him. They took long walks and ate chops cooked over an open woodfire accompanied by 'great chunks of cheese, new bread, great swills of beer, pipes, bed, and heavenly sleep'.[29]

The lure of the country for clerks and city men was expressed in essays of rural escape by writers such as Edward Thomas and Arthur Ransome as well as Grahame, and in a splendid poem, 'Week-End' by Harold Monro, which stood at the head of a hugely popular anthology of the 1920s and 1930s, *The Week End Book*.

> The train! The twelve o'clock for paradise.
> Hurry, or it will try to creep away.
> Out in the country everyone is wise:
> We can be only wise on Saturday.
> There you are waiting, little friendly house:
> Those are your chimney-stacks with you between,
> Surrounded by old trees and friendly cows,
> Staring through all your windows at the green.
> Your homely floor is creaking for our tread;
> The smiling tea-pot with contented spout
> Thinks of the boiling-water, and the bread
> Longs for the butter. All their hands are out
> To greet us, and the gentle blankets seem
> Purring and crooning: 'Lie in us and dream.'

The countryside was not for working in; it was a place for rest and recreation. Furnivall catches the mood, confiding that when editing the poet Hoccleve

I took my bundle of . . . papers down to the pleasant farm in which we spent our holiday month . . . But, alas, I never untied the string. Bother Hoccleve! where could he come in, with the sunshine, flowers, apple-orchards and harvest about?[29]

This romantic idea of the country relates both to the clubbable, roomy atmosphere of the all-male riverbank world, and to Grahame's oddly wrong-headed notions about his own book. In July 1908 he wrote a blurb for the fly-leaf, claiming that *The Wind in the Willows* was

a book of Youth—and so perhaps chiefly *for* Youth, and those who still keep the spirit of youth alive in them: of life, sunshine, running water, woodlands, dusty roads, winter firesides; free of problems, clean of the clash of sex; of life as it might fairly be supposed to be regarded by some of the wise small things '*That glide in grasses and rubble of woody wreck.*'[30]

He expanded on this in a letter of 10 October 1908 to Theodore Roosevelt:

Its qualities, if any, are mostly negative—i.e.—no problems, no sex, no second meaning—it is only an expression of the very simplest joys of life as lived by the simplest beings of a class that you are specially familiar with and will not misunderstand.[31]

The Wind in the Willows is a densely layered text fairly cluttered with second meanings (though not, as Grahame's phrase may imply, *double entendres*), but Grahame could not for his peace of mind afford to admit it. One of these second meanings, and one for which the book has come under considerable attack in recent years, is the political ethos. In chapter eleven, while Rat, Mole, Badger, and Toad prepare to storm Toad Hall, 'the bell rang for luncheon.' Grahame's 'character economy' enables him to evade the question 'who rings the bell?'[32] For his animal heroes form a leisured class which implies for its continuation a servant class, whom we never see. Instead the rough, uncouth 'Wild Wooders' are built up into a class enemy, uncomfortably like the Victorian working class. We find in *The Wind in the Willows* echoes of the middle-class hysteria consequent on the West End riots of February 1886, in which, as *The Times* put it, 'the great majority of those present were loafers and loungers of a pronounced type.'[33]

Yet though on one level the book encodes genteel Victorian paranoia about the mob, the anarchy Arnold and others felt heaving below the surface restraints of civilized society, to interpret the book in these simple political terms would be to read it perversely. For though the stoats and the weasels are on one level the beastly working class, they are also, more truly, the forces which for Grahame threaten and destroy the ideal life: the destructive part of human nature, and the inconvenient demands of human society. To consider the riverbank world as a working economy is to misread Grahame's escape fantasy, and mistake its implications. For in its paean to the simple uncluttered pleasure of friendship, it works to warm, not chill, the reader. While class prejudices may impinge on the book, human feeling drives it. And as George Sturt wrote in *A Small Boy in the Sixties*: 'One's mind easily forgets rubbishy opinions, while one's tissues take permanent growth from feelings.'[34]

'I love these little people,' said Grahame to the illustrator E. H. Shepard. 'Be kind to them.'[35] That love communicates itself; in *The Wind in the Willows* Grahame created, out of a thwarted and lonely imagination, one of the most companionable of all English classics: a book which enters and nourishes the mind, and whose plangent rhythms establish a resonance that enriches and enlivens one's sense of language, of landscape, of life.

Notes

An earlier version of this essay appeared in *Touchstones: Reflections on the Best in Children's Literature*, vol. i, ed. Perry Nodelman, Children's Literature Association (West Lafayette, Ind., 1985).

1. *A Hundred Fables of Aesop* from the English version of Sir Roger L'Estrange, with an introduction by Kenneth Grahame (1899), xi; Ezra Pound, *ABC of Reading* (London, 1951, 1968), 14; A. A. Milne, 'A Household Book', *Not That It Matters* (London, 1919), 85–9.
2. 'Child's Play', *Virginibus Puerisque* (London, 1881), 251–2.
3. Ibid. 253–4.
4. Ibid. 256, 243–4, 237; 'Prologue: the Olympians', *The Golden Age* (London, 1895), 4.
5. 'A Saga of the Seas', *Dream Days* (London, 1898), 164.
6. Patrick Chalmers, *Kenneth Grahame: Life, Letters and Unpublished Work* (London, 1933), 62.
7. Beatrix Potter commented 'Kenneth Grahame ought to have been an artist—at least all writers for children ought to have sufficient recognition of what things look like—did he not describe "Toad" as combing his *hair*? A mistake to fly in the face of nature—A frog may wear goloshes; but I don't hold with toads having beards or wigs! so I prefer Badger.' Quoted by Leslie Linder, *A History of the Writings of Beatrix Potter* (London, 1971), 175; *The Wind in the Willows* (London, 1908), 298, 9, 227; *Virginibus Puerisque*, 245–6.
8. Peter Green: *Kenneth Grahame 1859–1932: A Study of his Life, Work and Times* (London, 1959), 166, 284. Reissued in an illustrated abridgement as *Beyond the Wild Wood* (1983).
9. *The Wind in the Willows*, 130; *Virginibus Puerisque*, 245; Humphrey Carpenter, *Secret Gardens* (London, 1985), n. 133, 229.
10. *Virginibus Puerisque*, 256; *The Wind in the Willows*, 140.
11. 'Mutabile Semper', *Dream Days*, 611; 'The Magic Ring', *Dream Days*, 92.

12. See Hugh Brogan, *The Life of Arthur Ransome* (London, 1984), 395–6.
13. *The New Machiavelli* (London, 1911), 42, 43.
14. 'A Holiday', *The Golden Age*, 9.
15. *The Wind in the Willows*, 1–2.
16. Chalmers, *Kenneth Grahame*, 126.
17. 17 July 1907, reproduced in Elspeth Grahame, ed., *First Whisper of 'The Wind in the Willows'* (London, 1944), 60, and in facsimile in Kenneth Grahame: *My Dearest Mouse—'The Wind in the Willows' Letters* (London, 1988), 71; *The Wind in the Willows*, 237–8.
18. Sept. 1907, *First Whisper*, 82, *My Dearest Mouse*, 161; *The Wind in the Willows*, 287.
19. *The Wind in the Willows*, 272; 122.
20. *Cakes and Ale* (London, 1930), 122.
21. 'Pan Pipes', *Virginibus Puerisque*, 285.
22. 'The Pageant of Summer', *The Life of the Fields'* (London, 1884), 42–3.
23. *The Wind in the Willows*, 48–9.
24. 'The Devoted Friend', *The Happy Prince and Other Tales* (London, 1888), 59, 60.
25. Chalmers, *Kenneth Grahame*, xiii; 'The Fellow that Goes Alone' repr. in Peter Green, *Kenneth Grahame*, 5.
26. Constance Smedley, *Crusaders* (London, 1929), 150, cited by Peter Green, *Kenneth Grahame*, 17–18; J. M. Barrie, cited by Andrew Birkin: *J. M. Barrie and the Lost Boys* (London, 1979), 8.
27. Pierre Coustillas, ed., *London and the Life of Literature in Late Victorian England—The Diary of George Gissing, Novelist* (Brighton, 1978), 374–5.
28. Chalmers, *Kenneth Grahame*, 111.
29. Monro's 'Week-End' prefaces V. Mendel, F. Meynell, eds., *The Week-End Book* (London, 1924); F. J. Furnivall, ed., *Hoccleve's Works—The Regement of Princes*, E.E.T.S. extra series 72 (1897), xix–xx.
30. Chalmers, *Kenneth Grahame*, 145.
31. Ibid. 138.
32. *The Wind in the Willows*, 276.
33. Gareth Stedman Jones, *Outcast London* (Oxford, 1971), 293.
34. George Sturt, *A Small Boy in the Sixties* (Cambridge, 1927), 173.
35. Peter Green, *Kenneth Grahame*, 346.

Booklist

The following books by Kenneth Grahame are referred to in this essay:

Pagan Papers (1894).
The Golden Age (1895).
Dream Days (1898).
The Wind in the Willows (1908).

Elspeth Grahame, ed. and introduced, *First Whisper of 'The Wind in the Willows'* (London, 1944).

My Dearest Mouse—'The Wind in the Willows' Letters, introduced by David Gooderson (London, 1988).

Further Reading

Humphrey Carpenter, *Secret Gardens: The Golden Age of Children's Literature* (London, 1985).

Patrick Chalmers, *Kenneth Grahame: Life, Letters and Unpublished Work* (London, 1933).

Eleanor Graham, *Kenneth Grahame* (London, 1963).

Peter Green, *Kenneth Grahame 1859–1932: A Study of his Life, Work and Times* (London, 1959). Reissued in an illustrated abridgement as *Beyond the Wild Wood* (London, 1983). 'The Rentier's Rural Dream', *Times Literary Supplement*, 26 Nov. 1982.

Lois R. Kuznets, 'Toad Hall Revisited', *Children's Literature*, 7 (1978).

A. A. Milne, 'A Household Book', *Not That It Matters* (London, 1919).

Geraldine D. Poss, 'An Epic in Arcadia: The Pastoral World of *The Wind in the Willows*', *Children's Literature*, 4 (1975).

W. W. Robson, 'On *The Wind in the Willows*', *The Definition of Literature and other essays* (Cambridge, 1982).

K. Sterck, 'Re-reading *The Wind in the Willows*', *Children's Literature in Education*, 12 (1973).

Tony Watkins, 'Making a Break for the "Real England": The River-Bankers Revisited', *Children's Literature Association Quarterly*, 9/1 (1984).

Jay Williams, 'Reflections on *The Wind in the Willows*', *Signal*, 21 (1976).

15

Henry James's Children

BARBARA EVERETT

Henry James wrote in 'The Art of Fiction' (1884): 'The only obligation to which in advance we may hold a novel, without incurring the accusation of being arbitrary, is that it be interesting.' When in 1897 he published *What Maisie Knew*, returning after five hopeful, hopeless years in the theatre to the medium in which he now hardly even hoped for real success, he produced a novel which has remained ever since almost too 'interesting' to its critics. Found ambiguous, to all appearances scarcely enjoyed, this very remarkable work is the first by James to which a child is central.

In a section of his Life entitled 'The Little Girls', James's biographer Leon Edel traces the whole series of female children portrayed in the novels and stories, from the murdered infant Effie of *The Other House* (1896) to Maisie herself, then to Flora and Miles in 'The Turn of the Screw' (1898), last to a trio Edel groups together as 'adolescents': the central figure of 'In the Cage' (1898), then Aggie and Nanda in *The Awkward Age* (1899). On these characters Edel bases a thesis both simple and striking. James created this sequence of novels and stories in an act of unconscious self-therapy, revealing 'the astonishing fact that in his imagination he moved from infancy to childhood, from childhood to adolescence and then to young adulthood', thus making 'a series of parables, an extensive personal allegory'.

Because all writers write in some sense out of their experience, there is a large general truth in this, and Edel's ensuing account of *What Maisie Knew* is not unsympathetic. Yet James's imagination of children has a literary importance which Edel's theory can only obscure; the myths of biography may confuse the different chronologies of the artist. Perhaps suggestively, Edel's account is littered with curious small errors of fact. The first mention of

Maisie's age in *What Maisie Knew* calls her 'six', not Edel's 'five'. And, for that matter, so evident is the child's progression to emotional puberty, that at the novel's end the likelihood is that she is nearer to fourteen or fifteen than to Edel's 'seven or eight, or perhaps a bit older'. Again, Edel gives Aggie's age at the start of *The Awkward Age* as 'Sixteen'. But the book's opening pages actually make a point of Van's evasiveness concerning the girl's real maturity: when Mr Longdon sees Aggie's photograph and says drily, 'She's not a little girl', Van lets fall 'She's only seventeen or eighteen, I suppose, but I never know how old—or at least how young—girls are.' This suggests that Aggie is something more like her friend Nanda's rising nineteen. Again, Edel places before his 'sixteen-year-old' Aggie, in his careful chronological list, the intelligent sympathetic young woman who works in a Mayfair post-office in 'In the Cage'. But this girl's past experience, her social relationships, and her whole narrative tone—dry, stoic, and metropolitan—indicate someone nearer the age of the equally romantic but more provincial rectory-born young governess in 'The Turn of the Screw', whose story dates her precisely 'at the age of twenty, on taking service for the first time'.

Mere cavilling is not my purpose here. Edel's thesis seems to me against the meaning and feeling of much in James's work, and the biographer's attempt to push it home is bound to involve troubling discrepancies. This is a pity, because the novelist's fictive treatment of the young is of vital interest to his writing—but its importance cannot be rendered through these simple biographical patterns. The importance depends on seeing the year 1897 and its novel, *What Maisie Knew*, as a turning-point. I want to suggest that Maisie, and her more realistically presented successor Nanda, initiate James's 'last phase', so often located after the turn of the century; and that Maisie—with whom I am chiefly concerned here—in herself generates the peculiarly Jamesian heroes and heroines of the last novels. From this point of view she is very close to, but strikingly different from, the children of the stories. She is a novel's presiding consciousness and therefore heroic, and a heroic child is a radically new departure in James.

The children of the stories are only briefly treated and only externally viewed, and there is in a sense much less to be said about them here. But from one aspect they take the centre of the picture: they exist in their quite formidable power of pathos. Listing his 'little girls', Edel necessarily excludes the small boy in the painful earlier story, 'The Pupil' (1891), who in fact has a great deal in common with Miles and Flora in 'The Turn of the Screw'. All three are very powerful studies in pathos. As such, they are *foci* for an intensity of feeling which is at the heart of Henry James's work.

When in 1918 Ezra Pound commemorated the novelist in *The Little Review*, he took as topic Henry James's hatred of tyranny, 'the continual passion of it in this man who, fools said, didn't "feel"'. If James's 'coldness' as a writer was a theme of contemporary reviewers, not many critics since have been readier to recognize the centrality of feeling to his work. There is a kind of surprise in the fact that this most subtly urbane of novelists should number heroic children among his most original creations. But it is not unlike the surprise of that well-known letter which James's elder brother William wrote, when—visiting in England a younger brother unseen for half a dozen years—he relievedly found the cosmopolitan social reporter, the assured critic and novelist still 'the same dear old, good, innocent and at bottom very powerless-feeling Harry . . . caring for little but his writing, and full of dutifulness and affection for all gentle things'. William James himself was in process of becoming the distinguished philosopher and psychologist; and one of his own earliest essays, 'The Sentiment of Rationality' (which was to be sustained by much of his later and greater work) urges that in the human psyche, thought-processes are underwritten by far more potent, deep sources of feeling or sentiment. It may not be irrelevant that the rather saintly father of these two superficially different but brilliant men, Henry James Senior, was recorded to have had an obsessive love for children.

Henry James is scarcely a 'sentimental' novelist, in any of the available senses of the word. The truth of feeling in his work reaches us precisely because of the reticences and ironies

Alone in a new home, illustration by L. Leslie Brooke for Mrs Molesworth's *My New Home*, Macmillan, 1894.

involved, and all the countermanding social factors—the hard knowledge of class and money, the expertise in conventions and manners. James's genius is precisely to bring together human tenderness, moral idealism, with a never-relinquished social truth. It is this that makes the importance to his work of the 'social child'—the sophisticated innocent or 'smart' orphan. And these clear contrasting worlds, this sense of militant polarities in experience, took decades for the novelist to learn to grasp fully and to master inimitably. Most 'Jamesians' agree that the writer got himself into curious perplexities with his first considerable work of fiction, *Watch and Ward* (1871). This mild romantic tale of a man no longer young who adopts an orphaned female and educates her to be his wife, in an attempt to solace hurts given by social, romantic-erotic experience, takes on odd incidental or accidental shadows of the incestuous, as well as allowing the obtrusion of too frank and unrecognized a sexuality in the most innocently domestic imagery.

Watch and Ward is (for James) both a little inept and too often tedious. Yet it possesses a quietly large, even heroic vision, manifested in the description of its gentle bachelor, Roger Lawrence, as 'the most unobtrusively *natural* of men' (my italics); and when the child Nora, at first a pathetic ugly duckling, grows up beautiful and brave to love her guardian more than filially, she finds 'The secret of the universe was, that Roger was the only man in it who *had a heart*' (my italics again). It is an interesting fact that James's last completed novel, *The Golden Bowl*, written more than thirty years later, similarly works heroically to reconcile the two loves, *eros* and *agape*, love of husband and wife, and love of child and father; and this great book similarly cannot quite purge itself of troubled impurities. The most sympathetic and admiring reader senses problems (a near-incestuousness of relation, for instance, between the innocent father and daughter—whose enormous wealth casts its own shadow) deep within the nature of the fiction. But the trouble is now conscious, understood, and *becomes* the story—the separations and sacrifices are a part of the achievement, as the sophisticated Prince warns the child-like Maggie: 'Everything's terrible in the heart of man, *cara*.' 'Heart' is no simple factor. Of the three children in the stories of the 1890s, the two boys, Miles and the unnamed Pupil, both die of heart failure, torn apart by the demands and divisions of adults: Miles by the struggle of a possessive woman against ghosts, the Pupil by the departure of his loved tutor from his own noisy, selfish, 'lovable', Bohemian family. In their vulnerability these children may be felt to be more explicit, more satisfactory descendants of Hyacinth Robinson in *The Princess Casamassima* (1886), presented to us first as a child and thereafter, sometimes disturbingly, as a peculiarly child-like, small adult: one destroyed by the social and political objectification of the conflicts in his own birth and nature.

Hyacinth finally kills himself, rather than give himself to a political assassination in which he has no belief. This suicide consummates a certain painful melancholy heavy in the novel as a whole, a quality of feeling not untouched—despite all the work's absorbing interest and density—by the sentimentally masochistic or self-pitying. It is perhaps this strain in James's development which Edel interprets by his thesis in 'The Little Girls'. Yet that thesis hardly confronts a vital fact. In and through the child-stories and novels of the 1890s, James himself came to terms with and 'justified' these depths of feeling, converting social and personal defeats into true achievements, even triumphs. Self-pity transmutes to compassion, and compassion to courage. The very decision to write of girls, not boys (James thought of girls as tougher than boys, survivors) is a symptom of that gained objectivity. To say this is to counter that simple belief in James's homosexuality which seems now to have become current and fashionable, a subject too complex to be here tangled with—but one that is too often presented as crudely unliterary. The creation of Maisie seems to preclude confusion concerning gender: it suggests only that James's work in this period, while becoming in one sense more lonely, more obscure, is in another more self-denyingly or objectively large in its warmth. The pity for the Pupil and for Miles is indignant compassion, not self-obsession; and with Maisie, allowed by the wider novel format a fuller definition, authorial compassion gives way (as I shall go on to discuss) to something quite other. This odd, wise, plain little girl pities others, not herself, and makes it her business to discover something close even to the Wordsworthian 'comfort in the strength of love'. That strength the more fully-grown Nanda of *The Awkward Age* inherits, and she manifests it more positively and more practically. It is these two girls together, Maisie and Nanda, who may be said to head the line of peculiarly Jamesian heroes and heroines of the last novels.

This point I shall return to. For the moment, I want only to suggest that the strength of James's writing in the 1890s and after depends on his sense of what is 'terrible', but also of what is of 'comfort' in the life of feeling: a vision to which the figure of the child is vital. Support for this impression may be gained by pausing briefly and considering how radically different from all the post-1895 writing, and especially the late great 'feeling' achievements, is that strange sport *The Sacred Fount*—written just after *The Awkward Age* and before *The Wings of the Dove* and *The Ambassadors*, that is in 1901 (as if in self-clarification and self-confirmation). Though it is still often treated by critics as among James's serious work, *The Sacred Fount*—which the writer himself referred to in a warning letter to a reader as 'that profitless labyrinth'—exhibits Jamesian method purposively devoid of Jamesian feeling. Hence the reiteration in it of the word 'game'. However studied and rare an artefact *The Awkward Age* is, when Nanda's mother Mrs Brookenham stylishly quavers in her drawing-room, 'Oh I'm not *playing*', we should believe her—under her multiple ironies she tells the truth: she is a woman in love, and intensely, almost savagely absorbed in what she is doing. The pseudo-novelistic-narrator of *The Sacred Fount* (by contrast) makes Art, and studies Love, passionlessly, reducing them to meaningless secrets: 'The condition of light, of the satisfaction of curiosity, and the attestation of triumph, was in this direct way *the sacrifice of feeling*' (my italics). The novel's sacrifice of feeling, its deep refusal to suffer, may be summarized in a simple manner: at this weekend house-party which the fiction describes, with its narrator straining to tell who is emotionally destroying whom, it is impossible to imagine a child or a young person present. The great house Newmarch, despite its ironically promising name, is not for children: the phantasmagoric games of passion and the power-struggles to the death played out or not played out in the guesses of its observer are like the drawing-rooms of *What Maisie Knew* or *The Awkward Age*, before the children arrive or after they go. There is no heart here—an effect wonderfully reproduced in the eerie romanticism of this darkly incommunicative fable: 'The last calls of birds sounded extraordinarily loud; they were like the timed, serious splashes, in wide, still water, of divers not expecting to rise again.'

Early reviewers of *What Maisie Knew* (and some since) have protested at its 'obscenity', the pornography—as they read it—of a child's solemn contemplation of adult sexuality. But this is surely an interestingly total misapprehension. The book is the reverse of the future *The Sacred Fount*. With Maisie at its centre, the book is as unerotic as it is possible for a fiction to be; the *amours* of Ida and Beale Farange, of Sir Claude and Miss Overmore are inconceivable, unimaginable, beyond the aesthetic world of the work. Similarly, there is a chasm between the troublingly beautiful sterility of Newmarch, with its masks and pictures and its back-turned guests, and Maisie's growing life, her eager face, however dusty and desolate the houses between which she is hopefully shuttled. *What Maisie Knew* manages without even that faint taint of self-pity which touches the compassion of 'The Pupil' and 'The Turn of the Screw'. Hard as the child's fate is, her story has all the vigour and poise of true comedy. The book is powered by an objectivity which is present in its flamboyant logic of form and its thorough vitality of wit. In it, affectionate humour constitutes a kind of moral respect—respect tendered, across the chasm of age and gender and type, to a saluted equal. It is hard not to guess that through the profound disappointments that came to a climax in his preceding theatrical years, the writer reached some definitive ending of illusion: the iron, as we say, entered his soul, and he turned back to the fictive medium with a toughness and clarity dependent on lack of hope—toughness and clarity which however, given his generosity of moral nature, emerge as warmth of feeling, indignant defence of the vulnerable.

What Pound called the struggle for 'human liberty, personal liberty', articulated for instance in the political story of Hyacinth Robinson, had there hardly come off. But, translated into the comical yet heroic moral idealism of a skinny little girl abandoned by raffish Belgravian parents, the theme takes flight. When the public theatre failed James, he began to discover how to delineate boldly his most private themes. As a result, *What Maisie Knew* and *The Awkward Age* initiate Henry James's last phase, too often seen as beginning only after the turn of the century, and the child Maisie is the first and most simply original of the novelist's late protagonists.

The newness of *What Maisie Knew* is suggested by the fact that this is the first of the writer's novels to be found radically obscure by readers. *The Portrait of a Lady* and *The Bostonians* and *The Tragic Muse* have their subtleties and indecisions, but critics do not differ sharply about their essential moral bearings, as they do over Maisie and her world. This new ambiguity has its connections with a new clarity—the book's resolute schematization, the abstract formalism in its plotting. Maisie's parents abandon each other; Maisie is housed alternately by each parent with each new lover; Maisie's parents abandon their lovers; Maisie is invited to be housed by the paired lovers; Maisie at last abandons the lovers. The peculiar formal attributes of *What Maisie Knew* and the comparable if more realistic, larger and solider *The Awkward Age* are most often explained as 'dramatic', the effect of years of writing for the theatre. Yet the slightly earlier *The Other House*, a fiction written up from a play-scenario (and years later reconverted to the stage) has none of this abstract force—it is as merely factual as a melodrama can be and even has a certain real Ibsenite power in its portrait of Rose Armitage, a Kate Croy-like villainess.

The structural forms of *What Maisie Knew* (as of *The Awkward Age*) are more than 'dramatic'. They serve a new irrealism, which in its turn expresses a newly naked inward consciousness. The book's almost mathematical plot charts out the ways in which the feeling of an individual makes sense (or not) of the fantastic blind love-dance of society. There is both hope and desolation in the novel's paradoxical wit; there is a chasm between the deep, mute self of little Maisie and the brilliant, empty world which constitutes her experience, and the action of the novel is to bridge that chasm. At this point, in fact, James's intensely 'social' novels begin to take on the surprising depths and voids and disparities of a kind of symbolism—a method always extending and educating itself towards the at last almost out-of-touch silences of *The Golden Bowl*. It is, of course, not impossible to interpret psychologically—in personal terms, from the novelist's own viewpoint—this ambiguous retreat-and-advance into a form of symbolization. There is no doubt that, despite a small audience of mostly upper-class devotees, James was received in his own time with a neglect and even hostility earned by few novelists of his gifts; and in this sense he became as a writer as solitary as we see the child Maisie become. Yet her story is tragi-comic, and far from merely pathetic, and there was gain too in the writer's own situation. The life of feeling at once 'makes' society and yet depends for its survival on the inner resources of the lonely individual—a paradox which shapes James's later writing.

The peculiar schematization of *What Maisie Knew* justifies itself in a special fashion: as the natural and necessary embodiment of a life of feeling in itself formless, inarticulate, deeply reticent. From this point on, James's writing even assumes effects of metaphysical conceit, so inherent are its antitheses and contradictions. Interestingly, some of James's critics are happier to read more literally than metaphorically—to assume, for instance, that 'What Maisie Knew' is an item or subject that may be guessed or described, like the scholarly efforts to name the unknown source of the Newsome wealth in *The Ambassadors*. Thus, in his 'The Little Girls', glossing the biographical relevance of these stories and novels of the 1890s, and relating them to the assumed psychology of his subject, Leon Edel defines the shared essential history of all these young persons as 'their drive to attain omniscience'. Maisie knows something, and wants to know everything. And many readers and critics seem to agree with this presupposition. Otherwise able critical accounts of *What Maisie Knew* and *The Awkward Age* have seen the central subject of these fictions—the chief pursuit of the young people involved—as 'knowing'. The novels themselves are interpreted, one might say, as works in the tradition of *Bildungsroman*, novels of self-education. And there is of course some truth in this. But if this assumption were wholly true, we should probably have to agree with those who have protested at the 'obscenity' of the notion of a small child studying the sexual affairs of its elders. Moreover, we should perhaps note that such an interpretation comes close to identifying a novelist's characters with the novelist, and the novelist with the critic, whose business may be presumed to be primarily epistemological, a matter of 'knowing'.

I have suggested ways in which *What Maisie Knew* may be considered a new beginning. One last remains to be mentioned. It offers itself as perhaps a first case of what becomes the novelist's pervasive and striking use of irony in his titles; its title really needs to be read, *What Maisie 'Knew'*. This can be most briefly illuminated by a glance backward again at the basically unironical *Watch and Ward*, where James attempts, through his story of a man who adopts a little girl in order to marry her later, to harmonize in a love-story those primary relations of youth and age, innocence and experience, the individual and society, which were later to make the 'social child' such a vital personage to him. Near the end of *Watch and Ward* occurs one of its few very striking images, as the now grown child Nora, bewildered and confused by her relationships, is caught 'weeping in her ball dress those primitive tears': and the 'ball-dress', the 'primitive tears' are the promise of the profound and savage drawing-rooms of the later James. If there are grotesqueries as well as *longueurs* in this early story (the incest which obtrudes itself, and the too little accounted for sexuality which makes strange some pretty imagery) the cause is clearly only that the young writer does not know how to discipline materials already too powerfully unwieldy for his skills. *What Maisie Knew*, published nearly thirty years later, is a cooler and tougher novel as well as an incomparably more brilliant one. And it gains this power and this detachment from a pervasive and thorough irony. The writer inhabits absolutely a society distrusted absolutely. Beginning as it does (its very first sentence) with the divorce, the book takes off from the shock of a sanctity violated, a shock two pages later crystallized into paradoxical wit: 'They felt indeed more married than ever, inasmuch as what marriage had mainly suggested to them was the unbroken opportunity to quarrel.'

As with so many of the novel's coruscations (and it is an extraordinarily witty and entertaining book) this sentence works in terms of a civilized reticence. Writer and reader meet—or ought to meet—in a wholly silent agreement concerning what marriage 'mainly suggests' to *them*, a definition necessarily different from that of most of the novel's characters. The word *love* occurs strikingly rarely in *What Maisie Knew*, and then only in notably ironic or painful or farcical circumstances. But it is the factor that makes sense of Maisie herself, and of everything that happens to her, and of everything that everyone else does in the story. 'Kind' as many people try or pretend to be to her, Maisie is the loving child of an entire lack of love; her story is told when we recognize, by the end, that the more people Maisie 'knows', the more complex and crowded her acquaintance, the less love she finds. If the child knows anything, this is, by the end ('"Oh I know!"') what she knows.

James's title is in all other respects bitterly ironical. It permits him to phrase that hard obtuseness in society (replacing love by knowledge, as bread by a stone) in a style inherited from other ironical story-tellers—Defoe and Swift, for instance, both experienced the defeat of being at times mistaken at their face value. Certainly Maisie does in a sense 'learn'—the book is its own kind of *éducation sentimentale*; and certainly, too, she is a child of her world, giving up her hopes of a 'family' when she finds herself on the brink of falling in love (*faute de mieux*) with the beautiful but weak Sir Claude—just as poor straightforward Nanda, after her, falls hopelessly in love with the superb but empty Vanderbank. But all this acquisition of experience on Maisie's part is inset in a general apprehension about 'knowing' that goes deep into the later Jamesian work. It is perhaps best and most tellingly summed up in a sentence from the very late, very moral little story called 'Crapy Cornelia' (1909), which tells how a gentle, fastidious, perhaps craven American bachelor decides to settle for friendship with a dowdy, impoverished, slightly grotesque old maid (who however recognizes old fidelities) rather than marry a glamorous, rich and worldly soul who is always lethally knowing, '"up" to everything, aware of everything':

In his time, when he was young or even when he was only but a little less middle-aged, the best manners had been the best kindness, and the best kindness had mostly been some art of not insisting on one's luxurious differences, of concealing rather, for common humanity, if not for common decency, a part at least of the intensity or the ferocity with which one might be 'in the know'. Oh, the 'know' . . .

I am suggesting, in short, that *What Maisie Knew* has little to do with a 'drive for omniscience'. And the point seems to me an important one, because on it depends the full moral weight of the book, and to some degree of the sequence of novels which *Maisie* helps to generate. In James's creation of the child-heroine there is clearly a real originality which it can be difficult for some readers to come to terms with. The novelist's children don't 'drive' for omniscience, or indeed for anything else: in their entire impotence, their enforced passivity lies their moral character in James's eyes. They are social nobodies, nothings, 'not there'. If Maisie is (as of course she is) peculiarly intelligent, even dreadfully wise, this is because her existence is a non-existence, confined to what goes on in the forcing-house of the poor child's head. And even in that sphere there is a problem. Maisie's 'knowing' is limited to her virtuous '*not*-knowing'. Because marriage has (it seems) become 'the unbroken opportunity to quarrel', an erotic and romantic power-game in which someone has to be the loser, her sole function is to be a spy in unchangingly enemy country—she is invited only to contribute fuel to the camp fires of war. This she refuses obdurately, allowing herself to be thought a fool, a bore, disloyal; and she does so for the simplest of reasons.

Maisie is unconcerned with 'knowledge' or even experience—most of what she has, she would conceivably prefer to be without; it is only the avid adults round her who quest for experience, and who concern themselves with 'what Maisie *knows*', much as the more moral but equally wrong-headed young governess in 'The Turn of the Screw' does with her charges (the screw in question is presumably the torture-tool of Inquisition). Maisie's needs, in the name of 'common humanity'—even 'common decency'—are simpler: she must, to survive, love and be loved. The tragi-comedy of her story is that it is a love-story without love, a unique system of 'affairs' where nobody likes each other. There is in this whole thronged bookful of lovers only one human being around Maisie who actually knows what love is, the angelic and straightforward paid working-class nursemaid, Moddle, who within the book's first few pages disappears fast into tender memory, leaving the child clutching the cosy promise ('written on a paper in very big easy words') of '"a mother's fond love"' and '"a nice poached egg to your tea"'; she gets none at all of the first and little enough of the second.

Maisie's struggle, both cheerful and desperate, both pathetic and very funny, is to adjust to her circumstances her quite natural expectations of a person or persons who will permit her to do the 'common' thing, to love and be loved. Both prove difficult. At last, when the novel reaches its brilliantly-worked logical last phase, and the two new 'parents' propose themselves, time has passed and it is too late. Maisie has at last, unnoticeably, in the course of others' activities, grown up into a lonely self-dependent maturity. There is a hint that, however innocently, she loves the kind and exquisite Sir Claude (once her mother's lover and husband, now the lover of her father's ex-wife) now in a manner not totally filial, and cannot accept his coexistence with the attractive and hard and ruthlessly sexual Mrs Beale. Both moral instinct and perhaps some natural jealousy combine to drive her out, to return home to an England where adult existence awaits her, 'parented' only by the grubby grotesque Mrs Wix. The old lady's name is, I suspect, a cockneyfication of the Latin *vix*, meaning 'scarcely, hardly, only just': Mrs Wix offers a 'scarcely' or 'only just' love, the love of the hopeless person who at least—if she can offer little else—*needs* Maisie. Thus, out of his fascinating glimpses into the life of the late-Victorian hard-up rich, James invents a glittering legend of emotional making and breaking. His growing child, the reactor to a world of 'affairs', proves that feeling, the indomitable intelligence of the heart, can be a way of acting: and so creates a novel whose meaning is not far from Blake's ironic poem or epigram, 'Go, little creature born of joy and mirth,|Go, love without the help of anything on earth.'

At the end of her story, Maisie—half moral heroine and half social nuisance—may be going to grow up into someone not too unlike Lady Aurora in *The Princess Casamassima*: a tall, toothy, high-principled and touching humanitarian spinster who cannot either expect or deal with love, and who contents herself heroically with meeting human needs. As the child and Mrs Wix sail across the Channel, the old lady asks her if she looked back and saw Sir Claude, and Maisie says, 'He wasn't there'; when Mrs Wix questions, 'Not on the balcony?', Maisie adds enigmatically, 'He wasn't there.' After years of being lovingly 'not there' herself, Maisie is perhaps running out of love, starting to find even the beautiful, kindly but weak Sir Claude all too finally 'not there'. Maisie surely won't marry. But the novel leaves this issue wide open. Its story is only the making and unmaking of Maisie, who finds herself in the losing of others.

There is a very striking echo of this ending in *The Awkward Age*. The novel translates what is abstract and schematic in its predecessor into something more socially realistic: for in *The Awkward Age*, Maisie's inward growing-up becomes a young woman's 'coming-out', the now all-but-dead but then potent late-Victorian ritual or rite of passage. Nanda's hope is to 'come out' into marriage with Van, the splendid but vain and even shallow young man who is the star of her brilliant mother's Belgravian drawing-room circle: but a network of loves and hatreds, of loyalties and betrayals prevents it. At the end Nanda says 'Goodbye', but not quite to Van: only to the door that closes behind him. Like Maisie's 'He wasn't there', the gesture gives a sense of her new sad independence of images of love, her strong-minded self-knowledge. When her next visitor arrives, the elderly innocent bachelor with whom her future is to be spent, Nanda ashamedly bursts into tears, furiously denying that she loves Vanderbank. Critics invariably seem to take it that she lies. But

Nanda is essentially a truth-teller, to the point of solemnity, and she is here surely telling the simple truth. She has loved Van with a love she has now outgrown: something in herself is finished. She weeps because she has lost, not only Van, but her love.

The peculiar power of *The Awkward Age* lies in its subtle and original realism. We watch, not an intrigue, but a procedure whose meaning is to kill a love and to make a life, perhaps a soul. Undoubtedly Nanda changes and grows in the book's process. And here there is a difference from *What Maisie Knew*. One can hardly quarrel with any reader of that earlier novel who believes, as Edel does, that the story covers only a year or two and leaves its heroine at 'seven or eight'. For James, like all artists, invents his own chronologies. It would be as mistaken with this novel as with *Othello* to imagine a 'double time scheme', but seemingly Maisie lives through incommensurate periods. She moves psychologically, it seems, from six to sixteen, yet only a year or two passes. James has profited by a power of inwardness, of explored consciousness, to which time is highly material (the book is about a child's growing); yet the writer had never lost his novelist's hunger for the real, his loyalty to the social fact.

Just before James died, H. G. Wells directed against the elder novelist his disappointingly unpleasant and obtuse attack in *Boon*, describing *Maisie* as a book about 'what a little girl may or may not have noted', and focusing his contempt for James's unreality on the shortcomings of his characters, arguing that they 'never in any way *date*'. The single most important thing about Nanda is that she 'dates': eighteen or twenty months in her mother's drawing-room destroys her social image, changes her nature, and seals her fate. The novel's brilliant quiet time-scheme surely inspired Eliot's denotation of time passing in his early poems; winter drifts to spring, summer, autumn; leisurely seemingly 'timeless' social meetings succeed each other; 'too soon' becomes 'too late'. As June moves to June, Nanda is twenty, and her childhood is (in late-Victorian social terms) closed. She is 'out', and—to quote Sylvia Plath—'Somebody's done for.'

The marvel of this novel, a great interlocking chain of dramatic relationships, is that—as James's dislikers feel—'Nothing happens'. Time passes; and lives make and unmake themselves. Only with children, whose growing is the great process of their lives, could James effect this. By making his chief characters female children, 'mere girls', James withdraws his events further into the recesses of private life, inward consciousness, the world of feeling. Nanda thus, with Maisie behind her, forms a bridge to his highly original inventions in *The Ambassadors* and *The Golden Bowl*: novels which act out heroic existences on the part of human beings who are as good as, or as bad as children—nobodies, non-existers, 'unimportant' people, who none the less become the moral centres of their worlds. Strether and Maggie are not children: he is a grave middle-aged scholar-manqué in a world of business men, she a millionaire's daughter who marries a ruined Prince. But if *The Ambassadors* is, as it is, a profoundly moving and absorbing fiction, it is because Strether can act out in a larger world—a more public world, to which the novel's love-interest is in a sense subordinate—a life founded on the impotence, the accountability of James's children. ('I began to be young'—he tells Maria Gostrey—'the moment I met you at Chester, and that's what has been taking place ever since. I never had the benefit at the proper time'; and again, Strether sees himself, under the direction of the formidable Sarah Pocock, 'recommended to Woollett as juvenile offenders are committed to reformatories'). Strether is a child in his inability to play the power-game that finally traps him, ironically, between the worldly rivals, the American Puritanical 'business' Newsomes on the one hand and the European erotic Chad and Marie on the other. But, like Maisie and Nanda, he converts his weakness into heroism by making mere inability a principled refusal. He returns to America, accepting no gain from either side; and in that refusal there is a paradoxical, mysterious, and solitary existence, like that by which a child lives and grows and becomes itself.

The figure of the child clearly meant so much to James that it is (further) no surprise to find the Principino featuring on almost the very last page of *The Golden Bowl*. Because we are told that the Ververs will suffer the sadness of having no family, it is possible to feel that, strictly speaking, the Catholic Maggie and her Prince would (like the Jewish dealer at Brighton) have had a whole quiverful of children by now. The small boy's odd irreal solitariness therefore adds something to the novel: the sense of how hardly, at what a price, this quartet achieve their 'common humanity'. But the child's arrival at that remarkable tragi-comic last scene of meeting and parting forever—'I "ordered" him for half past five', Maggie tells her father—has peculiar effect. James causes the child's nanny to insert him into the great first-floor drawing-room, withdrawing herself and leaving him to advance alone, chattering, grown from a baby to 'the boy': an unknown factor, hardly any kind of character in the book, yet in a sense we feel, as the child brings its unambiguous presence into the extreme multiple ambiguities of the story's happy-painful ending, the reason for everything. In the book's last lines, Maggie has to recognize that, an inhabitant of what the novel's first paragraph calls the *Imperium* of London, she has conquered and even enslaved her husband, and from now on lives in a world of power. Yet always behind her she has the meeting of her small son with her father, who is parting for ever from the child he adores unequivocally:

'It's success. And even *this*', he added, as the Principino, appearing alone, deep within, piped across an instant greeting—'even this isn't altogether failure!'

The same devout if civilizedly ironic acclamation might be given by the admirer of James to the literary children he has created. I began this discussion with *What Maisie Knew*. A year or two after he wrote it, James spoke in 'The Future of the Novel' of the romance or novel of his time as peculiarly beloved by women and children, 'boys and girls'. He was writing, perhaps, with certain habitual ironies. None the less *What Maisie Knew*, like so much else that James wrote, has its connections with that high tradition of fiction that speaks to the adult in the child and to the child in the adult. Within the first few pages of *What Maisie Knew*, describing his protagonist, James says: 'She was at the age for which all stories are true and all conceptions are stories.' His sentence tellingly defines the area in which all literature is for children and all children's literature may be literature: the imagination of 'common humanity'.

Booklist

The following books by Henry James are referred to in this essay:

Watch and Ward (1871).
The Portrait of a Lady (1881).
The Bostonians (1885).
The Princess Casamassima (1886).
The Tragic Muse (1890).
The Lesson of the Master (1892), includes 'The Pupil' (1891).
The Other House (1896).
What Maisie Knew (1897).
In the Cage (1898).
The Two Magics: 'The Turn of the Screw' and 'Covering End' (1898).
The Awkward Age (1899).
The Sacred Fount (1901).
The Wings of the Dove (1902).
The Ambassadors (1903).
The Golden Bowl (1904).
The Finer Grain (1910), includes 'Crapy Cornelia' (1909).

16

The Child in Walter de la Mare

JOHN BAYLEY

IN 'The Turn of the Screw' Henry James could be said to have invented, inadvertently, a new concept of children. By some sort of intuitive process of his art he conveyed their essential dissimilarity from adults, and the way they live naturally in a world of their own, however ready they may be to seem to accommodate themselves to the ideas of grown-ups. His discovery is a by-product of the tale's technique, for in manipulating the ghostly atmosphere and apparatus he requires the behaviour of the two children exposed to it to seem curious and suspicious—even eerie—to their elders, and to their new governess in particular. Today we should think nothing of it; indeed it might be regarded as virtually the norm of childish behaviour, especially for children brought up as little Miles and Flora have been.

The further slant in the tale is that the ghosts—that sinister pair, the former valet and governess—seem, by dying, to have entered the childish world. They share the same dismaying inaccessibility as the couple who were once their young charges, and seem to merge into their ambiguous being. What frightens and horrifies the new governess seems quite normal and cosy to the children, an accepted part of their daily life, with its own small secret inventions and assumptions. Ghosts and children seem to understand each other, and to live on the same level of being, observing and frequenting the same covert runways. Walter de la Mare must have unconsciously absorbed this point. Children and the unseen live in the same world with him too. We know how much he admired James's stories, and his own reveal their unmistakable influence.

None more so than his masterpiece, 'A Recluse', from the collection called *On the Edge*. The sinister thing about this wonderfully bland and intricate tale, in which the young narrator has an involuntary experience in the house of a Mr Bloom, is that the theme of 'The Turn of the Screw' is both exploited and reversed. Mr Bloom, big, sly, ineffectual, copious of speech and manner, is an appalling parody of childhood, and its proper distance from the adult world. He plays a trick on Mr Dash, the brashly unsuggestible narrator, who has been drawn by what seems the deserted beauty of an English country house to do a bit of harmless trespassing. Sitting in his little sports car he contemplates the Palladian porch and the gracious front door, and suddenly there is Mr Bloom, materialized in its opening, contemplating him, and presently inviting him in to see the house. After a few moments of Mr Bloom's overwhelming affability Mr Dash is conscious above all of an equally overwhelming desire to escape. He himself is like the child now who longs to get away from a particular sort of 'grown-up' atmosphere; and this disturbing alternation of roles will continue throughout the story. The children's trick the old creature plays on his young visitor, and which the latter never for a moment suspects, is to purloin the ignition key of his sports car, and thus to acquire him as an unwilling guest for the night. Company is what Mr Bloom inordinately desires, for the 'company' that attends him in the house, as a result of his psychical research with the planchette and other false childish devices, he has found to be not the kind to be left alone with.

The point about these disquieting and enchanting stories of de la Mare is that they mingle, with great ease and a kind of eerie and dreamy naturalness, the world of childhood and adulthood, with an imaginative dimension in which both partake, but to which both are always having to say goodbye. No state in life is fixed: we live like strangers and revenants between the state of being old and being young; and in de la Mare's art we experience both in a poetic form to which we can uniquely respond. The poem 'The Listeners' carries its own gloss on this atmosphere, for who in it is what? The traveller is himself a ghost and the listeners are the vanishments of his own sensibility, to which return is only possible through the medium of art, frail but vivid. Like children listening on the stairs the disembodied ones can overhear the sounds of perpetual departure, and how the silence surges softly backwards.

In the best stories this commingling has the relish but also the power of parody. If the word were not so incongruous for the sensibility of de la Mare one would say that he positively gloats over it. The house, Montresor, in 'A Recluse' has all the aesthetic possibility of Henry James's Bly in 'The Turn of the Screw'. Its details are suave and pastoral—'lush, tepid, inexhaustible'—in an English May; and its master has, no doubt by intention, the physical stance, speech, and manner of James himself, James in whom the 'small boy—and others' acquires a new and disquieting perspective of meaning. To Mr Dash it seems incredible that this great simpering disconcerting creature could ever have been a little boy playing childish games at Montresor, but into the reader's reception the idea slips totally, for a version of those games is still going on.

The parody, and as it were the fixity of childhood, when that evanescent state should long have departed into consciousness and recollection, gives to Mr Bloom, as to Seaton's Aunt in the story of that title, something pathetic but also potentially appalling. Mr Dash escapes from the world of Mr Bloom, who is left in his gracious but also 'swarming' domain until the news of his decease comes in some oblique way to the young narrator. Arthur Seaton, already adult in childhood from his experiences, never escapes from the monstrous aunt who seems to have invested in herself the secret arrogance and egoism of one kind of childish world. He seeks to grow up and to enter the adult world of marriage and normality, but in some unnamed and unnameable way she destroys him. Yet he is not entirely 'worsted', for his presence remains to haunt her too, in the dreadful literalness of a perpetual intimacy. When the narrator, Seaton's one-time schoolfriend, calls at the house after his death, it seems quite natural that the rasping old voice should float down over the banisters saying 'Arthur? Is that you, Arthur?' In the same way the voice of Mr Bloom is heard in the small hours in the passages of Montresor, querulously calling 'Coming—coming' . . . at the behest of some domineering presence. The game in which adult, child, and 'presence' meet and conjoin was played too in the house and bedroom of Seaton's Aunt, when the old lady's dressing-gown was heard swishing softly back to her bedroom, and the two children fled into the cupboard where, as she lay serenely on her great bed, she knew very well they were hiding.

Childhood, for de la Mare, is a state of acceptance—acceptance of power and evil, joy and woe, the real and the feigned, the natural and supernatural—inhabiting the same dimension. Because, in consciousness, we never leave the childhood world, there is no special enclave for children. They take the adult world for granted, without attempting to understand it. The special intimation in both 'A Recluse' and 'Seaton's Aunt' is an exploring of this. Mr Bloom, whom the narrator finds impossible to imagine as a child, in fact has the childish faculty of acceptance to a most unnerving degree. Montresor, and its swarm of inhabitants and presences, is—or was—as natural to him as the book world of Henry Brocken was to him in de la Mare's early 'novel' of that name. Brocken was not in the least surprised to be talking to the girls from Herrick's poems, and to Gulliver in his stockade among the Houyhnhnms. Of course there is something slightly self-conscious about this, an echo of the deliberate 'for children— and also for adults' technique of Kipling's *Puck of Pook's Hill* and *Rewards and Fairies*. De la Mare's later stories are much odder and more business-like. Mr Bloom is indeed not a 'child'; but his activities and the atmosphere that surrounds him are seen as if through a child's sense of things—the grown-up perquisites, keys, and loose change lying on a dressing table, loose capacious armchairs of worn vermilion leather, seeming to blend with the presences who have come to live among them—the man with his back turned glimpsed standing under a tree outside, the beings to whom Mr Bloom querulously responded with his 'Coming— coming'—as if he were an adult summoned by a child, or a child by an adult. All this seems lost on young Mr Dash, the narrator, through whose medium it none the less becomes visible, and audible. When he wakes in the night, everything about him in the room looks peculiar, and he realizes it is as if seen by someone intensely afraid; yet he has himself no sense of fear. In the same way the writer manages it so that everything in the story is as if seen by a child, although there are no children in it, and no suggestion of their presence, no emphasis on their style of awareness.

Something of the same sort takes place in 'Seaton's Aunt', where the old woman, like Mr Bloom, seems isolated in a terrible parody of childhood. Both may remind us of the former governess and valet in 'The Turn of the Screw', who are united with the children, as Mr Bloom with his ghosts and Seaton with his infernal aunt. All three stories imagine with great skill and delicacy that debatable land where childhood and adulthood are joined by the nature of the imagination itself, a land from which the narrator in each tale is formally excluded. De la Mare has, in a sense, taken further the involuntary *trouvaille* made by James in the working out of his subject. If James perceived the difference of children, de la Mare's art sees the difference between all persons who still exhibit, in whatever context, the behaviour and assumptions of the childish condition, and those who do not. All three stories take it invisibly for granted, and in the most matter-of-fact way, that there is nothing serene or innocent in the child's world of vision, that anything seemingly angelic in it may belong to dark angels as well as bright ones. In the world of that imagination no distinction can nor need be made between the light and the dark. It is a pre-moral world, rather than a morally ambiguous one, in which monstrosity appears only in the eye of the narrator-beholder. The light and dark exist in their vividness, and their own matter-of-factness. There is something unnerving in all these stories, but there is also the deep satisfaction of something unswervingly true, rigorously unsentimental.

That lack of sentiment is a function of the fact that the three stories take childhood for granted, even as they 'expose' it. The stories are neither for children, nor about children, and yet they can only be fully appreciated by those readers by whom the child's world is naturally and involuntarily understood. When I said that Henry James accidentally invented the modern child in a literary context I also implied the paradox that it is *because* childhood is different that it cannot be isolated, contained, and understood by the vision in art of the adult world. That is exactly what the governess is attempting to do in 'The Turn of the Screw', and its sub-text tells how she fails. It is also what the narrators are seeking to do in 'A Recluse', and in 'Seaton's Aunt'; and there too the memorable figures in the tales elude the narrator, remaining for the reader (and no doubt for the writer too) in their own peculiar and compelling worlds of being.

There is another feature to the paradox. Because children are different, what they read is the same. They are falsified by stories intended for children and they falsify themselves (which they are generally perfectly willing to do) by accepting the idea of 'children's stories'. Naturally little actors, as the governess in 'The Turn of the Screw' finds out, they will accept any version of themselves, in literature as in life, but their real appetite is for whatever is read by persons who are both child and adult, that large category which only excludes (and there only notionally) James's governess and de la Mare's narrators. What matters is the sense in which we are all children when we read; and children as readers are, as it were, the same only more so.

The reader becomes child as he reads, and hence 'different'. That is perhaps the crux of the matter; and it is the matter which is in a sense analysed by the nature of the three tales I have discussed. Their form of secret imaginative analysis explains their peculiar resonance, and its success. De la Mare is a striking example here, because his work shows so subtly, and so conclusively, the difference between stories of childhood and 'children's stories'. The latter category, and the poems he wrote of the same kind, are frankly potboilers with their own sort of individuality and charm, but artistically not in the same class as his best poetry and prose. Many of his best stories, like 'Miss Duveen' and 'The Almond Tree', are specifically for and about childhood, but their art is far removed from his tales for children. *The Three Royal Monkeys* (or *The Three Mulla-Mulgars* as it was in the first edition) is a far better book than C. S. Lewis's *The Lion, the Witch and the Wardrobe*, with which it has something in common, notably the landscape in which summer has been transformed, as if by malign magic, into wintry snow. (Lewis may well have copied this or had an unconscious memory of it.) But although *The Three Royal Monkeys* is full of wonderfully memorable and imaginative scenes—like the great Gunga with his bow, the mountain Mulgars, and their subterranean cousins who impassively watch the voyage of the three travellers through the underground river—it suffers both from a repetition of the motifs and traditions of such books, from *The Swiss Family Robinson* to *The Coral Island*, and from an almost inevitable handing on of their general moral tone.

That general moral tone is one that might be considered suitable for 'children of all ages', a somewhat ominous concept, and one very different from the much more complex and indefinable feeling, which de la Mare's best stories give us, that children are different, and that we are sharing—even embodying—that difference in the act of reading. 'Children's stories' give us in a sense the feeling that we are all the same, all little adults, good, civic, virtuous, collective. That collective and communal atmosphere is common to *The Lord of the Rings*, *The Swiss Family Robinson*, *The Coral Island*, *Swallows and Amazons*, and most other such quest adventure tales, not excluding *The Three Royal Monkeys* and even *The Wind in the Willows*, although Kenneth Grahame's classic has the brilliant notion of isolating Toad from his civic-minded fellows. The wholly authentic aspect of *The Wind in the Willows*, which has kept it fresh for so long, is the perception that children take adult class attitudes and social activities for granted, as the reader takes those of the 'animals' in the story. Thus the animals appear like adults to the reader, who is not—by virtue of being reader—assumed to belong to the jolly gang involved, as he is in our other examples, but to accept them almost incuriously as creatures inhabiting the grown-up world of parties, clubs, and country houses. The irony of Toad's conversion at the end is that he has been the 'child' in the tale, and that he is now definitively joining the grown-up world, not by moral choice but because he has no choice. The book ends with the end of childhood, and the notional perpetuating of the 'grown-up' animal regime.

The most imaginative thing in *The Three Royal Monkeys* is somewhat similar. Nod, the youngest of the three, is accidentally

The three princes set out through the forest, illustration by Mildred E. Eldridge for *The Three Royal Monkeys*, Faber, 1949.

captured by a human castaway, Ben Battle, and frightens him by imitating the sounds of his voice. Nod, like a young child, is not just imitating, as would a parrot or mynah bird, but is naming after the man the things indicated by him. Battle's fear and wonder is caused by the unexpected loss of his own solitude, which seems threatened by the signs of independent intelligence in Nod, whom he had wanted as a pet, to be talked to but to remain uncomprehending. Nod's company, like that of the presences in 'A Recluse', or that of the children in 'The Turn of the Screw', suddenly seems to enter the realm of the uncanny. This goes to the heart of de la Mare's vision of childhood as a solitary state only imaginable in its aspect of solitude. When two solitudes meet, however reluctantly, 'strangeness' begins. This occurs in 'Miss Duveen', between the mad woman and the child, and in 'Seaton's Aunt', not only between the two persons named in that phrase, but between aunt and narrator. The process is most elaborately displayed in 'A Recluse', with its strong element of parodic buried humour where Mr Bloom talks interminably to his captive guest, majestically resenting any attempt by the guest to talk back. The real anguish which is so moving in that story—moving like a big fish far down in deep water—is Mr Bloom's adult imprisonment in a childhood solitude, once so exciting and so much to be revelled in. It seems like de la Mare's recognition of what is secretly equivocal—a possible source of deep personal trouble—in his own sources of literary inspiration. Like other writers for 'children'—Beatrix Potter for instance—he both displayed and relieved in the process something sad about himself. James, too, gives us the feel both of exclusion and of tenderness where children are concerned.

Yet de la Mare's story is also filled with a childish zest, a kind of private enthusiasm not unlike the one that lurks at times even in the most banal of de la Mare's 'children's tales'. What reader of the story can afterwards forget the wonderful supper conjured up by Mr Bloom for his reluctant guest? Mentally cursing the inexplicable loss of the essential car key, Mr Dash gloomily contemplates the deep green parterres from the terrace porch, and sourly imagines his insufferable host 'contemplating the broken meats in the great larder'. Mr Bloom had apologized in advance for what must of necessity be 'a lamentably modest little meal', but as usual he had shown himself to be incapable of 'facing facts'. Cold bouillon is followed by a pair of spring chickens, the white sauce on their breasts decorated in lozenges of cucumber and basil, 'hapless birds' who seem to have fed on the herbs of paradise. They are accompanied by an asparagus salad, 'so cold to the tongue as to suggest ice' and followed by a noble stilton and a bowl of dark rich wine jelly, thickly clotted with cream. 'After the sherry champagne was our only wine, and it was solely due to my abstemiousness that we failed to finish the second bottle.'

Children are fascinated by food in stories, but this is no childish meal. By what agency is it provided?—the old housekeeper vaguely mentioned by Mr Bloom as attending to his daily needs and departing well before evening? Why not, and yet there is more than a suggestion that some more magical and sinister agency must be involved. Everything in the fine old house is gracious and conventional and timeless, and yet everything is possessed by some occult force which never explains itself except through oblique hints and disquieting manifestations. The reassurance, the enchanted fixity of childhood, is suffused with some other force, which produced both childish excitement and absorption and a sense of some void beneath, the jaws of indifference into which everything is about to drop. De la Mare's inspiration, as always, is excited by the supernatural and yet finally disillusioned by it. Mr Bloom reminds him of a solitary spinster cousin with whom he used to play the planchette game, and it is her haunted yearning eyes which are the image in the story's last sentence. Wholly 'adult' as it is, the excitements and disillusionments of childhood underlie the story and insensibly penetrate all its levels.

And the food? Yes, food is magically important in this context. Ben Battle's homely supper, and how he eats it, is dwelt on at length in *The Three Royal Monkeys*, and both it and Mr Bloom's feast may remind us of those splendid matter-of-fact meals in *The Wind in the Willows*—the picnic, the extemporized Christmas dinner in the Mole's old home, the glorious pheasant stew Toad cajoled from the gipsy, the simple but sustaining lunch—'bacon and broad beans and a macaroni pudding'—eaten by the animals after Toad's return, before the serious business of recapturing Toad Hall. But it is vital to the enthralment of childhood that these should be all *grown-up* meals. I recall at an early age being attached to a book for children by Stanley Rogers, who wrote sea stories. It described the adventures of two boys who found themselves back in the past and aboard an Elizabethan galleon, commanded, rather improbably, by Sir Richard Grenville. They are offered a sumptuous meal 'in the cuddy', at which, as the captain explains, the fish only looks like fish but is really 'frozen lemon jelly'. (Curious, the association of ice with magical meals.) I remember at this point, however, my total disgust and disillusionment with the author's intention and method: he was writing for children and this was a children's tea-party. How could one go on any longer believing in the galleon and her crew and business?

De la Mare's characters, whether man, child, or beast, inhabit a very different world. 'Who said Peacock Pie?'—the poem and its query come from a collection of verses for children, but its sense is both complex and mysterious. The old king who uttered those ironic words to the sparrow makes one of the many confrontations which move the poet's imagination. The little poem 'Crazed' has three such—a blazing flower meadow, a nocturnal pool, a face that looks briefly out from the lattice of a toiling windmill:

CRAZED

I know a pool where nightshade preens
Her poisonous fruitage in the moon;
Where the frail aspen her shadow leans
In midnight cold a-swoon.

I know a meadow flat with gold—
A million million burning flowers
In moon-sun's thirst their buds unfold
Beneath his blazing showers.

I saw a crazed face, did I,
Stare from the lattice of a mill,
While the lank sails clacked idly by
High on the windy hill.

And no confrontation is stranger, or more rich in what it implies, than the child's with the man; or either with some force that dispossesses them from their normal state and status. A sense of ghostliness may do it. In any case what matters is that when immersed in de la Mare's world the reader loses distinction between a childish self and any other kind. When this magic fails, as it does in many of the poems and stories, the product becomes creepy or quaint in much the same way as with less individual and less original authors. Any undue emphasis on the nature or quality of childhood is usually fatal, dispelling that sense of a life lived naturally in a world of the seen and unseen. Forrest Reid is a writer with his own kind of originality and his own sense of childhood, but when he collaborated with de la Mare in a story called 'An Ideal Craftsman' the result was disastrous. The idea of a boy who 'arranges' a death in the most realistic and convincing manner may have appealed to the authors' more commonplace sense of the macabre, but it exaggerates and vulgarizes an original perception in much the same way as horror stories and films about childhood do today.

Children are more alienated from this world even than our adult selves. That one paradox which the best stories suggest, however lightly, even in the midst of delineating a consciousness which seems to take the seen and the unseen equally for granted. Sadness in that sense of things is almost indistinguishable from joy. When the traveller in *Ding Dong Bell* sees a human figure in the snow by a churchyard he knows it to be a version of himself, blessedly dispossessed from living, even as he assumes its ordinariness as a fellow mortal. Angels are creations of our own sense of not belonging where we are. De la Mare's best art is about that, as it relates to all our ages.

Booklist

The following books by Walter de la Mare are referred to in this essay:

Henry Brocken (1904).

The Three Mullar-Mulgars (1910), reprinted as *The Three Royal Monkeys* (1935, 1946).

Peacock Pie (1913) includes the poem 'Peacock Pie'.

The Veil and Other Poems (1921) includes 'Crazed'.

The Riddle (1923) includes 'The Almond Tree', 'Miss Duveen', and 'Seaton's Aunt'.

Ding Dong Bell (1924).

On the Edge (1930) includes 'A Recluse' and 'An Ideal Craftsman'.

17

Tolkien's Great War

HUGH BROGAN

Eventually an imaginary world is entirely without interest.

Wallace Stevens

In October 1919 Robert Graves, late Captain in the Royal Welch Fusiliers, went up to Oxford. He read English literature, but found the course tedious because of its emphasis on the eighteenth century.

It was also difficult for me, too, to concentrate on cases and genders and irregular verbs in Anglo-Saxon grammar. The Anglo-Saxon lecturer was candid about his subject. He said that it was of purely linguistic interest, that there was hardly a line of Anglo-Saxon extant of the slightest literary merit. I disagreed; *Beowulf* and *Judith* seemed good poems to me. Beowulf lying wrapped in a blanket among his platoon of drunken thanes in the Gothland billet . . . was closer to most of us at the time than the drawing-room and deer-park atmosphere of the eighteenth century.[1]

It would be nice to know who the lecturer was. He was certainly one of the jabberwocks later denounced by J. R. R. Tolkien in his '*Beowulf*: the Monsters and the Critics'.[2] But it is Graves's dissent from his views that matters; that and the nature of his reaction to Old English poetry. He and Edmund Blunden were young poets fresh from horror, and they were haunted:

Edmund and I found ourselves translating everything into trench-warfare terms. The war was not yet over for us. In the middle of a lecture I would have a sudden very clear experience of men on the march up the Béthune–La Bassée road . . . Or it would be a deep dug-out at Cambrin, where I was talking to a signaller; I would look up the shaft and see somebody's muddy legs coming down the steps, and there would be a crash and the tobacco-smoke in the dug-out would shake with the concussion and twist about in patterns like the marbling on books.[3]

The point does not need to be laboured. It is notorious that the Great War lay like a cloud on the consciousness of the English until it was eclipsed by the coming of an even greater conflict. It lay heaviest on the souls of those who had been combatants. Among them was Ronald Tolkien, late second lieutenant, 11th Lancashire Fusiliers.

The direct references to the war in Tolkien's published writings are few but significant. The most conspicuous occurs in the foreword to the second edition of *The Lord of the Rings*, in a passage where Tolkien is correcting the notion that his book is an allegory of the Cold War, or that its penultimate chapter, 'The Scouring of the Shire', is an allusion to the state of affairs in England in the wake of the Second World War.[4]

One has indeed personally to come under the shadow of war to feel fully its oppression; but as the years go by it seems now often forgotten that to be caught in youth by 1914 was no less hideous an experience than to be involved in 1939 and the following years. By 1918 all but one of my close friends were dead.[5]

And long before, in the Gollancz lecture, when defending the place of the dragon in *Beowulf*, he had remarked that 'Even today (despite the critics) you may find men not ignorant of tragic legend and history, *who have heard of heroes and indeed seen them*, who yet have been caught by the fascination of the worm.'[6] (My emphasis.) Plainly this is a reference to Tolkien himself, and to the heroism he witnessed in the trenches. It is significant that like Graves Tolkien finds something in *Beowulf* that appeals to the old soldier in him; though it is highly characteristic that he is attracted rather by the poem's fantasy than by its evocation of a warrior's life in the northern Heroic Age.

Graves and Tolkien overlapped at Oxford, but there is no reason to think that they ever met, or that they would have had much to say to each other if they had. (Years later, when Graves was Professor of Poetry at Oxford, Tolkien summed him up as 'a remarkable creature, entertaining, likeable, odd, bonnet full of wild bees, half-German, half-Irish, must have looked like Siegfried/Sigurd in his youth, *but* an Ass'.[7]) Each was a mythologizer, but their mythologies were radically different; and though each was a poet, their conceptions of Poesis were about as distinct as it was possible to be. However, they both loved *Beowulf*, and they had both been Fusiliers in France.

> By wire and wood and stake we're bound,
> By Fribourt and Festubert . . .[8]

It is reasonable to wonder whether Tolkien was also haunted by the war.

Neither his published letters nor Humphrey Carpenter's admirable biography throw much light on the matter. He was in the battle of the Somme and remained in France for some six months altogether. 'Trench fever' took him back to England and kept him there until the armistice. In the writings of the years that followed allusions to the war are rare. If Tolkien was haunted he kept the fact well hidden. There hardly seems to be a possibility to investigate.

And yet . . . compare these two passages. The first describes the downfall of Sauron:

. . . as the Captains gazed south to the Land of Mordor, it seemed to them that, black against the pall of cloud, there rose a huge shape of shadow, impenetrable, lightning-crowned, filling all the sky. Enormous it reared above the world, and stretched out towards them a vast threatening hand, terrible but impotent: for even as it leaned over them, a great wind took it, and it was all blown away, and passed; and then a hush fell.[9]

The second is from Siegfried Sassoon's *Memoirs of a Fox-Hunting Man*:

Against the clear morning sky a cloud of dark smoke expands and drifts away. Slowly its dingy wrestling vapours take the form of a hooded giant with clumsy expostulating arms. Then, with a gradual gesture of acquiescence, it lolls sideways, falling over into the attitude of a swimmer on his side. And so it dissolves into nothingness.[10]

The similarities between these passages cannot be coincidental. The very cadence of the prose is the same. It is possible that Tolkien used Sassoon's description as a model, but it is surely much likelier that he, as well as Sassoon, could remember what a shell-burst looked like, and could exploit it for literary purposes. There is something immensely fitting in using such an explosion as the visual symbol of the hateful war that the destruction of the Ring is bringing to an end; something triumphant in seeing it blown away for ever. And if the Great War could break through so vividly at such an important moment of *The Lord of the Rings*, may it not have manifested itself elsewhere? Here is a concrete problem to investigate.

Tolkien himself frequently denied that current or recent history had any influence on the plot of *The Lord of the Rings*; but he did acknowledge at least one direct link between his book and his war. 'My "Sam Gamgee"', he said, 'is indeed a reflexion of the English soldier, of the privates and batmen I knew in the 1914 war, and recognized as so far superior to myself.'[11] Considering the steadily growing importance that Sam assumed as *The Lord of the Rings* unfolded, this is a statement worth noting: 'Sam is the most closely drawn character, the successor to Bilbo in the first book, the genuine hobbit.'[12] It is therefore unarguable that the war had a profound moral impact on Tolkien in at least one respect; and as any reader of his letters will have seen, he was obsessed with the moral and religious significance of his book. At this level the relevance of the war is such that it is a pity we do not know more about Tolkien's relations with the actual soldiers who were his companions during his army days.

Yet it would smack too much of biographical reductionism to tour *The Lord of the Rings* (and *The Hobbit*, for that matter) looking for outcroppings of war experience. Tolkien was fully alive to the dangers of such procedures: 'I object to the contemporary trend in criticism, with its excessive interest in the details of the lives of authors and artists. They only distract attention from the author's work ... and end, as one now often sees, in becoming the main interest.'[13] Every work of the imagination may or may not be a concealed autobiography; even if it is that may not be the most interesting or valuable thing about it. Justifiably to discuss Tolkien's works in terms of their biographical purport, the critic must be able to show that some larger meaning, or pattern, may be discovered thereby. The works, not the author, must seem to be more truly known and understood by the demonstration. 'He that breaks a thing to find out what it is has left the path of wisdom.'[14] I think I can avoid that peril too.

Thus one of the main critical problems thrown up by *The Lord of the Rings* and still more by *The Silmarillion* is that of language. The main fabric of Tolkien's prose has dignity, strength, and flexibility; at its best it can compass a remarkable range of effects and affects. But it can run into excesses: for sensitive tastes there is surely too much of this kind of thing:

Many of the Easterlings turned and fled, their hearts being filled with lies and fear; but the sons of Ulfang went over suddenly to Morgoth and drove in upon the rear of the sons of Fëanor, and in the confusion that they wrought they came near to the standard of Maedhros. They reaped not the reward that Morgoth promised them, for Maglor slew Uldor the accursed, the leader in treason, and the sons of Bór slew Ulfast and Ulwarth ere they themselves were slain.[15]

And so on. Tolkien, the passionate philologist, was highly sensitive to criticism on this score, and defended himself vigorously and intelligently; but it is doubtful if he ever persuaded anyone that he was right. It is interesting to enquire why this should be.

Tolkien's apologia is put most trenchantly in his essay 'On Translating *Beowulf*':

We are being at once wisely aware of our own frivolity and just to the solemn temper of the original, if we avoid *hitting* and *whacking* and prefer 'striking' and 'smiting'; *talk* and *chat* and prefer 'speech' and 'discourse'; *exquisite* and *artistic* and prefer the 'cunning craft' and 'skill' of ancient smiths ... *well-bred, brilliant*, or *polite noblemen* (visions of snobbery columns in the press and fat men on the Riviera) and prefer the 'worthy brave and courteous men' of long ago.[16]

In setting up such acute antitheses Tolkien is surely arguing unfairly; but a different author's views on a similar point best indicate what has gone wrong:

I was always embarrassed by the words sacred, glorious, and sacrifice and the expression in vain ... There were many words that you could not stand to hear and finally only the names of places had dignity. Certain numbers were the same way and certain dates and these with the names of places were all you could say and have them mean anything. Abstract words such as glory, honor, courage or hallow were obscene beside the concrete names of villages, the numbers of roads, the names of rivers, the numbers of regiments and the dates.[17]

Most readers and writers since 1918 feel with Ernest Hemingway on this point; not with Tolkien. The American's view of language seems the truer.

In *The Great War and Modern Memory* Paul Fussell makes a related point in a way that might almost be direct ridicule of Tolkien's argument:

We can set out this 'raised', essentially feudal language in a table of equivalents:

A friend is a	*comrade*
Friendship is	*comradeship*, or *fellowship*
A horse is	*steed*, or *charger*
The enemy is	*the foe*, or *the host*
Danger is	*peril*
To conquer is to	*vanquish*
To attack is to	*assail*
Warfare is	*strife*
Actions are	*deeds*
To die is to	*perish*
Nothing is	*naught*
A soldier is a	*warrior*[18]

Taken together, these texts raise sharply the question of how it was that Tolkien, a man whose life was language, could have gone through the Great War, with all its rants and lies, and still come out committed to a 'feudal' literary style. His tenacity on the point looks like an act of deliberate defiance of modern history.

And so it was, but of a complicated kind. Tolkien had been at odds with his times long before 1914. The premature death of both his parents, especially of his mother, had left him with a deep sense of loss, of something having gone fundamentally wrong with the world. In Christian terms, the Fall of Man was a doctrine very real to him. As a lover of Old English he was inclined to date the catastrophe from the Battle of Hastings, when the right side lost; and he cast Shakespeare as the arch-villain, for his huge verbal innovations. The school-friends with whom he formed the little club known as the T.C.B.S. apparently shared, or came to share, his feeling that something essential had been lost; and before the war broke the fellowship by killing two of the four members, the T.C.B.S. seem to have hoped to convey this message to their countrymen in works of prose and verse.[19] Tolkien's pre-war—or, more precisely, his pre-Somme—verse is overwhelmingly elegiac, most impressively, perhaps, in his poem on Warwick and Oxford, 'The Sorrowful City', written in March 1916.[20] None of the verse is much good; the influence of Shelley, Poe, Tennyson, Keats, William Morris, and Swinburne is all too obvious, that of the Old English poets whom he knew so well, not at all; nor is the feeling for England, and sorrow for its fallen state, very unusual for its date; Georgianism is not far distant. What was individual was Tolkien's wish to incorporate his verse and insights in a mythology, and embody that, in turn, in an invented language. But, again, the spirit of his generation made itself felt. In its earliest form the mythology was to be dedicated 'simply: to England, to my country'.[21] It was going to fill the gap left by the loss of the myths of the Angles and Saxons; it was to have culminated in the coming of Hengest and Horsa; and it was to express Tolkien's sense of the Fall in the legend of the elvenfolk, alienated from men and retreating, after many cruel defeats, into the far, mythical West.[22]

This project did not survive the Somme unaltered. It is perhaps surprising that it survived at all; it might not have done so but for the advanced stage of the linguistic inventions with which it was bound up. As it was Tolkien, grieving for his dead friends, and himself convalescing slowly from trench fever, felt it more than ever necessary to work on the mythology; only it changed its nature. It became something he retreated into. The references to English history and geography were gradually dropped. It was not exactly an escape: 'The Fall of Gondolin', one of the earliest prose writings of the mythology, is full of bloody war; rather it became a world where he could master all the grief and horror and ugliness of the modern world, giving it dignity and significance. It was therapy for a mind wounded in war, and before that by deep sorrow in childhood and young manhood.

As such we may respect it (and respect Tolkien's defence of 'escapism' in *Tree and Leaf*); but that is not to say that *The Book of Lost Tales*, or even its later form, *The Silmarillion*, is a literary success, though it has many striking details. In literary terms, the stubborn adhesion to the values, as expressed in the language, of the Old English, and the attempt to revitalize them through sub-Tennysonian verse and prose, were bound to be failures. The way forward lay with the followers of Thomas Hardy (such as Robert Graves) and Ezra Pound. 'Make it new' was a good maxim; but Tolkien was temperamentally incapable of following it. In the end he could only solve the dilemma by evading it. He wrote *The Hobbit*.

This was the central event of his literary career, and the hardest to explain. Various minor writings, such as *Mr Bliss* and *The Father Christmas Letters*, show him getting his hand in as a writer for children; but the striking thing about *The Hobbit* is how accomplished it is, and how unlike anything which Tolkien (or anyone else) had written before. How he came to conceive such an elaborate and fecund fantasy can never really be made clear. Probably the nearest we can come is to say that in writing for children, and particularly for his own children, he could relax and play with his tragic themes; he could turn them into comedy, he could even mock them, or at least their first, failed expressions. Certainly the small, fat, earthy, and unimaginative hobbits are very like satires on the gossamer wee folk of his earliest, *Peter Pan* affected imaginings. And in writing about Bilbo and Gandalf and the Dwarves Tolkien gradually found his own literary voice. By the end of the book his style had become what it was to remain: capable of humour, irony, tragedy, and fast narrative, with only occasional lapses into cardboard grandiloquence. Without such a style *The Lord of the Rings* would have been impossible.

As has often been shown, *The Hobbit* opened the way in other

. The Front Gate .

Original drawing by J. R. R. Tolkien for *The Hobbit*, George Allen and Unwin Ltd., 1937.

respects.[23] It was a Quest-story, obeying the laws of quests: as such it provided a model for the later book, the plot of which can be viewed as no more than a vast elaboration of the *The Hobbit*'s, or as a tragic commentary upon it. By bringing hobbits into being, and then involving them in the world of Tolkien's mythology, their creator could as it were accommodate modernity without surrendering to it. The debate between the old world and the new could thus be put back where it belonged, at the heart of Tolkien's work; and it is notable that it is never resolved. For nothing can make the hobbits—not even Frodo—more than visitors to the antique world of Elvendom and Numenor; and nothing can stay the current of change. Tolkien's last, sorrowful verdict on his elves is that they fail because they cannot adapt to the inevitable alterations wrought by Time. They retreat to the twilight of the woods; but they remain Good People.

Another theme can be seen stirring in *The Hobbit*. The book does not end with the slaughter of the dragon, Smaug. It culminates in war. The significance of this can only be grasped after a consideration of the structure of *The Lord of the Rings*. For that too reaches a climax in war. More: it can be shown that the structure of *The Lord of the Rings* was determined by a particular war: the Great War, which has an obvious implication for the structure of *The Hobbit*, which is so similar.

In what follows I am entirely indebted to Paul Fussell. His survey of the literature of the Great War is not only comprehensive (he discusses almost all the writers affected by the war—not Tolkien, though, or this essay would not be necessary), it is also one of those rare works of literary criticism which startle the reader with a shock of recognition; he sees the world anew, but realizes he has always known that it was thus. Leaning in part on Northrop Frye's *Anatomy of Criticism* Fussell is yet deeply original as he explores the way in which traditions in literature—traditions of word, form, and value—shaped man's perceptions of the war, and the way in which the war, by its scale, intensity, and horror reshaped literature. It is not too much to say that, after reading Fussell, neither the twentieth century, nor the Great War, nor modern literature, will ever look the same again; and for admirers of Tolkien the book has this additional interest, that the 1914 war as Fussell describes it is unmistakably the War of the Ring.

So rich a book can hardly be paraphrased; but a few selected points should make its application to Tolkien plain. For example, one of the most effective literary devices of *The Lord of the Rings* is that the reader never meets the Lord; he exists, overpoweringly, offstage, until the epiphany of his destruction. Fussell, discussing the polarization of consciousness—what he calls 'the gross dichotomizing'—imposed by the war—the habit of reading the world and all experience as a struggle between our side and 'the enemy'—writes as follows:

'We' are all here on this side: 'the enemy' is over there. 'We' are individuals with names and personal identities; 'he' is a mere collective entity. We are visible; he is invisible. We are normal; he is grotesque. Our appurtenances are natural; his, bizarre. He is not as good as we are ... Nevertheless, he threatens us and must be destroyed ...[24]

'He', the reader of Tolkien must reflect, is Sauron, who never loses his name or his title 'the Dark Lord', but is nevertheless alluded to, more and more frequently, as 'the Enemy' as *The Lord of the Rings* proceeds.

It perhaps took an American to notice that English writing about the Great War is full of flowers and gardening, and that this reflects a deep-set national idiosyncrasy. 'When we go right through *The Oxford Book of English Verse*, we find that half the poems are about flowers and that a third seem somehow to involve roses ...'[25]. Fussell comes up with a touching anecdote of the trenches, of a battalion out of the line whose men set to competitive gardening, 'instinct with symbolism':

Each company ... marked out the pattern of its formal garden ... A platoon of A company ... enclosed a tent in a heart; a border of boxwood marks out the pattern of the heart—the plan is that the crimson of many blossoms shall blend to give a suggestion of passion and loyalty and suffering.[26]

'Gardeners camouflaged as soldiers', is the RSM's verdict; and we may immediately think of Sam Gamgee. Fussell also draws attention to the significance of the rose: the men's favourite song, according to Wilfred Owen, was about the roses round the door 'which make me love mother more'.[27] The rose was home, peace, England. It was also the name of Sam's sweetheart and eventual wife, Rosie Cotton, first mentioned when Sam, tormented by thirst, is in the desert at the foot of the volcano in Mordor—one of the many landscapes in *The Lord of the Rings* that, in their pitiless desolation, recall the wasteland of the Western Front, as Tolkien remarked himself.[28] Indeed, everything in Mordor, as might be expected, recalls the World Wars vividly—we hardly need Fussell to point it out: for example, the orc who snarls, 'Don't you know we're at war?' only because (surely) Tolkien felt it would be a lapse in taste to make him say 'Don't you know there's a war on?'[29] But it is Fussell who remarks that in this world of the trenches, day and night are reversed: it is the night which is filled with busy activity; and that again recalls Mordor:

> . . . the most easterly of the roads followed them . . . Neither man nor orc moved along its flat grey stretches; for the Dark Lord had almost completed the movement of his forces, and even in the fastness of his own realm he sought the secrecy of night.[30]

Fussell also brings out the significance of 'the Road'—one of the most potent of all symbols in Tolkien—for the soldiers of 1914–18. He quotes T. E. Hulme: 'You unconsciously orient things in reference to it. In peacetime, each direction on the road is as it were indifferent, it all goes on ad infinitum. But now you know that certain roads lead, as it were, up to an abyss.'[31] It can need no stressing that the road taken by Sam and Frodo leads them, precisely, to an abyss.

But it is doubtful if these, or many other details like them, would greatly change anyone's reading of *The Lord of the Rings* and *The Hobbit* were it not for Fussell's discussion of what he calls 'Myth, Ritual and Romance'.

Taking his terms from Erich Auerbach and Northrop Frye, Fussell shows not only how the experience of going to war in

1914–18 fitted easily into the patterns of heroic romance as written by Chrétien de Troyes and Thomas Malory, but that a mass of British soldiers knew it: many of them had read William Morris's *The Well at the World's End*, and all of them knew *The Pilgrim's Progress*.[32] They knew about the magical power of the number three; they knew what form a quest would take (and so, *a fortiori*, did J. R. R. Tolkien the medievalist). The pattern may be summarized thus: the hero begins in a world of pastoral bliss, such as Siegfried Sassoon's Kent. Enlisted in the Quest, his first journey is his training; he moves into a new landscape, enchanted, full of 'secret murmurings and whispers', quite distinct from his normal world. There are only two social strata: one is privileged and aloof, while the other, more numerous, is 'colorful but more usually comic or grotesque'[33] (officers and men). The hero receives his training and is admitted to the circle of the elect. That ends the first phase. In the second, he leaves his resting-place (the House of the Interpreter, or the regimental depot, or the base at Etaples) and goes forth to his great contest. He must travel through a wilderness, or an evil forest; he must face the Slough of Despond (one of the most popular of all images for men confronted with the evil mud of the trenches); he must enter the Valley of the Shadow of Death. And at the climax his burden will fall away, releasing him from guilt, fear, weariness, and crushing responsibility; when Private Anthony French got a Blighty one, he felt he was at the end of a pilgrim's progress: 'There was no pain. I felt at rest.'[34] That concludes the second stage. In the third stage, having proved his heroism, the hero is acclaimed, apotheosized; but he has been transformed by his experience, and, at any rate if he is a soldier of the First World War returning home on leave, or wounded, or after the armistice, he finds he cannot share what he has gone through with the people at home; he is no longer one of them.

It hardly needs saying that here is not just the plot, but even much of the geography of *The Lord of the Rings*.[35] The remaining question then is whether the parallels are no more than that, attributable solely, or mostly, to Tolkien's use of the Quest-pattern; or whether his use of that pattern was itself dictated by the dreadful memories of the Great War. The matter perhaps cannot be finally resolved, but it may be debated in various terms, and to my mind a heavy consideration must be the part played by war in all Tolkien's fictions.

A mythology does not have to be about war: Greek mythology is mostly about sex (a subject conspicuously missing from Tolkien's repertoire). Yet it is scarcely an exaggeration to say that *The Silmarillion* is about little else, which partly explains its aridity; and one of the latest of his writings is an account of the battle of the Fords of Isen which reads like nothing so much as an extract from the Official History of the War of the Ring (the appendix on the military organization of Rohan is even drier).[36] The topic would not leave him alone, which, in a veteran of the Somme, is hardly surprising. He was not a militarist, but his subject was as much war, and the pity of war, as was Wilfred Owen's. There is a great variety of approach, as well as form, in his writings; one of the most impressive on the war-theme is a short verse-play, *The Homecoming of Beorhtnoth, Beorhthelm's Son*. This prompts the reflection that the great superiority of *The Hobbit* and *The Lord of the Rings* lies in their form, the quest-form, for in that form Tolkien found what he was looking for: a means to express all that the Great War meant to him in a way that could reach out, even with hope, to his fellow men and women as the inward-looking, grieving mode of *The Silmarillion* could not.

If this interpretation is right, it shows how important a children's book can be, for without *The Hobbit* Tolkien might never have succeeded in unpacking his imagination. With it (even if *The Lord of the Rings* had never followed) he succeeded in saying much of what was in him, as he had not in earlier work; the book's drift is perhaps summed up in the sad farewell between Bilbo Baggins, the bourgeois hobbit, and Thorin Oakenshield, the great, passionate, covetous King of the Dwarves:

'I am glad that I have shared in your perils—that has been more than any Baggins deserves.'

'No!' said Thorin. 'There is more in you of good than you know, child of the kindly West. Some courage and some wisdom, blended in measure. If more men valued food and cheer and song above hoarded gold, it would be a merrier world. But sad or merry, I must leave it now. Farewell!'[37]

Two points may be made in conclusion. The first is that if my argument is correct, then Tolkien was much less of an anomaly among the writers of his generation than has usually been assumed. Fussell's conclusion that all poetry written since 1918 is war poetry applies to him. And the prodigious popularity of his fantasies suggests that, even if he is not a writer of the first rank— a designation which Fussell rather conventionally reserves for 'major innovative talents' such as Yeats, Virginia Woolf, Pound, Eliot, Lawrence, and Joyce—he has been at least as successful as, say, Owen, Graves, and Sassoon in communicating his vision of the Western Front and what it meant, and should be honoured in their company.

From which it follows that there is, perhaps, more to be said for his pessimistic and reactionary critique of modernity than is commonly supposed. 'Reactionary': he was that in the strongest possible sense. His belief that the wrong side won at Hastings was no joke; his disapproval of Shakespeare (though he could not help responding to his artistic power) had weighty foundations. It hardly needs saying that he was not a socialist;[38] he was hardly a democrat; he was certainly not a conservative:

My political opinions lean more and more towards Anarchy (philosophically understood, meaning abolition of control, not whiskered men with bombs) . . . There is only one bright spot and that is the growing habit of disgruntled men of dynamiting factories and power-stations.[39]

Saruman is perhaps the subtlest of all his inventions, and Saruman rules the world. Tolkien's vision is extremely bleak, but it is not depressing perhaps because it is realistic and courageous, with the realism and courage of the trenches. By this means we may come to recognize, not just what the war meant to Tolkien, but what it could still mean to us if we let it. For, as Paul Fussell ends his book by saying, what we recognize in writing about the war is a part, 'and perhaps not the least compelling part, of our own buried lives'.[40]

Notes

1. Robert Graves, *Goodbye to All That* (London, 3rd imp., 1929), 360.
2. J. R. R. Tolkien, '*Beowulf*: The Monsters and the Critics', the Sir Israel Gollancz Memorial Lecture to the British Academy, 25 Nov. 1936; subsequently printed in the *Proceedings* of the Academy and, more accessibly, in J. R. R. Tolkien, *The Monsters and the Critics and Other Essays* (London, 1983), 5–48. For the allusion to 'the jabberwocks of historical and antiquarian research' see p. 9.
3. Graves, *Goodbye to All That*, pp. 360–1.
4. I have often wondered whether this protest may not have been partially provoked by an article of mine that appeared in the *Cambridge Review* of 23 Jan. 1965. I sent a copy to Professor Tolkien, and he may have noticed the unhappy remark that 'some passages in *The Return of the King* were probably inspired by wartime and post-war experiences of bureaucracy and shortage'. If so, it was a *felix culpa*.
5. J. R. R. Tolkien, *The Lord of the Rings* (London, 2nd edn., 1966), i. 7.
6. Tolkien, *Monsters and Critics*, 16.
7. Tolkien, *Letters*, ed. Humphrey Carpenter (London, 1981), 353.
8. Robert Graves, 'Two Fusiliers', which I found in an anthology. It was originally published in *Poems, 1914–26* (London, 1927). It was dropped, with most of Graves's other war poems, from his subsequent collections.
9. *The Lord of the Rings*, iii. 227.
10. Siegfried Sassoon, *Memoirs of a Fox-Hunting Man*; quoted in Paul Fussell, *The Great War and Modern Memory* (London, paperback, 1977), 302.
11. Humphrey Carpenter, *J. R. R. Tolkien: A Biography* (London, 1977), 81.
12. J.R.R.T. to Christopher Tolkien, 24 Dec. 1944, *Letters*, 105.
13. J.R.R.T. to Deborah Webster, 25 Oct. 1958, ibid. 288.
14. *The Lord of the Rings*, i. 272.
15. J. R. R. Tolkien, *The Silmarillion* (London, 1977), 193.
16. *Monsters and Critics*, 55.
17. Ernest Hemingway, *A Farewell to Arms*, ch. 27.
18. Fussell, *Great War*, 21–2. I have greatly abridged this list.
19. For all this see Carpenter, *Life*, chs. 2–8, *passim*.
20. See *The Book of Lost Tales* (London, 1983–4), ii. 295–7.
21. J.R.R.T. to Milton Waldman, *c.*1951, *Letters*, 144.
22. This interpretation cannot be expounded here. It rests on a reading of *The Book of Lost Tales*.
23. Above all by T. A. Shippey in his *The Road to Middle-Earth* (London, 1982), This is far and away the most satisfying critical work about Tolkien to have appeared so far.
24. Fussell, *Great War*, 75. Sauron's invisibility is one of the chief positive reasons (the other being Frodo's prolonged anguish) why he seems so much more menacing and powerful a figure than Morgoth in *The Silmarillion*. The

chief negative reason is that Morgoth inevitably challenges comparison with Milton's Satan (not to mention the ancient tradition of the Devil) and as inevitably fails the challenge.

25. Fussell, *Great War*, 231.

26. Ibid. 233–4. The quotation is from Stephen Graham, *A Private in the Guards*.

27. Ibid. 245.

28. *The Lord of the Rings*, iii. 216. In a letter Tolkien writes: 'Personally I do not think that either war (and of course not the atomic bomb) had any influence on either the plot or the manner of its unfolding. Perhaps landscape. The Dead Marshes and the approaches to the Morannon owe something to Northern France after the Battle of the Somme.' (J.R.R.T. to L. W. Forster, 31 Dec. 1960, *Letters*, 303).

29. Ibid. 209.

30. Ibid. 211–12.

31. Fussell, *Great War*, 76.

32. Ibid. 125–31, and 135–44. In pp. 144–54 Fussell discusses David Jones's *In Parenthesis* in ways that unintentionally but strikingly bring out parallels between that work and *The Lord of the Rings*.

33. Ibid. 135.

34. Ibid. 138.

35. At *The Lord of the Rings*, i. 390, Tolkien actually makes Celeborn refer to 'the Noman-lands' lying between Cirith Gorgor and the black gates of Mordor and the river Anduin—that is, between the two front lines. At ii. 239 there is a reference to 'the arid moors of the Noman-lands.'

36. Which makes somewhat odd the remark, in the self-allegorical *Smith of Wootton Major* (London, 1967), 24, that 'Among all the things he made it is not remarked that he ever forged a sword or a spear or an arrow-head.'

37. *The Hobbit* (London, 1937), 294.

38. J.R.R.T. to Michael Straight (draft), 1956, *Letters*, 235.

39. J.R.R.T. to Christopher Tolkien, 29 Nov. 1943, *Letters*, 63.

40. Fussell, *Great War*, 335.

18

William Mayne

ALISON LURIE

ONCE upon a time children's books were the black sheep of fiction; like detective stories and westerns, they were tended mainly by specialists, critics of popular culture, or nostalgic sentimentalists. In libraries they were—and still are—herded together into a separate room, or quarantined from the rest of literature in the stacks under the letters PZ.

Recently, though, children's literature is beginning to be discovered by mainstream theorists and scholars. Learned volumes on its significance crowd the library shelves, and the professional journals are full of articles that consider every classic from *Alice* to *Charlotte's Web* as a 'text'.

And yet, except by the few people who write for these journals and the—I suspect—even fewer who read them, many of the most interesting children's books are little known. A case in point is William Mayne, one of the most gifted contemporary British writers. His thirty-five years in the field—in this case, you should probably picture a steep, stone-walled pasture in the Yorkshire dales, where Mayne has lived most of his life—have produced picture-books, family stories, tales of mystery and adventure, and some of the best fantasy and time-travel fiction to come out of England since Tolkien.

Mayne's dialogue has been likened to Pinter's, his 'exploration of sense experience' to that of Keats, his 'alienation effects' to Brecht's, and his sensitivity to landscape and primitive emotion to Lawrence's. By and large, these comparisons are not all that far off. Mayne also manages to treat extremely sophisticated ideas and subjects—including the ambiguities of perception and the shifting relations of present and past—in a lucidly simple manner, so that he can be read by children. If most of juvenile literature, however original and brilliant, was not still largely in quarantine, he would also be widely read by adults.

The first thing about Mayne's work that strikes most critics is the vividness and economy of his language and his acute, subtle sense of how the world looks and sounds. In *A Game of Dark*, a story about a boy who loses himself and finds himself again in an imagined medieval world, fallen leaves are 'circles of faded carpet along the streets . . . and between these circles with their unsewn edges lay the starlit desert of cloudless pavement' (*A Game of Dark*, p. 42).

When Mayne describes a train starting, the rhythm of his sentences is onomatopoeic:

Then there was a sort of small shake in the engine, and from the wheels there came a noise like sugar being trodden on, which was the rust on the rails being powdered. From the engine itself came a puffing roar and there was movement, and then there was going. (*Salt River Times*, p. 103)

Even the briefest simile can open out: 'There was [a bird] quite near, and he heard its wings flutter against the air like a book being shaken.' (*The Yellow Aeroplane*, p. 15.) The reader, if he or she chooses—and no doubt some do so choose—can test this comparison by shaking the volume in which it is printed, so that the book becomes the bird. It is the sort of odd reverberation that occurs often in Mayne's work.

He is also acute in describing mental phenomena, as in this meditation by a bedridden boy:

'What you see in a dream is like part of you, all the trees are like your own hands and all the ground is like your own feet and the sun is part of your own eyes. There were trees in the garden, but their shadows were just as important; there were birds flying in the air, but the air was just as important.' (*Max's Dream*, p. 27)

A related gift of Mayne's is the ability to enter sympathetically into the minds of a wide range of characters. It is perhaps most brilliantly demonstrated in *Salt River Times*, a series of interlocking sketches set in a working-class Australian suburb. With what seems effortless ease, Mayne reproduces the speech and thoughts of an elderly Chinaman, a squabbling married couple, and a whole gallery of children and adolescents, including Kate, who is fascinated by mortality:

Dead? says Kate. Bring them in, the death bed, the death sheet. Does anybody want them? I'll have them. I collect people, feathers, sharks, screams, ghosts. I am the collector. Bring them to me. (p. 160)

Though Mayne's portraits of adults are often skilful, his important characters are usually children or innocents— unsophisticated, half-literate people, separated from the contemporary world in some way: they are gypsies, uneducated servants, and labourers, farmers in remote Yorkshire villages, or inhabitants of an earlier period of history.

In Mayne's books such protagonists or narrators see nature and human relations uncontaminated by received ideas, and speak a language which is both simple and original. They also have the child's or the primitive's relation to time: it is not regulated by clock and calendar, but is free to expand and contract according to subjective perception. In the mind of the old serving-woman who remembers her girlhood in *Max's Dream*, today and sixty years ago melt into each other.

Several of Mayne's books are marked by an alliance between the very young and the very old, who have clear if idiosyncratic memories of the past, and speak to children as equals. Middle-aged people, such as parents and teachers, are often preoccupied and uncomprehending. Their interaction with the child characters is practical: they make rules, set tasks, and pack lunches. When children and parents (or teachers) speak to each other, the tone is detached and cool—sometimes, indeed, 'Pinteresque'. In *A Parcel of Trees*, for instance, Susan (age fourteen) is sitting on her bed reading one hot day, when her mother challenges her:

'I don't know how you're going to make out at all,' said Mum. 'Or I wouldn't if we didn't all feel the same. It's the weather.'
    'It's the dreadful life we lead,' said Susan.
    'What do you mean?' said Mum. 'You're the dreadful life, lying about like an old stump.'

371

'I haven't any branches,' said Susan. 'Do you think my soul's died first, and I'm going on automatic?'

'To think you used to be a sweet little girl,' said Mum. 'I enjoyed having you.' (p. 27)

Even between children real connection is unusual. What matters is not how they feel about each other, but how they feel about themselves and the country or town they live in, or the success of some common enterprise.

Though Mayne often stands back several feet from his characters, his descriptions of Yorkshire are close and loving: he knows its economy of farming and sheep-raising, its plants and animals, its weather and seasons. His preference seems to be for late autumn and winter, when the land is bare of leaves and of outsiders:

It snew the night through and it froze hard. But there were warm spots, like the shippon at milking time with the cows chewing and slopping and the milk cracking in the pail and coming in the dairy with hairy ice round the rim. . . . And there was always this aske wind, that never stopped. Most of the time it blew gentle, but there were days when it hurried on through our gates like the dog was on it, and the snow was stouring and banking up. (*While the Bells Ring*, p. 70)

As with many other British writers, Mayne's sense of landscape is intertwined with an almost archaeological sense of the past. He rejoices that every field has an ancient name, and that popular legends keep old beliefs and events alive. For him history is literally hidden beneath the landscape, and may appear at any time, as when Patty in *Underground Alley* discovers a five-hundred-year-old street of houses buried under a hill behind her cellar.

Occasionally the reappearance of the past is supernatural. In *Earthfasts* an eighteenth-century drummer boy called Nellie Jack John emerges into the modern world from beneath a ruined castle, carrying a candle that burns with a cold unextinguishable light. His interpretation of contemporary events transforms them: 'A car started in the market place, went up the steepness in a low gear. . . . "Wild boars," said Nellie Jack John. "They come up by the town of a night."' (pp. 17–18)

Illustration by Marcia Lane Foster to *Underground Alley*, Oxford University Press, 1958.

Mayne's fascination with the past is not unique. Much of the population of Britain today appears to be living in the shadow of history, and sometimes—to judge by films, television, and popular literature—heroism, virtue, relevance, even meaning, seem to have ended after the Second World War. For Mayne, however, history is sometimes dark. Patty's 'Underground Alley' turns out to be a decoy built to entrap and destroy a caravan of horses and men carrying treasure from Wales: the bricks of its pavement are gold, but behind the false fronts of its houses lie bones. What is concealed underground, in the past, is often both death and treasure.

William Mayne has now written over seventy books; as might be expected, his work is uneven. But at his best he is remarkable. Among his most interesting tales are *Winter Quarters*, a moving account of life among contemporary gypsies; and *A Game of Dark*, which can be read either as a time-travel story or the account of a boy on the edge of mental breakdown.

Winter Quarters, though a realistic narrative, is full of near-magical events. It is the story of the reuniting of a clan of 'fairground people' that has been separated and leaderless for fifty years. They have now lost their permission—possibly their right—to camp in a field by the sea for the winter. Lall, a gypsy girl, stays behind with 'houseys' when her people are turned away. Instead of attending school, she reads the landscape:

The sheep were walking, standing, in clumps, scattered, lying at random. She herself added a punctuation to the meaningless sentence by standing in a corner of the field . . . on a rustling carpet of frost, while wrens flew about the hedge and bluetits scolded, and she heard the grass tear in sheep teeth. (p. 90)

Eventually Lall discovers the buried secrets of her text, which as usual include both death and treasure.

Meanwhile a baby is born with birthmarks that proclaim him to be a chief, and the boy Issy is sent to search for the former chief, who was cast out by the tribe. In the course of his quest Issy meets many strange fairground characters, including one called Fish, who recites a fairground spiel that is also a metaphor of Issy's search:

'These are the original Sumatran Invisible Fish, and I had three this morning, but as you can tell there are now four, another one has hatched, what a sight, absolutely transparent except when they close their eyes, very rare. You get a better view if you close yours, that's it. . . . You understand, you are invisible to them when you have your eyes open. So blink gently.' (pp. 84–5)

The undernote of the book is semiotic: the need to name the world before it can be known. As Issy puts it, 'A thing is hard to see until you know what you are looking at. You have to be able to imagine it at the same time' (p. 111). In a hall of mirrors he has another kind of vision, a new reading, if you like, of his own being:

It was a tall, distorted, mangled reflection of himself, uncannily tall, a spindly stranger. When he put out his arm to its full length the pathetic monster in the glass put out a slow stub and could do no more.
And does this part of me, he wondered, try to come out from beyond the glass, being thrown back injured time after time? Am I like that, now and then? (p. 113)

Clearly, he is; and the old chief, too, turns out to have a strange, variously-named, shifting identity.

The hero of *A Game of Dark* also has two selves. He is a fourteen-year-old English schoolboy called Donald Jackson, deeply alienated from his narrowly religious parents. Though the book was published in 1971, it is prescient in its portrait of an adolescent out of touch with reality and absorbed in a Dungeons-and-Dragons type of imaginary world. It can also be read as a tale in the tradition of Borges or Garcia Marquez, in which fantastic events are simultaneously real and metaphoric.

Donald's mother is an exhausted, priggish, and disapproving schoolteacher whom he cannot seem to please. His father is a half-paralysed invalid, white-faced and white-haired, angry, disapproving, and rigid in his faith. He and his wife read his affliction as a judgement or test: '"There was never much wrong physically," said Mrs Jackson. "We knew it was a visitation from

God. . . . It was put upon us for our own good"' (pp. 124–5). Donald knows he should love and pity his father, but cannot: 'What he noticed most about the pain Mr Jackson had to bear was his own inability to appreciate and understand it. It meant to him a white-faced man of uncertain temper and dour disposition . . .' (p. 34). Later he begins to fantasize that he is not the son of Mr and Mrs Jackson:

If he had been taken in by them, adopted . . . that might account for the way he turned out not to please them. . . . If the man called Daddy was not his father, and the woman called Mum not his mother, then he had no need to feel guilty for no longer loving them as parents. (pp. 74–5)

When Donald goes to visit his father in the hospital he feels he is in a 'bedroom that he had no right to be in'. Mr Jackson, blurred by drugs, also denies his son's existence, though he remembers Donald's sister, who died before Donald was born; and Mrs Jackson reinforces the denial:

'Hello, boy,' said Mr Jackson, in a slow drawling tone. 'Where's Cecily?'
  'She's all right,' said Mrs Jackson. 'She couldn't come today.' (p. 95)

Finally, approaching the hospital on his next visit, Donald imagines his father lying inside and rejects him wholly: 'That patch of life was not even a person at present, not even intelligence, and most of all it had nothing to do with his own existence, he had nothing to do with it; he had no feelings about it except revulsion' (p. 107).

But though it increases during the book, Donald's misery and disorientation is evident from the first line: 'Donald heard Mr Savery shouting at him: "Jackson, what's the matter?" Donald tried to speak, but he had no throat to speak with and nothing to say, nothing that he knew about' (p. 7). 'The days are just happening,' he says at one point. 'I can't do anything about them' (p. 94). His surroundings seem unreal, and he seems unreal to himself: 'Donald sat in the vacuum of indoors and heard the weather being pumped past, as if it were emptying the building and increasing the internal vacuum' (p. 11).

While he goes passively through the motions of living, Donald moves in and out of another world in which he is known as Jackson and is active, competent, and loved. Here he comes upon a medieval town threatened by a huge dragon, or worm: icy cold, death-white, with an unbearable stench and a slimy track twenty feet wide. At first Donald realizes that this world is fantasy: 'One is real, he said to himself. Donald is real. The other is a game of darkness, and I can be either and step from one to the other as I like' (p. 27). Soon his two worlds become equally real. In the medieval town he becomes the trusted squire of the local lord, and then a knight. Naturally, he begins to prefer this world: '. . . he was seeing both places, and could again choose which to take. He chose the one with less shame and guilt to it' (p. 59).

It is clear that Donald's alternate world, real or not, is a metaphor for the real one. The worm stands for violence and hatred; but it is also a version of his father, a death-white, cold, crawling phallic horror (Mr Jackson, like the monster, cannot walk) whose entire will is towards destruction. The girl Carrica, whom Donald rescues from the worm, and who comes to love him, is both his mother at an earlier age and his lost sister Cecily.

The lord Donald serves is an idealized version of Berry, the good-natured Anglican vicar. Both of them stand for order and reason: 'an accepted way of doing things, a framework in which to live and achieve the best' (p. 109). It is a limited vision, which underestimates the power of evil. Gradually, Donald comes to see Berry's tolerance as senseless: 'The meeting [of the church Youth Guild] had been what Berry called an open-ended argument, so open-ended that anything put into it fell right through without affecting what was being talked about' (p. 133). The lord is equally limited. 'With a proper administrative set-up,' he remarks at one point, 'the worm would probably leave of its own accord' (p. 64).

The worm does not leave, but at first its taking of human life is controlled by providing livestock for it to devour. Eventually, however, the villagers begin to run out of cows and sheep, and the lord must fight the worm. He approaches it bravely in the traditional way, and fails: 'The orderliness had at last killed him,

because the accepted way of dealing with worms had been fatal,'
Jackson thinks (p. 133).

It is left to Jackson to destroy the worm, which he does by craft
at the very end of the book. Meanwhile, in his other life, his father
has come home from the hospital and is lying ill in the room next
door, breathing loudly and raspingly so that Donald cannot sleep,
haunting the place as the worm does the medieval town. 'The
whole life of the house, the whole intent of the day, seemed to
centre on him, or on something near him, his illness' (p. 132).

Jackson's triumph is flawed; the worm 'was slain in unfair
combat, and no glory from its death could come to him' (p. 141).
'It was not an honourable deed,' he says to Carrica (p. 142). Yet
afterwards Donald can see his two worlds clearly for the first
time:

Half of him watched the house in Hales Hill. Half looked at the girl,
Carrica. . . . She was his mother or his sister . . . and he knew that the
man in the other room was his father, whom he knew now how to love.
Carrica was a phantom if he wanted her to be, and the house in Hales
Hill was another, and he had the choice of which to remain with. (p. 142)

Just after he has chosen to return to the present-day world, his
father dies in the next room: 'There was no more breathing.
Donald lay and listened to the quiet, and went to sleep, consolate'
(p. 143). This is the end of the book; an ending that has puzzled
and disturbed critics. The supernatural explanation would be that
Doanld killed his father when he slew the worm; he will know
'how to love' Mr Jackson now because Mr Jackson will be dead.
A more naturalistic reading might suggest that once Donald
realizes his father is dying, he no longer needs to hate and fear
him.

On another level, we as readers repeat Donald's experience.
While we are engaged with the book we are passive in the 'real'
world and active in imagination: the bird flies as the pages are
shaken. When we reach the end of the story and return to reality
the characters become phantoms; in a sense, we have killed them.

One of the strengths of the story is that it holds all these
readings, and no doubt others, in suspension. *A Game of Dark*,

like all of William Mayne's best work, and most serious fiction, adult or 'juvenile', does not end neatly. Instead it opens out possibility and meaning.

This essay first appeared in the *New York Review of Books*, 18 Feb. 1988.

Booklist

The following books by William Mayne are referred to in this essay:

Underground Alley (1958).
A Parcel of Trees (1963).
Earthfasts (1966).
The Yellow Aeroplane (Reindeer Books, 1968).
A Game of Dark (1971).
Max's Dream (1977).
While the Bells Ring (1979).
Salt River Times (1980).
Winter Quarters (1982).

19

Children's Diaries

A. O. J. COCKSHUT

MANY thousands of children write diaries; of these very few are preserved, and of the few that are an infinitesimal proportion is published. The first of several problems with which the critic is faced is the unrepresentative character of the material before him. If we are considering (say) Victorian novels, we can be reasonably confident that time has done its editing for us with a rough fairness. If we read a novel by a minor figure like Rhoda Broughton we find, just as we expected, that it is much less interesting than one by George Eliot or Trollope; while the possibility of an unknown masterpiece is remote. Even if one were to be discovered today, it could not be expected to alter our mental map of a large subject more than a little. But it is possible, or even probable, that the best children's diaries have not been preserved, or if preserved, lie unread; and it is not a fantastic or absurd supposition that a new one discovered at any time might give us something better than anything we at present have.

While a great adult writer may appear from anywhere, maybe a country clergyman's daughter or the son of a man imprisoned for debt, a published child diary is likely to emerge from one of a few well-defined milieux. A well-knit, highly educated family with strong bonds of affection is the most likely source. Very often, the child will be encouraged and perhaps corrected by an elder sibling or relative. Often too the diarist died young. Young adults tend to destroy their earliest efforts; either they give up writing altogether, or, having ambitions to be recognized as adult writers they find childhood scribblings irrelevant or embarrassing. But if the child-writer dies, either in childhood or adolescence, early writings become the most precious and personal of relics, more imbued with personality than a lock of hair or a nursery toy.

It is easier too to be sure of authenticity in the case of early death. Adults may tamper with early efforts, as Alexander Pope was suspected of doing, either out of shame, or more probably out of the vanity of being thought exceptionally precocious. In some cases there may even be a real doubt whether the diary was written in childhood at all. In 1920, the diary of Opal Whiteley was published by Putnam with an introduction by a former Foreign Secretary, Lord Grey of Fallodon, who quoted passages to show that the diarist revealed the 'true Wordsworthian pleasure in common things'. But the documentary evidence of the diary's genuineness as the work of a child seems confused; and I doubt if anyone would endorse it with strong confidence on the evidence of the text itself. Perhaps Lord Grey forgot that the children in Wordsworth's poetry can only speak to us through the reflective adult mind of the poet. One of the most obvious and certain conclusions to arise from a modest amount of reading in the genre will be that there is a great gulf between the actual perceptions of a child and the child as seen by the adult writer, even when, as in *The Prelude*, that child is the author himself.

When precocious children write poetry or begin a novel or a *History of England* they are imitating adult models which are usually easy to trace. A child that has read Macaulay will write differently from one who has read Carlyle. But when a child writes a diary, adult diaries are unlikely to have been a leading influence. If the adults of the family keep diaries the children are probably not allowed to see them. Not many diaries are classics likely to fall into the hands of the young, and perhaps if they did they would not be found useful. In the children's diaries I have read there are no embarrassing traces of Pepys or Evelyn or Kilvert; but had the same children written poetry we may guess that it would be easy to detect signs that they had read Milton or Swinburne or Walter de la Mare. Here we have simply an extreme case of what is already true of adult autobiographies, and even more true of adult diaries. There is no school of autobiographies or diaries. If there are literary influences, they will probably be from other forms of writing, lyric poetry perhaps, or fairy story. A diarist, and especially a child diarist, is the least traditional of writers; there is no parody, no cunning imitation, no 'anxiety of influence'.

But there may well be anxiety of another kind. Does the child wish the diary to be read by others, or to keep it secret? Emily Shore,[1] reflecting near the end of her short life of nineteen years in her entry for 6 July 1838, was torn in both directions:

I have poured out my feelings into these later pages; I have written them on the impulse of the moment, as well as from the coolness of calm deliberation. I have written much that I would show only to a very few, and much that I would on no account submit to any human eye. Still, even now, I cannot entirely divest myself of an uncomfortable notion that the whole may some future day, when I am in my grave, be read by some individual, and this notion has, even without my being often aware of it, cramped me, I am sure. I have by no means confessed myself in my journal; I have not opened my whole heart . . .

But a moment later comes an entirely opposite consideration: '. . . should it hereafter happen that I should be married and the mother of a family, I think that much of these records of my own early life may be very interesting and instructive to *them*.' It seems likely that a similar inner conflict occurred in other cases where it is not recorded.

We may expect children's diaries, even when not private in the sense of being forbidden (or unknown) to other members of the family, will be private in the sense that they will ignore public events. But some children take a precocious interest in public affairs. Thus the Wynne diaries intersperse news filtering through from France in the revolutionary years with the ordinary concerns of family and childhood. Sometimes the child may overhear and record the unofficial prejudices of her elders, the things people say when they are sure of a sympathetic audience but might be ashamed to have recorded in enduring print. Thus Emily Pepys, daughter of an upper-class bishop of Worcester, shakes hands with the bishop of Hereford when she is ten years old, and records: 'he is only a tailor's son'.[2] A perfect instance of the way in which children adopt their elders' casual prejudices exactly while often remaining sceptical of moral and social lessons sedulously impressed upon them.

The weakness most likely to affect the child diarist is false quaintness. Clever children early become aware of the delight their elders take in their naïve precocities. Having been praised for early shrewdness or hugged for a delicious show of incomprehension of the adult world, the child may try out similar attractive features in the privacy of the diary. If an early reader of adult books, and accustomed to be praised for this, the diarist may assume a false air of modest ease in familiarity with the classics. Or—it is very difficult to tell—the ease may be perfectly unforced. What are we to think of a fourteen-year-old, who has become not merely a student of the classics but the stern taskmistress to another child? Thus Emily Shore:

Miss Harriet, finding that I noted down in my journal when she promised to begin Milton, desired me to note down today also that she had actually begun it, and has nearly finished the first book . . . I much doubt whether she will continue it . . . However, I feel very much pleased with her now for three reasons—first, for beginning Milton; secondly, because she saw the flock of wild geese; third, because she gathered the other day a nosegay of all the wild flowers she could find.[3]

Was that written with a thrill of pride at being such a young tutor? Or—perhaps more probable—is my last sentence only a late twentieth-century reflection of the fact that our literary classics have retreated into academic strongholds? In 1834 perhaps there was no self-consciousness about the great classics, because they were simply thought to be the most exciting books. Thus, a few years earlier, Jane Austen's Henry Crawford, obviously no serious student, had a good knowledge of Shakespeare. It is certainly heartening to find Milton bracketed with the flock of wild geese, which the most unobservant child might notice. It is better on the whole to give child authors the benefit of the doubt; to assume that they meant what they said. We shall be assisted in this by the presence of one theme which perhaps more than any other makes the differences between child and adult insignificant, the theme of death. Death was often a more pervasive presence for a child expecting to die young than for many a healthy adult; or the death of parent or relative unites all in a common grief.

The diaries of the Wynne sisters, my first example, begin in 1789, the elder of the two diarists having been born in 1779 and the other in 1780. They had an elder sister, who was married in 1789 to an Italian nobleman, and two younger sisters. The family was English, Catholic, aristocratic, and cosmopolitan. Betsey, the elder of the two, was the more simple and spontaneous, and Eugenia, the younger, cleverer, and more ruthless. They were used to travelling, sight-seeing, and a variety of amusements. The tremendous events in France reach them in scraps of surprise and horror; they feel a deep sympathy for the French royal family.

Both writers are notable for their lack of self-consciousness and their hereditary determination to call a spade a spade. The picture given of Catholic life in their own family and in the places they visit is authentically extrovert. Religion is experienced as objective, both in its unquestionable principles, and in the ceremonies and customs in which it is embodied. Thus Eugenia writes about priestly celibacy: 'There has been a dispute between Mr Jaegle and M l'Abbé of priests marrying and the validity of the vow made to God. One of them is according to me right and the other wrong ... I always despise the man who violates his oath to God.'[4]

The account of their confirmation and the preparation for it (18 and 20 October 1790) is unreflective, but sets the scene vividly, with shrewd touches, such as the bishop's need to restrain his laughter when girls curtsied and awkwardly repeated sonnets to him. (They were living near Venice; it is not clear which bishop confirmed them, perhaps the bishop of Padua.) On Shrove Tuesday, 1792, there are cool, detached comments about the drunkenness of the Carnival near Constance. On Ash Wednesday, after Mass and reception of the ashes, called 'cinders', there is a detached observant view of a peasant family working, which in its clear outlines and simple feeling suggests a genre painting. Yet it seems to come directly from observation: '... the old father mending his coat, two young girls embroidering a music stool which every peasant does well in this country, the boy making thick ribbon and the mother nursing her baby. It was touching to see how occupied they all were.'[5]

The process of growing up and learning about the world is rapid, perhaps because fed by several sources at once. Observation joins with reading of history, with sage reflections on the character of Charles VII and Louis XI of France, and listening to elders: 'Mamma and she [Mme de Bombelles] talked of marriage and of the jealousy of husbands and of the miseries that one suffers when one is married. How queer and wicked men are.'[6]

But this glimpse of horror is not a deep experience; nor, of course, does it inhibit love and admiration for Papa. Listening to sermons of Massillon read aloud produces a very mature reflection, not, so far as one can tell, suggested by an adult: 'What does not please me in Massillon are the praises he gives in all his sermons to Louis XIV (that was king then) and certainly does not merit them. For it seems to me that a priest in the pulpit ought always to leave flattery aside and to say rather the truth to kings than to put on a smooth air.'[7]

Touches of feeling are rare enough to be noticeable, the devotion of children at First Communion, the gratitude and joy of a boy pilgrim with broken arms to whom the children's mother gave six francs, the death of a child of six who had 'an excellent heart'.[8] But the entry ends calmly: 'We must all die.'

More often the reader is aware of a hereditary *nil admirari*. Everything can be coped with; the world is very old—people have always been dying and getting drunk; the class system is fixed. Justina, the youngest sister aged three, 'went to bed without supper because she gave the cook such a smack that for two hours she could not open her eyes'.[9] No shock, no sympathy, no pleading for the punishment to be remitted. Things are as they are and the consequences of them will be as they will be. The Augustan spirit is, in the wider world, already beginning to be an anachronism; but no whisper of this has reached the Wynnes.

Self-importance, which is found occasionally, though perhaps more rarely than in most children, is direct, self-interested and unillusioned; as in the entry for New Year's Day, 1791: 'After having been this morning to confess and to comun we went to wish Papa a happy new year. He gave me six ducats, but Mamma more generous gave me a gold piece worth 4 sequins. It was my wit that gained me this money for I wrote verses to them both.'[10]

Sometimes there is boredom. Eugenia, the quicker and the more impatient, suffers from it especially, and the diary entry often consists of saying that there is nothing to say. By the age of twelve she is beginning to be analytical and self-critical:

> How greatly am I inconstant in my thoughts! Now I love one thing, then a single chance word suffices to make me detest it. I thought Mr Vauchet was amiable, I abhor him at present, and really he has done me no personal wrong. I loved his sister, but now I have known her brother, I find a thousand faults where once I found graces. I am very stupid, but I cannot control my feelings. . . . I have two persons in me, one scolds me and disapproves of all I do, the other flatters my passions and counsels me to follow their dictates—indeed I am an enigma to myself and wish to know myself in vain. I have the vanity of a devil.[11]

The absence of false shame and emotional excitement is striking. The passage may have been formed on models of examination of conscience before confession, and maybe also on secular literary models (perhaps in French). But the grasp of reality is strong, despite the one touch of literary exaggeration in the last sentence quoted. The final impression is of a quality rare enough in adults, but much rarer in children, the power to look both outwards and inwards with unimpassioned intelligence.

Marjory Fleming was perhaps the first child diarist writing in English to become famous, and must be one of the youngest subjects in the *Dictionary of National Biography*. She was well known to the Victorians, and praised by R. L. Stevenson. Born in 1803, she lived less than nine years; so we are dealing here with the earliest phase of childhood in which literary production is conceivable. But, paradoxically, she is the most literary and derivative of them all. While the others wrote mostly for themselves, she was ever conscious of an authority both loving and stern, her cousin Isabella, who read her text, criticized her sentiments, and corrected her spelling. The uniqueness of the work lies in its mixing of schoolroom exercise and personal confession. It is odd that a cousin should so crowd out living parents and two elder siblings; but there can be no doubt of the fact.

The sense that everything she wrote would be read almost immediately by Isabella simplifies one of the most elusive aspects of diaries, whether written by children or by adults. Is the diarist imagining an audience? Is the reading of the diary by others contemplated as a distant possibility, or a likely event, or is it ignored altogether? It is rare for one particular reader to brood over the pages in the way that Isabella does here. And yet, it is still hard to be sure whether Marjory wrote 'Grandeur and magnificence makes one proud and insolent'[12] to please herself or Isabella. Did she really enjoy reading Ossian, or only wish to be praised for it? No doubt Isabella composed her reading lists in which the Augustan and the Gothic, Pope and Mrs Radcliffe, have equal status and produce equal enjoyment (or profession of it). But some things probably did not come from Isabella. The poem in couplets about the death of three turkeys, with its false rhymes which Isabella would not have tolerated, is obviously her own, both in the childish empathy with the sorrowing turkey parents, and the resounding but theologically inept phrase 'To eternity are they launched'.[13] At one point she shows an unusual power of putting herself into Isabella's place, and wonders if 'She is not tired to death with me . . . I would be quite Impatient if I had a child to teach'.[14] Isabella may have said she was tired to death, but is unlikely to have suggested the idea of Marjory teaching someone else.

Her self-reproach, though possibly inspired by the reproof of elders, nevertheless has a convincing air of inner reflection: 'I stamped with my feet and threw my new hat which she made me on the ground and was sulky and was dreadfully passionate but she never whipped me.'[15] In her own way she is aware of the strange mystery of the weakness of the will, of which Ovid and St Paul write: 'My religion is greatly falling off because I dont pray with so much attention when I am saying my prayers and my charecter [*sic*] is lost a-mong the Breahead people.'[16] She can move with a suddenness that Isabella would not have approved from a childish worry about the multiplication table to fancying herself the 'loveress' of a young man beloved by all his friends.[17] Another love fantasy is checked by the reflection 'O I forget Isabella forbade me to speak about love.'[18]

This constant yearning to grow up, to imitate sensations which cannot yet be felt in an adult way is one of the few constant features of the genre. No doubt precocity, another shared feature of all our examples, accentuates this longing; because to some limited extent, especially in literary enjoyment, the precocious child can share something of adult experience.

Emily Shore's journal makes a substantial and adult-looking volume, and one could read in it for some time without realizing that it had not been written by an adult. Born on Christmas Day, 1819, the daughter of a bookish Suffolk clergyman, she kept a journal from July 1831 until a few days before her death in July 1839. The precocity which she shares with our other diarists here takes a scholarly and enquiring form. She is knowledgeable about botany and art history; and at the age of eleven is already engaged on a history of the Jews, a conflation of biblical accounts and of Milman's semi-secular history. She is strongly aware of the political controversies of her day. But she is surprisingly independent at times of adult judgements. For instance: 'The boys in the street threw stones at us, and behaved very impudently, which my aunt attributes to Reform! What an idea.'[19]

It is a rare case of a mind prematurely stocked with knowledge, yet developing at the same time the beginnings of adult critical judgement. Nor does bookishness have the effect of making her unobservant. Of one of her father's aristocratic young pupils she writes: 'The newspaper is his inseparable companion . . . he is so employed with it at breakfast that Mr Gower . . . is often obliged to give him a little kick under the table to remind him that he must eat his breakfast.'[20] And later, in 1837, when she attended a Conservative election meeting:

I was much amused to read of 'the glorious phalanx of ladies who graced the orchestra, whose bright eyes and sweet smiles from behind the Old English heart of oak, told far more than words how deeply they felt the success of the Conservative cause.' Now, I was one of this glorious phalanx, and I think it would be more correct . . . to say that their broad grins and hearty laughter showed the high entertainment they derived from the scene.[21]

An early disciple of Pugin, she finds Gothic cathedrals 'infinitely nobler' than buildings of classical style.[22] But in her literary taste, precocity combines with a thoroughly childish set of preferences on hearing *Julius Caesar* read aloud: 'Brutus is my favourite . . . I am very fond of Portia also, but not Julius Caesar, nor Mark Anthony.'[23]

She is a shrewd and eloquent critic of clerical behaviour. In May 1835

The preacher was a very young man . . . His manner was such that it would not have been surprising if the whole congregation had burst into a laugh. He bowed; shook his head; sailed backwards and forwards; sank; rose; held one hand on his heart and stretched the other over the congregation or clasped them both together; waved his handkerchief; closed his eyes; smiled sweetly; shook his head; assumed a ludicrous sentimental tone, even when quoting a text; smiled sweetly; shook his head; jogged his sermon up and down; leant over his cushion; grinned; sighed;—in short, did everything he could to make himself offensive and ridiculous. I never saw such a preposterous display in all my life.[24]

Three years later, now in Jersey, she is a severe critic of the 'religious' party (probably this means evangelical) 'pervaded throughout with the essential spirit of gossip and scandal'.[25] But comments like these are moral and satirical, not theologically subversive. It is interesting to see a strong immature mind grappling with her evangelical training, sometimes unaware of her own inconsistencies. Thus she is exercised about the propriety of reading *Ivanhoe*, unknown to her uncle who was evidently stricter than her father. She probes for understanding of the rejection of all works of the imagination, asking: '. . . why has our Maker given us imaginations, if they are never to be indulged? I am sure papa would not object, for he has occasionally read us a novel himself . . .'[26]

A few days later she considers her uncle's view that the Ten

Commandments contain the whole of a Christian's duty. She is too young of course to analyse exactly that what is really troubling her is extreme Protestant Hebraizing and the tacit use of the idea of the chosen race to justify sectarian exclusiveness. But she makes enough shrewd comments to allow us to guess that had she lived a few years longer she might have understood the deeper reasons for her unease.

She throws herself strongly into the controversy aroused by the Hampden case[27] in 1836, no doubt repeating her father's views, which seem to have been a curious mixture of Low and Broad Church. She naturally misses the real issue as seen by the leaders of the Oxford Movement, that the Royal Supremacy gave Prime Ministers unlimited power to force heretical appointments on an unwilling church. Influenced more than she knew by the evangelical notions she had been questioning, she castigates Keble for denying 'the Divine authority of the Christian Sabbath' and complains that he 'will play at cricket on Sunday evening'. Here the interest of the text is perhaps more in its revelation of adult confusions than in her personal thoughts.

Very personal though and very touching are her meditations on death, both as something seen, and as anticipated for herself. Seeing the corpse of a young girl she records: 'The deadly pale of the countenance, the whiteness of the lips, and the unmoving look gives a dead body a very ghastly appearance.'[28] Soon she has to contemplate her own approaching death: 'I prayed earnestly for submission to the Divine will, and that I might be prepared for death; I made up my mind I was to be the victim of consumption.'[29]

After two more years to familiarize herself with death's approach, she shows a serene faith and courage: 'I feel no uneasiness on the subject, even if my ideas (I cannot call them fears) prove right. It must be my business to prepare for another world; may God give me grace to do so.'[30]

Emily Pepys, a collateral descendant of Samuel (though her branch of the family pronounce their name 'Peppis'), whose father became bishop of Worcester in 1841, lived to marry and died in middle age in 1877. Nevertheless her diary (or what we have of it) is restricted to six months in 1844–5, and the only event outside a serene upper-class life is a fire in the house on Christmas Day. Emily's precocity is different from Emily Shore's. It does not come from thought and study, but from her determination to project herself by force of will into adult sensation. Perhaps this is a normal result of being the youngest in the family, but it is extreme in degree. She is able to combine a dream of marrying a 'very nice pretty young *lady* . . . (the very idea!)'[31] with an aggressive courtship of an unimpressionable male contemporary who 'has not written to me for a very long time, but I have written to him very often'.[32] But she is sufficiently in command of her (perhaps partly imaginary) passion to reflect that 'my love for Teddy has rather gone down',[33] and to comment that 'if I do not see Teddy soon I shall give him up', though only a few lines earlier and on the same day she had been planning for Teddy to become a clergyman 'if ever he means to be my husband, for I have quite set my heart on being a clergyman's wife or the wife of an independent gentleman'.[34]

Mary Crawford would have thought she was reading a misprint, but in the episcopal household at Hartlebury Castle there was more sense of the likeness than of the contrast between the two conditions. A sign of growing up, more genuine perhaps than the passion for Teddy, is the moment when she prefers Mr Baker's sermons to Papa's, which previously she had naturally thought the best.

The death of a neighbouring young wife, though sad, is not felt as deeply moving, and the pious reflections hardly pierce through the conventional, but a wedding in prospect is the occasion for violent excitement. 'We heard today that *Miss Carless*!! was going to be married!!!!!!! to "Mr Tattersal"!!!!!!!! and to keep a "Carriage and horses"!!!!!! Only fancy!!! I believe she knew his first wife. He lives in Grosvenor Place, up a little dirty court, and no private entrance to his house.'[35] Yet perhaps the dominant impression is of a cool, confident temperament deliberately working up excitement lest the secure, predictable round of family life become dull.

Ellen Buxton's journal which she kept from 1860–4 and illustrated with lively drawings, beginning it when she was

The children going out for a walk.
Emily reading while I draw.
May 18 - 1866. Northrepps

Northrepps Hall

Drawings made by Ellen Buxton to illustrate her journal.

twelve, is also the chronicle of a large family, a record of which the editor remarks that it was not 'a receptacle for her private thoughts and feelings; it almost seems as if it did not occur to her to have any.' Her father was a prosperous brewer, and the family house was at Leytonstone, just south of Epping Forest but they spent several months in the year with their grandmother at Northrepps near Cromer where there were innumerable Buxton, Gurney, Barclay, and Hoare cousins. She shows her position as an elder in the family as clearly as Emily Pepys reveals herself as the youngest. Of her younger siblings at a christening she remarks: 'They were very good at the beginning, except that Barclay would kick against the back of the pew.'[36] The death of a little brother produces eloquence:

[Leo was] so beautiful and so perfectly at rest; but he did not look at all like himself, when he was alive; he was so changed I should not have known him . . . Papa told us to remember his dear face all our life and to look at him intently. He did indeed look lovely, and just as though he were asleep.[37]

After this the death of the Prince Consort has the comforting quality of a shared public event, more interesting than painful; 'the newspapers were all covered with black lines between each column'.[38] And when a child dies at a confirmation service Ellen records it with the detachment of a paragraph in a newspaper. Had she been able to read Emily Pepys she might have rebuked her for excessive and unladylike excitement about weddings, which for her have merely the insipid quality of being 'so charming'.[39]

Laura Troubridge, my last example, came from a similar world to the Buxtons, where a fortune derived from business has in a generation or two created an unselfconscious assimilation to upper-class manners. An orphan from the age of nine, she lived with her older and younger siblings with her Gurney grandfather (the brother of Elizabeth Fry) at Runcton in Norfolk, and many Gurneys, Barclays, and Buxtons feature in her journal. The disruption to her grandfather's life caused by this influx of seven high-spirited children seems never to have occurred to her. He was a widower of seventy-six when he took over the family of his dead daughter and son-in-law (who had survived his wife's death only by five weeks), but Laura in her adolescent self-absorption gave him no sympathy, merely grumbling at the old-fashioned restrictions Grandpapa sought to impose on them.

The diary begins when Laura is fifteen, and it is less a record of events than a portrait (showing some literary talent) of a family life, and a self-portrait as well. At eighteen, for instance, she is puzzled by her lack of susceptibility:

I can flirt now and have amused myself a good deal in that way. Last year I believe I fancied myself in love—a great mistake and I never mean to again. I have discovered a cavity in my left side instead of a heart. I much prefer it and hope it will remain, yet I'm awfully fond of men, I like 'em all—such dears.[40]

This did not prevent her from marrying later. We may guess that it was partly due to the fond memories of her parents whose death she had recorded with much poignancy in the memoir that is a prelude to the journal. In a long entry for 23 November 1873 she describes her tender dreams six years after the event.

... When I dream about Papa and Mama it is always that they have been dead and have come to life again, *never* that we are going on in the old way. But that is a dream I like so *very, very* much, it always makes me feel so glad and happy when I have dreamt about them, although they are sad too, for I always *beg* and *implore* them not to die in my dreams, and once I woke with, as I thought, my arms round Mama's neck ...[41]

The character-sketches of siblings and analysis of her own character are incisive and penetrating; perhaps a good biographer was lost in Laura Troubridge. She is capable of questioning prevailing assumptions. For instance:

Uncle Tum came to see us, raving about the Alhambra ... He said the *danseuses* were so indecent in the Ballet that he would not take us, though he was longing to himself. I thought it far more proper for *us* to see women with next to nothing on than him, but I kept this opinion to myself. However, he is so longing to take us that I think we will be able to work him up to the right pitch.[42]

On the other hand she is deeply embarrassed reading Evelyn's diary aloud to Grandpapa and concludes that 'Old books always are improper. People wrote coarse then . . .'.[43]

Her literary criticism, though crude and perhaps wayward, is entirely spontaneous and personal. She enjoys *The Newcomes*, which though delightful is unsatisfactory because it is better 'when people are unhappy in the beginning and happy in the middle and end'.[44] And it would have been amusing if Leslie Stephen and Swinburne, before composing their memorable castigations of the character of Stephen Guest in *The Mill on the Floss*[45] had been able to read Laura's artless and deeply felt opinion:

Oh, how I do *worship* that book, I really love Maggie and Stephen. Oh the breathless excitement of their elopement and how awfully disappointing the chapter called 'Morning' is; she really *ought* to have married him, she had gone *far* too far to draw back and Philip and Lucy did not matter in the least, and Stephen was so *awfully* nice and far more interesting than that old hunchback . . .[46]

It is hard and perhaps useless to generalize. Yet one reflection, to me entirely unexpected when I began to read the material, comes unbidden. I am struck by the independence of mind and power of detached criticism shown in so many entries. From the Wynne criticism of a preacher's sycophancy, and Emily Shore's questioning of Protestant distrust of the imagination, to Laura Troubridge's understanding that lustful male thoughts would be excited by half-naked dancers, there is a real testing of convention and conduct by principle. One might say this was due to the civilized and intelligent milieu shared by most of our authors; or attribute it mainly to natural intelligence. But perhaps the chief factor was religious training. The Gospel contains within it an implied criticism of the worldliness of those who inculcate in the young a convenient edited version. We have been dealing here with children perceptive enough to understand this.

Notes

1. *Journal of Emily Shore* (London, 1891), 262.
2. *The Journal of Emily Pepys*, ed. Gillian Avery (London, 1984), 70.
3. *Emily Shore*, 84–5.
4. *The Wynne Diaries*, ed. Anne Fremantle (London, 1952), 86.
5. Ibid. 88.
6. Ibid. 91.
7. Ibid. 92.
8. Ibid. 45.
9. Ibid. 12.
10. Ibid. 47.
11. Ibid. 118.
12. *The Complete Marjorie Fleming*, ed. Frank Sidgwick (London, 1934), 5.
13. Ibid. 29.
14. Ibid. 56.
15. Ibid. 41.
16. Ibid. 80.
17. Ibid. 47–9.
18. Ibid. 108.
19. *Emily Shore*, 16.
20. Ibid. 9.
21. Ibid. 213.
22. Ibid. 78.
23. Ibid. 22.
24. Ibid. 96–7.
25. Ibid. 249.
26. Ibid. 169–70.
27. R. D. Hampden's Bampton lectures of 1832 led to suspicions about his orthodoxy. As a result two controversies arose, the first (mentioned here) when Lord Melbourne nominated him Regius Professor of Divinity at Oxford, the second in 1847, when Lord John Russell nominated him as bishop of Hereford.
28. *Emily Shore*, 117.
29. Ibid. 142.
30. Ibid. 264.
31. *Emily Pepys*, 32.
32. Ibid. 29.
33. Ibid. 40.
34. Ibid. 45.
35. Ibid. 83.
36. *Ellen Buxton's Journal 1860–1864*, ed. Ellen R. C. Creighton (London, 1967), 45.
37. Ibid. 20.

38. Ibid. 41.
39. Ibid. 93.
40. *Life among the Troubridges*, ed. Jacqueline Hope-Nicholson (London, 1966), 147.
41. Ibid. 69.
42. Ibid. 143–4.
43. Ibid. 113.
44. Ibid. 64.
45. Swinburne wrote: '... the man ... does not exist who could make for the first time the acquaintance of Mr Stephen Guest with no incipient sense of a twitching in his fingers and a tingling in his toes at the notion of any contact between Maggie Tulliver and a cur so far beneath the chance of promotion to the notice of his horsewhip, or elevation to the level of his boot.' (*A Century of George Eliot Criticism*, ed. G. Haight (London, 1966), 127.)
46. *Life among the Troubridges*, 82.

20

Children's Manuscript Magazines in the Bodleian Library

OLIVIA BELL AND ALAN BELL

THE manuscript 'family magazine' was a relatively common feature of middle-class nursery life in Victorian Britain and up to the time of the First World War, and it is by no means extinct even today. Ill-typed pot-pourris of jokes, stories, news, and caricatures still circulate in some schools, though they rarely extend beyond a few issues revealing the temporary enthusiasm of a long summer holiday. Their predecessors were often much more elaborately conceived, and specimens frequently occur amongst the ephemera of family archives in county record offices. The Bodleian holds several in its Department of Western Manuscripts, and these will be discussed here; each of them is characteristic of schoolroom and nursery life in academic families.[1]

Usually such magazines are fated to languish in the 'miscellaneous' sections of family archives—often uncatalogued—to surprise and delight the occasional researcher. It is rare that any of these happy domestic compilations, essentially of local and family interest, ever achieves fame. Two well-known sets, the Dodgson family's Croft Rectory magazines and the Stephens' *Hyde Park Gate News*, share some characteristics with less famous specimens. *The Rectory Magazine*, *The Rectory Umbrella*, *The Comet*, and others produced in the Dodgson family home near Darlington in the late 1840s, saw the first appearances of Lewis Carroll's literary work. Most of Carroll's own childhood verses have found their way into the standard collections of his writings, but the manuscripts also contain some early and characteristic 'Difficulty's', such as the perennial problem of 'When does the day begin?', which foreshadow his mathematical-logical work.[2] Like most other family magazines, the Croft Rectory series were open to contributions by any of the children (eleven of them in the Dodgson parsonage), but regular appearance depended on one determined literary character. It was Lewis Carroll himself who provided the bulk of the text and kept a flagging enterprise alive.

It was almost inevitable that households with a strong adult literary tradition should produce some corporate effort in the nursery. *The Hyde Park Gate News*, compiled by Sir Leslie Stephen's children between 1891 and 1895, is perhaps the best known of late Victorian examples of the genre. Its double columns on Monday, 21 November 1892 ('Vol. II, no. 45') led off in Miss Virginia Stephen's hand with some significant local intelligence:

Mr. Leslie Stephen whose immense litterary powers are well known is now the President of the London library which as Lord Tennyson was before him and Carlysle was before Tennyson is justly esteemed a great honour. Mrs. Ritchie the daughter of Thackeray who came to luncheon the next day expressed her delight by jumping from her chair and clapping her hands in a childish manner but none the less sincerely. The greater part of Mrs. Stephen's joy lies in the fact that Mr. Gladstone is only vice-president. She is not at all of a 'crowy' nature but we can forgive any woman for triumphing when her husband gets above Mr. Gladstone. We think that the London library has made a very good choice in putting Mr. Stephen before Mr. Gladstone, as although Mr. Gladstone may be a first-rate politician he cannot beat Mr. Stephen in writing. But as Mr. Stephen with that delicacy and modesty which is always eminent in the great man's manner went out of the room when the final debate was taking place we cannot oblige our readers with more of the interesting details.[3]

It was through the *Hyde Park Gate News* that Virginia Stephen first experienced the special thrill of being recognized as an author. As her sister Vanessa later recalled:

Naturally we produced a family newspaper . . . Virginia wrote most of it . . . She was very sensitive to criticism and the good opinion of the grown-ups. I remember putting the paper on the table by my mother's sofa while they were at dinner, and then creeping quietly into the little room to look through the window and hear the criticism. As we looked, she trembling with excitement, we could see my mother's lamplit figure quietly sitting near the fire, my father on the other side with his lamp, both reading. Then she noticed the paper, picked it up, began to read. We looked and listened hard for some comment. 'Rather clever, I think,' said my mother, putting the paper down without apparent excitement. But it was enough to thrill her daughter; she had had approval and been called clever, and our eavesdropping was rewarded.[4]

The *News* contains Virginia's first efforts in fiction, and one finds in references to Talland House, the family's Cornish holiday home, the *donné* of *To The Lighthouse*. Like others of its kind, the *News* stimulated rivalry. 'Mr. Adrian Stephen,' the London Library issue commented, 'who as perhaps our readers remember produced a little newspaper (which however did not have a very long existence) at St. Ives has now begun another similar journal. We hope that it will get the success it deserves.' Adrian Stephen's papers were all the more characteristic of nursery emulation for being short-lived efforts. In the *Hyde Park Gate News*, the charm and fun gradually diminish as more adult aspirations replace the literary ingenuousness of childhood.

There is probably a distinction to be made between nursery magazines, spontaneous confections started by the children them-selves, and drawing-room magazines, possibly governess-inspired, which used the talents of any adults of literary or artistic pretension who were prepared to allow themselves to be pressed into contributing. The 'drawing-room' variety is more akin to the 'visiting books', those albums that young ladies took on country house visits, soliciting verses, caricatures, water-colours, and humorous contributions from fellow guests. These flourished in Edwardian days, especially when wet weather favoured the non-shooting gentlemen of the party; elaborate examples survive in some country house libraries.

The Miscellany, compiled by members of the Bradley family (Bodleian, MSS Don.e.35, d.96–101) belongs to this 'drawing-room' tradition. It is thus a good deal more sophisticated than others, partly because of the literary talent available to the family of George Granville Bradley (1821–1903), Headmaster of

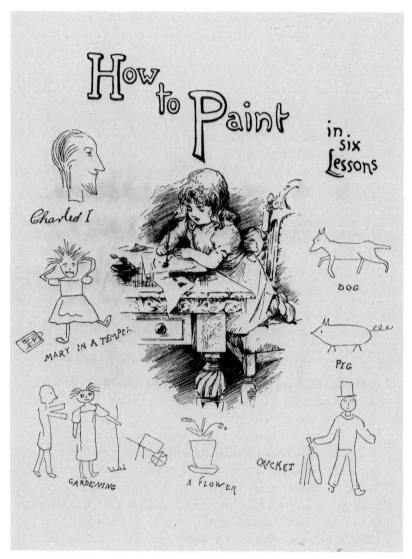

From *Nister's Holiday Annual*, 1895.

Marlborough, later Master of University College, Oxford, and finally Dean of Westminster. The extended Bradley family, which fits into academic and clerical groupings as neatly as parts of Noel Annan's Cambridge-based 'intellectual aristocracy', passed the volumes round with elaborate postal arrangements between the contributors. It circulated from Ashton-on-Mersey to Torquay, Lydney to Kingsbridge, but it was G. G. Bradley's daughters Daisy (Margaret Louisa, 1846–1945, later Woods) and her older sister Edith Mabel (d. 1936, later Birchenough) who were the animating spirits of the whole enterprise.

Not all the contributors are identifiable; initials do not always correspond to the list of subscribers. There is a sprinkling of adult, or precocious, contributions. The Dean's half-brother, later the Shakespearean critic A. C. Bradley, provided articles from the start of the *Miscellany*. A. C. Bradley was eighteen when in 1869 he wrote on 'Palgrave's corrections of Shelley's text' (rather, one likes to think, in the manner of the headmaster Waterbury submitting 'Some Little Known Aspects of Tacitus' to the *Mayfair Gazette* during Sipperley's brief editorship). Fortunately the *Miscellany* did not become a *Notes and Queries* of the nursery world, and its other articles and stories are less grown-up in tone. 'The Ridiculous Story Again' is an instalment of a serial involving Arthurian characters, skeletons, ghosts, and white mice.

The Bradleys' Philpot cousins enquire within on many things. A. W. P[hilpot] 'would be glad to know if it is possible to teach a bullfinch to wash himself regularly, as he has to be dipped periodically'. Later on, the same enquirer 'would be glad to know if when *one* feather appears in a bullfinch that has no tail, it is a sign he is going to have one?' (The reply is 'Annie! How can you be *so* absurd?') There is a prize page, with anagrams, riddles, double acrostics, and other word games, though in later editions there is often a dearth of entries. Most of the editorial comment is by Edith Bradley, who copied out most of the contributions.

The *Miscellany*'s poetry is generally sombre in tone, often about death or loss, and there are one or two hymns. Prose includes history (such as the death of Wolsey, or the naval battles of Lord Howe), but there are also domesticated contributions such as tatting patterns. Illustrations are few to begin with, but in later volumes (particularly from July 1868) water-colours are pasted in, with decorated initials and small pen-sketches.

By January 1872, after the Bradleys had moved to Oxford, Andrew Lang becomes a contributor: his stories are of interest to readers of *The Blue Fairy Book* and its successors, and his illustrations complement the text. Some of the drawings and water-colours are of a very high standard (Selwyn Image, the Ruskinian artist, was a contributor); others have obviously been drawn by children. The 1872 volume includes photographs, not related to literary articles, generally of mountain landscapes or foreign scenes.

The *Miscellany*, even in its early days, is a very polished production, and was very possibly conceived with adult help. From the beginning it would have interested adults of the family as well as children. It is no surprise that the later issues were printed: 'Having long past [*sic*] the term of years usually allotted to Manuscript Magazines, the Miscellany has at last ceased to be numbered among such periodicals.' By its thirtieth (and final) issue in 1875 it had acquired a subscription list of 120, but topical printed debates on 'the position of women' show that it had grown away from its probable origins as a governess task.

Starting up and circulating a private periodical did not of course require a large family. Maurice Platnauer (1887–1974), the son of a museum official in York (and later a classical scholar, and fellow and Principal of Brasenose College), dedicated five notebooks compiled between 1896 and 1900 to his cousin Hugh Stott. These amusing literary compilations (which are now Bodleian MSS Eng.misc.e.854) were not conceived exactly as a magazine, but their contents are so similar to those of other family creations that they merit discussion here. The first of the varied series, with a front cover decorated with many colours of sealing wax and diamond-shaped pieces of mother of pearl, is entitled 'Maurice's New English History, Dedicated to Hugh Stott, from his Cousin M. Platnauer', with a globe in curlicues as 'trade mark'. 'Maurice's Educational Series. Short Stories from The History of

England', written in 1896–7, covers the reigns from William I to Edward III. The Conqueror's entry, concise and spirited, obviously owes a lot to the tradition of Lady Callcott's *Little Arthur's History of England* before it had been confused by Sellar and Yeatman:

William duke of Normandy afterwards called Willian the conqueror came to England in the year 1066 he gathered a large fleat & sailed over to England, Harold, who had gone to fight the fierce king of Norway (who had been brought over by Harold's brother, who was there himself) he had just won a glorilus victory when news reached him that the normans had landed he could not take the 6.30 o'clock train doon to London, but had to travel doon all night & reached there early in the morning the normans had not landed yet so his men dug a dich on a little hill at Hastings near the sea & set up a fence all round it & in the middle of the dich, waving in the morning breeze stood the banner of *Harold*, as soon as the normans saw how strong the saxons position was they thought they would play them a trick so they pretended to run away & Harold's men rushed opon the norman troops as soon as the normans saw the men were *out* of their strong-hold they rushed upon the Saxons in return. Harolds men fought bravely but were defeated & harold was killed by an arrow in his eye, William was crowned king as William I on Christmas day in the year 1066. He was not a very wicked king but treated the poor saxons very crully. He built the tower at london and ordered the doom's day book to be written, the doom's day book is a book that told him the state of the grount & the state of all the country, an other thing that did not please the people very much was the curfew bell this was a bell that was rung in the tower of all the churches at 8 o'clock at night which told people that they were to put out their fires and candles because the houses were made of wood. Willilam died at rouen his horse trood on a cinder (while he was besieging a castle at mantes) his horse plunged and reared & william was thrown off & carried to rouen where he died P.S. he made the new forest in hampshire he pulled doen houses & churches to make it.

Later reigns, lacking the excitement of Hastings, are dealt with more summarily:

Henry II was good & kind but rather hasty, when I tell that he shut his wife up in a tower & did not even allow her children to see her. Henry was not a wise king like the other henry I have told you about he

married a french princess who was very wicked & this of course was not
right . . .

Maurice Platnauer's second notebook is a compilation of
disparate facts, '50 Commonly Mistaken Ideas', followed by fifty
more. Earwigs, volcanoes, measles, lightning, and mad dogs are
all adduced for a gallimaufry of misapprehension, and it is
remarked that 'perspiring and sweating are not the same thing'.
The fourth volume sees him in literary mood, writing short
stories during summer term at Bramcote, Scarborough, in 1900.
The three short stories include 'How I Caught a Nihilist' in which
a boy sets a trap for his ghost-playing friend, and (by mistake)
catches a Nihilist who was intending to murder his father; it is set
in a castle on the Yorkshire moors. Maurice notes his own
fondness for blood-and-thunder stories.

The final volume of the Platnauer series is very different:
'Monograph of British Ferns. To the Yorkshire Philosophical
Society, This book is respectfully dedicated, By the author, M.
Platnauer. Scarbro' 1900.' This is a fairly technical (or 'technecal',
as the author puts it) discussion of the subject. In a way quite
characteristic of older private-school boys, information has taken
over from fancy.

Another pleasing minor example is the *Weekly Magazine* (two
volumes) and *St. George's Magazine* (six volumes), compiled in the
family of the archaeologist O. G. S. Crawford in 1862 (Bodleian,
MSS Crawford 116). Although obviously a nursery production
from the start, there is a somewhat didactic tone about many of
the contributions, for example an essay on 'The Cat' in volume I
which starts: 'Having made the history of the cat and other
domestic animals the study of a long lifetime I feel that I shall not
fail to write most interesting articles.'

'A Sonnet' in the same issue begins:

> To write a sonnet for a new magazine
> 'Tis a nervous thing to do
> And I very much fear the public jeer
> Which I am not accustomed to.

Later, there are the usual elaborate rules drawn up, better presentation with a decorated cover and list of contents, and entries copied out by a single editor which show the rapid dominance of one pertinacious contributor.

There are calendar entries well chosen from standard diaries: '5 Th. S.Agatha, a Sicilian Virgin suffered under Decius at Catanea A.D.253. 6 F. Sow 2nd crop of peas'. As always, competitions fail to attract the requisite number of entries, and editorial frustrations tend to show unduly as the enterprise advances. A continuing essay on 'The Kettle' contains in part II:

the heat from the boiling water pours into our hand the moment we touch it, the very thoughts of this makes us long for a kettle-holder and a thick one too so the editor not trouble himself if the one he is making proves rather massive. He may feel quite sure it could not be made of better material as our next article will prove, the writer hopes the editor will not mind this public allusion to his works in progress.

It is in their nature almost inevitable that these magazines of childhood should be short-lived, their existence only occasionally prolonged by a younger brother or sister showing an interest in continuing the enterprise. The 'Unique Manuscript Magazine', also in the Bodleian (MSS Eng. misc.d.872–3, e.737–8) is justified in its title as being a rare exception to the rule of evanescence; its compilers, the Dixey family, kept it up as a family magazine for no less than seventy years.

In 1912 Giles Dixey (1893–1974) wrote in the 'Unique Magazine' an account of its beginnings eight years earlier, when he and his younger brother Roger, then aged nine, had bought an inviting pad of paper during a seaside holiday. Roger became editor and Giles, who produced much more copy, was sub-editor of what was originally called 'Our Own Magazine' but adopted its new title a year or so later. The first issue was all their own work, but a few neighbouring friends from the Oxford Preparatory (later Dragon) School were soon let into the secret. The magazine originally appeared three times a year (January, April, and October) but from April 1910 to August 1912 it managed to come out monthly. The early issues were quite substantial, but they thin out as contributors went off to their public schools or found other interests. In 1907–8 the 'proprietors' were driven to offering to pay contributors, according to merit and 'not by length or quantity, but by quality'. 'Please bear in mind the rule of Copyright', they added efficiently, for the pretence of running a real, businesslike office is part of the great tradition of juvenile editorship.

Rules, especially those enjoining confidentiality, were central to the enterprise, and were periodically revised and consolidated with due attention to standing orders:

I. If any keeper of any portion of the U.M.M. returns it to the Office damaged in any way, he shall be fined in proportion to the offence.

II. Further, no person may keep the U.M.M. more than 7 days at once without special leave from the Editor or Sub-Editor.

III. Stories must be original. Pictures mostly, if not always so. Riddles and Puzzles, if not original, must be ones that are very rare or unknown. Details in this respect must always be arranged with the Editor.

IV. Secrecy is required. Curiosity cannot be satisfied in certain matters.

V. No person except the Editor may invite or join any person to the U.M.M. without special leave; nor expound anything to anybody without leave.

VI. Contributions and all correspondence should be addressed to:- The Secretary, The U.M.M. Office, 24 Museum Road, Oxford. Changes of address will be notified beforehand.

VII. *N.B. The Editor's Copyright must be respected.*

If any further rules be made, they will be communicated to the members and contributors. Rules IV and V are considered binding even after all connection with the U.M.M. be severed. *Signed*: R. N. Dixey *Editor*. H. G. Dixey (Hon. Sec.) *Sub. Ed.*

[9 April 1908]

Elaborate rules like these seem characteristic of the Dixey boys, who were later to provide their magazine with cumulative indexes.

The contents grew up with the principal contributors. Roger Dixey's insubstantial 'A funny story from China' in the first issue is commended as 'verry exitting', but the brothers soon developed a better fictional manner. As in practically all such

36A

NOTICE.

IMPORTANT.

THE Editor and Subeditor have been ~~exceedingly~~ MERCIFULL in matters Conserning Rule I.
The Editor has spent hours over putting the ~~new~~ 2nd Annual into Repair and has had to take off the pictures and stick them on another piece of paper for the back cover.
Hence forward they will not be mercifull and will fine ~~heavilly~~ and not unjustly.

R. U. & A. J. Dixey

A Dixey editorial notice.

magazines, serial stories are usual, often in the 'Unique Magazine' with strong elements of the 'surprising' or 'improbable'. Roger had a predilection for railway stories, and Giles soon showed a fascination for boats and the sea that was to become the main interest of his life. The two boys differ in their verses, Roger trying to be humorous but showing himself rather derivative, Giles revealing himself as much more serious and by 1907 trying to write in dialect. Topical verses, as on mishaps at the Oxford pageant of July 1907, with participants falling into the river, are characteristic too.

There are competitions, but the limited circulation of the Magazine, with only about half a dozen junior households participating in 1906, meant that there were few entries. Religious articles creep in as a reflection of public-school attitudes, some pieces being obvious sermon derivatives. There is still, however, plenty of humour, puns, and tortuous jokes to alleviate the adolescent priggery. 'Stories, Rymes, Rydles, Puzels and all those kind of things' which were asked for in 1904, fortunately continued to be submitted. *Punch*-like cartoons (collapse of juvenile party) occur from time to time, and holiday topography of course supplies subjects for pencil and crayon illustrations, none of great significance.

Most of the preparatory school-friends who had contributed were killed in the First World War; only Giles and Roger (who both served in the War) and one other contributor survived. Their sister Maud kept 'the U.M.M.' going for the duration— 'The office-boy has become acting sub-editor'—and it was a matter of family pride to sustain it, if only intermittently. Even before the War, senior members of the Dixey family had written for it, none older than a grand-aunt Elizabeth, aged ninety-eight in 1914. The father, F. A. Dixey, an entomologist and long-serving Fellow of Wadham, had a complete Royal Institution lecture on 'Seasonal Dimorphism', about the colour variations of butterflies hatching at different times of year, included in 1912. This is an indication of how the magazine was becoming a record of family activities rather than of aspirations to turn into a learned journal.

It becomes increasingly a combination of family log and commonplace book, with drawings and sketches stuck in. Giles enjoyed a short period as a merchant seaman (there are descriptions of his voyages to South America), and he eventually settled down to a long career as an idiosyncratic and unmistakably nautical master at the Dragon School, sharing his magazine contributions with the *Draconian* as well as including select pieces from the school magazine in his 'Unique Magazine'. (John Betjeman's precociously ecclesiological 'A Stained-Glass Window', from the 1920 *Draconian*, is an example.) Giles Dixey also had a number of volumes of verse privately printed throughout his lifetime (some poems were transcribed for the 'Magazine'), thus continuing a childhood habit for a slightly larger audience. Roger Dixey became a research officer in agricultural economics, and there are descriptions of his own travels in connection with his work on milk. His own *Recollections* were privately printed in 1974.

Even though in its later years it drew largely on adult family contributions and was far removed from the tentative efforts of its prototype 'Our Own Magazine', the whole enterprise, sustained for no less than seventy years and owing its inspiration to the brothers' seaside holiday efforts of 1904, must indeed be reckoned 'Unique'.

Seventy years of consistent compilation may well be a world record in domestic magazine editorship. Even in its truly juvenile period, the 'Unique Manuscript Magazine' may seem to reflect all too clearly the precocious verbalism of North Oxford. The fact that several of the examples discussed here come from academic families of course accounts for their survival in a university library. But, as mentioned at the outset, many a county record office could provide comparable specimens. The genre, moreover, is far from dead. One can see that the computer may well help to keep alive a long-established tradition of inventiveness.

Olivia Bell and Alan Bell

Notes

1. This essay was originally conceived by Bodley's Librarian, David Vaisey. We are very grateful to him for his advice and encouragement, and to the Bodleian Library for permission to quote from manuscripts in its keeping. We would also like to thank Ruari McLean, a late contributor to the 'Unique Manuscript Magazine', for sharing with us his memories of Giles Dixey, its joint editor.
2. There is a good discussion of the Rectory magazines in Roger Lancelyn Green's 1953 edition of the *Diaries*, i. 19–28.
3. Facsimile in *Adam*, Nos. 297–400 (1977), 19.
4. Vanessa Bell, *Notes on Virginia's Childhood* (New York, 1974), 10–11.

INDEX